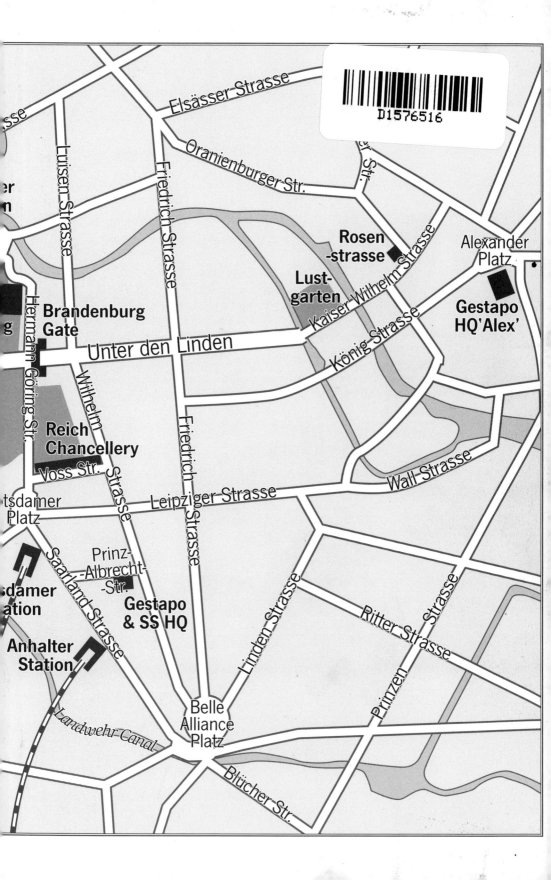

Berlin at War

Life and Death in
Hitler's Capital, 1939–45

Microcosm:
Portrait of a Central European City
(with Norman Davies)

Killing Hitler:
The Third Reich and the
Plots against the Führer

Berlin at War

*Life and Death in
Hitler's Capital, 1939–45*

ROGER MOORHOUSE

THE BODLEY HEAD
LONDON

Published by The Bodley Head 2010

2 4 6 8 10 9 7 5 3 1

First published in Great Britain in 2010 by
The Bodley Head
Random House, 20 Vauxhall Bridge Road,
London SW1V 2SA

www.bodleyhead.co.uk
www.rbooks.co.uk

Addresses for companies within The Random House Group Limited can be found at:
www.randomhouse.co.uk/offices.htm

The Random House Group Limited Reg. No. 954009

A CIP catalogue record for this book
is available from the British Library

ISBN 9780224080712 (HBK)

The Random House Group Limited supports The Forest Stewardship
Council (FSC), the leading international forest certification organisation. All our titles that are
printed on Greenpeace approved FSC certified paper carry the FSC logo. Our paper procurement
policy can be found at www.rbooks.co.uk/environment

Mixed Sources
Product group from well-managed
forests and other controlled sources
www.fsc.org Cert no. TT-COC-2139
© 1996 Forest Stewardship Council

Typeset in Dante MT by Palimpsest Book Production Limited
Falkirk, Stirlingshire

Printed and bound in Great Britain by
Clays Ltd, St Ives plc

For

Amelia

in the hope that she
will never have to experience
times such as these

and for her great-grandparents

Paul & Hildegard Schmidt

who did

Contents

List of Illustrations

Clearing the rubble (*Bundesarchiv Bild 183-L09712*).

Gestapo HQ: Prinz-Albrecht-Strasse (*Bundesarchiv Bild 183-R97512*).

Beppo Römer (*Gedenkstätte Deutscher Widerstand*).

Otto Weidt (*Gedenkstätte Deutscher Widerstand*).

Johanna Solf (*Gedenkstätte Deutscher Widerstand*).

Stella Goldschlag (*akg-images/ullstein bild*).

The Invalidenfriedhof, autumn 1942 (*Bundesarchiv Bild 183-J04378,
Fotograf: Schwanke*).

Victims of an air raid, autumn 1944 (*Bundesarchiv Bild
146-1970-050-31*).

Night scene, Jerusalem Strasse, July 1944 (*Bundesarchiv Bild 183-
J30142*).

Survivors clamber through the rubble, February 1945 (*Bundesarchiv
Bild 183-J31345*).

A soup kitchen for those bombed out, August 1943 (*Bundesarchiv
Bild 183-J07449, Fotograf: Ernst*).

The flak tower close to Berlin Zoo, 1943 (*akg-images/ullstein bild*).

Building barricades on a Berlin street, March 1945 (*Bundesarchiv
Bild 183-J31385*).

Combat in the capital's streets, April 1945 (*akg-images*).

A Soviet T-34 passes Berlin civilians (*akg-images/Voller Ernst*).

Surrendering German soldiers (*akg-images*).

Berliners butchering a dead horse (*Bundesarchiv Bild 183-R77871*).

Two old men (*akg-images/Voller Ernst*).

Acknowledgements

Any work of research carries many debts along with it and this book is certainly no exception. Many people have helped along the way, amongst them Philipp Rauh and Saskia Smellie, who helped with ancillary research in Berlin; Kinga Boruc at Carta Blanca (Warsaw), who designed the maps; and Phil Berks at Digital Services (Tring), who rescued my manuscript from a potentially catastrophic hard-drive crash.

Thanks are also due to all those friends and colleagues who answered specific queries and kindly shared their knowledge, amongst them Norman Groom, Cord Pagenstecher, Michael Foedrowitz, Gregers Forssling, Giles MacDonogh, James Holland, Nick Stargardt and Nigel Jones.

Special mention must of course be reserved for all those Berliners of the wartime vintage with whom I spent so many enjoyable and enlightening hours conducting interviews. Without their reminiscences, their manuscripts and their diaries, this book would simply not have been possible, and I am only sorry that the march of time has robbed some of them of the satisfaction of seeing the finished product.

In setting up that programme of interviews, I incurred a number of significant debts, not least to Wieland Giebel of 'Berlin Story' and to Thessi Aselmeier and all those at the excellent Zeitzeugenbörse.

I would also like to extend my thanks to some of the institutions in which the research and writing of this book was carried out, amongst them the Deutsche Tagebucharchiv in Emmendingen, the Landesarchiv Berlin, the National Archives in Kew, the British Library and the excellent German Historical Institute in London. In addition, the guides of Berliner Unterwelten deserve credit for making my visits to some of the more esoteric sights of the German capital so enlightening.

Lastly, mention must be made of all those others who made this project possible: my agents, Peter Robinson in London and Jill Grinberg in New York, and my editors Lara Heimert and Brandon Proia in New York and Will Sulkin and the incomparable Jörg Hensgen in London. I am indebted to all of you for your insight, your perseverance and your unflagging enthusiasm for this project. Thank you.

Convention dictates that I dedicate this book to my daughter Amelia, but I would also like to acknowledge two other familial debts. The first is to my wife's grandparents, Paul and Hildegard Schmidt, who experienced life in Nazi Germany – albeit not in Berlin – and whose reminiscences spurred my interest in the subject. The second is to my wife Melissa, without whose love, support, patience – and occasional impatience – this book would scarcely have seen the light of day.

Roger Moorhouse
May 2010

Introduction

For all its breezy modernity, Berlin is a city that positively reeks of history. If one were looking for a single location – a focal point – for the bloody trials and tribulations of the twentieth century, then one would have to look no further. From the bullet-scarred buildings to the lingering shadows of totalitarian regimes, Berlin experienced world events not as something remote or imperceptible, but rather as immediate, tangible and very real. Last year the city celebrated the twentieth anniversary of the fall of its hated Wall, the moment in which it became the crucible of the death spasms of communism. A generation earlier it had been the plaything of the squabbling superpowers, serving as the backdrop to earnest speechifying and sinister spy swaps. And a generation further back, the then capital of the Third Reich had been the very epicentre of Nazi power – the canvas upon which Speer's architectural dreams and Hitler's racial vision would be made real.

Berlin was one of the very few European capitals to experience the horror of the Second World War at first hand. Not only was the city subjected to the full wrath of the Soviet ground offensive and siege in 1945, but it also found itself in the very front rank of the air war. Its wartime military history, therefore, is a catalogue of superlatives. As the most important Allied target, Berlin attracted more air raids, more aircraft and more bombs than any other German city. It was the most aggressively defended target, employing the largest number of personnel in the most elaborate network of defences and costing the largest number of Allied airmen's lives. It also outstripped its rivals in its civilian death toll: with an estimated 200,000 casualties it suffered the largest non-military loss of life of any city of Western and Central Europe.

Yet though Nazi Germany and the Second World War are subjects that continue to occupy and fascinate historians, the story beneath those superlatives – the story of civilian life in Berlin during the war – is one that has remained curiously unwritten.

There are a number of reasons why this apparently obvious subject should have become one of the few remaining lacunae in the historical record of Nazi Germany. Historians have traditionally tended to pay comparatively little attention to the social history of Nazism, preferring the 'top-down' approach of analysing the role of Hitler, the Nazi elite or the military. The result is that few of the volumes in the ever-burgeoning canon of literature on the Third Reich shed any light on civilian life at all.

Other factors serve to reinforce this bias. Most important, perhaps, is the fact that those historians that do venture into the social sphere of the Third Reich often tend to concentrate their attentions on the persecution and destruction of the Jews. This is, of course, right and proper, but it has also led to a profound imbalance in our understanding of German society as a whole. We know little about the challenges posed to the German people by living in a dictatorship, the compromises demanded and the principles that, in some cases, had to be abandoned. We know little about the ways in which consent was engendered, how it was maintained and what happened when it broke down. In short, there are a plethora of books explaining how a minority died under Nazism, but there are very few that explain how the majority lived.

Happily, there are a number of factors that strongly encourage an examination of the social history of wartime Berlin. Historiography has been shifting in this direction in recent years, as historians look beyond the bare facts to discern popular reactions to events. Where once grand strategy and high politics were the dominant themes of history, nowadays much more humble everyday subjects and sources begin to proliferate. One might call this process the democratisation of history, marking as it does the shift away from 'the great and the good' in favour of the 'view from below'. This trend is also illustrated by the many published memoirs and diaries that now seem to be ubiquitous in the bookshops.

The most urgent argument in favour of this approach, however, is that this is the final opportunity we have to allow those that experienced the war directly to tell their stories. Many of the 'voices' that I have used in this book are from published sources, but I also wanted to make use of the personal accounts of ordinary Berliners, which have never been recorded for posterity. To this end, I undertook a programme of interviews in the German capital, in which I crisscrossed the city to meet people for whom 'Berlin at War' forms part of their personal story.

Yet as time marches on – this spring saw the sixty-fifth anniversary of the end of the Second World War – those that experienced the war even as adolescents are now well into their seventies. Sadly, some of those elderly Berliners whom I interviewed have passed away in the interim. Many of them are still in rude health, a few quite astonishingly sprightly, but there are some, I fear, that will not see the publication of a German edition. The generation that experienced the war at first hand is gradually slipping away. And as the African saying runs: 'When an old man dies, a library burns to the ground.'

Over coffee and cake in *gemütlich* surroundings, I would often hear the most hair-raising tales of personal pain, loss and survival; occasionally there were tears as long-suppressed memories were brought to light once again. Though it was never demanded or requested, I felt obliged to render such contributions anonymous, out of respect for the privacy of those who I interviewed and whose unpublished memoirs and diaries I have quoted.*

Needless to say, I gleaned far more material in this process than I could ever sensibly use in the writing of this book. Much of it was also very subjective, unverifiable, occasionally misremembered or accompanied by the whiff of self-exculpation. But in spite of those caveats, the experience demonstrated to me that eye-witness testimony has a vital role to play in history; personal accounts and anecdotes can bring a fresh perspective, colour or context to even the most hackneyed and well-trodden narrative. Some purists wax rather sanctimonious about this 'personalisation of history', which they perceive as the elevation of the personal above the political and empirical. But I would suggest that if it is done correctly and responsibly, then this personal approach not only has a role to play, it is an essential ingredient of the historian's art of bringing the past to life.

Of course, other primary sources are readily available. There is a wealth of published memoirs, ranging from the well-known works of Missie Vassiltchikov or William Shirer to the vast number of obscure volumes never translated into English. Countless unpublished diaries kept by ordinary Berliners during the war were subsequently bequeathed to

* For stylistic reasons pseudonyms are employed in the text, while the authors are cited in the endnotes with only their first name and an initial of their surname.

relatives or donated to the archives. It is this mass of primary material that has been my constant companion in writing this book. Here too I have been able to incorporate only a fraction of those 'voices' into my narrative, but their words have shaped my understanding of the subject.

Yet even with the best possible research and the richest 'raw material', it is still a hugely complex task to tell the story of a city of five million souls over six years of warfare. In the circumstances, my approach has been necessarily *pointillist*, seeking to give a flavour of events, rather than make any grand claims to comprehensiveness. The book's structure also required a degree of ingenuity. Given the complexity of the story that I wanted to tell, I dispensed early on with the idea of a unified linear chronology and realised that some nod towards a thematic approach would be necessary. The result is an attempt to combine both the thematic and the chronological in a single narrative arc. I would willingly concede that this has sometimes been a difficult balance to strike and I beg the reader's indulgence if occasionally he or she has to rewind a little between chapters.

The result is something rather novel: a 'Berlin-eye view' of the Second World War, telling the story of that conflict as ordinary Berliners would have experienced it. It gives a flavour of everyday life in the German capital, charting the violent humbling of a once-proud metropolis – the fear, the cruelty, the petty heroism and the individual tragedy. What emerges most vividly, I believe, is the rich political diversity of Berlin society. The German capital was never a natural constituency for the Nazis: its left-wing traditions, vibrant Jewish community and cosmopolitan elite saw to that. Consequently, it witnessed more opposition to the Nazis – on every level – than any other German city; more Jews survived in the underground there – aided and abetted by ordinary Berliners – than anywhere else in Germany.

I hope the book will demonstrate that we are fundamentally missing the point if we imagine wartime Berliners to be an indoctrinated mass of Nazified automata, sleepwalking into catastrophe. As numerous interviewees made clear to me, Berlin was a city where minorities of active Nazis and active anti-Nazis flanked an ambivalent majority, who were often simply motivated by self-preservation, ambition and fear. In this respect, at least, it strikes me that wartime Berliners had much more in common with ourselves than we would care to concede. 'They' are really not so very different from 'us'.

Prologue: 'Führerweather'

Unbroken sunshine was forecast for Thursday 20 April 1939, *Führerwetter* as it was known in Nazi Germany. Across the city, Berliners woke that morning in eager expectation of what promised to be one of the highlights of the year. It was the fiftieth birthday of the German Chancellor and Führer of the Greater German Reich, Adolf Hitler, and a series of events, parades and receptions would mark the occasion. A public holiday had been decreed, a grand spectacle was in the offing and the forecast of good weather would only have heightened the party mood.

Across the capital, therefore, thousands of ordinary Germans prepared for a day out. Veterans of the First World War would polish their medals and pin them proudly on their chests. The women would take care to select stout shoes and carry coats and some refreshments: bread rolls, perhaps, and cold meats. The better prepared among them would take folding chairs or stools. Some even packed a mirror periscope to ensure a good view of proceedings. The younger generation, meanwhile, mostly members of the various Hitler Youth organisations, would don their neatly pressed uniforms, shine their belt buckles and check their complement of badges. Boys would comb their hair; girls would wear plaits or neat 'German' braids. For all of them, the excitement of that morning would have been palpable.

Before setting off for the city centre, those attending the celebrations would have been wise to read the official directions that were published in every newspaper. They were advised not to stray too close to tracked vehicles during the parade and warned to stay well clear of horses. The instructions of police and Party officials, they were reminded, were to be heeded without delay and without contradiction. During the parade itself, photography was strictly forbidden.[1]

The official preparations for the day were no less thorough. The administrative centre of the city was closed to traffic from 7.00 in the morning. The Tiergarten railway station – close to the site of the parade – was also shut. Those travelling into the centre of Berlin to enjoy the festivities were advised to alight as close as possible to the restricted area and continue their journey on foot. Finally, due to a planned fly-past that afternoon, the airspace over central Berlin was to be closed to air traffic for the entire day.[2]

Large numbers of participants and visitors would require overnight accommodation in the capital. The majority of the 50,000 or so military personnel who were directly involved in the parade could be housed in the barracks at Lichterfelde and Potsdam, or at the various other military installations that surrounded the capital. VIPs and special guests, meanwhile, were given rooms in two of Berlin's best hotels; the Adlon and the Kaiserhof, where they were even afforded an SS guard.[3] The many thousands of ordinary visitors, who had come from all over the Reich and abroad, found accommodation – if they were lucky – in Berlin's many less renowned hotels and guest houses. For the lowliest among them, the city's numerous parks offered ample opportunities for pitching a tent.

Hitler, meanwhile, had wanted for nothing that morning. He had risen unusually early. As his valet, Heinz Linge, later recalled, 'The Führer donned his brown Party uniform . . . [and] put on the golden dress belt of a German general as Supreme Commander of the Wehrmacht. He stood before the mirror in his bedroom for ages, feasting his eyes on his own image like a peacock and repeatedly adjusting his jacket.'[4] His staff, standing to attention in the marbled halls of the Reich Chancellery, had been similarly preened. 'Servants stood at the doors', Linge went on:

> wearing magnificent uniforms with silver lanyards and medals on their chests . . . the adjutants and liaison officers were lined up, together with Hitler's bodyguard and the pilots from his own flight. Then there were the soldiers from the *Leibstandarte* in their black SS uniforms, their new belts made in imitation of Kaiser Wilhelm's guards. Officers from the *Leibstandarte* – like those from the Wehrmacht – wore silver lanyards and dress-uniform belts.[5]

At 8.00 that morning, the band of the SS-*Leibstandarte* performed a short recital in the garden of the Reich Chancellery, playing '*Deutschland, Deutschland über Alles*' and the 'Horst Wessel Song'. Hitler, standing beneath the elegant classical portico, listened intently before thanking the performers and returning inside. There, he perused the vast accumulation of gifts that was presented on the long negotiating tables. He had received a selection of presents from his inner circle at midnight the previous evening, but most would be presented this morning. As his secretary Christa Schroeder wrote to a friend that week:

> the number and value of the presents this year is staggering. Paintings (Defregger, Waldmüller, Lenbach, even a glorious Titian), then wonderful Meissen sculptures in porcelain, silver table- and centre-pieces, magnificent books, vases, drawings, carpets . . . aircraft and ship models and similar military items which give him the greatest pleasure.[6]

Yet, in addition to such treasures from his political colleagues and admirers, Hitler also received countless more modest gifts from ordinary Germans: pillows and blankets embroidered with swastikas, handicrafts, huge cakes, boxes of sweets and local delicacies. 'How many thoughts from fanatical, adoring women', Schroeder mused, 'had been woven into this handiwork!'[7]

An hour or so later, after a short breakfast, Hitler left the Chancellery to review a parade on the Wilhelmstrasse, where the *Leibstandarte*, the SS-*Totenkopf* and a battalion of *Schutzpolizei* marched past in perfect order, to the blare of a military band. The streets – festooned as they were with swastikas and thronged with well-wishers – gave an impressive foretaste of what was to follow.

The next hour was taken up receiving the congratulations of esteemed guests, delegations and the representatives of foreign powers. The first to attend was the Papal Nuncio, bringing the best wishes of the new Pope, Pius XII. He was followed by the President of Bohemia and Moravia, Emil Hácha, and the President of Slovakia, Jozef Tiso. Next, Hitler received the congratulations of the Reich Government, a delegation of senior Wehrmacht personnel, and a visit by the Lord Mayor of Berlin, Dr Julius Lippert. Telegrams were also delivered, among many others from King George VI and from Henry Ford. Lastly, at 10.20, Hitler was formally awarded the Freedom of the City of Danzig, presented by the city's Gauleiter, Albert Forster.

Then, shortly before 11.00 that morning, Hitler once again climbed into his Mercedes Tourer to be driven to the reviewing stand, located on the East-West Axis. For the duration of the short journey, as he passed the countless columns of troops mustered for the parade, he stood impassively in the footwell of the Mercedes, his right arm outstretched in salute.

The majority of Berliners, now thronging the route of the parade, had probably endured a rather less hectic morning. They might have listened to the radio, or taken the opportunity offered by the public holiday to enjoy a leisurely breakfast. Those preparing to visit the city centre would have discussed which vantage points to head for. Those who planned to stay at home could listen to proceedings from the comfort of their armchair, as the entire occasion would be relayed by a team of radio commentators, with light music punctuating the action. Listeners with a trained ear would even notice the usual musical choreography at work; the jaunty 'Badenweiler March', for instance, which signalled the imminent arrival of the Führer.

Special editions of the news magazines were crammed with pictorial accounts of Hitler's life and achievements. The newspapers, too, published special editions to mark the occasion. All of them would have reproduced the text of the congratulatory speech given by Joseph Goebbels, who had exhorted the previous night that: 'no German at home or anywhere else in the world can fail to take the deepest and heartiest pleasure in participation. It is a holiday of the nation, and we want to celebrate it as such.'[8]

Most newspapers also carried a large selection of congratulatory letters and poems sent in by readers. The SS paper *Das Schwarze Korps* quoted readers expressing their 'eternal pride' in 'the miracle' of Hitler, or lauding Berlin as the 'epicentre of events at this momentous time'.[9] Another paper followed suit, printing the dubious poetic musings of an eighty-year-old reader, who, it was claimed, was 'delighted to have experienced these times'.[10] Goebbels' Berlin paper *Der Angriff* carried a saccharine piece expressing the congratulations of three 'unknown Berliners' – a policeman, a housewife and an SA man.[11]

★   ★   ★

For those who ventured into the city centre that morning, a genuine spectacle awaited. All Germans were obliged to hang out a swastika flag on such an important day, and it was an instruction that few dared to contravene. Nonetheless, many Berliners went beyond mere perfunctory compliance. In the suburbs, countless balconies and windows were adorned with flags, photographs or elaborate garlands. The city centre was extravagantly festooned. In the commercial districts, almost every shop and office building had photographs or busts of Hitler mounted in their windows, surrounded with flowers and wreaths. All ministries and state-owned enterprises, of course, competed with each other to demonstrate their devotion. Nazi Party offices cast restraint to the four winds and hung portraits and framed slogans on their outside walls. Central streets of the capital – especially in the main administrative district – were barely recognisable. Wilhelmstrasse, for instance, where the Reich Chancellery was located, was a sea of swastika banners, while Unter den Linden and Friedrichstrasse were also decked with flags, bunting and festive garlands. One publishing house even sought to outdo its rivals by erecting an enormous 25-foot portrait of Hitler, complete with flood-lights and flags, bearing the words 'Our Loyalty: Our Thanks'.

The centrepiece of the celebrations was the East-West Axis; a newly-constructed boulevard running for seven kilometres west of the Brandenburg Gate. According to one eyewitness, on both sides of the carriageway stood 'dazzling white miniature temples of wood . . . orna-mented with clusters of scarlet, white and black swastika flags . . . At other prominent points forests of masts displayed the devices of all the districts of Greater Germany.'[12] The American correspondent William Shirer could not help but be impressed by the scene: 'I've never seen so many flags, standards, golden eagles and floodlit pylons in my life', he wrote, 'nor so many glittering uniforms, or soldiers, or guns. Nor so many people at a birthday party.'[13]

Shirer's excitement was understandable. With 50,000 troops poised to participate in the parade and as many as two million spectators ready to watch, it was to be the largest ceremonial event ever staged by the Nazis. The most fortunate, or best connected, would have secured a seat in one of the large grandstands surrounding Hitler's reviewing platform. On either side of the East-West Axis, close to the Technical High School, a pair of large tribunes had been constructed.

The first, on the south side of the boulevard, was open to the public. The other, on the north, contained a VIP enclosure to accommodate Hitler's special guests and assorted representatives of the military and the Party. Each grandstand had been built to hold approximately five thousand spectators, and was flanked by enormous pillars, each topped with a gilded eagle clutching a swastika in its talons. Those who had managed to find a seat would have had every reason to feel extremely pleased with themselves. From there, they could watch the afternoon's proceedings in relative comfort.

One spectator who had done especially well was a young Wehrmacht lieutenant, Alexander Stahlberg. As he recalled in his memoirs, a simple ruse was all that was required to get a seat in one of the grandstands:

> I learned that thousands of tickets were being issued solely to Party members and prominent personalities, so (quite without authority) I put on my new made-to-measure dress uniform, hung the sword of the Pasewalk Cuirassiers at my side and went down to the [grandstand]. There I simply followed the signs to the individual groups of seats on the stand. CD – Corps Diplomatique – seemed to me the best chance, and in the twinkling of an eye there I was amidst all the pomp and circumstance of the foreign military attachés.[14]

Most spectators, however, had no such luck. They lined the route of the parade dozens deep, waiting. There was much pushing and shoving, as ever more Berliners joined the throng and all had to be held back by the lines of smiling SS and SA men with their arms linked. Some children complained of tiredness and asked incessantly whether the Führer was there yet. Others wriggled through to the front rank of the crowd, where they could watch proceedings through the legs of the men in the police cordon. As the tension rose, some spectators fainted and had to be revived by the nurses of the Red Cross; a few – despite the imprecations and threats of the police – bravely perched on windowsills or climbed the still-bare trees of the Tiergarten to get a better view. Nonetheless, despite the strain and the excitement, the crowd was generally in excellent humour. William Shirer described it as 'a pure holiday mood . . . The Führer's birthday was a national holiday, with the result that all the youngsters of the

city were in the front row . . . with the elders, usually the whole family
– father, mother, uncle, aunt – grouped behind.'[15]

The crowd was a microcosm of Nazi Germany. Alongside Berliners,
it included representatives of every district, province and *Gau* of the
Reich. Regional accents and dialects proliferated; Rhinelanders rubbed
shoulders with Saxons, Bavarians with Frisians and Sudeten Germans
with East Prussians. Every uniform imaginable was represented, from
the dark brown overalls of the *Reichsarbeitsdienst* to the short trousers
of the Hitler Youth and the smart field-grey parade dress of the
Wehrmacht. In the hours before the spectacle, the crowd entertained
themselves listening to martial music piped through the network of
loudspeakers. They would have swapped stories, compared notes
perhaps on how many times they had seen their Führer in the flesh,
or maybe tentatively expressed their concerns about the precarious
international situation. Most, however, would have simply been happy
to be there, to enjoy the holiday atmosphere and participate in such
a memorable occasion. Then, as Hitler first appeared – making his
way to the reviewing stand – the crowd was briefly hushed before
erupting into a chorus of cheers and hurrahs.

Of course, there were also some present who did not support the
Nazis and had turned out in the Tiergarten merely to witness what
they had rightly expected would be an historic spectacle. One such
Berliner recalled that, as the crowd roused itself to acclaim Hitler's
arrival, she and her partner dived into a side street to avoid any
accusation of recalcitrance. 'Behind us', she wrote:

> the crowd stretched out the 'German Greeting'. 'Sieg Heil! Sieg Heil!'
> we hear them shout. Those who don't raise their arm are arrested. Yet,
> as we look around, we see around fifteen or twenty people who, like
> us, have managed to extricate themselves from the crowd and have
> hastily disappeared into the calm of the side street. 'Good day', we say
> as we pass. 'Good day', they reply genially. One of them even raises
> his hat with a smile. [16]

Some were not so cowed, however, and dared to register a protest.
'On a kitchen stepladder in the middle of the push sits a workman',
one eyewitness wrote, 'lean, unshaven, in blue mechanic's overall. He
looks pensively at the rolling trucks. "You take all that, and no gas,"

we hear him growl, "and it's just junk." People around look up at him, horrified. When they see that no one is protesting, they venture an approving smile.'[17]

The majority of the spectators, however, would scarcely have noticed such independently minded protest. Most of them were doubtless lost in the moment, enjoying seeing their Führer at close quarters and revelling in the enthusiasm exuded by the rest of the crowd. The cult surrounding Hitler was very much in place by 1939, with all Nazi ceremonial being minutely stage-managed so as to consciously and deliberately invoke wonder and reverence in the watching public. Many of those witnessing events that day in Berlin would have felt euphoric emotions akin to a religious experience.

After the initial excitement of Hitler's arrival and the progress of his motorcade along the East-West Axis, a hush descended as the Führer reached the reviewing platform. As Alexander Stahlberg recalled: 'Then came the great moment when the birthday boy drove by, standing in his big 7-litre Mercedes. The good company into which I had so successfully insinuated myself rose, as is proper on the arrival of a Head of State, and saluted in silence.'[18] There, opposite the heavy Wilhelmine backdrop of the Technical High School, Hitler alighted from his Mercedes and climbed a few steps to a central dais where a plush red and gilded chair awaited him. Above him, his personal standard hung stiffly, and to his rear – behind the grandstand – an enormous gilded eagle was flanked by six large banners, all bearing the swastika. He greeted his guests. To his left sat the representatives of his latest territorial acquisition – the 'Protector' of Bohemia and Moravia, Konstantin von Neurath, and the province's diminutive President, Emil Hácha, looking forlorn in a sober dark suit and a top hat. To Hitler's right sat the President and Foreign Minister of the newly independent Slovak republic along with the German Foreign Minister, Joachim von Ribbentrop. Behind him, the bemedalled commanders-in-chief of Germany's armed forces were arranged: Hermann Göring for the Luftwaffe, Admiral Raeder for the Navy and Generals Brauchitsch and Keitel for the Wehrmacht. In a large VIP enclosure to the rear of them sat the serried ranks of the senior military in a mass of grey uniforms, broken only by patches of black for the Navy, whose white hats gleamed in the sunshine. Behind and on either side of the military, another enclosure contained more special guests including the representatives of foreign powers – military attachés, ambassadors and consular staff – as well as numerous lesser Party and state functionaries, accompanied by their coiffured wives. For the ordinary spectators, gathered in the grandstands to either side, or across the boulevard, it was all a most impressive sight.

After a brief lull, the proceedings began with a display of German air power. Berliners craned their necks skyward as squadrons of Heinkel bombers and Messerschmitt fighter aircraft droned past in tight formation. Hitler acknowledged the display, nodding to himself with satisfaction and sharing a word with Göring.

Following this aerial prelude, the procession proper could begin. First, the three hundred or so colours and standards of all the participating regiments were paraded, their bearers marching in step to the repertoire of the *Leibstandarte* military band. This was followed by divisions of infantry and marines goose-stepping in immaculate order past the tribune. When the paratroopers appeared, marching in close formation wearing their camouflage jumpsuits, a buzz went through the crowd: this was the first time that this new elite formation had paraded in public.

Next came the motorised units, first, the panzer-grenadiers, loaded into Opel trucks that trundled past the podium four abreast. They were followed by motorcycle sidecar units, each carrying three men and pedantically arranged in number-plate order. Armoured cars came next, followed by reconnaissance vehicles and searchlight teams. All the latest machinery was on display. Panzers followed; some clattered along churning up the fresh road surface, others were mounted on low-loaders, their crews – resplendent in black uniforms and berets – perched on the accompanying trucks. One young spectator was especially enthused. Watching the soldiers and machinery, he was struck by how precisely the ranks were drawn up and the tremendous discipline that was demonstrated as they marched or drove past the reviewing stand. 'It was a feast for the eyes', he recalled, 'and the applause never seemed to end.'[19]

Lastly, all manner of artillery filed past. Every type was in attendance, from the smallest horse-drawn field howitzer, to the 88mm anti-aircraft gun and the massive K-3 cannon, hauled by an equally massive 18-ton FAMO half-track. For the grand finale, the colours of the participating regiments were returned to the saluting base and were massed before the Führer. As a commander – precariously mounted on a skittish grey – gave the orders, the flags were dipped in solemn salute.

From the first bugle call to the last hurrah, the parade had lasted almost five hours. If arranged in a single line, its troops and machinery would have formed a queue over 100 kilometres long.[20] It had been the largest peacetime display of military might ever seen. Throughout, Hitler acknowledged the passing regiments and divisions in his trademark manner: his left hand resting on the belt buckle at his waist, while his right arm was outstretched in salute. Only occasionally – when a lull in proceedings would allow – he would sit for a time and exchange a few words with those around him. But mostly he stood, stern-faced, watching his military machine pass by. Hitler liked to boast of his ability to stand and salute much longer than any of his fellow Nazis,[21] and on this occasion his claims were well proven. Christa Schroeder was one of those who marvelled at his stamina. 'It is simply amazing to me where he gets his strength from', she wrote. 'Hours without a break standing and saluting are damned tiring. Just watching we got dog-tired.'[22]

The reaction of the crowd to this martial spectacle, however, was anything but tired. Those that opposed the Nazis or were unnerved by such demonstrations of military might would generally have stayed away, so the vast majority of those present surely felt nothing but a surge of pride at the very visible restoration of German power, and – as they saw it – German honour. Their reaction was simply one of enthusiasm, wonder and occasional amusement. The appearance of the cavalry squadrons raised a cheer, for instance, not least as the occasionally wild-eyed horses injected a spirit of glamour and unpredictability into proceedings. At other times, the sheer scale, complexity or novelty of the military hardware on display prompted exclamations of amazement. One journalist reported that the phrase 'Neee . . . sowat!', which roughly translates to 'Well, I never!', was a commonly heard response.[23]

Naturally, the entire event would be thoroughly exploited for the purposes of propaganda. Official photographers had lined the route and dutifully captured every sight and vista, many of which would later appear in commemorative volumes, a must for every German coffee table. In addition, Goebbels had selected twelve cinematographers to record the procession. Their brief was clear. 'Transcending the present', it said, they were to:

> create a historic document for the future, to capture in pictures the greatness of this day for all to see. This parade must become a paradigm of film reporting. It is not simply a matter of outward form – the spirit of the hour must be captured also, the whole atmosphere of discipline and concentrated power. Every second of the action must be captured as it occurs.[24]

They would not disappoint. Between them, they would shoot over eight kilometres of film,[25] material which would be used – accompanied by appropriately martial music – in the newsreel of the day.

As the parade concluded and Hitler returned to the Reich Chancellery to receive foreign delegations in a private reception, the crowds that had thronged the East-West Axis or packed the grandstands began to drift away. A few would have moved on to other celebratory events elsewhere. Many with young children, meanwhile, would have found themselves magnetically drawn to the tanks now parked up on the East-West Axis, whose crews allowed eager young boys to clamber aboard and peer inside, wide-eyed. The majority, however, simply made for home or else sought refreshment in the crowded bars and restaurants of the city centre. Inevitably, as the hostelries filled to overflowing, the revellers spilled out into the street where they sang and danced the night away, restrained only by the cordons of jovial SS and police, who sought to keep the main thoroughfares open. For many of them, the party would only end with the break of dawn.

The mood among the revellers was optimistic. Germany's military and political might had been demonstrated to full effect that afternoon, and it was all a far cry from the humiliations of Versailles, the grim years of the Depression and the political chaos of the 1920s. Hitler, it appeared, had delivered what he had promised and had restored German prestige and self-confidence. That afternoon, it must have seemed to the Berlin public as though their Führer had made good on his prediction expressed in *Mein Kampf*: 'It shall be a greater honour to be a citizen of this Reich, even as a street-sweeper, than to be the King of a foreign state.'[26] Even William Shirer, not a natural ally or admirer of the Nazis, would have agreed with that assumption. That afternoon, he recorded: 'you get the impression from the people in the street that they feel pretty good about these things, and certainly proud of them. They seem to feel that they have got somewhere and are going places, as a nation.'[27]

Such optimism was not misplaced. In the spring of 1939 Hitler's Germany was at the very peak of its power. In the preceding few weeks, German troops had marched into Prague, occupied what had remained of Czechoslovakia and annexed the disputed Memel territory from Lithuania. Of course, such events had injected a rather fraught tone to international relations, but the vast majority of Germans fervently believed that Hitler was committed to peace and would be able to negotiate such tensions away.

Greater Germany, therefore, was a reality and – crucially for the German public – it was at peace. Straddling the continent from the North Sea to the Danube Basin and from the eastern Baltic to the Rhine, it was the largest and most populous state in Europe. Beyond its borders, Germany wielded enormous influence. It had successfully overcome the worst effects of the Depression. Its economy was booming – having already reached full employment – and was drawing much of central Europe into its 'area of influence'. Germany's political model, meanwhile, was proving increasingly attractive to those nations seemingly hamstrung by democracy and struggling with political extremism and unrest. Even the overt display of military might seemed to have done little to dampen the enthusiasm. As one commentator noted that day, the crowd at the parade 'didn't strike you as thinking much about war, even though they were looking at the men and the machines which will fight it, if it should come'.[28] Little wonder, perhaps, that so many Berliners viewed the future with unbridled optimism.

I

Faith in the Führer

The 1st of September 1939 was a day that began like any other. A bright, late summer morning had dawned, with a sprinkling of dew on the ground and a cool breeze blowing down off the Baltic. Early risers opened their curtains and readied themselves for the day ahead. It was a Friday and work and school beckoned for most. The morning ablutions would be completed; clothes for the day would be selected and put on. Children would be hurried along, encouraged to follow the established routine. Then there would be breakfast: coffee pots would be placed on hobs, dark rye bread carefully sliced, and meat or cheese prepared.

Those reading their newspaper over breakfast would have learned little about the momentous events then unfolding two hundred or so miles to the east. Though the main dailies would later produce an 'extra', hawked noisily in the heart of the capital, the regular editions carried no information about the events of that morning. Some printed stories suggesting that the ongoing crisis with Poland was coming to a head, listing Polish 'outrages' of recent months or giving details of a hand-grenade attack carried out against ethnic Germans there.[1] Some news stories were rather peculiar, the products perhaps of fevered speculation or the imagination of a Propaganda Ministry official. One suggested that the Polish army was moving against Lithuania and Latvia,[2] while another reported that a Polish claim had been made to the city of Berlin itself.[3]

Most reports in the newspapers, however, portrayed a city in which life appeared to be continuing very much as norm... link to Dresden was declared to be close to... Zoo announced that children would be adm... coming weekend. Book serialisations vied fo... and reports from the financial markets. Enter... prominently displayed. The premiere of the film...

('The Merciful Lie') – a peculiar tale of a love triangle set during a German expedition to Mongolia – was scheduled for that evening in the UFA cinema on Kurfürstendamm. German cinema's darling, Olga Tschechowa, meanwhile, was appearing in a stage production of the comedy *Aimée* at the Künstlertheater. Wagner's *Meistersinger* was being staged at the Volksoper. In sport, a report on practice for the Belgrade Grand Prix noted with satisfaction that a German driver in a Mercedes had posted the fastest lap time.[4]

Yet, at some point, the realisation would have dawned that this was not just another day. For some, word might have come from their neighbours, perhaps only a shouted and half-understood exchange across a stairwell. For those in the city centre, raised voices might have drifted up to them from the streets below. Hungry for information or clarification, they would have switched on their radios. The same announcements were broadcast across all stations – an official proclamation containing a flurry of phrases, such as 'frontier violations', 'defence of German honour', 'duty to the last' and 'force being met with force'.[5] Berliner Günter Grossmann was sixteen at the time. His description of hearing the news that morning was typical:

> 7 a.m., I wake and turn our 'Volksempfänger' on to listen to the early concert. But, instead of that, I hear the voice of the Reich Chancellor, Adolf Hitler; a declaration of the Reich Government, that since 4 o'clock that morning German troops have crossed the Polish frontier and are on the advance . . . With that, our worst fears are realised: It is war! . . . I wake my parents and tell them what I have heard. There is consternation.[6]

The dawning day would be one that few Berliners would ever forget. Heinz Knobloch remembered with particular clarity how he had heard the news. When he arrived at school that morning, he had been told that there would be no lessons and that he was to return home. 'Fantastic!' he recalled thinking, but neither he nor his classmates asked why.[7] On arriving home, he was still none the wiser and was happily anticipating a day off school when a family friend called down from the next floor: 'You should turn on the radio', he was told. 'There is something going on. The *Führer* is giving a speech.'[8]

* * *

At that very moment, Hitler was delivering one of the most important speeches of his life. He was ill prepared; he had not slept well
and looked tired and drawn, despite receiving a stimulant injection
from his personal physician.[9] The stresses of recent weeks had taken
their toll, and, as was usual, he had been up late the previous night,
dictating the text of his speech to his secretaries. His usual ailments
were also affecting him that morning: stomach pains, headaches,
insomnia. His halitosis had been so bad, one member of his entourage
recalled, that those around him had struggled not to step backwards
in revulsion.[10]

Shortly before ten o'clock that morning, Hitler had climbed into a
Mercedes limousine and had been driven the short distance from the
Reich Chancellery to the Kroll Opera House, where the Reichstag had
been called for a special sitting. From the Chancellery, Hitler's convoy
would have wound its way north onto Wilhelmstrasse, before turning
west onto Unter den Linden, heading for the Brandenburg Gate.
Hitler's mood would scarcely have been lightened by the sights that
greeted him on the way. From around eight o'clock that morning,
units of SS and SA had been dispatched to hold back the crowds that
were expected to line the route after hearing the news. But there were
no crowds. Almost all of those who witnessed the scene testified to
the peculiar emptiness that echoed around Berlin's central district. The
Swede Birger Dahlerus recalled that 'the streets seemed rather deserted
and as far as we could see . . . the people with few exceptions stared
in silence as Hitler passed by'.[11] Even Albert Speer conceded that the
area of the Chancellery, which was usually besieged by people whenever Hitler was there, was 'strikingly quiet'.[12]

Passing through the Brandenburg Gate, Hitler's car would have
turned north and skirted around the Reichstag building – now largely
abandoned after being burnt out in the infamous fire of 1933 – before
entering the manicured lawns and parkland of the Königsplatz. To
the south, the tree-lined Siegesallee, or 'Victory Avenue', disappeared
into the Tiergarten, flanked with white marble statues of the Prussian
kings. Ahead stood the Kroll Opera House.

Originally constructed in 1844 to provide Berlin with a venue for
diverse cultural and festive events, the Kroll was a most impressive
building. Looking like an elegant Roman *palazzo*, it had once boasted
three large halls, fourteen function rooms, a generous veranda and a

resident orchestra of sixty musicians. In its heyday, it was said, there
was space to accommodate fully five thousand Berliners.[13] The Kroll
had earned its greatest fame in the late 1920s for producing challenging
contemporary works, such as those of Hindemith, Stravinsky and
Schönberg, but had been closed in 1931 by those conservative forces
who despised its modernistic licence. Thereafter, the building had stood
empty for two years until 1933, when Hitler needed a replacement
venue for the Reichstag. After the necessary alterations had been made,
the Kroll Opera became the new home of the German parliament.

Yet, in this capacity, the Kroll served as little more than the backdrop for the death throes of an ailing democracy. It was there, in
March 1933, that a cowed Reichstag passed the 'Enabling Act', which
empowered the Nazi government to legislate without its consent –
thereby providing Hitler with, in effect, dictatorial power. After that,
the Kroll Opera saw only sporadic Reichstag meetings, in which the
deputies – shorn of their communist and socialist contingents –
dutifully passed whatever legislation was put before them. As one
historian has written, the formula for such meetings was always the
same: 'Göring, as President, greeted the members; there was a moment
of silence for the Nazi martyrs; Hitler spoke; Göring thanked the
Führer; laws were rubber-stamped; the 'Horst Wessel Lied' was sung.
Then they all went home.'[14] With that ignominious development, the
Kroll Opera House should perhaps finally have faded into obscurity.
But its most famous – or infamous – hour was yet to come.

Hitler arrived outside the Kroll in bright sunshine. Stepping from
his car, he was met by members of his entourage – Heinrich Himmler,
Martin Bormann and his adjutant Julius Schaub. He briefly inspected
an SS guard of honour before walking the fifty or so yards to the front
steps. Entering the main hall, he passed the ranks of Reichstag deputies,
all now standing in silence with their right arms raised in the 'Hitler
greeting'. There were no dissenters. All those of independent or
oppositional mind had long since been intimidated, co-opted or otherwise removed from the chamber. Even those deputies who had been
unable to get to the capital at short notice had been replaced by
members of Hitler's bodyguard.

In its Nazi incarnation, the main hall of the Kroll was little changed
and the Reichstag deputies were seated, like the opera audiences before
them, in the stalls and in the two grand tiers above. The only real

changes were on the former stage, where an enormous stylised eagle rose – its outstretched wings reaching the full width of the fire curtain – with the rays of the sun seemingly emanating from the swastika held in its claws. On either side were two massive swastika banners. Beneath that, in the area once inhabited by the orchestra and choir, members of Hitler's cabinet were arranged in seated banks facing out into the hall itself. In the centre, Göring – as Reichstag President – sat in a high leather-backed chair, overseeing proceedings. Below him stood the lectern with a bank of microphones, where Hitler would speak – standing – flanked by seated Gauleiters and ministers.

After a brief introduction from Göring, Hitler arrived at the podium and composed himself. As a hush descended, he began to speak. Sounding hoarse and tired, even hesitant at the outset, he nevertheless quickly warmed to his task, presenting a masterful portrait of feigned innocence. He outlined his spurned proposals for 'peaceful discussions' with the Poles, his attempts to find mediation and his 'patient endurance'. He railed against Polish 'provocations' – border incidents and acts of terror allegedly perpetrated against innocent German civilians – before speaking of the perfidy of the Poles and their unwillingness to commit to a nego-tiated settlement of the crisis. In response, he warned that 'no honourable Great Power could calmly tolerate such a state of affairs' and stated that his 'love of peace and endless forbearance' should not be mistaken for 'weakness or even cowardice'. He was resolved, he said, 'to speak to Poland in the same language that Poland has employed towards us in the months past'. Hitler then revealed what most people already knew:

> We have now been returning fire since 5.45 a.m.* Henceforth, bomb will be met with bomb. He who fights with poison gas shall be fought with poison gas. He who distances himself from the rules for a humane conduct of warfare can only expect us to take like steps. I will lead this struggle, whoever may be the adversary, until the security of the Reich and its rights have been assured.[15]

He went on to outline the sacrifice that he was demanding of the German people; a sacrifice that he, too, had been ready to make in

---

* Whether by accident or design, Hitler had misrepresented the time at which his forces had opened fire. The first shots had actually been fired an hour earlier, at 4.45 a.m.

the Great War. 'I am from now on', he proclaimed, 'just the first soldier of the German Reich.' Referring to the field-grey tunic he had donned for the occasion, he said, 'I have once more put on that coat that was most sacred and dear to me. I will not take it off again until victory is secured, or I will not survive the outcome.'[16] After the requisite chorus of *Sieg Heils*, Hitler left the chamber.

If he had been hoping to convince the people of Berlin and the wider Reich through the force of his delivery, Hitler was mistaken. Though the Nazi Gauleiters and Party men had given their predictably enthusiastic verdict, the general public was not so easily swayed. A young diplomat in the American Embassy recalled watching workmen from his office window that morning, while Hitler's speech was being broadcast. 'They were unimpressed by the fact that their Führer was speak-ing', he recorded; 'they did not even stop their work to listen.' The end of the speech, with its admission that the war against Poland had begun, was met with similar apathy. Even the lusty rendition of the national anthem left them unmoved. 'The workers across the street had almost finished', he recalled. 'They were undisturbed by the declaration of war. After all, nobody had asked their opinion about it.'[17]

A depressed atmosphere greeted Hitler as he returned to the Reich Chancellery that morning, where a small, somewhat grim-faced crowd had gathered on the Wilhelmstrasse and on the Wilhelmplatz. His arrival was met not with the usual chorus of cheers and slogans, but, rather, with an eerie silence; with some silently raising their right arm in a Nazi salute. The Gauleiter of Swabia, Karl Wahl, who had been present at Hitler's Kroll Opera speech, confirmed this negative mood in the capital. 'I have not seen a trace of that which I experienced in 1914', he wrote in his memoir, 'no enthusiasm, no joy, no cheering. Everywhere, one encountered an oppressive calm, not to say depression. The entire German people seemed seized by a paralysing horror that made it incapable of expressing either approval or disapproval.'[18]

As Hitler dismounted from his car, the band of the *Leibstandarte* did their best to maintain a martial air, but the mood was distinctly downcast. Before he disappeared behind the heavy doors of the Chancellery, Hitler cast a perplexed glance towards the hushed crowd. Watching the scene, one eyewitness remembered hearing the distinctive sound of women weeping.[19]

★   ★   ★

In spite of the momentous events unfolding at the Kroll Opera, most commentators noted the sheer ordinariness of the day. A little less traffic on the streets, perhaps, and a few more uniforms in evidence on the pavements, but otherwise the buses, trams and trains were full, and everybody went about their business as they had done before, albeit occasionally huddling around a radio to listen to the latest announcements. William Shirer summed up the public mood in Berlin:

> The people in the streets, I noticed, were apathetic despite the immensity of the news which had greeted them from their radios . . . Across the street from the Adlon Hotel the morning shift of labourers had gone to work on the new I. G. Farben building just as if nothing had happened, and when newsboys came by shouting their extras no one laid down his tools to buy one.[20]

This apparently relaxed attitude was partly due to the fact that Berliners had already experienced a number of international crises over the past few years and all of them had blown over without conflict. Hitler, after all, had made his reputation and career by his piecemeal and peaceful dismantling of the so-called 'Versailles System'; he had blustered and threatened, even annexed disputed territories, but he had always stopped short of war. And this was how the German people wanted him to continue. As they saw it, he had been restoring German honour, restoring Germany's status as a sovereign Great Power, but avoiding the outright warfare that had been the root cause of her malaise. Far from appreciating that the invasion of Poland would be the prelude to an all-consuming conflagration, therefore, most saw it merely as an isolated skirmish, more akin to the Austrian *Anschluss* or the recent occupation of Bohemia and Moravia. A discussion one Berliner had with a taxi driver, early that weekend, showed this thinking with particular clarity:

> 'You know,' he went on, 'Hitler is really a great guy. With the [Nazi–Soviet] pact the Poles haven't got a chance. I bet you not one of these boys,' and he pointed to the heavy tanks now rattling by, 'will have to fire a single shot, or maybe just a few bullets to clean up the place. But this time there won't be any dead lists in the papers, and we'll have plenty to eat. No sir, Hitler won't get us into war.'[21]

The Berlin public was well primed, therefore, to accept the officially proclaimed fiction that Germany was the innocent party and was now 'returning fire' in what was being billed as a limited, punitive campaign. 'If Germany had been attacked', many would reason, 'she must defend herself.' Erich Neumann saw evidence of this attitude at Innsbrücker Platz in the south of the city, that morning. He was changing trams as Hitler's speech was broadcast and he heard a ripple of applause run through the crowd, while a few bystanders cursed the Poles or muttered 'finally!'[22]

Elsewhere, however, the news was received with contemplation and, in many cases, a profound sense of foreboding. Seventeen-year-old schoolgirl Else Diederichs recalled the mood on a Berlin train that morning: 'I remember that we all sat there with these frightfully serious faces. We were depressed. We had the feeling that something quite terrible was coming . . . I can still see them before my eyes, how all those faces looked.'[23]

The crowds watching the newsreels that day also failed to respond with their usual enthusiasm. As one eyewitness remembered:

> I walked into one of the inexpensive movie houses around the Friedrichstrasse station. The newsreel was on. There were a few pictures of manoeuvres of the English navy, but they were not hissed. Göring reviewing air-force troops caused applauding murmurs and consenting smiles. Goebbels, shown as he opened some party gathering, was met with dead silence. Hitler, photographed as he rode up to the new chancellery building, received a few female 'Heils', but the crowd remained tensely quiet.[24]

It was the first time in years, the author noted, that the image of the Führer had not caused 'wild and roaring applause'.

For some, the day brought forth unwelcome recollections of the Great War. Dorothea von Schwanenflügel recalled her parents looking at one another in terror when the invasion of Poland was announced: 'My God', her father exclaimed, 'wasn't one war enough in our lifetime?'[25] Others had more immediate fears: particularly for sons, husbands and brothers in the armed forces, many of whom had already been called up for active service.

For the younger generation, the outbreak of war caused genuine consternation. One young Berliner recalled hearing the declaration that 'German troops were returning fire', but could only ask himself 'who are they shooting at?'[26] Theodore Willmann, meanwhile, was more bewildered still, not least by the sudden air of seriousness at home. 'One day', he remembered, 'my mother and aunts Annuschka and Heide gathered at the window of my bedroom and gazed out in agitation. My mother said – in a voice that almost made me scared – "It is war". I stood on my bed and strained to see out, beyond the grown-ups, but I couldn't see anything.'[27]

For most Berliners, therefore, the mood on the outbreak of war was one of shock. Yet, though many had not yet realised the horrors the invasion of Poland portended, there was nonetheless a quiet determination to adapt to the new reality. That same afternoon, for instance, the first ration cards were distributed and many Berliners immediately set out to the shops to stock up on necessities. Heinz Knobloch was dispatched by his mother to a department store by the Hallesches Tor to buy something – anything – exempt from the rationing. He managed to return with two tins of sardines.[28] He was lucky to have escaped with his booty intact: the new legislation against hoarding meant that some of the more punctilious shopkeepers were already insisting on opening all tins immediately upon purchase.[29]

Sandbags were also distributed, which were to be filled and stacked against cellar and ground-floor windows, to protect against bomb blasts. To this end, large piles of sand swiftly materialised across the city, in private courtyards and in public spaces. Each block diligently set to work, dividing their labour so that the women would sew the hessian sacks, while the men would fill them, tie them off and stack them for use. One young man described the scene behind his home.

> Everyone met down in the yard. Even those whom we'd never noticed or spoken to before all lent a hand. The men reinforced the cellar windows with wooden boards. The women sewed the sandbags. One by one they were filled. 'Don't hurt yourselves lifting those!' the porter called to us boys as we set to with the bags.
>
> . . .
>
> Those who couldn't help, made coffee. And then cakes appeared from somewhere. It was like a holiday . . . an atmosphere that I had never experienced . . . The war seemed somehow harmless.[30]

As afternoon turned to evening another novelty made itself known. While the news of the outbreak of war was being solemnly digested across the city, the air raid sirens wailed into life for the first time. One foreign correspondent noted, quite correctly, that that first air raid brought the war home to the inhabitants of Berlin far more effectively than the countless announcements and decrees of that day.[31] As the opening drone of the warning siren sounded, many reacted with no little panic, unsure of where they should go. One diarist recalled the confusion: 'Outside a strange noise is heard – up and down, down and up, a long-drawn howl. Andrik springs up. "Air raid alarm!" he cries startled. We look around not knowing quite what to do.'[32]

In spite of the confusion, that first raid on the evening of 1 September passed off without serious incident. No bombs fell and it is unclear whether the 'raid' was a propaganda exercise or just the result of a lone plane that strayed too close to the capital. Whatever its origins, the regime took advantage of the event to sing Berliners' praises. According to officials, the alarm was greeted by a 'remarkable calmness and discipline' among the civilian population of Berlin. 'Within a few minutes', the newspaper articles claimed, 'the streets of the capital were completely deserted.' The mood in the cellars was 'serious, but calm and optimistic'. Within a mere quarter of an hour of the 'all clear', they claimed, Berliners were back on the street, going about their business 'as if nothing had happened'.[33]

The reality was rather different. One Berlin diarist found that the alarm caused the greatest unease. It was all 'most disagreeable', she wrote, 'and almost makes us feel as if we'd disgraced ourselves'.[34] Another remembered eating with her father in a Berlin restaurant, when the siren sounded for the first time. She was immediately gripped by fear:

I panicked and thought 'now there'll be mustard gas and phosgene'. I ran into the restaurant, opened the case, pulled out an item of papa's underwear and hurried towards the buffet. I wanted to wet the underwear in the sink so that I could cover my mouth and nose if there was a gas alert . . . I just wondered why the other guests all sat calmly at their tables and continued eating and drinking.[35]

She soon discovered, to her embarrassment, that her fellow diners had
all assumed that the siren was a test.

For those waking to a bright autumn morning the next day, 2 September,
it might have been possible to imagine, albeit briefly, that the momentous events of the previous day had been no more than a bizarre dream.
That is until the German press and radio wrenched them back into
the new reality of military offensives, artillery bombardments and
'Polish perfidy'. The newspapers that morning triumphantly recorded
that German forces had advanced all along the line; Danzig had been
welcomed back to the Reich, Teschen on the Polish–Czech frontier
had fallen and the rail link to Gdynia had been severed. The only
problem, it seemed, was that the British and French were still declaring
their support for their beleaguered Polish ally. Though they had not
yet declared war, both had ordered a general mobilisation.

The world's politicians also went into action. President Roosevelt
had issued an appeal the previous evening to all the governments
caught up in the European crisis. 'The ruthless bombing of civilians
in unfortified centers of population', he wrote, had 'sickened the hearts
of every civilized man and woman and [had] profoundly shocked the
conscience of humanity.'[36] In response, he asked all would-be combatants to affirm their determination to desist from bombing civilian
populations or undefended cities. He requested an immediate reply.

Mussolini, too, sought to exert his influence. Despite previously
pledging to support Germany in the event of war, the Italian leader
now prevaricated and tried instead to broker a peace conference, clearly
hoping to pose – as he had done at Munich the previous year – as the
voice of moderation. When this idea foundered – scuppered by Hitler's
unwillingness to be pacified and the British insistence that German
troops withdraw from Poland prior to any talks – he chose neutrality,
dressed up for his domestic audience as 'non-belligerence'. Though
the German press indulgently neglected to mention the Duce's decision, Hitler was privately furious.

While the diplomatic storm raged worldwide that weekend, Germany
presented an image of outward calmness. Hitler busied himself reading
situation reports from the front and refused to hear what he called 'bad
news' about the wider crisis. Foreign Minister Ribbentrop, therefore,
assumed temporary control of what remained of German diplomacy.

His primary objectives were to forestall the creation of a united front against Germany, and to shift the blame for any widening of the war firmly onto the shoulders of the British and the French. To this end, he prevaricated and obfuscated to the best of his ability, repeatedly sending the Italian ambassador, Bernardo Attolico, to act as an intermediary with the British and French, while simultaneously hoping that any such exchanges would be overtaken by events. He also attempted to undermine Britain's new-found assertiveness by inviting Chamberlain's adviser, Sir Horace Wilson, to Berlin for talks.[37]

In Britain, meanwhile, Prime Minister Chamberlain also prevaricated, hoping to the last to prevent war, while the British cabinet and parliament pushed for a robust response to Hitler's invasion of Poland. An initial British warning, sent on the evening of 1 September, had brought no response from Hitler, and, on the afternoon of 2 September, cabinet met and unanimously decided that an ultimatum should be communicated to Berlin. Chamberlain, however, was more cautious and sought to clutch at the straws offered by Mussolini. That evening in the House of Commons he suggested the possibility of an international conference to resolve the crisis, if the Germans agreed to withdraw their forces from Poland. In a 'short and fierce debate',[38] he was shouted down, however. And when cabinet met again later that evening, it was resolved to convince the Prime Minister of its will. Chamberlain gloomily agreed. The ultimatum would be delivered to the German capital the following morning.

The population of Berlin, meanwhile, carried on as best they could. William Shirer, for one, believed that he discerned a slight improvement in morale on the morning of 2 September. People were, he wrote, 'a little more cheery' now that the first night of blackout and air raid was behind them. Berlin 'had a fairly normal aspect', he recalled, 'shops were open . . . work on the new buildings went on as usual.'[39]

Other commentators disagreed with this rosy assessment, however. The British ambassador, Sir Nevile Henderson, was one. 'In order to see for myself the mood of the people', he wrote in his memoirs, 'I went for a walk down Unter den Linden, the main street of Berlin. Few people were about, and everyone seemed completely apathetic.'[40]

Henderson was heartened to record that Berliners did not vent their discontent in displays of hostility towards the British. 'I happened to want a drug called "Codeine"', he recalled:

and went into a shop to buy it. The chemist glumly told me that he could not give it to me without a doctor's prescription. I mentioned that I was the British Ambassador. He repeated that he was sorry, but the regulations on the subject were quite definite. So I said again, 'I don't think you understand, I am the British Ambassador. If you poison me with your drug, you will get a high decoration from your Doctor Goebbels.' The chemist's lugubrious face lit up with pleasure at this feeble joke and he at once gave me all the codeine that I wanted.[41]

Even so, he noted that 'The whole atmosphere in Berlin was one of utter gloom and depression.'[42]

Certainly, considering the fine weather of that weekend, it was apparent that few Berliners were enjoying the city's parks or waterways. One memoirist, for instance, recalled being told by a friend that she had been the only pedestrian on Unter den Linden, at 11.30 that morning.[43] Racked with anxiety or confusion, most were busy stocking up on food supplies, making the necessary alterations to their cellars, or checking their precautions for the blackout. Some of the city's children found themselves being swiftly dispatched to relatives or friends in the country, out of harm's way. They appeared at the capital's railway stations, looking pale and anxious, wearing tags around their necks bearing their names and destinations.

At 9.00 a.m. the next day – Sunday 3 September – Nevile Henderson entered the Reich Chancellery to deliver London's ultimatum to the German government. He was met by Hitler's interpreter, Paul Schmidt, who had been asked to officiate by Ribbentrop, as the latter was unwilling to be the recipient of such bad news. Schmidt, who had overslept that morning after the feverish activity of the previous week, recalled that Henderson bore a serious look when he arrived punctually on the hour. The pair shook hands; they had come to know each other quite well over the months of Henderson's residence in Berlin. Henderson declined the offer of a seat, and stood solemnly in the middle of the room. As Schmidt recalled, he announced, in a voice betraying genuine emotion:

I regret that on the instruction of my Government I have to hand you an ultimatum for the German Government. More than twenty-four

hours have elapsed since an immediate reply was requested to the
warning of September 1st, and since then the attacks on Poland have
been intensified. If His Majesty's Government has not received satis-
factory assurances of the cessation of all aggressive action against Poland,
and the withdrawal of German troops from that country, by 11 o'clock
British Summer Time, from that time a state of war will exist between
Great Britain and Germany.[44]

When he had finished, Henderson handed the ultimatum to Schmidt.
The two expressed their regrets, shared a few heartfelt words and then
bade each other farewell. As Henderson departed for the British
Embassy, Schmidt took the ultimatum to Hitler.

After negotiating an anteroom packed with most of the German
cabinet and a number of senior Party functionaries, Schmidt entered
Hitler's office. Both the Führer and Ribbentrop looked up in expectation. He stopped a short distance from Hitler's desk and slowly
translated the document. When he had finished, there was silence:

> Hitler sat immobile, gazing before him. He was not at a loss, as was
> afterwards stated, nor did he rage as others allege. He sat completely
> silent and unmoving. After an interval which seemed an age, he turned
> to Ribbentrop, who had remained standing by the window. 'What now?'
> he asked with a savage look.[45]

That afternoon, after the ultimatum had expired and war had been
formally declared, the news was broken to the German people. For
those listening on the radio in the capital, the announcement interrupted a broadcast of Liszt's sombre Hungarian Rhapsody No 1.
Immediately afterwards, in a speech that was relayed via loudspeakers
in the streets of Berlin, Hitler attempted once again to justify his
actions and to put the blame for the conflict on the 'British warmon-
gers'. He spoke of his 'peaceful efforts to secure bread and labour for
the German people', and his difficulties in finding an understanding
with the British, who sought 'new, hypocritical pretexts' for limiting
Germany. He concluded by warning that the British 'shall find out
what it means to wage war against National Socialist Germany',
and reminded his listeners that 'Germany will not capitulate ever
again'.[46]

Although it was altogether rather perfunctory, one might have expected that Hitler's speech would at least have stirred patriotic emotions and mobilised Berliners to leap to the defence of their country. Yet, as Shirer noted, when news of the declaration of war was relayed to the German people that day, there was little obvious reaction. 'I was standing in the Wilhelmstrasse', he wrote, 'when the loudspeakers there suddenly announced that England had declared a state of war with Germany. There were I should say about 250 people standing there in the sun. They listened attentively to the announcement. When it was finished there was not a murmur. They just stood there like they were before. Stunned.'[47]

That afternoon, the German newspapers were hurrying to catch up with events. Many of them produced extras, which were then eagerly hawked in the city's streets. One of the headlines blared:

BRITISH ULTIMATUM TURNED DOWN
ENGLAND DECLARES A STATE OF WAR WITH GERMANY
BRITISH NOTE DEMANDS WITHDRAWAL OF
OUR TROOPS IN THE EAST
THE FÜHRER LEAVING TODAY FOR THE FRONT
GERMAN MEMORANDUM PROVES ENGLAND'S GUILT[48]

Though the extras were distributed free of charge, there were few takers.

Later that day, as British Embassy staff prepared to leave Berlin, Sir Nevile Henderson noted that a small crowd of Berliners had gathered outside the embassy building and was watching as the staff's luggage was loaded onto military trucks. 'It was an absolutely silent crowd', he wrote later, 'and if there was hatred or hostility in their hearts, they gave no single sign of it.'[49] One might dismiss this account as an example of British wishful thinking, but his observations were confirmed by Helmuth James von Moltke, a Berlin lawyer who would later become one of the most prominent members of the German resistance. In a letter to his wife that week, he described the scene of Henderson's departure:

This war has a ghostly unreality. The people don't support it. I happened to pass when Henderson left the Wilhelmstrasse yesterday. There were about 300 to 400 people, but no sound of disapproval, no whistling, not a word to be heard; you felt that they might applaud at any moment. Quite incomprehensible. People are apathetic. It's like a *danse macabre* performed on a stage by persons unknown; nobody seems to feel that he'll be the next one crushed by the machine.[50]

The broad mass of the German people reacted to the outbreak of the Second World War proper, on 3 September 1939, with horror. As William Shirer noted: 'there is no excitement here in Berlin . . . no hurrahs, no wild cheering, no throwing of flowers – no war fever, no war hysteria . . . make no mistake, it is a far grimmer German people that we see here tonight than we saw last night or the day before.'[51] If there had been some who, two days earlier, might have been excited by the prospect of a limited skirmish against the Poles, few relished a wider war against the British and the French. For the vast majority, even those born after 1918, the First World War loomed very large indeed. Not only had its human cost been enormous, but its political consequences had racked Germany, leading to revolution, political unrest and territorial truncation. The desire of Germany to avenge itself was strong – and had, of course, been one of the primary wellsprings of Nazi support – but for most this meant stopping short of war. The prospect of returning to the fray two decades on against the same enemies was one that seems to have left most Germans in something approaching a state of shock. As one Berliner wrote that day, the mood in the capital was profoundly depressed. 'The atmosphere here is terrible', he said, 'a mixture of resignation and mourning . . . It could not be worse.'[52]

Christabel Bielenberg, as an Englishwoman married to a German and living in Berlin, perhaps felt the pain of the new war more than most. She recalled listening to Neville Chamberlain's Downing Street radio broadcast on 3 September, which contained the fateful words 'this country is at war with Germany'.

I sat motionless on the sofa. The voice carried on with its message but I was no longer listening. . . .

The room seemed very small, much too small, and I got up suddenly and went out through the French windows into the garden . . . The air outside was gentle and warm. A pungent smell of pine trees from the Grunewald hung over the garden and it was very dark.

I sat down on the low brick wall which separated our flower beds from the lawn, and stared into the darkness. Ahead of me a narrow shaft of light from the sitting-room window pinpointed my path through the dew, some dahlias beside me, the rough bark, the shadowy branches of an apple tree beyond. . . .

An electric blue flash from the S-Bahn lit up the blacked-out sky, our little house, the billowing curtains of the room upstairs where the children were sleeping. An apple slithered through the branches of the tree behind me and fell with a soft thud on to the flower bed beneath. It was very peaceful and very still in the garden.[53]

That peace, it seemed, was soon to be shattered.

After the Polish campaign was completed, in early October 1939, the German people might still have imagined that the chances for peace were good. After all, the Poles had been defeated and, with that – cynics would have argued – the Allied *casus belli* had effectively been removed. Moreover, as no open conflict had yet erupted on the Western Front, it was reasonable to assume that a settlement was possible.

This certainly was the logic adopted in Berlin's government circles, even by Hitler himself. On 6 October, after returning from Warsaw, where the last pockets of Polish resistance were being subdued, the Führer stood before the Reichstag – once again assembled in the Kroll Opera House – and made what became known as a 'peace offer' to Britain and France. He began with a long, rambling piece of self-justification: summarising the successful campaign in Poland, pouring scorn on his opponents and praising Nazi–Soviet cooperation. He summed up his own thinking by asking:

> Why should there be war in the West? To restore Poland? The Poland of the Treaty of Versailles shall never rise again. This, two of the world's greatest states guarantee. The final structure of this area, the question of the restoration of a Polish state, are problems which cannot be resolved through war in the West, but rather solely by Russia on the one hand, and Germany on the other.[54]

Though he made it abundantly clear that any supposed settlement would have to be on his terms, Hitler nonetheless proclaimed his readiness for

peace. He hinted vaguely at the possibility that an international conference might settle Europe's problems and that a new Geneva Convention
might regulate warfare 'among civilized states': prohibiting the killing
of the injured, for instance, or the use of poisoned gas. He concluded
with the *faux*-pious hope that God might see to it that the Germans 'and
all others [may] find the proper path, so that not only the German Volk
but all of Europe may rejoice in the new happiness of peace'.[55]

Four days later, while Germany waited for Britain's response to
Hitler's peace offensive, a curious episode tested German resolve
to the full. When Christabel Bielenberg visited the market that
October morning, she noticed immediately that something was
afoot. 'What had happened?' she asked herself:

> There shouldn't have been a cabbage-leaf left, instead the stalls were
> only half cleared, only the do-or-diers were queuing and the other
> ladies were standing round in animated groups. As I passed down
> between the rows, one or two heads nodded smilingly in my direction.
> It was the baker's wife who enlightened me as she clipped off my bread
> coupons and recklessly pushed an extra loaf into my old string bag.
> 'We won't be needing these much longer, Frau Dr,' she said. '*Wieso?*'
> 'Why, haven't you heard? Peace, they say, peace negotiations are going
> on at this very minute.'[56]

The same scene played out countless times across Germany that
morning. The rumour of peace spread like wildfire, overwhelming
the telephone system with the increased traffic. Though it had not
emanated from the German media, it nonetheless quoted reliable
sources, such as the Air Ministry and German radio. Wild claims were
trumpeted: Chamberlain's government had fallen; the British King had
been forced to abdicate; peace had returned to Europe.

A few managed to remain circumspect. Helmuth James von Moltke,
for instance, wrote to his wife on 10 October of 'a suggestion . . . that
the war may come to an end'. If it were true, he said, it would come
as a 'welcome relief', but, he conceded, 'I don't know if there's anything
in it.'[57] The majority of Berliners, however, rejected caution in favour
of celebration. According to William Shirer, there was tremendous
rejoicing all over Berlin. 'The fat old women in the vegetable markets',
he wrote, 'tossed their cabbages in the air, wrecked their own stands

in sheer joy, and made for the nearest pub to toast the peace with *Schnaps*.'[58] In a market in the suburb of Prenzlauer Berg, it was said that traders abandoned the usual rationing procedure in the mistaken belief that such pettifogging was now redundant.[59] Christabel Bielenberg recalled the scene in her suburb of Dahlem:

> I was soon the centre of a chattering group all eager to tell me exactly what was going on. Peace negotiations, oh yes, with the British of course, a special envoy . . . No one seemed to know any precise details. Most had got the news from someone who'd had it from someone else; but one thing was certain: everyone . . . was beside themselves, and our joy reached its peak when the police sergeant, on duty guarding the market, pushed through the crowd and added his voice, behind which was all the authority of the law, to our babbling conjectures.[60]

The peace rumour was certainly not confined to the 'babbling' housewives at market stalls. In the university, it was relayed during lectures with no doubts expressed as to its authenticity. Factories stopped work to discuss the news, and even those in government ministries began to celebrate.[61] Cheering crowds of civilians greeted troop transports returning from the Polish campaign: 'You can go home!' they cried, 'The war is over!'[62]

An American observer noted that the Germans he saw on the streets of the capital that morning were smiling in a way that he hadn't seen since the time of the *Anschluss*. 'On Potsdamer Platz', he wrote, 'I saw people who had gone crazy with joy. Strangers grabbed strangers by the arms to tell them the wonderful news. "Peace, brother, peace!" Other people grabbed strangers and embraced them in a delirium of joy. It looked like New Year's Eve in the daytime.'[63]

As the rumour spread, it was embellished still further. Eden, it was said, would take over from Chamberlain. The Duke of Windsor would accede to the British throne and a special plane was due to land at Tempelhof that very day, bringing a British envoy and a draft peace treaty. Then, as if to give final confirmation to the rumour, word spread that Hitler would speak that afternoon at three o'clock. In response, jubilant crowds began to gather outside the Reich Chancellery on the Wilhelmstrasse chanting *'Wir wollen unseren Führer!'* – 'We want our

Leader!'[64] Across the city, pubs were filled to overflowing and radios were switched on everywhere at the appropriate moment. Berliners, like Germans elsewhere in the Reich, waited with bated breath to hear the good news. For those sober enough to realise it, the reaction was all very different from that of barely a month earlier, when war had been declared.

The American William Russell witnessed the Berlin public as they eagerly gathered to hear Hitler's speech. 'It was already three o'clock', he wrote:

> I stopped in front of a radio shop, where a large crowd was collected on the sidewalk to listen to an outside loud speaker. Martial music blared from the radio. The Germans talked happily amongst themselves.
>
> We waited for an hour, hearing the stirring music all the time. Finally, not at three o'clock but at four, came the voice of Adolf Hitler. The crowd on the sidewalk was deathly quiet.
>
> *Der Führer* spoke.
>
> . . .
>
> The Voice spoke for forty minutes.
>
> It had finished, and the sound of rousing '*Sieg Heil, Sieg Heil, Sieg Heil!*' came through the noisy loud speaker.
>
> There was no mention of the new peace in any sentence.
>
> The Germans on the sidewalk around me were puzzled. Could it be that everybody in Germany knew that peace had arrived except Hitler?
>
> Had nobody told him?
>
> The crowd was bewildered, and disappointed.[65]

That disappointment, it seemed, proved to be just as infectious as the jubilation that had preceded it. An SS security report, for instance, noted a 'profound dejection' evident in the populace following the official denial.[66] Christabel Bielenberg retrospectively chided herself for believing in such a 'ridiculous affair'. She vowed, from that point on, 'never to believe anything that I had not seen with my own eyes or heard with my own ears'.[67] William Russell commented on the 'gloom' that settled on Berlin that night. 'The faces which had been alight with joy all day were secret and hurt . . . Berlin was completely blacked out. Just like every other night. But in the hearts of the people it was blacker still.'[68]

Even the more sober observer Helmuth James von Moltke was crushed by the sudden realisation that Germany was in the war for the long haul. In the following days, he wrote once again to his wife in Silesia: 'The catastrophe is rushing towards us. I've reached the point where I can no longer see anything standing between us and this catastrophe. Only a miracle can give us a brief respite.'[69]

Goebbels, meanwhile, set about tracking down the source of the rumour. In a radio broadcast he vehemently denied the stories, directing his trademark venom at the 'peace-loving rumour mongers' who had fallen victim to 'fishwives' gossip'[70] spread by the British Secret Service. In truth, there is no evidence that the peace rumour originated in Britain. The subsequent investigation traced its immediate origin to the German Post Office, and its director was duly hauled over the coals.[71] But Goebbels was incensed: 'There must be exemplary penalties', he raged in his diary. 'It will rain punishments.'[72]

Whatever its precise origin, the peace rumour had clearly struck a chord with the wider German public. As the crowds listening in expectation to Hitler's speech that afternoon had demonstrated, the country was gripped by a fervent enthusiasm for peace. To the dismay of the Nazi leadership, it was clear that Berliners and the German people as a whole were not ready for war.

2

A Deadly Necessity

As the people of the German capital accustomed themselves to the reality of the war, they also had to come to terms with one of its defining features: darkness.

Blackout regulations were issued on the very first morning of the conflict. They stated that all light sources in Berlin were to be extinguished, filtered or shaded during the hours of darkness. Lights in shop windows, advertisements, railway stations, buses and trams were also to be switched off or covered with a blue filter. All windows and doors – from factories to restaurants to homes – were to be shuttered and curtained. Skylights and cellar ventilators were to be sealed with waxed paper or sandbags. According to the wording of the decree, no light was to be visible from a height of 500 metres.[1] If the cities and towns could not be seen from the air, so the reasoning ran, then they could hardly be bombed.

To minimise the inevitable disruption, a number of additional measures were introduced to aid pedestrians. Phosphorescent paint was liberally employed: kerbstones, street corners, crossings and assorted pavement obstacles were marked with a stripe; steps were painted with a zigzag.[2] Luminous arrows were painted on walls giving directions to the nearest air raid shelter. Scaffolding or earthworks, meanwhile, were to be marked by red-filtered lamps.[3]

Naturally, Berlin's road users were targeted with a raft of new rules. Their vehicle headlights were to be screened, and only a rectangular opening, no larger than five by eight centimetres was permitted. They were also informed that they should use their horns more frequently. Cyclists, too, were ordered to shield their lights with red cloth or paper. Green and blue filters were not permitted for the public, as they were the colours used by the police and the fire brigade.[4]

William Shirer noted the effect of the new measures in his radio
broadcast to America on the very first night of the war, 1 September
1939: 'It's just quarter after one in the morning Berlin time', he said,

and we're half way through our first blackout. The city is completely
darkened, and has been since seven o'clock.

It's a little bit strange at first, and takes some getting used to. You
grope around in the pitch-black streets and pretty soon your eyes get
used to it, and you can make out the white-washed curbstones – and
there's a blue light here and there to guide you – and somehow you
get along.[5]

Though the experience was disquieting, the results were nonetheless impressive. The Berlin press enthused that, on that first night,
compliance with the blackout had been 'exemplary'. 'The 4 million
inhabitants of the city', one report swooned, 'adjusted to the new situation with incomparable ease . . . Berlin was ready and the Berliners
did their duty.'[6] Even the city's contingent of foreign correspondents
shared this positive judgement. One American reporter noted the
assessment of a neutral diplomat with experience of both the German
and the French capitals, who told him that 'the blackout [in Berlin]
was one hundred percent, really pitch black . . . By comparison, what
the French call a "blackout" has left Paris still *La Ville Lumière*.'[7]

One diarist marvelled at the scope and efficacy of the new measure:

Berlin was a no-city city out there in the black. I could see occasional
flashes of light from the S-Bahn and the subways. There were noises of
unseen automobiles passing along the street by the Tiergarten. I even
heard guttural little scraps of conversation drifting up to me, and saw
the lighted ends of cigarettes bobbing along the black sidewalk.
Over there, where the beacon used to flash from the top of the radio
tower, there was blackness. There were no lights from the apartment
windows; Berlin was as though some giant had placed a thick blanket
over it, to hide the light.[8]

Aside from the journalistic hyperbole, Berlin and its inhabitants
genuinely adapted well to the new regulations. Pedestrians took
to carrying torches (with an appropriate filter), or pinned small

phosphorescent badges – sometimes in the shape of cloverleaves or horseshoes – on their clothing to avoid collisions. Others adopted more imaginative measures. According to an American correspondent, 'to keep from bumping into one another on the sidewalks at night, Berliners . . . were rattling canes on the pavements or imitating old-time auto horns with guttural cries of "Honk, honk, honk"'.[9]

A few saw the legislation as a business opportunity. For a fee, entrepreneurs and small businessmen offered advice on how best to meet the new requirements. Sales of kerosene lamps, thick card and blackout curtains multiplied, and some who had previously struggled to make a living selling items such as roll-shutters suddenly saw demand hugely outstrip supply. Big business was not slow to get in on the act either. The German chemical giant BASF, for instance, developed an additive called Lumogen, which would lend luminescence to almost any colour of paint, as well as to dyes, polishes and waxes. One report enthused: 'He who cleans his shoes with Lumogen and crosses the street in the dark, will see them all lit up.'[10]

Some ordinary Berliners received the blackout with similar enthusiasm and a few commentators were even moved to lyrical outbursts by the sudden darkness that descended on a previously brightly lit and colourful metropolis. The writer Carl Haensel may have set the mood with a newspaper article in which he described the blacked-out capital in the most romantic tones – from the 'Morse-code' of the street markings to encounters with other pedestrians 'like ships passing in the night'. Berlin, he rhapsodised, was like a 'city of dreams' bathed in a soft half-light that liberated the imagination. He claimed that he had no desire to return to the garish brightness of the 'old world'.[11]

Another Berliner recalled in her diary how brightly the stars seemed to shine over the city. 'We see stars over Berlin for the first time', she wrote, 'not paling behind gaudy electric signs, but sparkling with clear solemnity. The moon casts a milky gleam over the roofs of the town. Not a spark of electric light falls upon the streets.'[12]

Most other observers eschewed such purple prose, but were no less enthusiastic. One eyewitness recalled the party mood that descended on the city in the early weeks of the blackout, with sightseers crowding the city centre:

The streets, which otherwise would be quiet so late at night, were overflowing with a happy, excited crowd keen to experience the blackout.
This unusual darkness was the cause of great amusement and some
incidence of violence. One heard giggling, curses and laughter. The
huge buses, with their blue-painted windows, rocked along the narrow
gorge of the Friedrichstrasse like enormous sea-monsters.[13]

Yet, whether they liked it or not, Berliners had little choice but to
comply with the order. To help them, the government produced an
official booklet in 1939, entitled *Verdunkelung – Aber wie?*, 'Black out –
But how?', which contained a host of tips, suggestions and sketches
showing how the order might best be implemented. 'Nobody', it
reminded its readers,

> should say that the chink of light escaping from his dimly lit room is
> not dangerous, or that it doesn't matter if the blackout measures leave
> a little gap, through which a tiny shaft of light can shine. If many
> thought that way, then the lights would be clearly visible from high-
> flying aircraft, and pilots would know for sure that they were over a
> poorly blacked-out city.[14]

Propaganda posters also reminded Berliners to be on their guard.
Perhaps the best known was produced in 1940. Above the silhouette
of a person standing in an undarkened doorway, an RAF bomber
appears to dive out of the clouds, with a grotesque skeleton riding
atop its fuselage, holding a bomb which it is about to hurl down onto
the house below. It bore the chilling reminder: 'The enemy sees your
light – black out!'

For those who still contrived to forget their duty, air raid wardens
were always on hand to remind them, patrolling the streets and bellowing
'Lights Out!' at those who contravened the blackout order. Wardens –
who were usually Party members – also had the power to inspect all
blackout measures in any property within their jurisdiction. Repeat
offenders were publicly humiliated. As an initial punishment, wardens
affixed a placard to the offending property bearing the words 'This
House Is Poorly Blacked Out', reminding the building's inhabitants that
compliance was a communal responsibility and warning that they could
endanger the entire district. The placard would only be removed when

all apartments, the stairwell and the rear of the building were satis-
factorily blacked out.[15]

Subsequent transgressions might earn the offenders a visit from the
authorities, or a personal lecture from the local air raid warden. In
time, a fine would be levied by the authorities, specifying the date
and time of the offence, and even the particular window that was
insufficiently blacked out. The standard fine was 10 Reichsmarks, which
was to be paid within a week. The impecunious, however, could opt
instead for a two-day stay in a police cell.[16] In extreme cases, offenders
were liable to have their electricity supply cut off for eight days.[17] The
most persistent among them could even earn themselves a spell in a
concentration camp.

For many, however, the greatest risk from the blackout did not come
from the threat of prosecution. A spate of accidents in that first autumn
of the war swiftly highlighted the dangers involved in the sudden
switch to darkness. In September 1939, Berlin police reports concluded
that nine out of ten accidents involving trains had been directly caused
by the blackout.[18] A serious rail crash in Berlin that autumn was also
attributed to the new legislation. On the evening of 8 October, an
intercity train overran a set of signals before ploughing into the back
of a commuter service near the Gesundbrunnen Station in the north of
the capital. In the mêlée that followed, the wreckage caught fire and
twenty-four passengers were killed. The accident was initially attributed to the driver's inattention, combined with the new and difficult
conditions of the blackout. However, when the driver was subsequently cleared of negligence, only one cause remained.[19]

Berlin's roads were not much safer. Driving in such conditions was
fraught with danger. Cars crawled along the street, picking their way
through the darkness, while other vehicles appeared as scarcely visible
hulks with only pinpricks of light emanating from their darkened
headlights. In open squares, such as Wilhelmsplatz or Potsdamer Platz,
it was not unusual for drivers to become completely disorientated as
they lost sight of the rooftops and trees that might mark the approx-
imate direction of the road. In consequence, though most private
traffic had disappeared from the streets with the outbreak of war, due
to the strict rationing of petrol, road accidents rose by 82 per cent in
Berlin between August and November 1939. And although an increase
in alcohol consumption was considered to be a contributory factor in

that rise, the blackout was deemed to be the dominant cause. In October, 28 out of 33 serious traffic accidents were attributed to the new legislation; the following month, it was found to have been responsible for 12 out of 15 road deaths.[20]

Curiously, the high rate of deaths did not fall, as the city grew used to the new measures. Rather, it continued to climb, reaching new heights in winter, when the public's exposure to the enforced darkness was greatest. In January 1940, for instance, 43 of the 162 accidental deaths registered in Berlin were attributed to the blackout;[21] in December that year, the rate was 75 out of 221.[22]

Aside from the evident dangers on the city's streets and railways, the blackout was implicated as a factor in a number of crimes. Police files suggested that Berlin's criminals saw the darkness as an opportunity rather than a nuisance. Most prominently, a spate of widely publicised murder cases in the autumn of 1939 caused alarm and fascination in equal measure. One of them concerned a man who had apparently murdered his wife in a fit of rage. To dispose of the evidence, he bundled the body into a packing case, which he perched on the back of his bicycle. Under cover of the blackout, he then rode across the city to dispose of the corpse in the Havel River.[23]

The second case was more gruesome. In early October 1939, a dismembered female body was discovered in three locations across the city. The arms and legs were found in the stairwells of apartments on Elsässerstrasse and Auguststrasse, while the torso – minus its head, breasts and internal organs, which were never found – was discovered at the Circus Busch on Monbijouplatz. It later transpired that the victim; one Käthe Kessler, an eighteen-year-old girl from Breslau, had been murdered in a crime of passion. The murderer – who had dismembered the body with a pocket knife and disposed of the head by baking it in his oven – confessed to two similar murders under interrogation and was duly sentenced to death. His attempt to conceal his victims' identities, by scattering their remains across the capital, had certainly been aided by the blackout.[24]

The incidence of mugging, robbery and crimes against property also showed a marked increase in that first winter of the war.[25] In late December 1939, for instance, three Czechs – named Zikmund, Oplatek and Zalenka – were sentenced to death for a spree of crimes in the German capital. They had stolen from a shop window in Tempelhof and snatched a handbag from a passer-by in Leipziger Platz. In both instances, the news report stated, they had 'exploited the blackout' in carrying out their crimes.[26] The following month, another mugger, Karl Ratzke, was executed for committing a street robbery under cover of darkness. He had escaped with a mere 18 Reichsmarks.[27]

The blackout certainly came as a boon for Berlin's prostitutes. Not only could they escape arrest easier, the enterprising among them could even turn the new legislation to their advantage. As one observer recalled: 'certain girls made easy pickups . . . even the old girls, the wrinkled ones, stood on street corners with their ugly features safely hidden in the darkness and shone their flashlights on their legs in invitation'.[28] The downside was that women were also more liable to be raped than before. Indeed, in the first year of the war, fully thirty-five rapes would be reported in the capital, a dramatic increase on the previous year's figure.[29]

In consequence, the enthusiasm and bravado shown by some Berliners in the first few weeks of the blackout soon dissipated, and most began to feel uneasy about travelling through their city at night. Women, especially, tended to stay at home, but the unease was universal. As one commentator noted:

> walking home in the dark is not only adventurous but distinctly uncomfortable . . . Many Berliners are saying to themselves, 'I don't want to come home in the dark' and have given up going out at night for this reason . . . It is no fun to walk down the Friedrichstrasse or Unter den Linden in darkness so complete you scarcely see your hand before your face.[30]

One of the most common and peculiar effects of the blackout was that it made people whisper and speak in hushed tones. The silence that resulted was all-pervading, seemingly deepened by the accompanying darkness. It could be profoundly unnerving. 'At night', an American visitor reported,

> the silence deepens. To drive in the main streets in the blackout is like driving through a dark country lane. The buildings are completely blotted out and no sound issues from the invisible doors and windows. Groping along the tunnel-like streets you almost never hear a voice. Other gropers are just shadows and footsteps.[31]

According to some commentators, there was another, rather more sinister, consequence of the blackout. One socialist critic, for instance, complained that the darkness had encouraged 'the unmistakeable symptoms of a collapse in moral standards' in the city, and that drinking and 'pleasure-seeking' had increased exponentially once the lights had been turned off.

> From all parts of the city, it is reported that bars . . . of all types are suddenly being placed under exceptional pressure. In this way, the face of the city centre is being changed. Everybody remarks with astonishment, that they have never in their lives seen so many drunk people on the streets as at this difficult time.[32]

An American commentator agreed, concluding that the blackout represented the suspension of civilised life in the capital. 'Civilisation', he wrote, 'has turned back a century or more and Edison's electric lamp may just as well be the foolish pipe-dream it was considered to be fifty years ago.'[33]

Though such prognostications of doom were doubtless exaggerated, it should come as no surprise that the capital felt a sense of unease in the gathering gloom. Berliners had been forced to adapt to many novelties in those first months of the war – rationing had been introduced and the threat of air attack was ever present – but it was the blackout that gave every one of them a jolting, chilling reminder, night after night, that Germany was at war.

As if such concerns were not enough, Berliners soon found a new peril stalking the night-time streets of their city. In the autumn of 1940, a woman's body was discovered in her home in the eastern suburb of Friedrichsfelde. The victim, a twenty-year-old mother of two named Gerda Ditter, had been strangled and stabbed in the neck. Her home, a small wooden building in an area of allotments, shacks and summer houses, showed no signs of robbery or forced entry. There were no witnesses.[34]

To make matters worse, the murder appeared to be part of a pattern. Three other women had been stabbed in the same district over the previous year. None of them had been robbed or sexually assaulted and all had survived – but the coincidence of location and method suggested that a single suspect might be responsible for all four crimes. In addition, two further assaults had taken place nearby; one woman had been dazzled by a man with a torch, before being beaten unconscious; and a second had been throttled and then thrown from a moving train. All the offences had been committed under cover of darkness, with the attacker exploiting the blackout to facilitate both his approach and his subsequent escape. As a result, no useful description of the suspect was available, other than the fact that he was male, of slight build and of average height.[35]

A month later – on the night of 4 November 1940 – the suspect struck again. This time, a thirty-year-old woman was attacked on a train travelling between the stations of Hirschgarten and Köpenick in the south-east of Berlin, not far from the location of the previous attacks. As before, the victim had been hit over the head in the near darkness of the blacked-out carriage and thrown from the moving train. Fortunately for investigators, however, she had survived and was able to tell police that her assailant had been wearing the uniform of German Railways. In addition, the weapon used in the attack – a length of lead piping – was found in a nearby rail carriage.

Another month later, and two more cases confirmed to the detectives of the Berlin serious crime bureau, the *Kriminalpolizei* – or Kripo – that they were dealing with a vicious serial killer. In the early morning of 4 December, a woman was found unconscious by the roadside, close to the railway lines in Karlshorst. Nineteen-year-old Irmgard Frese's skull had been fractured with a blunt instrument, and she had been raped. She died later that day in hospital without regaining consciousness.

That same day, just as news of this latest victim was circulating at Kripo headquarters, investigators received reports of the discovery of a second body, barely 500 metres away from the first. Elfriede Franke – a twenty-six-year-old nurse – was found close to the railway line at Rummelsburg. She had been thrown from a train and had suffered a fractured skull.

Accidental deaths on the railways during the blackout in Berlin were a rather common occurrence. In December 1940, as the *Kriminalpolizei* investigation was getting under way, there were twenty-eight deaths registered on the capital's railways, twenty-five of which were directly attributed to the blackout.[36] They were caused by people unwittingly stepping off platforms in the darkness, or being hit by speeding trains while crossing unlit tracks and sidings. Typical of such cases was that of one Gerda May, who slipped on the darkened platform at Bellevue that December and fell into the path of an oncoming train. Her mangled body, like those murdered in Karlshorst and Rummelsburg, was found next to the tracks.[37] It could be argued, therefore, that the officers of the Kripo were not only hampered by the fact that their suspect was operating under cover of darkness. They also found it difficult to sift accidental deaths, or even suicides on the railways, from those that might feasibly be considered as murders. The blackout, it seemed, was obstructing them at every turn.

For this reason, perhaps, the killer's next victim was initially misinterpreted as a suicide. Three weeks after the double murder, on 22 December, another female corpse was found, also close to the railway tracks and also with a fractured skull. Investigations determined that the victim, thirty-year-old Elisabeth Büngener, had a history of serious illness and had been diagnosed with depression. Moreover, her body had been found at Rahnsdorf, fully eight miles east of Karlshorst and Rummelsburg, where the other victims had been found. Accordingly, the initial Kripo report concluded with the suspicion that the cause of death was suicide – that the victim had died jumping from the S-Bahn train.[38]

This was no suicide, however, and, within a couple of weeks, two additional victims demonstrated as much. First, on 29 December, the body of forty-six-year-old Gertrud Siewert was found close to the railway at Karlshorst. Like the others, she had a fractured skull and appeared to have been thrown from a train. A week later, on 5 January 1941, the body of twenty-eight-year-old Hedwig Ebauer was found in similar circumstances near Wuhlheide. Both cases, the Kripo concluded, fitted the profile of the previous four murders and the earlier assaults, and were assumed to have been the work of a man already known to all Berlin as 'the S-Bahn Murderer'.

The realisation that a serial killer was stalking the darkened streets of the capital caused considerable alarm in Berlin. With the majority of the city's menfolk away serving in the armed forces and many women now drafted in to work long hours in factories and businesses, it was easy to see how a form of mass hysteria might have resulted. Well aware of the public's concerns, the authorities were forced to

tread a fine line between providing adequate information and
provoking panic. As one senior police officer warned at the time: 'We
should not exaggerate the whole thing, [and] drive the people of Berlin
crazy.'[39] So, though the popular press covered the murders, at least in
their essentials, it is worth noting that the more serious *Deutsche
Allgemeine Zeitung* did not. Its Berlin edition failed to make any mention
of the murders in December 1940, in spite of the fact that four women
had been killed in that month. The *Völkischer Beobachter*, meanwhile,
mentioned only one case – that of Gertrud Siewert – and averred that
it was most likely to have been an accident.[40] It is not clear whether
there had been orders from on high to this end, but it stands to reason
that there would have been a policy of not reporting news stories that
would reflect badly on German society.

In truth, a certain dose of hysteria was already in evidence, not
least in the Kripo investigation, which had begun to reflect the racial
and political prejudices of the time. One officer, for instance, suggested
that the suspect might be a Jew, explaining himself with the contention
that large numbers of Jews were then working on German Railways.[41]
Others, it seemed, speculated on whether the killer might be a British
agent.

More plausibly, the Kripo had to consider whether their suspect
could be a foreign labourer. By the autumn of 1940, after the successful
Blitzkrieg in the west, Berlin was awash with foreign workers, shipped
in – usually against their will – to meet the manpower demands of
the city's industrial and commercial sectors. Coincidentally, that foreign
presence was particularly noticeable on the stretch of railway where
the murders and assaults occurred. Not only were Italian, French
and Polish labourers a common sight in the factories of the area –
especially working for German Railways – but at nearby Wuhlheide,
there was an *Arbeitserziehungslager*, a form of concentration camp for
foreign workers who had committed crimes. It did not take an enormous leap of imagination to conclude that one of those countless
labourers might be the culprit. The Kripo acted accordingly. Nearby
foreign labourers' camps were placed under a nightly curfew, requests
for information in numerous languages were distributed, and identity
checks were made on the foreign personnel working for the railway.[42]

In addition, the authorities took some practical steps both to protect
women travelling on the S-Bahn and to catch their killer. A reward of

10,000 Reichsmarks was offered for information leading to an arrest. Fingertip searches of the various crime scenes were carried out and a number of large-scale, night-time sweeps of the area were undertaken. The police presence on the railway was also increased. Officers patrolled the stations and platforms and even volunteered to accompany woman travelling alone at night. Meanwhile, investigators examined the shift patterns of over five thousand railway employees to see which ones coincided with the times of the murders.

Kripo methods were more imaginative still. Male officers in drag were first placed on the trains to pose as 'bait', riding the S-Bahn at night so as to draw the murderer into an attack. When this failed, their female colleagues were asked to fill the role as well. Though they were not armed, they were at least equipped with reinforced headwear to protect them from attack.[43]

These measures were not entirely unsuccessful. They did not lead directly to an arrest, but it seems they might have given the murderer a fright. One night that winter, a female Kripo officer, acting as 'bait', was travelling alone in a second-class carriage on the S-Bahn when she was approached by a man matching the description of the killer. Following a brief exchange, however, the man became alarmed and bolted out of the train as it was approaching a station. After evading the police pickets on the platform, he disappeared into the darkness. In another incident, a police patrol discovered a man hiding in a train carriage in a siding at Erkner, at the end of the line that ran through Karlshorst and Rummelsburg. When he was approached by police officers, he ran off.

Perhaps because of these heightened measures, the killer – who had struck five times in barely a month – became much more sporadic in his attacks. The next assault took place fully five weeks after the last of the murderous spree that had filled December and early January. On the night of 11 February, a woman's body was found by the rail tracks near Rummelsburg. Johanna Voigt was thirty-nine and had suffered horrific head injuries before being thrown from a train.

As if to confirm this new-found caution, the killer made his next – and final – attack five months later, in early July 1941. He also changed his *modus operandi*. Switching away from making his assaults on the trains, he reverted to his earlier tactic of attacking women in the alleys and allotments in Friedrichsfelde – the same place where he had killed his first victim, Gerda Ditter, nine months earlier. There, in the early morning of 3 July 1941, the body of thirty-five-year-old divorcee Frieda Koziol was discovered. She had died from a fractured skull inflicted by a single blow with a blunt instrument. The Kripo investigators concluded that she had been hit from behind and then sexually assaulted. She had had no chance to defend herself.[44]

At this point, the detective work of the Kripo at last began to bear fruit. For one thing, the latest crime scene had given investigators a crucial piece of evidence: an impression of a rubber-soled shoe, presumably from the suspect. In addition, as a result of the painstaking analysis of the shift patterns of railway employees, eight suspects were brought in for interrogation. One of these was a twenty-nine-year-old assistant signalman, Paul Ogorzow, who had been employed on the S-Bahn between Rummelsburg and Karlshorst since 1938. Upon initial interview, Ogorzow had impressed his interrogators. Confident and coherent, he was described as 'assiduous and industrious' and 'happily married with two children'. A Nazi Party and SA member to boot, Ogorzow appeared to be such a solid, upstanding member of German society that the primary interrogation concluded: 'After these obser-vations, further enquiries regarding Ogorzow are suspended.'[45]

However, in the ongoing investigation Ogorzow's name kept coming up. He was labelled by colleagues as an outspoken misogynist. And, more importantly, one of his workmates stated that he had seen him jumping the perimeter fence of the railway and wandering off while on duty. On 12 July 1941, Paul Ogorzow was arrested and formally questioned again. Alibis were checked, forensic evidence gathered and shoeprints compared. Six days later, after a lengthy interrogation, he finally admitted to eight cases of murder, six cases of attempted murder and a further thirty-one cases of sexual assault.

By way of a defence, Ogorzow attempted to chime with the Nazi *Zeitgeist*, claiming that his predatory and sexually aggressive behaviour had been caused by an unconventional treatment for gonorrhoea prescribed for him by a Jewish doctor. He might feasibly have had some success with this anti-Semitic line of argument. After all, at least one member of the Kripo investigating team – Georg Heuser – would go on to forge a murderous career as commander of one of the *Einsatzgruppen*, the Nazi execution squads that slaughtered Jews en masse across eastern Europe.[46] However, the *Kriminalpolizei* gave

Ogorzow's defence little credence, and cast him instead as a simple sexual predator. In their final report, on 22 July 1941, they described him as being 'of a completely cold and calculating nature, without any nerves or any inhibitions when it came to satisfying his sexual urges'.

Barely two days later, at dawn on 25 July 1941, Paul Ogorzow was executed by guillotine in Plötzensee prison. He expressed no regrets.[47] The Kripo report concluded that he had 'willingly and consciously exploited the blackout' in carrying out his crimes. The enforced darkness of wartime Berlin, it said, 'had given him greater opportunity for his attacks . . . and had facilitated his escapes'.[48] The blackout, it seems, had been his ablest and most accommodating accomplice.

Of course, for the majority of Berliners the perils they faced during the blackout were much more commonplace and mundane than those represented by the 'S-Bahn Murderer'. But, crucially, they were no less deadly. Deaths attributed to the blackout continued to be shockingly high for the first two years of the war: through 1940, for instance, thirty Berliners died, on average, every month from blackout-related accidents. One victim for every day of the year.[49]

Yet, curiously, those statistics drop off sharply during 1941. Though accidental death rates remained fairly high – with average figures in winter of around 100 per month – the numbers attributed to the blackout dropped to only a handful. Either the figures were being massaged, or the Berlin public had finally come to terms with life in the darkness.

Throughout the war, the German authorities did not relax their guard and continued to remind Berliners of the correct application of blackout measures. Month after month, instructions, reminders and new regulations poured forth, all of which were communicated to Berliners through public information leaflets, articles in the press, or just the bawled orders of the air raid wardens.

The supreme irony, however, was that, just as the blackout regulations were being heightened, they were becoming irrelevant. Technological advances, such as the development of radar, would soon supersede the rationale given for the blackout in the first place, and render all such efforts rather superfluous. Though radar had been in development in Britain as well as Germany for many years, the emergence of the British 'H_2S' apparatus provided the significant breakthrough. With this system – which became operational in 1943 – radar was able to reveal different types of terrain on the ground and thereby provide a crude image of the land below the aircraft. The images were far from perfect. The Chief of Bomber Command, Arthur 'Bomber' Harris, for instance, learned early in 1943 that 'there was sometimes little or no relation between the real shape of a town and the image of it that appeared in the H_2S apparatus'.[50] Some quipped that the technology's code name (the same as the formula for hydrogen sulphide) was coined because 'it stinks'. Nonetheless, H_2S picked up water very well, allowing the competent navigator to find his targets by examining the rivers, coastlines and other patterns appearing on the small five-inch screen before him.

This technology was to have important consequences for Berlin, a city whose extensive network of rivers and lakes made it, potentially at least, an easy target to identify. A chart produced in the summer of 1943 showed some of the features that an RAF navigator might expect to see; and – ominously for Berliners – it revealed a surprising amount of detail. The city's rivers and lakes were clearly visible: from the Müggelsee to the east, with the River Spree snaking towards the city centre, to the Havel River to the west, opening into a complex of lakes – Wannsee, Havelsee and Tegelersee – before disappearing to the north-west. Though the city centre was largely an indeterminate mass of white, some more defined built-up districts, such as Potsdam, Spandau and the industrial area of Siemensstadt, could also be easily made out. Most importantly of all, perhaps, the city's numerous green spaces and parks were also visible. Not only could the airport of Tempelhof to the south-east be seen, but even the oblong of the Tiergarten – in the very heart of the city – was clearly defined.[51] Any one of these locations could easily be used by an attacking bomb crew for orientation, or as an aiming point.

H_2S was not the radical breakthrough in radar technology that some have suggested.[52] It was certainly useful for crews attacking in darkness or confronted by heavy cloud cover, as it meant that they were no longer entirely dependent on the normal, visual, points of reference. But, though an improvement on traditional night-time navigation methods, it was vastly inferior to visual aiming. It could not lead its crews to a particular spot, or even to a particular suburb, but it could help them to find a particular city – and even, once arrived, to adequately navigate their way around it. And in this sense at least, H$_2$S was of profound importance. Though they couldn't have known it, the people of Berlin – dutifully carrying out their blackout measures, trying to make their city invisible from the air – were wasting their time.

Despite this, the German authorities did not relax their vigilance. In the summer of 1944, for instance, the body responsible for such measures, the *Reichluftschutzbund*, or 'Reich Air Defence Corps', was complaining to the German press that 'in spite of its long existence, the blackout was still not being carried out carefully enough'. 'This neglect', it went on, 'is primarily to be attributed to idleness, thought-lessness, even irresponsibility.'[53]

Such reminders fell increasingly on deaf ears, however. Despite their conscientious compliance with the blackout legislation in the early phase of the war, some Berliners were clearly starting to ignore the instructions. As the Wehrmacht's 'mood reports' of the final months of the war make clear, there were many complaints that the blackout was being imperfectly applied. As one complainant recorded:

During an air raid on 2 January [1945], one could observe how a stream of people emerged from the bunker in Fichtestrasse in Kreuzberg; almost all of them with brightly lit torches. It was like a torch-lit parade. Even when the flak started firing, it did not change. The police are not bothered by it. The same scene could be observed that same night near the bunker in Rosenthal.[54]

By that time – with Berlin exposed to night and day air raids, France and Belgium liberated, and the Soviet army poised on the River Vistula – Nazi Germany was standing on the very edge of the abyss. It seems reasonable to conclude that the people of Berlin had other, more pressing worries, than the filters on their pocket torches.

3

A Guarded Optimism

After the excitement and upheaval of those first days of the war, life soon settled down for the majority of Berlin's population and, once again, assumed a veneer of normality, which the conflict – initially at least – only rarely disturbed. Despite the profound shock that most had experienced with the outbreak of hostilities, the differences that they witnessed to their everyday lives were, in practical terms, really rather subtle.

Indeed, for the opening phase of the war, it appears that a conscious effort was made in Berlin to maintain some sense of normality, with entertainment and sporting schedules enjoying more emphasis and interest than in peacetime. 'You can feel the effort here to make life as normal as possible', wrote William Shirer that October:

> Berlin today has one of the heaviest sport programs of the year. The races at Hoppegarten will attract a big crowd this afternoon. Besides this the following events are scheduled in Berlin alone: one track-meet, a bicycle race between Germany and Hungary, two hockey matches, two rugby-football games, one wrestling match, one amateur boxing show, one weight-lifting contest, two hundred handball games and one hundred soccer matches.[1]

He was not mistaken. On the orders of the 'Reich Sport Leader', the gloriously named Hans von Tschammer und Osten, sporting events were, as far as possible, to remain unaffected by the war. An international rowing regatta scheduled to take place at Berlin-Grünau in early October went ahead as planned. The high point of the racing calendar – the Berlin Grand Prix – was held that autumn over 2,400 metres in the Hoppegarten, with a purse of 100,000 Reichsmarks.

Football, as one of the most important mass sports in the Third Reich, was not slow to follow suit. Though the regional and national championships were temporarily suspended with the outbreak of the war, Berlin's football clubs embarked on a cup competition of their own, which – appropriately for the times – was named the Danzig Cup.

Aside from sport, there was a veritable plethora of other events to distract Berliners. That autumn, the capital's cinemas saw a number of highlights, such as the courtroom drama *Sensationsprozess Casilla*, starring Heinrich George, which was intended to mock the American way of life. Most notable, perhaps, was a film about the life of the biologist Robert Koch starring Emil Jannings in the title role. Jannings, who was one of Nazi Germany's foremost stars of the silver screen, had starred opposite Marlene Dietrich in *The Blue Angel*, and had been the very first recipient of an Oscar for Best Actor.

Elsewhere in the capital, there was much to entertain: from *Aida*, *La Traviata* and *Il Forza del Destino* in the city's opera houses, to variety at the Winter Gardens, and a performance of the Goethe play *Götz von Berlichingen* at the Schiller Theatre. It is little surprise, therefore, that Shirer concluded, 'reading the sports pages and the theatre pages of the morning papers today, you would hardly believe there was a war on'.[2]

Shirer was right, but there were many other pages that would have left the reader in little doubt that he was living in momentous times. All newspapers had been subjected to additional editorial requirements with the outbreak of war, which aimed at preventing their reports from unwittingly giving any assistance to Germany's enemies. In practice, these rules led to some subtle but nonetheless noticeable changes. No longer, for instance, could newspapers feature a weather forecast, for fear that such information might aid enemy air forces. Nor was it permitted to publish anything that would reflect negatively on the progress of the war or the state of morale on the home front. Those readers who wanted something beyond the boasts and platitudes of the Propaganda Ministry had to become expert in the art of reading between the lines.

That first autumn and winter of the war were profoundly interesting times. It had begun with the successful conquest of Poland, a decisive victory that would have been unthinkable twenty years before.

There were other successes. Much was made in the German press that winter, for instance, of the heroic return of Günther Prien, the commander of *U-47*, which had sunk the British battleship *Royal Oak* at anchor in Scapa Flow in October. Prien became an instant celebrity and was awarded the Knight's Cross, the first sailor of the Kriegsmarine to be so honoured. Yet, Germany had not had things all her own way. For all the back-slapping that surrounded Prien, it was also known that one of Germany's most famous battleships, the *Graf Spee*, had been scuttled in the River Plate that December, after being caught by a British fleet in the South Atlantic.

As a result, even though Poland had been roundly defeated, few were minded to see the international situation wholly positively. Germany's two primary enemies – the British and the French – were still in the field, and though hostilities in the west had not yet broken out, they were popularly considered a formidable military force. Optimism, therefore, was a rather rare commodity.

With the nation at war, the majority of Berliners naturally rallied round and, whatever their opinion of Hitler and the Nazis, complied with the new strictures of rationing and the blackout and supported the government and the armed forces. Yet, though comparatively rare, dissent was not entirely absent from the political landscape in the early months of the war. In fact, Berlin witnessed a resurgence of political protest that was more marked than elsewhere in the Reich.

Protests mainly took the form of symbolic action. Political graffiti and anti-Hitler slogans were a favourite – especially if they could be daubed on a highly visible, moving placard, such as a railway wagon. Other protesters chose to make more radical statements. In early November, the Berlin office of Hitler's personal photographer, Heinrich Hoffmann, was targeted, and a shop window containing portraits of the Führer was smashed.[3] More seriously, bomb attacks were carried out against high-profile targets in the capital. In mid-September, explosive devices detonated outside the Air Ministry and in the entrance to the police headquarters in Alexanderplatz.[4] The perpetrators were never apprehended, so their precise motives are unclear. But by their actions they had demonstrated that the Berlin *Volksgemeinschaft* – the national community – was perhaps not as united as the Nazi leadership would have liked.

As a result of such tensions, the first Christmas of the war was a curious affair. The regime certainly did its best to raise the public's spirits, with the usual smattering of festive concerts being staged across the capital, from a Bach recital in the music school to a performance by the choir of the *Gross-Berlin* guard regiment.[5]

Senior Nazis were also obliged to donate at least a little of their time and energy. Rudolf Hess spoke to the nation by radio that Christmas Eve, from the naval base at Wilhelmshaven. Goebbels, meanwhile, was the special guest at a celebration in the Berlin *Theatersaal*. 'Many children present', he wrote in his diary, adding optimistically, 'the public is in good fettle despite all their troubles.'[6] Göring's baby daughter, Edda, also made an appearance, surrounded by dolls in a Berlin toyshop, where her mother was selecting gifts to be donated to the children of soldiers killed in the Polish campaign.[7] Only Hitler seems to have abdicated his wider festive responsibilities, repairing quietly instead to the Rhineland, where he visited troops stationed on the Siegfried Line and enjoyed a Christmas dinner in Aachen with the motorised regiment of the SS-*Leibstandarte*.[8]

The public mood that Christmas was a mixture of forced cheer and depression. Berliners did their best to get into the festive mood, and, for many, this centred on seeking the right food for the occasion. Those with contacts, and sufficient funds, would have got hold of a carp – the traditional Christmas Eve fare – which would be baked or filleted and fried. For some children, therefore, one of the great excitements of Christmas was having the live carp swimming in the family bath for a couple of days, so as to cleanse the fish and keep it fresh. For the vast majority, however, carp was not on the menu, and the ration allowance scarcely allowed for any festive spirit.

The situation was not helped by widespread fears that Germany's food reserves were not quite as extensive as the Nazi leadership had claimed. One report, from the underground Social Democratic movement, noted that the Berlin public had expected that the restrictions of rationing would be loosened slightly in the run-up to Christmas. When this did not happen – and when the only extra allocations were rather paltry, amounting only to an additional 125 grams of butter, 125 grams of artificial honey and one egg per consumer per week[9] – many interpreted this as a symptom of a more general malaise. After all, if the reserves were there, why wouldn't Göring and Goebbels want to spread a little Christmas joy?[10]

Others were irritated by the intrusion of the Nazis' pagan pretensions into the traditional ceremonial. The most zealous Nazi supporters would not celebrate Christmas at all; rather, they would observe *Julfest*, a time to remember their Germanic ancestors and soldiers fallen in the service of the Fatherland. Even the less ideologically observant would have noticed the admixture of pagan symbolism, such as tree decorations or wrapping paper bearing the swastika.[11] Traditional Christmas carols would even have their lyrics altered to excise their Christian content. Ruth Andreas-Friedrich noticed a reworking of the staple Christmas carol 'Silent Night', in a volume entitled *Christmas in the Third Reich*:

> Silent night, Holy night,
> All is calm, all is bright.
> Only the Chancellor stays on guard
> Germany's future to watch and to ward,
> Guiding our nation aright.
>
> Silent night, Holy night,
> All is calm, all is bright.
> Adolf Hitler is Germany's star
> Showing us greatness and glory afar
> Bringing us Germans the might.

It was, she noted bitterly, for a 'work of art' such as this, that Stefan Zweig had to leave the country, 'for this Heinrich Heine's poems have been prohibited for seven years past'.[12]

Despite such aberrations, some things did not change. Christmas trees remained a priority, and were eagerly sought across the city. 'No matter how tough or rough or pagan a German may be', William Shirer noted, 'he has a childish passion for Christmas trees.' For some, it seemed, it became a point of principle to maintain the old traditions, in spite of the difficulties of the war. 'People everywhere', Shirer noted, 'are bravely trying to make this Christmas seem like the old ones in the time of peace.'[13] Fortunately, Christmas trees were still plentiful and relatively easy to procure.

Buying gifts for one's family and friends was more problematic. Not only was there little leeway for purchases beyond the limits set by the ration card, but there was also precious little disposable income spare for the few luxury goods that were still available. One commentator noted that the restrictions imposed by the rationing had had a profound effect on people's buying habits: 'Germans usually give wearing apparel and soaps and perfumes and candy to one another for Christmas', he wrote,

> but this year, with these articles rationed, they must find something else. In the shops, which are crowded, they were buying today mostly books, radios, gramophones, records, and jewellery. I tried to buy some gramophone records for the four secretaries at the *Rundfunk* who have been most friendly and helpful to me, but found that you could only buy new records if you turned in your old ones. Having none, I was out of luck.[14]

The American William Russell noted in his diary:

> [In] Berlin, I had found it almost impossible to buy Christmas presents. To my closest friends I had given coffee ordered from the free harbour in Hamburg. A pound of coffee was a princely gift. For my friends at the Embassy, I had had to search harder. Everywhere in Berlin I met the same answer – 'all sold out'.[15]

For many, therefore, the result was a rather gloomy Christmas, in which a meagre diet conspired with the blackout and the insecurity of not knowing the whereabouts of family members, to create an atmosphere that was remembered as deeply depressing. As one young Berliner recalled:

> That first Christmas of the war was sad. On Christmas Eve, which I usually couldn't wait for, I already wanted it all to end. Daddy and Uncle Willy were somewhere. The Polish campaign had ended long ago, but we still didn't know where they were . . . We had received the last letter from Daddy on the first of December. It said little of interest, but at least we knew that he was still alive. We didn't have a Christmas tree. Mother just sat at the table and knitted a jacket for my little brother.[16]

William Shirer, ever alert to the public mood, summed up the atmosphere:

> On many a beautiful night I have walked through the streets of Berlin
> on Christmas Eve. There was not a home in the poorest quarter that
> did not have its candlelit Christmas tree sparkling cheerfully through
> the uncurtained, unshaded window. The Germans feel the difference
> tonight. They are glum, depressed, sad.[17]

The irony was that, for the following few years at least, most Berliners
would look back on the Christmas of 1939 as a time of peace and
plenty.

As winter turned to spring in 1940, the mood in Berlin lifted a little.
Warmer weather and an end to the harsh winter that had plagued the
capital brought Berliners out onto the streets once more. At the weekends, people once again flocked to the city's lakes and parks. Life appeared
to have returned to something approaching normality.

Even so, the public mood was hardly optimistic. The spectre of the
Great War, which had scarred a generation, hung over Germany like a
dark cloud. Once again, Germany was facing her most implacable
enemies. When would the British attack? they wondered. When would
the shadow-boxing give way, once again, to slaughter? As Christabel
Bielenberg noted that spring, 'We were watching and waiting, they were
watching and waiting, even Hitler seemed to be watching and waiting
– nothing moved. It was as if the bitter relentless cold had seeped its
way into the very fibre of events.'[18]

Though the Western Front appeared to be calm, other theatres of
war were far from peaceful. On the seas, the tit-for-tat sinking of
merchant vessels and navy ships was accelerating. In February 1940,
five German U-boats had been sunk, while the British had lost two
destroyers, *Exmouth* and *Daring*, and the minesweeper *Sphinx*, as well
as numerous merchantmen.

In the air there were even more ominous developments. Most previous
air attacks had been limited to seaborne targets, but in the early months
of 1940 a decisive shift occurred. First, in March, the Luftwaffe launched
an attack on the Royal Navy base at Scapa Flow, causing the war's first
British civilian deaths. In retaliation, the RAF abandoned their previous

campaign of merely dropping leaflets over Germany. Three days after
the attack on Scapa Flow, British aircraft targeted a German naval base
on the island of Sylt. The first raids on the German mainland were now
only weeks away.

Yet, many still hoped that Hitler could engineer some diplomatic
miracle to wrest peace from the jaws of conflict. The Führer's benign
public image had suffered some damage the previous autumn, not least
among those few Germans who had seen through the tissue of lies with
which he had attempted to justify the Polish campaign. But, to the
majority of Germans, Hitler was still viewed as 'a man of peace'. After
all, they would have argued, he had stopped short of war at Munich in
1938 and had left the conference table with most of the concessions that
he had demanded. And, in the years before that – when he had raised
Germany from the ashes of defeat and restored her, proud and independent, to the world stage – was that not achieved through diplomacy,
rather than warfare? And when war had finally erupted the previous
autumn, was it not true, they reasoned, that Hitler's hand had been
forced by the perfidy of the British and the stubborn intransigence of
the Poles? And was it not Hitler who had then offered generous peace
terms to the British after the defeat of Poland?

Yet for all these considerations, the primary concerns for most
Germans during the 'Phoney War' were much more mundane,
centring on the restrictions of the rationing system, and their fears
for their brothers, husbands and sons serving in the armed forces.
But despite such undoubted hardships and worries, life continued
much as before. As the American reporter Howard Smith noted, Berlin
in the spring of 1940 was remarkable primarily for its continued order-
liness, cleanliness and normality. A few essentials had certainly disappeared, he noted, such as coffee and chocolate, but beyond that
'the whole atmosphere was incompatible with the strain Germany
had undergone preparing for war'. Smith noted that the 'gargantuan
performance' of raising several million troops to fight in Poland had
'had no more effect on the German home front than the wash of a
motor boat on a giant liner at sea'. His impressions seemed to be
confirmed when he accompanied a German officer down Unter den
Linden that spring: 'Look around you, Herr Smith', the officer said,
'nowhere a sign of war. Not the slightest difference from two years
ago. Is that not the best argument for our strength? We shall

never be beaten.' 'It was heartbreaking', Smith wrote, 'but it seemed true.'[19]

Such apparent confidence was little shaken when German troops marched into Denmark and Norway in April 1940. Hitler had dressed the invasions as a necessary action to secure his northern flank and ensure the uninterrupted supply of iron ore from Sweden. But, though the mood reports of the Nazi security service dutifully recorded that the German people were 'enthusiastic' about the invasions,[20] some Berliners were clearly unsettled by an attack on countries that had little record of hostility towards Germany. William Russell recalled listening to the radio with a German friend when the occupation was announced. As Goebbels finished telling the people of Denmark and Norway how the invasion was for their 'own protection', Russell glanced across at his companion. 'She had tears in her eyes', he recalled. '"That hateful damn liar!" she said bitterly. "That hateful damn liar!"'[21]

Others were fundamentally unimpressed by what they saw as a minor skirmish in a peripheral theatre. A scene recorded by a journalist on the morning of the invasion was perhaps typical of the low-key reaction of the Berlin public. He watched as a man walking his dog through Berlin Zoo approached the barrier, where his entry ticket was clipped: 'Morgen', said the doorman,

> 'See we invaded Norway this morning?'
>   'Ja,' said the visitor, removing his cigar from his mouth, 'and Denmark too.'
>   'Ja,' said the ticket-taker handing back the punched ticket.
>   'Auf Wiedersehen.'
>   "Wiedersehen.'[22]

It may well be that this laconic exchange was due to a natural caution of discussing events with strangers, for fear of denunciation. But this was clearly a muted response, even for the famously phlegmatic Berliners.

When the Norwegian campaign was successfully concluded in early May 1940, there was an upsurge in enthusiasm, not least because the British and French had finally been engaged in the field and defeated. As William Shirer noted after the German victory against the Royal Navy and an Allied expeditionary force in Norway, 'it would be hard to exaggerate the feeling of triumph in the Third Reich today . . . as they see it, Germany has at last met the great British Empire in a straight fight and won hands down.'[23]

The mood reports compiled by the exiled German socialist party concurred. One dated April 1940 noted:

> An atmosphere has developed that is quite optimistic about the progress of the war. It does not even occur to most people that Germany could lose. The bourgeoisie, for instance, has not the least inclination to wonder whether the war could end with something other than a German victory. Very few people are concerned.[24]

In line with this assessment, the first newsreel with images of the campaign in Norway was received with tremendous enthusiasm and played to packed cinemas across Germany. For some at least, the victory against the British and French at Narvik seemed to exorcise the spectre of 1918 and fostered the belief that, this time, Germany might emerge victorious.

But, for the majority, the invasion generated comparatively little interest. Most German civilians understood that the conquest of Denmark and Norway would not decide the war. Though there was a certain sense of relief that the British and French had finally been engaged, few believed that battle had been joined in earnest. That campaign, they realised, was yet to come.

When German troops marched across Belgium and into France in May 1940, the reaction in Berlin was initially one of stubborn caution. Despite the blaring headlines from the Nazi press, most of the 'extras' produced to commemorate the attack went unsold and lay stacked and bound in the streets.

Most Berliners, in fact, took the attack on France as phlegmatically as they had taken the previous attacks on Poland, Denmark and Norway. William Shirer noted that Berlin's streets exuded a calmness and normality that did not fit with the fact that the war had now entered its supposedly decisive phase. 'Yesterday and today have been so normal here', he wrote. 'People going about their business just as usual. No excitement in the air . . . repair work on the streets was going on just as before. Workers were busy on the new buildings. No excitement

discernible in them.'[25] Nazi mood reports perceived a 'profound seriousness', even 'a certain scepticism' in the German population.[26]

The reason for such seriousness and scepticism was obvious. With
every step the German armies took that summer, they were reawak-
ening memories of the First World War. The mention of Verdun or
Arras, or any number of other towns so bloodily fought over a generation before, sent shivers down German spines and provoked the fear
of a similar catastrophe. Howard Smith recalled a visit from an older
fellow resident in his guesthouse on Kurfürstendamm:

> An ageing Prussian came to my room as soon as he had read the
> headlines on his paper. He sat down and looked worriedly and intently
> at me.
> 'It's begun,' he said. I acknowledged it had.
> 'Now it will really get started,' he said, peering again at his folded
> newspaper.
> 'We didn't want this war. We really didn't.' Tears welled in those
> hard, old eyes as he proceeded to argue the oft-repeated German case.
> This was typical of the World War generation; no faith in German
> strength, believing more fully than any Englishman or Frenchman in
> German inferiority, praying for mercy to the only foreigner within reach.[27]

In the face of such apparent pessimism from some sections of
German society, the Nazi regime sought to encourage more belligerent
attitudes in the population. One young Berliner recalled attending a
lecture in a cinema entitled 'Hatred towards England':

> The speaker told us again how good we Germans were. We have
> achieved so much and will achieve more, because we have the Führer.
> There was one thing, however, that we couldn't do: we could not hate.
> We lacked hatred for England. So we had to learn how to hate. But
> how that was to be achieved, he did not say. Should we murmur 'I hate
> England' three times whilst brushing our teeth? Or whilst going to bed?
> Or when being tested on English vocabulary? The speaker did not say
> what I was to do.[28]

Yet for all the imprecations to hatred on the home front and the relentless advance of German troops across northern France, the mood in

the capital remained one of caution, at least until the campaign in the west was successfully concluded.

Indeed, even after the fall of France in late June 1940, the public mood in Berlin was hard to gauge. On the one hand, there was un-bridled jubilation, with a number of high-profile parades and proces-sions, and a three-day public holiday to celebrate the fall of Paris. The festivities did not end there. As was customary on public holidays in the Third Reich, flags were ordered to be displayed, and church bells were to be rung. The mood on the streets, it seems, was exultant: 'crowds cheered hoarsely in Berlin', it was reported, no doubt spurred by the 'deafening radio fanfares' which blared out 'at all important points of the city and in all shops, stores, offices and factories . . . Martial music filled the air.'[29]

When Hitler returned to his capital in early July, after the successful conclusion of the French campaign, he was driven to the Reich Chancellery on a carpet of flowers. According to press reports, 'the mile-long route from the Anhalter Station to the Chancellery was a perfumed avenue of greens, reds, blues and yellows flanked by cheering thousands who shouted and wept themselves into a frantic hysteria as the Führer passed'.[30]

Though Nazi Germany had a track record of minutely stage-managing such events, the enthusiasm demonstrated that day was most certainly genuine. Indeed, the throwing of flowers at Hitler's convoy had even been expressly forbidden on security grounds, but the crowds ignored the instruction. The celebrations continued at the Reich Chancellery, where the streets were again blocked by the massed ranks of Hitler Youth and the German Maidens, who filled the air with their 'incessant . . . shrill cheering'. Twice Hitler appeared on the balcony of the Chancellery to greet the enraptured crowds. The press report concluded: 'Caesar in his glory was never more turbulently received.'[31]

On the other hand, apathy – even anger – was also in evidence. Ruth Andreas-Friedrich was one of those unimpressed by the overt celebration of war. In mid-June, she confided to her diary:

Three and a half months have passed – fourteen weeks, during which the German nation has been reeling drunk with one victory after another. Put out the flags; take in the flags. Every window, every gable, every tower, all a sea of swastika'd flags. Order for display of flags: 'As of today, for a period of one week.' Ringing of church bells: three days. Once again Christian tongues have to join in praising the bloody victories of arms.[32]

This reflective tenor seems to have been shared by others in Berlin. Though the Nazi mood reports from the end of the French campaign paint a picture of public jubilation across Germany, some of those recording events in the capital described a very different scene. One Berlin journalist recalled sitting down to lunch in her office canteen when news of the surrender in Paris was announced over the radio.

Everyone looks unhappily at his plate. Two fat tears fall into Karla's raw eel and parsley sauce.
'Hurra!' comes a sudden shout from the corner. Everyone winces. 'Hurra!' again, but this time with less authority. One of our scrubwomen has jumped up, grabbed her glass and is cheering 'Long live the Führer!' Icy silence at every table. She sits down again, disconcerted.[33]

Missie Vassiltchikov would have concurred. A Russian émigrée, who had found refuge in Berlin, she noted in her diary: 'Paris surrendered today. Strange how lukewarm the reaction is here. There is absolutely no feeling of elation.'[34]

William Shirer, as ever, was able to see both sides. He warned, 'it would be wrong to conclude that the taking of Paris has not stirred something very deep in the hearts of most Germans. "Germans Capture Paris" are magic words to so many here.' But he went on to say, 'In fact, Berlin took the capture of Paris as phlegmatically as it has taken everything else in this war.' To illustrate the point, he claimed that of the five hundred people he observed enjoying the afternoon at a popular bathing beach in the city, only three bought a copy of the newspaper in which the fall of Paris was announced.[35]

It may be, of course, that such sources were mistaken in their assessments or were reporting opinions that were not representative of the majority of Berliners. However, the fact that these contemporary commentators all make the same point makes their testimony rather difficult to dismiss as anomalous. A recent study of selected 'mood indicators' would seem to back up the conclusion that June 1940 did not represent a peak in enthusiasm for war – or, indeed, a high point in support for Hitler or the Nazi Party.[36] And, as Howard Smith observed, civilian morale in 1940 was resolutely downbeat, only lightened by the prospect of an end to the fighting:

> The graph of German morale is not a graceful, snaky thing which slithers upwards in long rises and downwards in slow, calm declines, like the graph of almost any people living in peace. It is a low, jagged line, which leaps spasmodically upwards in one instant and collapses into sharp depressions in the next. The reason for its abrupt contours is the unmitigated fear of this war . . . and [the people's] gullible readiness to believe anything, however fantastic, which indicates an early end to it.[37]

Foremost among the pessimists were those few who actively opposed Hitler. Their attitude is a little easier to justify. Many of them were hoping, that summer, for a military setback to dampen the popular enthusiasm for Hitler and, in turn, to strengthen the calming hand of the General Staff. One of those who typified this belief was Colonel Hans Oster, a senior officer of German military intelligence, the *Abwehr*, and a leading member of a group that had been actively plotting Hitler's downfall. Oster had even been passing military secrets to the Dutch since the previous autumn, in the hope that it would stiffen Allied resistance to the German advance.[38] For all those like Oster who opposed Hitler, the fall of France in 1940 was a hammer blow. As Oster's colleague Reinhard Spitzy recalled, the entry of German troops into Paris that summer caused all the critics of the Nazi regime to suddenly 'fall silent'.[39]

Whatever their reasoning, it is clear that, for all the thousands thronging the government district and cheering Hitler in July 1940, there was also a minority in Berlin who felt little reason for jubilation.

Even if there were some small sectors of Berlin society that were ambivalent about Germany's success, the return of the victorious troops to the capital seems to have been a cause for unalloyed and uninhibited enthusiasm. Howard Smith noted that 'it was the only occasion in the better part of six years that I have spent in Germany that I saw . . . Germans weeping and laughing from pure spontaneous joy'.[40]

Even so, the event was meticulously stage-managed: grandstands were erected on Pariser Platz, a public holiday was proclaimed and church bells were to be tolled while the parade was in progress. As if in recognition of the slightly ambivalent response to previous victory announcements, Goebbels reminded the Berlin populace to provide a 'tumultuous welcome for your sons, husbands, fathers and brothers who won the great victories in Poland and France'.[41]

Berliners did not disappoint. They lined the streets cheering and throwing flowers, their 'good humour equalled only by that of the soldiers themselves'. William Shirer noted that 'nearly the whole town turned out to welcome [the soldiers] back' and that the crowds 'yelled and yelled until they were hoarse'.[42] Indeed, at times it seems that traditional military discipline threatened to break down entirely as the parading troops broke ranks to be reunited with their loved ones, while children escaped the police cordon to run to their fathers clutching small bouquets of flowers.

According to Howard Smith the parade was 'a real, tangible sign of victory and the end of the war Germans detested and feared. Sons, husbands and fathers, sun-tanned and healthy after long military training, happy as kids after the great triumph, were returning home to their families to stay.' 'It was', he concluded, 'truly a glorious day and in every happy heart lived the belief that this was the end of it all.'[43] This last sentiment was perhaps one which every Berliner – even those unmoved by previous celebrations – could share.

Some Germans, while not immune to Germany's strategic and military success, were also enthused by the prospect of the material improvements they hoped would follow. Thus, while Göring toured the museums and galleries of Paris in search of titbits to add to his personal art collection, many Berliners were also anticipating their own share of 'war booty', in the form of chocolate, silk stockings and coffee.

Yet, though such material concerns may certainly have helped generate enthusiasm, the sentiment registered by the vast majority of Germans in the summer of 1940 was one of overwhelming relief. The First World War had loomed large in German public life in the previous two decades and, measured by the experiences of that conflict, 1940 was an enormous success. Germany was the master of continental Europe. Her age-old enemies had been defeated: Poland had been crushed and France had capitulated. And, best of all perhaps, the meat-grinder of trench warfare had been avoided. German casualties in the French, Scandinavian and Polish campaigns of the previous ten months had amounted to 200,000, of whom some 60,000 had been killed. And, while this total may seem shocking to twenty-first-century ears, it represents about half of the German losses incurred in a single battle of the First World War – the Battle of the Somme in 1916.

The fly in the ointment was Britain. Routed in France and forced into ignominious evacuation off the beaches of Dunkirk, the British had been roundly defeated and, though they were still at war with Germany, were no longer considered to pose a serious threat. Indeed, the battles of 1940 were widely believed to have neutered the British for good. For one thing, the military materiel left behind at Dunkirk filled ten acres of the French countryside, and it was thought unlikely that it could be replaced in short order. In addition, the Germans held little respect for British troops them-selves, whom they considered, for the most part, to be ill-trained, ill-led, ill-disciplined and far inferior to the already routed French.[44] Newsreel images of puny, gap-toothed 'Tommies' alongside strapping, bronzed German infantrymen did much to convince the German public that their troops really were biologically, as well as militarily, superior. Even the British blockade of Germany, which had been so devastatingly effective during the First World War, held no fear any more. As the German people were keen to stress, with most of the western seaboard of Europe – from the North Cape to the Pyrenees – in German hands, who was it that was being blockaded anyway?[45]

In the summer of 1940, this flowering of popular optimism was bolstered by a peculiar form of celebrity mania, as the heroes of the recent military campaigns were lauded and fêted in the capital. One of the first had been the U-boat captain Günther Prien. He was followed by others who had won their spurs in the French campaign, such as the pilots Werner Mölders and Adolf Galland. In most cases, the accession to celebrity status in the Third Reich was swift. First, press conferences would be called, where the would-be celebrity would recount his heroic deeds for the waiting press and public. This would be followed by promo-tion, the award of high military honours and an invitation to private meetings with the Führer. In time, if the candidate proved sufficiently malleable and photogenic, he would join the 'A-list' and be seen at all the best events.

An essential part of the celebrity culture in the Third Reich was the production of photographs and postcards. In an age before television, this was seen as a vital way to extend the celebrity appeal beyond the traditional circles of those who read the newspapers or listened to the radio, and especially to target the young. Postcards had long been a part of the Nazi propaganda effort, from those commemorating the Nuremberg rallies or the movement's martyrs to the ubiquitous, stern-faced image of Hitler. But with the advent of war, and especially the victories of 1940, the medium really came into its own.

The rise to fame followed a familiar pattern. The dashing war hero would be required to sit for a photographic portrait, perhaps even by Heinrich Hoffmann himself. The resulting images would be printed as postcards and then either be sold or sent out, upon request, to the adoring public. Field Marshal Rommel's adjutant, Hans-Joachim Schraepler, recalled the process in a letter sent to his wife from the North African desert in the summer of 1941. 'Yesterday', he complained, 'I wrote and dictated a vast amount of letters on the general's behalf, and sent the new photos which were well done. I am afraid that not hundreds but thousands will ask for a photo. This is the price of glory. It is of no use to become a famous man.'[46]

Perhaps the best examples of this celebrity culture were the cards produced by the prolific artist Wolfgang Willrich. Willrich was already well established prior to 1939, with numerous exhibitions and publications to his name. Among other commissions, he had been engaged to produce collections of sketches of the Nazi leadership, ethnic Germans abroad (*Volksdeutsche*) and German peasants. His portraits typically consisted of a head and shoulders, often viewed in profile, showing the contours of the face and the bone structure of the subject to best advantage. Executed in pencil and charcoal, but sometimes wholly or partly overpainted in watercolour, they portrayed the same bluff heroism – all cheekbones and rippling muscles – common to much Nazi art. Those earlier pictures were generally published with commentary in bound volumes, appealing to collectors and those with a passion for German ethnography.[47]

Willrich seems to have come into his own with the outbreak of war. After petitioning Rommel, asking to be permitted to accompany the troops as a war artist, he took part in both the Polish and the French campaigns, sketching senior personnel and ordinary soldiers as he went. In time, he also produced sketches of the military heroes of the day, including Prien and Mölders. One of Willrich's portraits of Rommel would even find its way into the possession of British general Bernard Law Montgomery, who gave it pride of place in his battlefield caravan.[48]

Such pictures, reproduced as postcards for the Propaganda Ministry, proved enormously popular. Sold for around 20 pfennigs apiece, sales particularly spiked when entire platoons of Hitler Youth were encouraged to write off requesting signed examples. One collector was the young Christa Riemann. Her bedroom wall was festooned with pictures of Mölders and Galland: 'We were crazy about the pilots', she recalled, 'they had these chic uniforms and received medals and high awards . . . all very impressive.'[49] These cards would be eagerly collected, or might be swapped in schools and playgrounds, but their propaganda value was incalculable.

So, Berlin's optimism was palpable that summer, but it would prove to be short-lived. In August 1940, the RAF began night bombing over Berlin and, although the early raids tended to be rather inconsequential, they nonetheless reminded citizens that they were still at war and gave them a grim warning of things to come.

That autumn there were further unsettling shifts. The state visit of Soviet Foreign Minister Vyacheslav Molotov to Berlin in November had been strained and, despite public expressions of friendship, the perceptive observer would have discerned a new chill in German–Soviet relations. Political developments thereafter only strengthened the suspicion that Stalin was being cut adrift. The Tripartite Pact, signed earlier that autumn between Italy, Germany and Japan, gained a number of new signatories – Hungary, Romania and Slovakia – in November 1940. Though the text of the Pact explicitly stated its peaceful intentions towards Moscow, it was obvious that the countries of central Europe were taking sides.

The following spring, the balance of power appeared to shift still further. In March 1941, Bulgaria too joined the Tripartite Pact and was immediately occupied by German troops. In April, German forces launched the simultaneous invasion of Yugoslavia and Greece, thereby at a stroke cutting the Gordian knot of Yugoslav politics and clearing up the Italian-inspired military quagmire in Greece. When the German–Turkish friendship treaty was signed early that summer, Germany had

gained effective control of all of continental Europe and, most importantly, her south-eastern flank was secure. The scene was set, it
seemed, for the next phase of the war.

Yet, this is – in part at least – to read history backwards. Seen from
the perspective of ordinary Berliners in the early summer of 1941, these
were heady days indeed. Germany, it appeared, had already taken on
her primary, historic enemies and had emerged victorious: France had
been defeated and the British had been driven from the continent. The
German Reich was bound by treaty with the other major powers in
Europe – the Soviet Union and Italy – and had entered alliances with
almost all of the other lesser players. Greater Germany was a reality:
it bestrode the continent, its economy was the strongest and its political model was the most dynamic. Militarily, too, the perception of
German invincibility was creeping into even the most sceptical hearts.

And yet, for all the optimism, a profound sense of unease seemed
to persist. This was not helped by the regime's rather clumsy attempt
to distract attention from the build-up of German forces on the eastern
border of the Reich, by obliquely suggesting that an airborne invasion of Britain would be the next operation.[50] Whether the public
believed the ruse or not, it did little to raise the mood as it indicated
that the 'lull' of 1940–41 was merely the pause between two battles,
rather than the end of the war.

The result was a combination of confusion and suspicion in which
rumour and hearsay flourished. As the New York Times noted on 20
June, a Nazi spokesman complained in a press conference of the
'tremendous flood of rumours'[51] that had erupted surrounding
German–Russian relations. Though he took pains to deny them, he
offered little else by way of confirmation or contradiction. Nazi mood
reports, meanwhile, relayed more of their substance. Across the Reich,
it was noted, 'the Russian question is being discussed incessantly'. In
general, the opinions expressed were optimistic: Stalin would travel
to Berlin, some suggested, to negotiate with Hitler face to face; others
believed that Ukraine would be granted to Germany on a ninety-nine-
year lease. 'Only a minority', the report concluded, suspected the
scenario that would soon transpire to be the truth; 'that German–
Russian negotiations had come to nought and that an invasion of
Russia would begin around the end of the month.'[52]

★   ★   ★

The 22nd of June 1941 fell on a Sunday. Coming at the end of a period of fine, dry weather, many Berliners found the day a good excuse for packing a picnic and heading for the parks and lakes of Berlin. There they could try to forget about rationing and escape the war that had seemed, of late, to have reached stalemate.

As the sun came up that morning, a few early risers were already preparing rolls, sandwiches or flasks of ersatz coffee to take with them for their excursion. They would head out of the city in their droves, perhaps to go boating on the Havelsee, or stroll around the shores of the Müggelsee, where children would happily splash in the water. Some would head further afield, perhaps to Potsdam, where they would visit Frederick the Great's palace of Sans Souci to walk in the gardens or view the royal art collections. Others would simply take a tram to the Tiergarten in the heart of the city, where it was still quite possible, both literally and metaphorically, to lose oneself.

For some, that Sunday morning offered a chance to sleep off the exertions of the night before. Though in the middle of a war, the German capital had few restrictions on entertainment, especially after the ban on public dancing, which had been imposed with the outbreak of war, had been lifted a couple of weeks earlier. Consequently, there would have been much to entertain night owls. Some might have taken in a Richard Strauss opera – such as *Wiener Blut*, playing at the theatre on Nollendorfplatz, or *Ariadne auf Naxos*, which was running at the Staatsoper across town on Unter den Linden. Others might have visited one of the city's many cabaret shows, such as the famous *Kabarett der Komiker*, or 'KadeKo', on Kurfürstendamm, hosted that summer by the renowned cabaret star Willi Schaeffers. In addition, the UFA cinemas across the capital offered a host of other attractions that weekend, from *Der Weg ins Freie*, starring Zarah Leander, to the drama *Carl Peters*, a swipe at British imperialism set in late nineteenth-century East Africa.

Early that Sunday, however, all Berliners would have become dimly aware that something was afoot. They might have listened to the radio, or heard snatches of conversations from the street or the stairwell. Had they done so, they would have learned that Hitler had finally turned on his erstwhile ally: Operation Barbarossa – the German invasion of the Soviet Union – was under way.

At 5.30 that morning, Goebbels read the Führer's proclamation across all radio stations from his office in the Reich Ministry for

Propaganda. It was a strange document. 'German People! National Socialists!' it began: 'Weighted down with heavy cares, condemned to months-long silence, the hour has come when at last I can speak frankly.' The average Berliner up with the lark would have been confused as to what precisely he was listening to. And that confusion was unlikely to have been dispelled by what followed, as the first half of the proclamation was aimed, almost exclusively, at the British, whose perfidious methods of waging war by proxy and seeking to decimate the German population, Hitler claimed, had forced Germany into this 'act of self-protection'.

When the proclamation finally switched to the Soviets, Hitler claimed to harbour 'no hostile feeling against the peoples of Russia', but was unswerving in his condemnation of their 'Jewish Bolshevist rulers'. There then followed an exhaustive, point-by-point refutation of Soviet claims and demands, the intricacies of which would doubtless have been lost on the majority of his audience. However, Hitler's proclamation ended with words that few would have failed to understand:

> German people! At this moment a march is taking place that, as regards extent, compares with the greatest the world hitherto has seen . . . The German Eastern Front extends from East Prussia . . . to the shores of the Black Sea. The task of this front, therefore, no longer is the protection of single countries, but the safeguarding of Europe and thereby the salvation of us all . . . May God help us in this fight![53]

This proclamation, read and broadcast live on all German radio channels, would be repeated throughout the day. Half an hour later, at 6.00 a.m., Foreign Minister Ribbentrop gave a similar address to domestic and foreign journalists in a press conference at the Foreign Office. Later in the day, Hitler promulgated another declaration, this time to the soldiers of the new Eastern Front. 'German soldiers!', he proclaimed, 'You enter a fight that will be both hard and laden with responsibility because the fate of Europe, the future of the German Reich, and the existence of our people rests solely in your hands.'[54] Once again, uncharacteristically, he invoked God's help in the struggle to come. This proclamation, too, would be broadcast relentlessly through the day – both on radio and via loudspeakers in the streets – and would be published verbatim in the newspapers.

While the politicians pontificated, 700 kilometres to the east soldiers of Hitler's Wehrmacht were embarking on the largest military operation in European history: 3.5 million men, supported by nearly 4,000 tanks and over 2,500 aircraft, were advancing along a 2,000-kilometre front, stretching from the Baltic to the Black Sea. They were opening the most decisive theatre of the war in Europe, the theatre in which the lion's share of Germany's five million military deaths would occur.

The public reaction to the commencement of Operation Barbarossa was mixed. Officially, the Berlin public was stoical, demonstrating 'complete trust in our Wehrmacht' and 'facing the coming events with calmness and martial determination'.[55] The reality was slightly different, however. There was a profound sense of shock, not least among those who had not seen it coming. Lutz Ritter recalled that his father had organised a sailing trip with friends on the Müggelsee that morning. As the would-be sailors were gathered on the landing stage waiting to board, the announcement came through on the radio. 'It was as though they had been struck by lightning', Ritter reported, 'nobody spoke.'[56]

There was also a sense of liberation. Goebbels, for one, described feeling 'totally free' with the invasion, as 'the burden of many weeks and months'[57] was finally lifted. Ordinary Berliners would have felt a similar sense of relief, not only because they could now move on from the rumour and hearsay of recent weeks and face the new challenges, but also because Germany could at last engage with what many of them regarded as their country's most dangerous opponent. Even the less ideologically committed would have absorbed the vehement anti-Soviet rhetoric of the early 1930s and adjusted only with difficulty to the tactical alliance with Moscow which had opened the war. The American Henry Flannery noted:

> The war against Russia was the first popular campaign that had been launched. None of the Germans had been able to understand why a treaty should have been made with the Soviets, after they had been the main object of denunciation since 1933. Now they had a sense of relief, a feeling of final understanding. I listened to their conversations around

the news-stands and on the subways. I talked with a number of them.
For the first time, they were excited about the war.

'Now,' they said, 'we are fighting our real enemy.'[58]

Tellingly perhaps, the extra editions of the newspapers were purchased
with particular alacrity that morning[59] – in sharp contrast to earlier
points during the war.

Berlin's communists undoubtedly felt the same sense of relief, albeit
for a very different reason. With the Nazi attack on the 'bastion of
world revolution', they were finally free from the ideological gymnastics that they had been obliged to perform for the past two years. No
longer did they have to bite their tongues when they read about the
'eternal friendship' between Nazi Germany and the USSR. With Hitler's
attack on Stalin, they now knew on which side they stood: the Soviet
Union, the 'home of the proletarian revolution', had to be defended.
To this end, numerous underground groupings in the capital – among
them those run by 'Beppo' Römer and Robert Uhrig – began to plan
their part in the struggle to come.[60]

Many Berliners were simply stunned. The most perspicacious among
them foresaw that the campaign against the Soviet Union would bring
with it new hardships, new privations. Helmut James von Moltke was
excited about the invasion – of which he had received advance word
through his military contacts – but was nonetheless filled with foreboding. He wrote to his wife the day before the invasion was launched,
to warn her that 'tomorrow everything will look different, and many
things will assail us which we must arm ourselves against'.[61] Others
warned that a swift victory of the kind that had been achieved up to
that point was unlikely. As one of Ruth Andreas-Friedrich's friends
noted grimly that day: 'Don't be deceived gentlemen . . . Russia has
never been suited to lightning wars. What's the good of our being in
the Urals? They'll just go on fighting beyond the Urals. No, that
mouthful is one we can't chew.'[62]

For this reason, perhaps, those who ventured out of town for a walk
in the park or a visit to Potsdam that Sunday were a little preoccupied.
Yet, with the sun shining and nature in the full flush of summer, their
mood would probably have lightened somewhat. As Berliners had
learned by now, in wartime one had to take one's pleasures where and
when one could and learn to block out the wider picture. This was

certainly the mood that a Swiss journalist detected in Berlin that weekend, writing: 'Out there [in the parks and lakes], nothing reminds one of the war, as it is an unwritten rule that such free time out in the countryside should not be diminished by thoughts of war.' He continued that 'the fateful invasion of Russia has not prevented Berliners from enjoying the beautiful summer weather with gay abandon . . . [and] many thousands were out in the woods and on the lakes around Berlin.'[63]

With the benefit of hindsight, it is tempting to see the invasion of the Soviet Union as the beginning of the end of Nazi Germany. But from the perspective of Berlin in the summer of 1941, the new theatre of the war was just that: another theatre, another act in the ongoing drama, another list of unpronounceable locations on a map, another excuse for hyperbole from the Nazi regime's propagandists.

To most Berliners, Operation Barbarossa would not have been considered in strategic or political terms, but on a much more human level; in terms of the sons, brothers, fathers and friends who were now fighting for Hitler, for Germany and for their lives. The first of more than three million men crossed the Soviet border that morning. Every household and every family in Berlin would have known somebody who was there.

4

Marching on their Stomachs

Enjoying the snow on New Year's morning 1940, few Berliners would have suspected that they were witnessing the first flurries of one of the worst winters in European history. As the snow fell that January, temperatures dropped also, reaching levels not experienced in living memory. With little respite, winter would hold the continent in its icy grip well into the spring. Germany's waterways, from the smallest canals and lakes to the greatest arterial rivers, froze solid. The Danube was impassable for most of its length; the Rhine, Elbe and Oder were also blocked with ice. Road and rail traffic ground to a halt.

The German capital was also grievously affected. Temperatures regularly fell as low as minus 20°C reaching an absolute low point of minus 22.5°C in mid-January.[1] For many, however, it was not the extremes, rather the duration of the cold that was most trying. For days on end, daytime temperatures struggled to rise above minus 5°C and night-time would generally bring with it a further 10° drop. Snowfalls, too, were substantial, with as much as three feet of snow falling on a number of occasions. Initially, the sudden irruption of winter had been greeted with considerable enthusiasm. The capital's waterways were transformed into impromptu skating rinks; its numerous parks became playgrounds for skiing and sledding. As William Shirer noted that January:

> you would have found it difficult to believe that a great war was on ... The streets and parks are covered deep with snow now, and in the Tiergarten ... there were thousands of people this afternoon, old and young, tobogganing on the knolls and skating on the ponds. The place was a paradise for children, and they were in the park in droves.[2]

At around the same time a marathon ski course was marked out in the city's forests and parks, in preparation for a race that was to be open to all-comers. Yet it seems the exuberance of the Berlin populace was to be the event's undoing. As competitors began to lose their way in the woods, it became obvious that many of the marker posts and direction flags had been removed by mischievous spectators. The race had to be abandoned.[3]

Despite such apparent levity, reality soon bit. Travel in the capital became impossible, with railway points freezing and snow piling high on the city streets. Berlin's authorities reacted as best they could. A strict emergency snow removal programme was instituted, with all home owners being required to clear and grit the pavements outside their property before 6.00 a.m.[4] In addition, snow-shovelling gangs were mobilised, consisting mainly of press-ganged residents, Hitler Youths and the city's Jews, whose task it was to keep all other streets and pavements as clear as was possible.[5]

Official placards were posted in the capital, proclaiming optimistically: 'NOBODY SHALL HUNGER OR FREEZE'. Yet as far as the last word was concerned, that is precisely what happened. In mid-January, a man was found frozen to death on a Berlin street – the first such casualty for over ten years.[6] He would not be the last. The capital's wits quipped that even freezing to death was *verboten* now. Others suggested that Germany's new allies, the Russians, had thrown in the Siberian weather, gratis, along with the friendship pact of the previous autumn.[7] Most, however, were simply too cold to see the funny side.

In such conditions, the most immediate difficulty the city faced was a lack of coal. Germany's coal supplies were either stranded, en route, on the frozen waterways of central Europe or else sitting in the paralysed railway sidings. The urban centres were the first to feel the pinch. And, as the supply collapsed entirely that January, even those who had managed to put aside small amounts of fuel for the winter found their reserves swiftly exhausted.

On 11 January the crisis came to a head when the city authorities invited Berliners to come and collect the remaining coal reserves, piled up in the rail yards. As William Shirer recalled: 'This afternoon, you saw the precious coal being hauled through the streets in every imaginable kind of vehicle – street-cars, private autos, horse-carts, even in wheelbarrows.'[8] Another eyewitness recorded, 'it got to be a common sight to

see an old man of seventy-five or eighty years trudging along the streets
with a heavy coal sack slung over his shoulder. Beside him usually walked
a youngster pulling a toy wagon full of lumps of coal.'[9]

After the dwindling reserves had been distributed, most of Berlin's
coal merchants simply hung out a sign saying 'sold out' and closed their
doors. Some of them would not be resupplied for well over a month.[10]
The authorities attempted to make the most of what little coal remained.
Berlin's schools, for example, were ordered to surrender any coal supplies
that they had managed to stockpile. Fourteen days' supply was considered an adequate reserve; anything beyond that had to be surrendered
for redistribution to the civilian population.[11] Churches, meanwhile, were
instructed to return all coal to their distributors, as all places of worship
were to remain unheated until further notice.[12] All factories not engaged
in war production, moreover, were informed that they would receive
no coal at all.[13] Most controversially, the city authorities decreed that all
domestic central heating boilers were to be switched off and that hot
water was only to be made available at the weekends.[14]

The lack of fuel meant that many buildings and businesses across
the capital were forced to close. The University, for instance, closed
its doors from mid-afternoon; the Technical High School, meanwhile,
closed completely, as did Berlin's City Library. Many beer halls, cafés,
restaurants and theatres followed suit. Countless factories closed their
doors, while some offices generously permitted their employees to
take work home with them. Schools opened, when at all, for only a
couple of hours a day, long enough for homework to be collected and
new assignments to be set.[15]

Berliners had to survive as best they could. The worst affected were
those – estimated at as many as one in four of the city's population
– who had to endure that winter with no heating at all.[16] In such
households, water supplies would freeze solid and thick crusts of ice
would form on the inside of the windows. A report by the security
service of the SS, the *Sicherheitsdienst*, or SD, noted one such flat in
the Berlin suburbs, in which the temperature dropped to minus 10°C.[17]

Most Berliners were not so badly affected and were able, at the very
least, to heat a single room. Yet they too became, in effect, refugees
within their own homes, huddled around whatever meagre source of
warmth they could muster. Some sought out long-neglected electric
heaters. Others used a stove or oven, ignoring the official instruction

that kitchen appliances were to be used exclusively for cooking. Those
with a grate in their apartment and a sense of adventure could forage
for firewood in the city's parks and forests. When those supplies ran
out, they would have to consider sacrificing items of furniture.

Many simply resorted to wearing their winter clothing indoors. One
diarist visited a friend that January and found her sporting a fur coat
and gloves, trying to keep warm by the kitchen stove.[18] The city's
contingent of journalists faced particular difficulties in this respect.
Fred Oechsner, correspondent for United Press, and newly arrived in
Berlin that January, recalled the struggle of trying to type wearing
gloves while sitting 'half-frozen, muffled in overcoats, woollen scarves,
several pairs of socks and innumerable pullovers'.[19] William Shirer,
meanwhile, found that his room at the prestigious Adlon Hotel – with
its constant supply of hot water – soon became a haven for journalists who were unable to work in the severe weather:

> an American correspondent came to my room to get warm – we still
> have heat in my hotel. He said he'd kept dipping his hands all morning
> in a pan of warm water on his kitchen stove. It was the only way he
> could keep his fingers warm enough to typewrite his dispatch. He didn't
> realise you're not supposed to heat water except at weekends.[20]

With the restriction on domestic water heating, Berliners found that
they now had to live without regular washing as well. Twenty-three-
year-old Missie Vassiltchikov recorded the fact soberly and succinctly:
'This [new decree] is quite a blow, as one gets amazingly dirty in a big
town and it is one of the few ways to be warm.'[21] Fortunately, there
were ways to circumvent the proscription. Bathhouses, for instance,
enjoyed a huge increase in business; one Finnish bathhouse in the capital
was fully booked for the whole of January.[22] The American Embassy
even went so far as to install two steel bath tubs for the use of its
personnel. Due to the high demand, those wishing to avail themselves
of the facilities had to book a day in advance, and were given a twenty-
minute slot in which to have their bath.[23]

For ordinary Berliners the cold weather could prove to be more than
a mere inconvenience – it could be lethal. Berlin's roads were more
treacherous than ever and accidents multiplied, even given the dramatic
fall in traffic volume. In January 1940 the number of accidents on the

capital's streets rose considerably, and according to police files the rise
was to be regarded exclusively as a by-product of the unusually cold
winter. Berlin's mortuaries, meanwhile, processed nearly five hundred
bodies that month, an increase over the previous month of over 20
per cent.[24]

It was little safer to stay at home. For those huddling around gas
fires and ovens, for example, the risk of gas poisoning was ever present.
In February, an elderly couple were found dead in Charlottenburg.[25]
It appeared that they had been sleeping in the kitchen with the stove
lit to provide warmth. When the flame went out, the gas overwhelmed
them in their sleep.

There were other perils. Many house fires that winter were caused
by ovens and gas fires left burning by residents desperate to keep warm.
There were also cases of residents attempting to thaw frozen pipes in
their apartments by lighting charcoal fires, which subsequently burned
out of control.[26] The cold spell wrought havoc with Berlin's ageing
network of water pipes. In the suburb of Stahnsdorf, a burst water
main caused the entire road surface to collapse, leaving a hole fully six
metres across.[27] Pipes bursting inside apartment blocks were less spectacular, but no less destructive. In one instance, a burst pipe in a third-
floor flat in Steglitz not only damaged the two floors below, but also
flooded the cellar.[28]

Yet, aside from the immediate and practical concerns of the people,
the cold and the lack of coal posed a profound challenge to the authorities. For one thing, the coal shortage meant that locomotives were
often left stranded, with the result that marshalling yards descended
into chaos and the city's transport network rapidly ground to a halt.
In one instance, a short commuter train ride across Berlin, which
would normally have taken a mere twenty minutes, took in excess of
nine hours.[29] In retrospect, one might conclude that the commuters
were lucky to have arrived at all. One SD report claimed that workers
attempting to travel into the capital from the outlying areas were
spending as much as fifteen hours travelling per day.[30]

The next problem was that when supplies were finally restored they
were often unevenly distributed. Growing public discontent at such conditions was not easily stilled. When the first trickles of coal supply finally
made it to the capital, for instance, it was found that those merchants
who were prepared to pay cash were often given priority. The resulting

inequality of supply – where one Berliner received coal from his whole-saler, but his neighbour did not – stoked class and political antagonisms and spawned a number of pernicious conspiracy theories.

In addition, the difficulties of supply coupled with an increasingly desperate public demand inevitably put tremendous upward pressure on coal prices. Though consumer prices were fixed, many in the coal industry began – with some success – to demand a revision of pricing to reflect the increased transport costs that they were being forced to bear.[31] When the government also ordered additional restrictions on the consumption of gas, the result was widespread public dismay that the authorities could have had so little understanding of the hardship already being endured in the capital.[32]

Such conditions were not conducive to the maintenance of public confidence and order either. At first, complaints proliferated about what was perceived as the improper use of transport infrastructure during the coal crisis. Berliners were 'astonished' to see official trucks used for clearing snow in suburban side streets, at a time when the shortage of coal had been publicly blamed on a lack of delivery lorries.[33] More seriously, it was reported in late January 1940 that as many as sixty trucks had been standing idle at Tempelhof airfield for over two weeks, instead of being used for the distribution of coal.[34]

In time, the coal crisis led to a minor crime wave. SD reports highlighted a 'considerable increase' in the theft of coal from cellars, factories and coal yards. Most tellingly, they concluded, many of the thefts were committed in broad daylight, with passers-by and eyewit-nesses failing to intervene.[35] Inevitably the Berlin rumour mill was soon alive with stories of demonstrations across the city, protesting about the coal shortages and the apparent indifference of the author-ities. Nazi security sources characteristically suspected that such rumours were the work of their opponents, attempting to incite the German populace to revolt.[36] This interpretation may have been accurate, although it is difficult to imagine that feelings of discontent had not already entered Berliners' heads.

Beyond coal, two other staples whose scarcity became worrying were milk and potatoes. Milk was already in short supply, due to an outbreak of foot-and-mouth disease in Saxony, and transport compli-cations caused reserves to sink to around half the normal volume.[37] In response, Göring announced a price rise for milk and butter in an effort to spur production, while dairies in the capital responded by distributing only to their regular customers.[38]

The shortage of potatoes was more serious, primarily because the humble potato was a traditional standby for the German housewife in times of hardship. The problem in this case was the weather. Though the breakdown in the transport infrastructure that winter did little to help matters, the shortage of potatoes actually dated to the previous autumn, when heavy rains and an unseasonal chill had conspired to ruin much of the domestic crop. Thus, already in December 1939, the supply of potatoes to Berlin had fallen by about half, and it would fall by about the same again the following month.[39]

By that time, new concerns compounded the existing shortages. Farmers were often unwilling to disturb their stores of potatoes for fear that they might be ruined by the cold weather. As a result, many areas – and especially the urban centres – simply went without. Berlin saw no potatoes for more than two weeks that winter and, when supplies finally began to trickle through again, many of those that did reach the capital had already been spoiled by the frost. Though the authorities claimed that there had only been a tiny disruption to the supply, it was privately acknowledged that the crop lost that winter amounted to over 30 per cent of the annual average.[40]

In response to this crisis, the authorities sought to reassure the civilian population that everything possible was being done to secure adequate supplies. It was even claimed that third-class rail wagons would be requisitioned to transport potatoes to the capital, as they could be heated so there would be no risk of frost damage.[41] Berlin housewives, meanwhile, were advised on the best way of using potatoes that been spoiled by the cold – if soaked in salt water, or vinegar water, prior to cooking, it was suggested, such stocks could still be used for human consumption.[42]

Regardless of these efforts, however, the result for many was a winter lacking all but the most basic foodstuffs. One diarist summed up the difficulties experienced by an ordinary Berliner:

'I couldn't buy a single potato in this neighbourhood', she apologised, ... 'Green vegetables won't be available until the summer and of course fruits are out of the question. Even salt is hard to get.' ... 'Yesterday, I waited at the market for two hours and finally got a head of cauliflower,' she continued. 'Many women waited that long and got nothing. I was more successful because I told the clerks that I have four children and had to have something to feed them.'[43]

Most were never in danger of starvation; rather, the main peril was the lack of vitamin-rich fruit and vegetables. Ironically, some Berliners found themselves putting on weight, as their enforced carbohydrate-rich diet of pasta and bread took its effect. As one newspaper reporter noted that winter: 'The Germans, especially the women, are getting stouter, rather than the reverse.'[44]

In the end, nature took its course and the crisis was eased by the thaw and the consequent restoration of Germany's transport infrastructure. At the end of February, snow began slipping from the roofs and the ice that had accumulated on the city streets started to melt. This, in turn, brought new challenges: the Berlin fire brigade was employed to remove icicles – some over four feet long – before they fell to earth of their own accord. Meanwhile, the police and Hitler Youth were charged with the job of ensuring that all the city's gutters, storm drains and culverts were clear, in anticipation of the flood of meltwater.[45]

Amid this flurry of activity, William Shirer was dismayed to hear the air raid sirens sound, once again, over the city on 1 March. He was relieved to learn that it was merely a test, ordered by the authorities to see how the system had stood up to the rigours of an extraordinary winter. 'Judging by their sound', he concluded, '[the sirens] had stood it very well.'[46] The Berlin public, it seemed, had stood the test, too.

A harsh winter – even the harshest for some decades – should not have presented too much of a problem to the inhabitants of central Europe, where snow and freezing winters were very much the norm, but the winter of 1940 *was* exceptional. Not only was it the severest winter witnessed in northern Germany for over a century, it also coincided with a German society and economy still finding its feet; still learning to prosecute a war and still wrestling with the problem of rationing.

Nazi Germany had introduced rationing a few days before the outbreak of war, on the morning of Sunday 27 August 1939. From that point on, the supply of most foods, as well as clothing, footwear and coal, would be strictly controlled. It had been a controversial, if not daring move. For many of the older generation of Berliners, rationing brought back uneasy memories of the First World War, in which nearly a million Germans had perished on the home front from malnourishment. Thus, its reintroduction in 1939 had to be handled with considerable sensitivity. The announcement was accompanied, therefore, by a flood of government-sponsored newspaper articles giving fulsome details of Germany's (largely mythical) food reserves.[47] Some were even less subtle – one report, for instance, proclaimed with trademark Teutonic directness that 'Starving is impossible!'[48]

The rationing system was infernally complex and inevitably unpopular. As one commentator noted, during the first winter of the war: 'the Germans are saying that even if they do survive the war, they will undoubtedly end up in a lunatic asylum as a result of the rationing system. Trust the Germans to devise the most complicated system possible.'[49]

All German citizens and permanent residents were categorised. Adults were divided into three categories, based on the physical intensity of their work: an office worker, for instance, would be classed as a 'normal consumer', while a train driver might be classed as a 'heavy worker' and a coal miner would fall into the category of 'very heavy worker'. Additional categories were established for infants, children and youths.

All such individuals were registered with the municipal authorities and then issued with seven colour-coded ration cards, which were valid for four weeks. There were blue cards for meat, yellow for fat and cheese, white for sugar and marmalade, pink for flour, rice, tea and oatmeal, orange for bread, green for eggs, and purple for sweets and nuts. Ration cards were printed on stiff paper, which was perforated into small, tear out coupons – known as *Marken* – each of which carried the name of the product and the quantity allocated.

Berliners could exchange these *Marken* – along with the necessary payment – for their allocated ration; receiving, for instance, 500 grams of meat, 270 grams of fats and 290 grams of sugar and jam per week. In this way, it was calculated that a 'normal consumer' would receive 2,400 calories per day, while supplements would provide a 'heavy worker' with an additional 1,200 calories daily, and a 'very heavy worker' would receive a daily total of 4,200 calories.[50] Ration cards would be reissued every month, thereby giving the authorities the chance to revise allocations according to supply. Special arrangements were made for temporary residents and for shops, canteens and restaurants.

Germany's Jews, too, were subjected to special arrangements. Their ration cards – overprinted with red 'J's – allowed only a vastly reduced allocation and permitted their holders to shop only at certain times, normally the half-hour before the store closed, by which time most goods had been sold. The result, as Berliner Rachel Becker noted, was that 'hunger became a permanent bedfellow'. Despite her mother's best efforts to find food for the family, she recalled that 'turnips and a few potatoes usually had to suffice for supper'.[51]

A few Berlin Jews were fortunate enough, however, to have amenable shopkeepers. One of the latter was the so-called 'Vegetable Lady' of Lichterfelde, whose Jewish customers were permitted to hang a bag on the back of the shop door in the morning, which could then be collected – complete with their order – at the allotted time. In this way a few Jewish families were able, temporarily at least, to stave off the worst ravages of hunger.[52]

In addition to food, soap, footwear and clothing were also rationed. The latter was arranged by a points system. Each consumer was allocated a fixed number of points – 100 for an adult, 60 for teenagers and 70 for a small child – which were available to them for purchases during an average period of around eighteen months. The items rationed all had a points value; 80 points, for instance, for a suit, 18 for a skirt, 14 for a child's pullover and 10 for a pair of underpants. Whatever one purchased, however, the total points value could not be exceeded. On this basis, it was envisaged that a 'normal' wardrobe would consist of the following:

> Men: 1 suit, hat or cap, shirt, tie, collar, vest, pair of underpants, nightshirt or pair of pyjamas, pair of socks, and 3 handkerchiefs.
> Women: 1 dress, petticoat, shirt, pair of knickers, brassiere, nightgown or pair of pyjamas, pair of stockings, and 3 handkerchiefs.[53]

Shoes, too, were strictly controlled, with only two pairs generally permitted to each consumer, and with a permit for a new pair only being issued upon submission of a declaration that one of the older pairs had worn out.

The system was both onerous and unpopular. It is certainly not

surprising that the first thing Berliners did when they mistakenly
believed that peace had been restored in October 1939 was to ignore
the restrictions and dispose of their ration cards. But in spite of its
inevitable unpopularity, the rationing system worked tolerably well;
Berliners got on with their lives and, most importantly, no one
starved.

The generosity of the system should not be overstated, however.
Although examining the bare statistics, it would be an easy conclusion to make. It has been said, for instance, that in some cases ration
allocations actually exceeded the average pre-war consumption.[54]
Certainly, allowances were comparable to those available under the
British rationing system; and though bread was rationed (which it was
not in Britain), the German fat allowance, for instance, exceeded the
British until 1945.[55] At first sight, at least, it also appears that the German
system held up rather well until the end of the war. There were fluc-
tuations in the allocations permitted, and the general trend is a down-
ward one, but beyond those two caveats one might conclude that
supplies were maintained throughout.

This is certainly the story that the official statistics tell. At the beginning of the war, the weekly ration allocation for a 'normal consumer'
was set at a generous 2,400 grams of bread (approximately two and
a half loaves), and a less than generous 500 grams of meat, 270 grams
of fats and 290 grams of sugar. And, according to archival records,
these figures subsequently dropped, but only very slowly. The weekly
bread ration, for instance, dropped to 2,250 grams late in 1940, then
to 2,000 grams early in 1942. The meat ration, meanwhile, dropped
to 400 grams in 1941, then to 300 in 1942.[56]

Yet to accept these statistics at face value – as most historians of the
period tend to do – is to ignore the central fact that they represent the
amount to which each consumer was *entitled*, not the amount that each
consumer actually *received*. The difference between the two was often
significant. The complaints of one American in Berlin in 1940 summed
up the situation for the general population. 'Every month', he wrote,

the Germans tighten up on our ration cards – which were jokes anyway.
We started out with four pounds of meat a week and later got two. We
started out with four pounds of rice a month, which was cut to one
pound – and not a store in Berlin had any rice to sell. We had ration

cards for oil, eggs, peas and beans. None of these articles was to be found, ration card or no ration card.[57]

The reality, therefore, was that the rationing allocations were often largely theoretical – especially after 1941 – and that most 'consumers' in the capital were forced to make do with reduced allocations, inferior alternatives and long queues.

The primary indicators of the shortages were the rows of empty shelves that were often to be seen in Berlin's shops. Though this was a problem throughout the city, it was perhaps most remarkable in the expensive department stores in the city centre. As well as a shortage of foodstuffs, Berlin suffered serious shortages of just about everything else, from material goods to consumables and toys. One shopper, for instance, complained after searching for two hours to find something of use in the elite Ka-De-We store on Wittenberg Platz: 'That big barn is empty', he said. 'It is a feat of skill to get rid of fifty pfennigs on all seven floors.'[58]

Shortages were quickly felt across the board. William Russell noted how many everyday items were already unavailable in the early months of 1940:

It is difficult for me to write down all the things one could not buy in German shops.

Just think of anything that you would like to buy, anything at all. It was a cinch that it wouldn't be in the store when you asked for it. Or if it was, it wouldn't be for sale.

Shoe strings. None.

Toilet paper. None.

Suspenders. None.

All canned goods. *Verboten*.

Rubber bands and paper clips. Sold out.

Other things which one could not buy in German stores: shaving soap, electric wire, candles, any metal object, phonograph records . . ., typewriters, electric razors, electric water heaters, clothing of all kinds . . ., furniture, thread (one spool a month), many kinds of paper and stationery, color film, vanilla, spices of all kinds, pepper, gelatine, leather goods, buttons, cigars.[59]

The list went on. Soap was already a rarity, with Germans being permitted to purchase only one cake of so-called 'unity soap' per month, which was supposed to cover all requirements, from washing dishes to laundry and personal hygiene.[60] In addition to such household items, many foodstuffs were also becoming scarce. Coffee had already begun to assume the status of an ersatz currency. Fruit and vegetables, though unrationed, were also increasingly hard to find, with more exotic items, such as tomatoes and oranges, swiftly disappearing altogether.

Despite the shortages, many shopkeepers did their best to maintain the façade of normality and kept elaborate window displays to tempt customers. One observer claimed this was a propaganda ruse ordered by the authorities, to reinforce the domestic myth that there were unlimited supplies in the Reich all stored away for eventual use.[61] Whatever its precise origin, the paradox of having empty shops with well-stocked window displays often led to frustration. One eye-witness noted: 'The shop windows were stacked full of things, but in the right hand lower corner was the now familiar sign: "GOODS DISPLAYED IN THE WINDOWS ARE ABSOLUTELY NOT FOR SALE".' At the same time, he said, 'Everywhere in Berlin I met with the same answer – "all sold out".'[62] Another would-be consumer noted that the sign in his local shop window stated that the contents of the window would not be sold until the decorations were changed. However, he observed, 'the decorations simply did not change . . . I put in a bid at one shop for a pair of red pyjamas . . . Six months later, the decorations – i.e. my pyjamas – still had not changed.'[63]

Berlin's hotels and restaurants colluded in a similar deception. The bar of the elegant Kaiserhof Hotel, for instance, contained a large display of many-coloured liqueurs and bottled spirits from around the globe. However, as one customer commented, 'it caused visible pain to the old bar-tender to answer an order for a cocktail saying that he was dreadfully sorry but today, precisely today, he had run out of ingredients'.[64] The truth, it seems, was that many of the bottles were filled with coloured water.

Naturally in such times of shortage, queuing became something like a national pastime. Berliners had to queue for almost everything, meaning early mornings, late nights, and long hours standing in line, waiting – often in vain – for whatever was at the end of the queue. Howard Smith would gauge the availability of a particular item – in

his case tobacco – by recording the length of the queue which formed
in the street outside his apartment:

> One could make observations like this, for the queues generally
> remained a fairly consistent length while the tobacco shop had cigar-
> ettes and cigars, from the time the door was opened until, about half
> an hour later, when the door was closed and the 'sold out' sign was
> hung on it. The queues increased from around twenty yards in length
> in the second month of the Russian war, to ninety yards the evening
> I left [in December 1941].[65]

Missie Vassiltchikov spoke for millions of Berliners in May 1940 when
she recorded her frustrations at the meagre fare available when one
finally got to the front of the line. 'I sometimes get desperate', she wrote
in her diary, 'at having to queue up after the office, just for a piece of
cheese the size of one's finger.'[66]

Given these attendant irritations, some Berliners developed ingenious solutions so as to supplement their official allocation. Theft was
the simplest answer, but it was not treated lightly if discovered. A
Berlin housewife who stole three ration coupons from her neighbour
in December 1939, for instance, was sentenced to three months in
prison.[67] Some were bolder still. One woman was sentenced to two
years' hard labour in the spring of 1944, after it emerged that she had
fooled the authorities into believing that she had a child. She had been
collecting food rations for two for over a year.[68]

Few were quite so brazen, however, and most restricted themselves
to smaller-scale measures to ensure that they were not left empty-
handed after a hard day's queuing. It helped enormously if one had
a regular source where items might even be reserved for favoured
customers. Christabel Bielenberg stressed the vital importance of such
contacts: 'Unless you were known to some shopkeeper, some whole-
saler or better still a farmer, and were able to come to a deal by dint
of the ingratiating smile, the tender enquiry after wife and children,
[then] cows no longer had livers, hearts, kidneys or tails and hens had
vanished off the face of the earth.'[69]

Others were rather more inventive. One observer noted how Berlin
housewives developed a cooperative system of 'rotating queues', whereby
one individual could effectively stand in more than one queue at the

same time, thereby giving them the chance to get different items from
the markets on a single day. 'The scheme operated this way', he wrote:

> Frau Schmidt reached the market early in the morning and got a place
> in the potato line, the most important of them all. She immediately set
> about making friends with Frau Mueller behind her. When relations
> were cemented and an oral pact made, Frau Mueller agreed to hold
> Frau Schmidt's place in the potato line while the latter went over to the
> carrot line and repeating the procedure, succeeded in inducing Frau
> Hinkel to hold her place while she returned to the potato line in order
> to hold Frau Mueller's position, while Frau Mueller went over to the
> carrot line. At length Frau Schmidt's turn for potatoes arrived, and after
> she had bought her potatoes she rushed over to take her position, by
> now at the head, in the carrot line. Thus, and thus alone, could one
> buy two vegetables.[70]

Consumers were also obliged to expand their cooking repertoire
and experiment with new, exotic – and sometimes not so exotic –
ingredients. In this way, chicory, endive, aubergines and Jerusalem
artichokes all made an appearance in the German diet. Similarly, the
definition of meat became increasingly elastic as the war progressed,
encompassing anything from assorted cuts of offal, such as lungs and
brains, to pigs' tails and baked udder. In the winter of 1940, one Berliner
was surprised to see a dead donkey being carried into the back door
of his local butcher – he recognised it by its hooves and ears, which
were sticking out from under a tarpaulin.[71]

Bread, as an essential staple of the German diet, was adulterated with
just about anything to stretch the limited supply. As the war went on,
the quality gradually deteriorated and loaves began to get increasingly
grey, even green, in colour, as more additives and alternative ingredients were included. Some claimed that sawdust was being added, while
others suspected darkly that bonemeal was now included in the recipe.
Whatever the additions used, the flavour did not improve. With a gritty
texture and a taste reminiscent of cardboard, wartime bread was barely
palatable.[72]

Manufacturers of all manner of products began to show similar
ingenuity and many items for which there were the most serious shortages were soon replaced by an ersatz alternative. Berlin consumers

had the choice of ersatz honey, ersatz egg powder derived from fish and ersatz sugar made from sawdust. One observer noted that the icing used in Berlin bakeries 'tasted like a mixture of saccharine, sand and cheap perfume'.[73] He was probably not far from the truth.

The fashion-conscious could – theoretically at least – also avail themselves of ersatz items of clothing that were not subjected to the rationing restrictions. There were wooden clogs to be had, for instance, women's shoes made from straw and even overcoats made from fish skin.[74] Ersatz wool was spun using cellulose from wood pulp, sugar cane or even potato peelings. Even more bizarre experiments were made with ersatz products for the military: pistol holsters were fashioned from laminated paper, and uniforms were made from leftover food and wood fibres.

Such peculiarities gave rise to a rich seam of popular humour. According to one joke that did the rounds in 1942, a man 'who is tired of life tries in vain to hang himself – impossible: the rope is made of synthetic fibre. Then he tries to jump into the river – but he floats, because he's wearing a suit made from wood. Finally he succeeds in taking his own life. He has been existing for two months on no more than he got from his ration card.'[75] Another Berlin wit imagined a conversation between a Dutchman and a German:

The Dutchman, who had plenty of food in his belly, was sympathetic with the plight of his hungry neighbour.
   'I hear that it's so bad in Germany,' he said to the German, 'that you're even eating rats.'
   'Gosh, and were those rats good!' the German exclaimed reminiscently. Then his face fell. 'But now they're all gone, and the government is feeding us *ersatz* rats!'[76]

Few Berlin consumers were laughing, however. Though the novelties of ersatz were widely publicised, the fact for most German consumers was that even these products were not available. The reality after 1941 was that clothing shops stocked neither the genuine articles nor the much-trumpeted ersatz alternatives. The grim truth was that – as one would-be consumer complained – 'clothing rationing became purely theoretical. Clothing simply ceased to exist.'[77]

In the few examples where ersatz products actually reached the market, meanwhile, the most common complaint was that they rarely met the standards expected by the buying public. Wooden clogs or wooden-soled shoes were uncomfortable and straw fell far short of the strength and durability of leather. Moreover, the ersatz products made for the military were often useless. In some cases, the dyes ran in wet weather, staining the wearer bright green. In others the material began to smell or simply dissolved.[78]

One of the most common – and unpopular – ersatz products was coffee. Made from roasted malt or chicory and known colloquially as *Muckefuck* – from the French *mocca faux* – it was a poor, caffeine-free alternative. Christabel Bielenberg summed up the criticisms by contrasting the advertising slogans with the reality. Where the advertisements promised a product that was 'healthy, strength giving, tasty' and 'indistinguishable from the real thing', she noted sourly that *Muckefuck* was indistinguishable except in one vital respect: 'that one produced coffee and the other a nauseating brown mess'.[79]

Complaining about such products was not only futile, it could also be perilous. Ruth Andreas-Friedrich noted the fate of a woman who complained about the quality of skimmed milk, which she described as 'slop'. Denounced to the authorities for the remark, the woman had to report to the police station every day for three months, where she had to repeat aloud before the assembled officials and police officers: 'There is no skim milk. There is only decreamed fresh milk.'[80]

There were a couple of state-sponsored alternatives to the endless queuing and ersatz. The first was the Army Day commemoration, each March, during which Berliners could buy soldiers' rations without having to part with ration coupons. Rather less popular was the ubiquitous *Eintopf*, or 'one pot meal', a simple catch-all stew that was ordered to be served by every household once a month. The idea was that the *Eintopf* would be consumed by Gauleiters and ordinary workmen alike, enhancing a sense of national solidarity, while the resources thus saved would benefit the wider economy. Though primarily intended to be prepared within each household, the *Eintopf* was also served in restaurants, hotels and even al fresco by the Nazi welfare organisations. On Berlin's streets, vast wheeled soup kitchens – colloquially known as 'goulash cannons' – would appear, from which the steaming stew would be ladled out to the waiting public.

Theory aside, the *Eintopf* did not prove popular with many. William Shirer – used to dining in style at the best hotels – complained in his diary about the 'cheap stew' that he was occasionally obliged to eat. Missie Vassiltchikov was also unimpressed. On one occasion, she had arranged to eat out with friends, but then realised what was on the menu: 'We had hoped to have a good meal, but it turned out to be *Eintopf* day.' The 'tasteless stew' left her 'much disgusted'.[81]

Those who could afford it could go out to a restaurant to eat, at least until Goebbels' austerity drive, in the aftermath of the Battle of Stalingrad early in 1943, forced the majority of them to close. Before then, Berlin's restaurants, bars and cafés continued to trade, with ration *Marken* merely exchanged – along with payment – for the appropriate quantities and categories of food. To this end, waiters were generally armed with scissors to be able to clip the necessary coupons from the customer's card, when a meal was ordered.

Eating out had its advantages. Foremost was that one could avail oneself of those items that – subject to availability – were not restricted by the rationing, such as fish, fowl and pasta. Strangely, many delicacies – including lobster and champagne – were not rationed and were available to those that could afford them right up to 1943. Missie Vassiltchikov, who seems to have spent much of her time in Berlin frequenting the best restaurants, recalled dining on 'lobster and other plutocratic delicacies . . . at Savarin's'.[82] The anti-Nazi plotter Hans Oster, meanwhile, famously wagered a lunch of oysters and champagne at the Berlin Cavalry-Guards Club with his colleagues, claiming that Hitler's armies would be defeated in France in 1940. When proven wrong, he kept to the bargain.[83]

There were two main problems with eating out, however. The first was the cost. A meal, with wine, in a decent restaurant cost almost as much as the average Berliner made in a week. The second problem was the indifferent quality offered by the majority of Berlin hostelries. As the war progressed, the quality of restaurant food suffered, and, as many diarists attest, the dishes actually available rarely coincided with those on the menus. A menu from 1943 for the prestigious Berlin restaurant Borchardt shows what inroads the shortages had made into the fare available to the ordinary paying customer. The restaurant offered one basic dish: red cabbage, mashed potato and an unspecified cut of meat. In addition, there were two soups available

– a 'special' soup and a vegetable consommé – as well as 'field kitchen' dishes, such as 'Pork with Bavarian cabbage'.[84]

Yet if the prestige establishments found their menus restricted, the majority of less salubrious restaurants were often unable to supply even the most basic fare. Howard Smith recalled a visit to the 'Pschorr Haus', a large brewery-restaurant on Potsdamer Platz, which he described as '*the* typical, average, big Berlin restaurant'. After noting how run-down the building was, with dingy interiors, dirty tables and the lingering smell of 'bad fish', Smith described what was on offer:

> There are only two meat dishes on the menu, one of which is struck through with a pencil mark . . . The other is generally two little sausages of uncertain contents, each about the size of a cigar butt. Before the meat they give you a chalky, red, warm liquid called tomato soup . . . With the meat you get four or five yellow potatoes with black blotches on them.[85]

In addition to such obvious shortcomings, it seems many restaurants were also cutting corners in the kitchen and were cheating their customers of their ration allowance. In an internal SS mood report from March 1943, complaints were aired that, although restaurants demanded fat coupons from customers, fat was evidently not used in the cooking. The report quoted a chef who had worked in a number of restaurants in Berlin and Potsdam, and who had confirmed to investigators that the practice was widespread. He claimed that one of his employers had demanded a coupon for 15 grams of fat, for a dish of fried plaice, when in fact no fat was used in the cooking and food colouring was applied instead.[86] In this way, it seems, unscrupulous restaurateurs could make their own supplies go much further.

For those lacking the necessary funds, or unwilling to sacrifice their ration allocation for such questionable fare, there were alternative sources of food available. The most obvious option was to try to grow your own. To this end, those with access to a garden would start a vegetable patch, to produce carrots, potatoes and other essentials. By 1942, most of the city's open spaces and parks had been converted in this way. Benedikt Dietrich recalled that his family received pumpkin seeds from relatives abroad, which were duly planted in their small garden and in time made an important – if rather monotonous – contribution to the family diet.[87] Those without access to a 'kitchen garden' made do as best they could, often searching for fruit, weeds and wild plants that might be used in cooking, such as rosehips, apples, nettles, dandelions and, of course, fungi.

Some were more adventurous. The rearing of chickens – for meat and eggs – was widespread, especially in suburban districts. Christabel Bielenberg, who was then living in the elegant western suburb of Dahlem, recalled the initial displeasure of her middle-class neighbours when she and her husband started keeping hens. 'Did she not know', she was asked, 'that Dahlem was a very respectable residential area?' In time, however, such complaints would be silenced:

> As the thermometer began its descent to unheard of depths and the food rations seemed bent on the same downhill path, the sepulchral cluckings from our cellar, which echoed regularly across the hedgetops, made havoc of our neighbours' status qualms. We noticed discreet wooden structures being erected in bushes and behind unused garages, and felt assured that by spring our corner of the smart residential district would greet the dawn as merrily as a busy barnyard.[88]

Rabbit keeping also became popular. Larger breeds such as the Flemish Giant and the German Grey were favoured, as they yielded the greater portion of meat. Angoras, too, were much prized for their wool. An official breeding programme was even begun in a number of concentration camps, to produce Angora wool for use in the lining of Luftwaffe flying suits.[89] The needs of the average civilian rabbit keeper were much more mundane. But, as rabbits bred swiftly and could be used both for their meat and their skin, they proved so popular that the authorities decreed that only one animal was to be permitted for each member of the household. As they could even be kept by those living in apartments with no access to a garden, they were often referred to as 'balcony pigs'.[90]

For those unwilling or unable to keep chickens or 'balcony pigs', the alternative was to make an arrangement with someone who did. To this end, many Berliners would travel – on so-called *Hamsterfahrten*, or 'hamstering trips' – out into the countryside surrounding the city to deal directly with the local farmers and smallholders. There they would make cash purchases or – increasingly – barter anything they could

take with them for ham, eggs, bacon or vegetables. One Berlin mother
traded a ring, bracelet and necklace set with garnets in return for a
kilo of bread and a small jar of marmalade.[91] This activity, though
widespread, was illegal and those caught would have to reckon with
the confiscation of their 'haul' as well as a fine, or worse.

There were more legitimate ways of achieving the same result.
Some would request food packages from relations in rural areas,
where the shortages were not so severe and access to meat and fresh
produce was easier. Others would look to exploit the evacuation of a
child to the countryside to secure additional food. For many Berliners,
such supplies – whether legitimately obtained or otherwise – made
the vital difference and helped to stave off the pangs of hunger.

Though such activities were more or less constant features of Berlin
life, there were a few food sources that were rather more sporadic or
unusual. The Allied bombing briefly provided a boon for Berliners,
when the city's zoo was hit in the autumn of 1943. In the aftermath,
there was a short-lived glut of meat – most of which, thankfully, was
unidentifiable. Lutz Heck recalled:

> We had meat coming out of our ears. Many of the edible animals
> which had fallen victim to the air raid ended up in the pot. Particularly
> tasty were the crocodiles' tails; cooked tender in big containers, they
> tasted like fat chicken. The dead deer, buffalo and antelopes provided
> hundreds of meals for man and beast alike. Later on, bear ham and
> bear sausage were a particular delicacy.[92]

Also, to most people's astonishment, the meat ration in Germany
was periodically doubled in 1943 and 1944.[93] Consumers, naturally, were
delighted. Fifteen-year-old Dieter Borkowski initially took the news as
evidence that the war was progressing well for Germany, and made the
mistake of expressing his enthusiasm for the measure while collecting
his family rations from the butcher. He was soon put straight. 'You fool!'
said the butcher:

> You will see what becomes of it. Those are the calves and cows from
> the Ukraine, and we won't have them next year! Emergency slaugh-
> tering due to planned withdrawals by the Greater German Wehrmacht!
> That's what they call it. You'll see, my boy, next year we will be slicing

everything thinner and tightening our belts. After all those retreats, we'll be happy to have some dried bread![94]

The butcher was right. But in the meantime, the 'emergency slaughtering' lasted for some months and provided a much-needed fillip to hard-pressed Berlin housewives. Even in the summer of 1944, as the German Eastern Front began to collapse, large numbers of cattle were still being herded west and slaughtered to keep them from falling into the hands of the Soviet army.

Dwarfing even those not inconsiderable supplies were the vast amounts of goods sent home to the Reich by German soldiers serving in the occupied lands of Europe. Much of this was the result of simple plunder, especially that which originated on the more lawless Eastern Front. However, the vast majority of it was legitimately purchased and sent home from comparatively well-supplied areas such as France, Belgium and Denmark. German soldiers stripped occupied western Europe bare, like a plague of field-grey locusts. Either sending it by post or carrying it themselves, they transported enormous amounts of foodstuffs and consumer items to the Reich: bacon and butter from Denmark, fish and fox furs from Norway, eggs from Ukraine, tobacco from Greece or honey from Russia. Often soldiers would receive a 'wish list' of foods and consumables from family members and friends, which they subsequently endeavoured to fulfil.

This state of affairs was tolerated, even encouraged, by the military authorities. All of the controls by which such transactions were traditionally kept within reasonable bounds – from currency exchange rates and purchase restrictions to transport limits and soldiers' financial allowances – were abolished or set to the advantage of German soldiers, with the clear aim of facilitating purchasing. Göring even formulated what became known as the *Schlepperlass*, or 'Schlepp Decree', in October 1940, which stated that German soldiers abroad could take with them on home leave whatever they could carry so long as it was intended for their personal use.[95] They were effectively given carte blanche to strip bare the shelves of occupied Europe.

More than anywhere else, occupied France was viewed as the mother lode. One contemporary observer noted that the fall of France in June 1940 'yielded a wide-open treasure chest to the German civil population' as the 'contents of the rich boulevard shops of Paris and the

well-stocked pantries and the wine-cellars of the French countryside'
were systematically emptied by Wehrmacht troops.[96] Göring was even
said to have urged German troops in France to 'transform yourselves
into a pack of hunting dogs and always be on the lookout for what
will be useful to the people of Germany'.[97] Such avarice was clearly
not confined to necessities, however. One historian has reported that
German soldiers leaving France on home leave were 'loaded down with
heavy packages . . . Their luggage crammed with lingerie, specialities
from Paris and luxury goods of every description.'[98]

Consequently Berlin saw a temporary but nonetheless obvious jump
in material wealth. As Howard Smith noted in 1942:

> the first effects of the war were not the traditional ones of decay and
> scarcity, but a sudden leap upwards in visible prosperity. Berlin charwomen
> and housemaids, whose legs had never been caressed by silk, began wearing
> silk stockings from the Boulevard Haussmann as an everyday thing – 'from
> my Hans at the front'. Little street corner taverns began displaying rows
> of Armagnac, Martell and Courvoisier Cognac from the cellars of Maxim's
> and others. Every little bureaucrat in the capital could produce at dinner
> a fine, fat bottle of the best French champagne.[99]

Though there was a certain amount of hyperbole in such observations, the principle behind it was certainly accurate. Berlin, it seems,
survived – even flourished – for a season, on the enforced largesse of
occupied Paris.

Not all the goods thus acquired abroad and brought into the Reich
were consumed or used by their primary recipient. Silk stockings and
eau de Cologne were of little immediate use to those enduring the
pangs of hunger, but they could be exchanged or bartered for food.
In this way, many a farmer's wife became well supplied with luxuries.
Some, evidently, were rather too well supplied. One farmer near
Potsdam refused the offer of four pairs of stockings in return for some
fruit. 'What am I supposed to do with those?' he exclaimed, 'my wife
already has thirty-eight pairs of them lying around.'[100] Indeed, Ruth
Andreas-Friedrich complained in 1943 about the greed of rural farmers
who 'trade bacon for dress goods, eggs for jewellery, butter for stockings'. 'Their abundance', she wrote rather haughtily, 'doesn't suit our
distress; their smug materialism is . . . alien to us.'[101]

Though such supplies made a tremendous difference to the soldiers' families who received them, much of the material also found its way onto the black market. Any political system that seeks to control the supply and pricing of goods will develop a black market, and wartime Germany was no exception. In Berlin, the area of Alexanderplatz was the very heart of the illegal trading network – ironically right under the nose of the *Kriminalpolizei*, whose headquarters was nearby.

One example of black-marketeering in the German capital is that of fifty-five-year-old Martha Rebbien. Arrested in November 1944, Rebbien admitted under interrogation that she had lived from the black market for the previous four years, exchanging foodstuffs, luxuries and household essentials. It emerged that she had a circle of around sixty people with whom she did business, each of whom had a similar circle of their own.[102] Networks such as these spread right across the city, from the humble tenement blocks of Friedrichshain to the elegant villas of Dahlem. It has been estimated that the black market in Nazi Germany accounted for at least 10 per cent of average household consumption.[103] Nationally, this may well be the case. But for larger urban centres such as Berlin – where the competition for 'home-grown' produce was that much greater – the black market would have been considerably larger. Everybody would have had their 'source'. Everybody would have known a street corner, or a bar, where one could purchase something illegally, or – as the Berliners put it – *schwarz*, 'black'.

The growing black market criminalised large sections of normally law-abiding citizens. One observer of this development was the Norwegian journalist Theo Findahl, who was based in Berlin until 1945, as a correspondent of the Oslo *Aftenposten*. In the latter stages of the war, he noted that the atmosphere in the city was something similar to that of a detective novel, with suspicion ever-present, directed especially towards foreigners like himself. 'We are all criminals', he wrote,

all of us, and the more sensitive amongst us never enjoy a clear conscience. It's not enough that we are all, more or less closet 'enemies of the state', who are of the opinion that Hitler is insane and is leading his people into oblivion, rather we all do something, almost everyday, which is illegal; small transactions with Swedish, Swiss, Danish or Norwegian currency, purchases of petrol or similar from the black

market, bribes to government officials. Small things, of course, but in
Hitler's Reich black marketeering is punishable by death![104]

Though he was talking specifically about the few foreign correspondents who were permitted to remain in wartime Berlin, his
comments could well have applied to almost any Berliner.

In the vast majority of cases the black market was a small-scale
affair, consisting of individuals taking advantage of the shortages and
restrictions to sell or exchange a few items. But in some cases the
black market in Berlin spilt over into the more serious realm of outright
corruption. Many senior Nazis, it seems, were not averse to profiting
from the war. It has been claimed, for instance, that three German
ministers – Wilhelm Frick, Bernhard Rust and Walther Darré – as well
as two commanders-in-chief – Walther von Brauchitsch for the army,
and Erich Raeder for the navy – were involved in the foodstuffs black
market in Berlin.[105]

The Nazi hierarchy easily found ways to avoid its own rationing
restrictions. One of the most famous examples was that of Horcher's
restaurant, which was one of the renowned haunts of Hermann Göring
and Joseph Goebbels, and where – according to one diner – they scorned
the 'very idea of rationing coupons'. Horcher's was well protected by
the regime. Its staff were exempted from conscription, and when closure
was threatened in 1943 – as part of a post-Stalingrad austerity drive –
Göring responded by reopening the restaurant as a private club for the
Luftwaffe.[106] Of course, for establishments such as Horcher's, and for
the Nazi elite, there was always enough food to go round. And though
Hitler's own tastes were decidedly Spartan, his fellow Nazis did not
share his frugality and moderation. Indeed, greed among the senior
personnel of the regime was to lead to one of the most notorious
corruption cases of the war.

August Nöthling ran a delicatessen from his premises on Schlossstrasse
in the southern Berlin suburb of Steglitz, and soon gained a reputation
for supplying to the Nazi elite of the capital, without the bothersome
question of ration cards being raised. Nöthling, for instance, had 25
pounds of chocolates, 120 kilos of poultry and 50 kilos of game delivered to the home of the Interior Minister, Wilhelm Frick.[107] When the
authorities ordered a clampdown on consumption in the aftermath of
Stalingrad, therefore, Nöthling would have had good reason to believe

that his contacts in the Nazi elite would be able to protect him from prosecution.

That was not to be the case, however. Complaints about Nöthling, it seems, had grown too numerous to ignore. As the official investigation discovered, the Berlin grapevine was alive with stories of Nöthling – who was known as *Tütenaugust*, or 'shopping bags August' – and damning opinions of what the case said about wartime German society. The investigation concluded that the case had caused 'considerable damage' to public morale, and to the belief in justice and order in the Third Reich.[108]

So *Tütenaugust* was 'hung out to dry' by his esteemed customers. Although Foreign Minister Ribbentrop refused to cooperate with the police enquiry, others were much less punctilious, pleading ignorance, or blaming Nöthling for persuading their wives, or their cooks, to place large, unnecessary grocery orders. The chief of Berlin police, Wolf von Helldorf, was the driving force of the prosecution, in spite of the fact that he had been one of Nöthling's most enthusiastic customers. Fined and imprisoned for five months, Nöthling hanged himself in his cell in the summer of 1943.[109]

For the remainder of the war, the food supply situation in the German capital continued in much the same way. The ration allocation – though in many cases largely theoretical – continued to supply the very basics for sustenance, such as poor-quality bread and meat of sometimes dubious origin. The system staggered, certainly, but it did not collapse. However, the average Berliner would have struggled to survive solely on what the ration cards allowed. Diets had to be complemented by items purchased by relations abroad, 'hamstered' from the countryside, or traded illegally on the black market. By the end of the war, indeed, most Berliners relied to some extent on illegal means to feed their families and themselves.

Yet, for all the hardship, no one had yet starved to death in wartime Berlin. In the last winter of the war, a Wehrmacht mood report from the capital noted that 'the overwhelming majority [of the population] were of the opinion . . . that the food situation [had been] much worse during the old World War'.[110] Such praise, however faint, must have been music to the regime's ears.

5

Brutality Made Stone

In the late autumn of 1941, a peculiar construction began to take shape high on a railway embankment in the southern district of Tempelhof. The structure was about the same size as a three-storey detached house, except that it had no windows or doors and consisted instead of layer upon layer of concrete, poured by French prisoners of war. Once finished, it resembled a vast champagne cork, with a circular 'head' standing 14 metres (45 feet) high with a diameter of 21 metres (68 feet), and a narrower concrete base below it descending over 18 metres (59 feet) into the ground. Except for three vertical maintenance shafts built into the base, the structure was completely solid and weighed over 12,600 tons – about the same as a Royal Navy cruiser. Officially, it was known as the *Schwerbelastungskörper*, or 'heavy load-bearing body', but the local population christened it 'the mushroom'.[1]

It is highly doubtful whether those locals, or indeed the French POWs who built the 'mushroom', were ever told what it was for. In fact, it was an enormous measuring device. Its base had a surface area of precisely 100 square metres, thereby facilitating the necessary calculations, while the shafts built into its base were fitted with precisely calibrated equipment to measure how much the structure sank into the ground. It was intended to help Nazi scientists and architects to gauge the ability of the sandy soil of Berlin to support massive buildings. Far from being an obscure technical exercise, 'the mushroom' was an essential component in one of the most ambitious building projects ever devised. It was to serve as the test bed for a gargantuan remodelling of the German capital, a project that was intended to transform Berlin into 'Germania'.

The plans for 'Germania' had been of long gestation. Originally dating back to a municipal redevelopment project from the early 1920s, they had been seized upon by Hitler, who was then a frustrated architect and struggling politician. Finding the official proposals inadequate, Hitler had made some sketches of his own, which he squirrelled away for a later date.

Hitler had also committed his thoughts on the subject to paper in *Mein Kampf*, in which he elaborated, at some length, on the need for new architectural showpieces to define the 'new' Germany. He bemoaned the lack of 'cultural building' in the nineteenth century, which, he said, had reduced Germany's cities to 'mere human settlements', which were 'culturally insignificant'. Where Germany's cities had once seen towering cathedrals, he noted, now they possessed nothing to dominate the skyline, no buildings which 'might somehow be regarded as the symbols of the whole epoch . . . [and] reflect the greatness and wealth of the community'. Hitler had nothing but contempt for the 'pettiest utilitarianism' that characterised the architecture of his own era. 'If the fate of Rome should strike Berlin', he concluded, 'future generations would someday admire the department stores of a few Jews as the mightiest works of our era and the hotels of a few corporations as the characteristic expression of the culture of our times.'[2]

Hitler argued that public buildings were necessary to define the new Germany and to inspire what he called the 'sense of heroism' in the German people. 'We are the first since the time of the medieval cathedrals', he told a confidante, 'to provide the artist with important and imposing tasks. Not homes and little private buildings, but the most tremendous architecture that has been seen since the gigantic buildings of Egypt and Babylon.'[3] To this end, after 1933 large-scale building projects would eventually be devised that spanned the entire country – from the Prora holiday resort on the Baltic coast to the SS training school at Sonthofen in the foothills of the Alps.[4] As the capital of the Greater German Reich, Berlin would always be of special significance, however. Berlin was foreseen by the Nazis as the new Rome.[5]

The construction programme began soon after the Nazis seized power. Göring's new Air Ministry, for instance, was completed in 1936. Extending more than 250 metres along Wilhelmstrasse, in the heart of Berlin's administrative district, its seven storeys, four thousand windows and seven kilometres of corridors made it the largest office building in Europe. Its vast scale was only matched in newsworthiness by the starkness of its architecture, a curious amalgam of neo-classicism and art deco, which came to be known as 'Luftwaffe modern'.

Nineteen thirty-six saw two further notable additions to the Berlin landscape. The Olympic Stadium was built as the centrepiece for the Olympic Games of that year and was intended – like the Games themselves – to serve as a showpiece for Nazi Germany. It was hugely impressive, with a dramatic sweep of unbroken terracing providing seats for over 100,000 spectators. Besides the stadium itself, the site consisted of a number of other structures and open spaces, whose form and function were undoubtedly influenced by Nazi design concepts. The largest of them, the Maifeld, was an enormous field, with capacity for over 250,000 participants, and a stand for 60,000 spectators at one end. Though it served as a venue for gymnastic displays and polo during the Olympics, it was clearly conceived as a stage for political rallies. Beyond that, lesser amphitheatres and more than 150 additional buildings offered facilities for both sporting and political events. The entire area, over 300 acres in total, was adorned by a series of large, heroic sculptures by noted Nazi sculptors. Quite obviously, the Olympic complex served a purpose that far surpassed the mere sporting requirements of the XI Olympiad.

The second project, Tempelhof airport, was no less ambitious. Designed by Ernst Sagebiel, the architect responsible for Göring's Air Ministry, it was equally immense. Begun in 1936, it consisted of a main terminal building stretching in a 1.2-kilometre-long arc around the north-western corner of the airfield. This opened into a large central hall, whose clean lines and simplicity would not have failed to impress the visitor. On the outside, meanwhile, the building's grand, neo-classical frontage of shell-limestone echoed the stark architectural styles that were then so current in the German capital.

For all their monumental grandeur, however, all of these new architectural icons of Nazi Berlin would be dwarfed by the scale of the Germania project. The plans were so massive in conception, indeed, that they would challenge even the most hyperbole- and superlative-prone of Nazi commentators. Hitler foresaw nothing less than a new heart for the capital, centred on two intersecting, central axes, one running north–south and another east–west. Along these thoroughfares, over a hundred new public and ceremonial buildings would be located, all of them conceived on a grand scale, including an 'Arc de Triomphe' to commemorate Germany's dead of the Great War, and an enormous domed hall for political events.

Initially, Hitler had considered that the plans could be carried out by Berlin's existing city administration. However, he soon tired of what he perceived as their incompetence, obstructionism and lack of a grand vision. By way of encouragement, he suggested starting from scratch, constructing a purpose-built capital away from Berlin, reckoning that the threat would bring the city fathers to their senses. He even claimed to have found a suitable site – on the Müritzsee, 100 miles north of the capital in rural Mecklenburg.[6] In the end, however, he decided to bypass the existing planning authorities altogether. The reconstruction of Berlin, which Hitler considered 'the greatest building assignment of all', would be handed to Albert Speer.[7]

Albert Speer remains one of the most fascinating and controversial figures of the Third Reich. Born in Mannheim in 1905, he was educated, sophisticated and urbane, in sharp contrast to many of the senior Nazi cadres in whose circles he moved. His rise was swift. After attending a Nazi rally in Berlin in 1930, Speer had joined the Party, and was soon being rewarded with small architectural commissions. As his reputation grew, so did the scale of the contracts he won. In the spring of 1933, only weeks after the Nazis came to power, he was charged with renovating the Leopold Palace, the home of the new Ministry of Propaganda. The design for the Party Rally Grounds in Nuremberg followed, and in 1937 he was asked to design the German pavilion for the Paris Exposition.

Speer was by no means the only architect favoured with commissions from the leaders of the Third Reich; there were many others, such as Paul Ludwig Troost, Hermann Giesler and Roderich Fick. But, by the late 1930s, Speer had already emerged as Hitler's architect of choice. There has been much speculation about the relationship between the two men. Hitler, for his part, was doubtless impressed by Speer's erudition and confidence, and possibly saw in the young architect an inkling of how his own destiny might have played out had he been able to realise his artistic ambitions. Speer, meanwhile, was no doubt intoxicated by his sudden proximity to the epicentre of power in the new Reich, and believed in Hitler's supposed 'genius' with all the fervour and certainty of the acolyte.

Moreover, Speer seems to have known, almost instinctively, how best to interpret and realise his master's architectural desires. He persistently played up to Hitler's megalomaniacal desire for size. Knowing how Hitler resented the fact that other architects and planners seemed intent on scaling his ideas down to more manageable proportions, Speer did the opposite. If Hitler demanded a specified scale, he would be more likely to exceed it. Gerdy Troost, the widow of Paul Ludwig Troost, reported that if Hitler had told her husband to design a building of a hundred metres, 'he would have thought it over and replied that for structural and aesthetic reasons it could be merely ninety-six metres. But if Hitler had given a similar order to Speer, the latter's reply would have been, "My Führer, two hundred metres!"'[8]

Part of this was down to arrant sycophancy, but Speer also understood what underpinned Hitler's monumentalist taste. In the first instance, he realised that it was motivated at least in part by petty jealousy and one-upmanship. Hitler never tired of comparing Berlin to other European capitals. 'Berlin is a big city', he once said to Speer, 'but not a real metropolis. Look at Paris, the most beautiful city in the world. Or even Vienna. Those are cities with grand style. Berlin is nothing but an unregulated accumulation of buildings. We must surpass Paris and Vienna.'[9]

Yet, there was also something more substantial, more philosophical, feeding Hitler's gigantism. Hitler saw himself not as building a city for his own day, but for posterity; indeed, for generations to come. As he explained in a speech in 1937, 'these buildings of ours should not be conceived for the year 1940, no, not for the year 2000, but like the cathedrals of our past, they shall stretch into the millennia of the future'.[10] Hitler was rebuilding Berlin as the capital of Germandom and the Aryan race, the centrepiece of the civilised world. Given the enormous historical importance of such a task, he could not be expected to build according to the needs and mores of the *current* generation of Germans. In designing Germania, therefore, Hitler took little heed of the petty concerns of the planners, or of trivial realities on the ground.

Speer took this vision to heart. Indeed, he appears to have run with it, developing his own, related theory of 'Ruin Value', wherein each building was to be constructed with one eye on its future aesthetics as a ruin. Even in a state of decay, he reasoned, hundreds or even thousands of years into the future, his buildings would mirror Roman and Greek models. To this end, steel girders and ferro-concrete would be shunned in favour of sandstone and marble, and buildings would be constructed so that the walls did not require a finished roof to brace them. (One might speculate in this regard whether Speer was anticipating the Berlin of 1945, where there was scarcely a roof left intact.)

This was a potentially risky strategy. Though it certainly dovetailed with Hitler's key idea, it also seemed to equate Hitler's grand plans with the hubris and futility of Ozymandias. Yet, surprisingly perhaps, Speer's theory found favour with the Führer. 'To illustrate my ideas', he wrote,

> I had a romantic drawing prepared. It showed what the reviewing stand on the Zeppelin Field would look like after generations of neglect, over-grown with ivy, its columns fallen, the walls crumbling here and there, but the outlines still clearly recognizable. In Hitler's entourage, this drawing was regarded as blasphemous. That I could even conceive of a period of decline for the newly-founded Reich destined to last a thou-sand years seemed outrageous to many of Hitler's closest followers. But he himself accepted my ideas as logical and illuminating. He gave orders that in future the important buildings of the Reich were to be erected in keeping with the principles of this 'law of ruins'.[11]

With such philosophical underpinning in place, Hitler began to plan for the wholesale reorganisation and redevelopment of Berlin. Speer had already been working on Hitler's plans when, in January 1937, he was appointed as the *Generalbauinspektor* ('GBI' or Inspector General of Building) for the German capital. In theory, at least, Speer's new position was only of equivalent rank to a junior minister; in reality, it was far more important. Responsible only to Hitler, Speer held the right of veto over *all* building and planning projects in Berlin. He also had the power to expropriate *any* necessary properties and was en-titled to subordinate *all* government departments and state offices in carrying out his task. Almost overnight, Speer had become one of the most important men in the Third Reich.

Thus empowered, Speer pressed on with the job of redesigning Berlin. Though the plans would develop and be finessed over the coming months and years, a project of works – complete in all its essentials – was presented to the public only a year after Speer's appointment, on 28 January 1938. The reaction within Germany was predictably enthu-siastic, with newspapers carrying detailed explanations of the plans. *Der Angriff* stated that the designs were 'truly monumental . . . far exceeding all expectations'.[12] The *Völkischer Beobachter* proclaimed grandly that 'from this desert of stone, shall emerge the capital of a thousand-year Reich'.[13] The foreign press, though less effusive, nonetheless concurred.

The *New York Times* described the project as 'perhaps the most ambitious planning scheme of the modern era'[14], while *The Times* noted that the scheme promised 'to turn a substantial area of Berlin into an excavation [*sic*] for 10 years to come'.[15]

Speer's plans certainly did not want for ambition. In accordance with Hitler's original designs, they centred on a grand axis, which was to run from north to south for around five miles, linking the city's two new rail termini. This grand new boulevard would begin at the South Station, which would serve as one of the primary interchanges between local commuter services and regional rail traffic approaching from the south. Though it demonstrated uncharacteristic flashes of modernism in its conception, with its framework of steel and copper sheeting visible through a partially glazed frontage, the South Station at least conformed to type in its scale. At over 1,000 feet wide, it comfortably surpassed New York's Grand Central Station.[16]

By design, the visitor stepping out of the South Station would be dazzled by the vista that opened up before him. He would find himself on an enormous plaza one kilometre in length and over 300 metres wide. In the distance to the north, the epicentre of Nazi power, the Great Hall, would be visible. The plaza itself would be lined by trees and a two-lane thoroughfare, while at its heart a ceremonial drive would be laid out, flanked with manicured gardens – or, as was later proposed, captured weaponry.[17] To either side, elegant, four- or five-storey, neo-classical buildings would frame the plaza; hotels, restaurants, a swimming-pool complex, and the 'KdF block' – a site to provide entertainment for German workers.

After proceeding to the northern end of the plaza, the visitor would encounter one of the key features of the project – the *Triumphbogen*. This enormous Romanesque arch was essentially a gigantic version of the Arc de Triomphe, which – at over 100 metres high – would have dwarfed its Parisian counterpart. Square in profile, it was topped with an ornate balustrade and an equine statue, while its 80-metre arches would have housed a network of elaborate cloisters at ground level.

According to Speer, the *Triumphbogen* was 'the heart of [Hitler's] plan'. It was, he wrote, 'the classic example of the architectural fantasies [Hitler] had worked out in his lost sketchbook of the 1920s'.[18] Like its Allied equivalent, the Menin Gate at Ypres, it was intended to serve as a memorial to the fallen of the First World War. Decorated with seventy-five bas-reliefs, it was to bear the names of the nearly two million Germans who had died in that conflict.[19] It was specifically in preparation for this massive edifice that the 'mushroom' had been constructed in 1941, to test the load-bearing capability of the Berlin soil.

Leaving the arch, the visitor would follow the axis north, through the administrative heart of the new capital. This area would be home to many of the most important offices of the German state, including the headquarters of the SS, and the ministries of Justice, Propaganda, Foreign Affairs, Economics and the Interior. In order to counteract the potential lifelessness of such a bureaucratic quarter, Speer reserved a majority of the sites on the street for private buildings. Also, alongside the ministries, he planned for

> a luxurious movie house for premieres, another cinema for the masses accommodating two thousand persons, a new opera house, three theatres, a new concert hall, a building for congresses, the so-called House of the Nations, a hotel of twenty-one stories, variety theatres, mass and luxury restaurants . . . There were to be quiet interior courtyards with colonnades and small luxury shops set apart from the noise of the street and inviting strollers.[20]

Continuing north for around three miles, through this curious mix of grey officialdom and brightly coloured hedonism, our visitor would arrive at the Circus. Over 200 metres in diameter, the Circus was foreseen, in essence, as a large roundabout marking the intersection of Potsdamer Strasse with a new North-South Axis. Its focus would be an elegant fountain, with a central sculpture of Apollo mounted on a stepped dais, surrounded by water fountains in a wider circular pool. Skirting the outer edge of the fountain would be a further six bronze figures, all by the noted Nazi sculptor Arno Breker. Surrounded by a ring of six-storey, neo-classical buildings, including a casino and a cinema, the Circus was intended to serve as the entertainment hub of the new district. However, it would have been overshadowed – quite literally – by a number of nearby edifices, whose purpose and significance were far from entertaining.

Firstly, to the west, in an enormous block bounded by the Tiergarten to the north and the Landwehrkanal to the south, the supreme headquarters of the German Armed Forces was to feature a large tower looming over a central parade ground. To the north, meanwhile, the monolithic Soldiers' Hall was to be constructed. Though its precise purpose was never explicitly stated, Speer suggested that the Hall would serve in part as a military museum and in part as an ossuary for Germany's fallen, containing a crypt for the tombs of the country's field marshals. Its design, devised by the prominent architect Wilhelm Kreis, represented the purest Nazi neo-classicism. Flanked by two single-storey colonnades, with bas-reliefs of martial scenes and equine statues, the front entrance of the Hall was a mass of vertical twin columns rising over three storeys to support a flat stone roof.[21]

North from the Soldiers' Hall, the boulevard continued for another 750 metres, through the comparative peace and tranquillity of the Tiergarten, the former hunting forest of the Hohenzollerns, before arriving at the East-West Axis – the first stage of the project, which had been completed for Hitler's birthday in 1939. Beyond lay the political heart of the new capital. Two identical buildings, the Army High Command and the new Reich Chancellery, would form an imposing entrance. But the visitor's eyes would inevitably be drawn to the massive domed building beyond. The Great Hall, inspired by the Pantheon in Rome, would be the largest building in the world. Standing over 1,000 feet tall, topped with an enormous copper-clad dome, it was designed to hold up to 180,000 of the Party faithful. The square over which it towered was similarly immodest. Paved with granite, Adolf Hitler Platz encompassed over 50 hectares and was intended to be large enough to hold a million people. On its eastern side, the square would incorporate the old Reichstag building – the former icon of the German capital, now reduced to insignificance by the sheer scale of the buildings planned to surround it.

Beyond the Great Hall, the line of the development, which previously had run along a north-south axis, shifted some 30° to the west to match the orientation of the existing streets and to incorporate the now redundant railway sidings. Here a grand rectangular lake would be built, one kilometre in length and containing crystal-clear water, rather than the polluted flows of the nearby Spree. On its western and eastern edges, the lake would by bounded by further huge buildings, including the Berlin Town Hall, the city Police headquarters and the Navy High Command. All of them would be constructed in the stark, relentless symmetry of Nazi neo-classicism, or what Albert Speer

called 'our Empire Style'.[22] Finally, to the north of the lake, beyond
two 100-metre stone obelisks set in manicured gardens, the visitor
would arrive at the North Station – the second new rail terminus, just
as grand in scale as its counterpart seven kilometres to the south.

Though Hitler's interest in the Germania project was restricted
almost exclusively to the dramatic main thoroughfare described above,
Speer incorporated those glamorous headline plans into a wider, more
thoroughgoing reorganisation of Berlin's infrastructure. Firstly, and
most importantly, the rail network was to be overhauled. In fact, the
entire project was actually predicated on this one aspect, as much of
the land required for the North-South Axis was to be reclaimed from
the redevelopment of railway sidings approaching the Lehrter Station
to the north, and the Potsdamer and Anhalter Stations to the south.
In the revised plans, these three stations, which handled much of the
capital's local and national traffic, were to disappear and be replaced
by the two new termini. In addition, the other existing rail termini
were to be downgraded or removed entirely, while the two new stations
would be linked by a circular line which would skirt the city centre.[23]

The capital's roads, too, were to be redrawn. The two new boulevards – the North-South Axis along which the majority of the new
building was planned, and the East-West Axis already completed in 1939
– were seen by Speer as the centrepiece of a radical redevelopment.
Where it had previously grown organically in a fairly haphazard fashion,
Berlin was now to be rationalised by the addition of a series of four
concentric ring roads, intersecting with the two radial axes. The innermost ring road would encircle the city centre and the Tiergarten, while
the outermost one was envisaged as sweeping around the entire metro-
politan area of the capital.[24]

One of Speer's overarching intentions was to clear the city centre
slums and provide modern housing stock in the suburbs.[25] To this end,
the *Südstadt*, or 'South Town', was designed to house over 200,000
Berliners and provide work for around 100,000. It was to be located just
inside the outer ring road, strung for around 15 kilometres along the
southern reaches of the extended North-South Axis, with a series of
monolithic apartment blocks alternating with smaller developments
of villas and family houses. Nearby, a military academy was planned, as
well as the headquarters of the Waffen-SS, a Reich Archive, numerous
industrial concerns and one of Berlin's new airports.[26]

The planning was not restricted to stone and concrete, however. Though Berlin already had plenty of parks – such as the Tiergarten, Humboldthain, Friedrichshain and Grunewald – it was nonetheless to be further provided with green spaces for the amusement and recreation of its inhabitants, and also to define the city's suburbs and districts. With this in mind, one planning document of the time anticipated that no Berliner should have more than fifteen minutes' walk to reach a park, a forest or a public garden.[27]

Furthermore, the very nature of those proposed green spaces was subjected to the closest scrutiny. Speer instructed a leading horticulturist to draw up a list of shrubs and trees, outlining which of them were suitable for planting at the roadside, on river banks or in marshy ground.[28] Beyond the city limits, he even had large numbers of deciduous trees planted to restore the original eighteenth-century flora of the region.[29]

The entire plan was extraordinarily ambitious. Given carte blanche and an almost unlimited budget, Speer had designed a city that was intended to become the very centrepiece of the civilised world – a city whose scope and scale would bear comparison with the likes of Rome. When Speer's father, himself an architect, saw the plans, he summed up the thoughts of many of his contemporaries succinctly: 'you've all gone completely crazy'.[30]

Certainly, there was a substantial dose of arrogance and megalomania in Speer's plans. The enormous scale of the designs – 'incomparably monumental'[31] as Goebbels put it – neatly expressed the puffed-up, self-aggrandising misanthropy of Nazism. It is notable, for instance, that the human dimension is almost completely absent. As Speer recalled, Hitler had absolutely no interest in the social aspects of the planning that he oversaw; his passion was for the buildings themselves, rather than for the human beings who might one day inhabit them.[32] Indeed, it has been plausibly suggested that the plans for Berlin's reconstruction betrayed Hitler's megalomaniacal desire to reduce cities and even individuals to the status of mere playthings.[33] When one recalls the images of Hitler stooped like some malevolent deity over his architectural models in the Reich Chancellery, this interpretation becomes instantly and chillingly persuasive.

However, for all its overweening ambition, its megalomania and its misanthropy, the rebuilding of Berlin was *not* a Nazi pipe dream. As Speer recalled in his post-war diary:

It seemed to all of us that with every passing month we were almost effortlessly drawing nearer to the reason for the arches of triumph and the avenues of glory. The Great Hall and the Berlin Palace of the Führer suddenly acquired a real background: the victories in Poland and Norway, the conquest of France. In the crypt of the Soldiers' Hall innumerable places were reserved for the sarcophagi of the commanders of these campaigns.[34]

From the perspective of 1941, Germania was very real indeed. Hitler himself was obsessed with the project. When he learned that Stalin was unveiling plans for remodelling Moscow, he was so outraged that it was on his mind on the day his armies invaded the USSR in the summer of 1941. In spite of the fact that his soldiers had just embarked on the largest military campaign in history, a struggle that would make or break the Third Reich, Hitler, it seems, was musing once again on architecture. 'This', he said to Speer that day, 'will be the end of *their* building for good and all.'[35]

Indeed, by 1941, the translation from theory to reality was already well under way. The first part of the realisation was the demolition of those buildings that, by dint of their insufficient grandeur or the accident of their location, were slated to be destroyed. This process had begun in 1938, when labourers had started clearing the area of the Spree bend – the projected location of the Great Hall – as well as the streets surrounding the planned Circus near Potsdamer Platz and the proposed South Railway Station in Tempelhof. Already by the end of that year, some seven thousand properties had been demolished. A further 62,000 demolitions were considered necessary.[36]

Initially, the affected buildings were painstakingly dismantled, with each one requiring an average of sixty days of intensive and often specialised labour in order to preserve building materials that could be used elsewhere and to protect remaining buildings in close proximity.[37] After the outbreak of the war, however, Speer began to despair at the slow progress. In May 1940, he advocated that dynamite should be used so that prisoners of war and concentration camp labour could be more effectively utilised in clearing the debris.[38]

Indeed, in time, the methods advocated – or tolerated – by Speer and his staff would become more brutal still. A cartoon drawn by one of Speer's department chiefs showed the capital's suburbs being blasted away with an enormous cannon.[39] It was not really a joke. On 26 April 1941, Rudolf Wolters, one of Speer's lieutenants, wrote that the British bombing raid of the previous night, which had hit the area around Potsdamer Platz, close to the site of the proposed Circus, had 'achieved valuable preparatory work for the purposes of the rebuilding of Berlin'.[40] That same month an internal memo noted that over 53,000 properties had already been demolished in the capital – it amounted to only 3.6 per cent of the total.[41]

Alongside the demolition, construction was also under way. Beneath the Tiergarten, for instance, a network of road tunnels was built, which were intended to ease traffic flow around the intersection of the two main boulevards, just west of the Brandenburg Gate. Other sites were rather more obvious. In the area of the planned Circus, the first new block had already risen from the rubble. The *Haus des Fremdenverkehrs*, or 'Foreign Travel Office', occupied the site where Hitler had laid the first foundation stone for the reconstruction of Berlin in the summer of 1938.[42] Completed at least in its essentials by the outbreak of war, it soon dominated the local landscape. Its one concave, arcaded frontage faced the wasteland that was foreseen as the Circus, and was complemented by two wings extending for around 100 metres along the side roads. Imposing in both in design and execution, it was intended, quite explicitly, to impress and intimidate foreign travellers arriving to register in the German capital.

All of this came at a human cost. Thousands of POWs and forced labourers were housed in often substandard conditions and made to work in all weathers. Despite his later protestations of innocence, Speer was never shy of using POWs as labour. Indeed, in November 1941, after the opening successes of the war against the Soviet Union, he petitioned Hitler with a request for some 30,000 Soviet POWs specifically for use in the construction of the 'new Berlin'. Hitler acceded to the request, thereby bringing the total workforce overseen by Speer's staff to around 130,000.[43]

In addition, most of the stone and bricks that were prepared for the project came from the network of concentration camps dotted about Nazi Germany. It is little appreciated that many of the most infamous concentration camps of the Nazi era – Dachau, Gross Rosen and Buchenwald among them – were established close to quarries. The camp at Mauthausen, for instance, was set up alongside the granite quarry that had supplied much of the stone used to pave the streets of Vienna, while that at Sachsenhausen, outside Berlin, was host to the largest brickworks in the world. The camp-quarry at Flossenbürg in northern Bavaria, meanwhile, was the source of much of the white-flecked granite that was foreseen for use in Berlin, especially in the construction of the Soldiers' Hall.[44] Even as the rebuilding of Berlin was superseded by the demands of the war and in effect suspended from around 1942, the production of granite and bricks continued unabated. Thus, the Germania project was not only central to the Nazi aesthetic; it also played a vital role in the establishment and maintenance of the concentration camp network. Nazi architectural planning, it seems, had meshed perfectly with the interests of the SS.

The rebuilding of Berlin also left its mark on the city's civilian population. Most Berliners who were affected were treated decently. Marianne Meier's family, for instance, was evicted from their home on Schellingstrasse, just to the south-west of Potsdamer Platz, on 1 September 1939 – the day war broke out. They were informed that all removal arrangements and costs were to be covered by the state, and were offered a choice of new flats elsewhere, and chose one in the quiet neighbourhood of Friedenau, a couple of kilometres to the south.[45]

Yet, in many cases, it was at this point that the building plans collided with cold realities. Though Speer promised to house all the 200,000 or so displaced Berliners, in reality he was hardly in a position to do so, as the Berlin housing market was already seriously under-supplied and he could not build new properties at anything near the necessary speed. This situation, coupled with the Berlin housing stock already lost to RAF raids, led to a genuine housing crisis in the German capital, a crisis that would have profound ramifications.

As perhaps is natural in a crisis – and especially so in a dictatorship – the solutions to problems are often found with society's weakest members. In Berlin in 1941 the answer to the housing crisis was sought in a stepping up of the official persecution directed towards the city's Jews: if there was insufficient housing stock to accommodate those relocated as well as those bombed out, then the Jews would be forced to make way.

Berlin's Jews – like those elsewhere in the German Reich – had already been subjected to growing persecution. By the outbreak of war, they were effectively isolated from everyday German life, banned from most public places and facing severe restrictions on their movement and employment. But events would soon take an even more ominous turn.

In fact, the idea of forcibly evicting Berlin's Jews dated back to September 1938, a full year before the outbreak of the war. At that time, Speer suggested that the capital's Jewish community should be moved into smaller properties, thereby freeing up larger ones for the use of those Aryan Berliners displaced by the ongoing demolition works.[46] Speer's idea was at least partially incorporated into the revised rental law of April 1939, which decreed that Jewish tenants could be legally evicted if it could be demonstrated that replacement housing was available elsewhere. This decree opened the way for a series of piecemeal evictions of Jews from those areas that Speer had earmarked for his building projects. In 1940, one thousand Jews were removed from the area to the south of the Tiergarten, which was required for the construction of new Danish, Swiss and Spanish embassies.[47] The following summer, a further five thousand Jewish properties were ordered to be cleared.

In time, the rules regarding Jewish housing were tightened still further.[48] In 1941 it was decreed that all vacant properties in Berlin were to be registered with Speer's office, which would then decide on whether, and to whom, they could be re-let. With this move, all remaining rights of Jewish tenants were suspended, and it became possible for the authorities, in effect, to decide where to house Jews.[49] This resulted in the establishment of so-called *Judenhäuser* – 'Jew houses' – often dilapidated blocks in insalubrious areas, where large numbers of Jews would now be concentrated, subletting individual rooms and sharing the meagre facilities. As if to make matters worse, homeless Jews now also had to be taken in by existing Jewish households.

Life in the *Judenhäuser* was difficult. Overcrowding was endemic, with families often living in a single room, sharing bathrooms and kitchens and enduring the inevitable conflicts. Inge Deutschkron described some of the everyday problems in her 'Jew house', on Bamberger Strasse in Schöneberg:

> Eleven people lived there, in 5½ rooms, according to the rules; one room for every 2 Jews. In the flat, there was only one bathroom and one kitchen. The mornings there were terrible. Everyone wanted to get to work on time, as lateness could be taken as grounds for deportation.

To do more than was required appeared to promise security, or relative security at least. Anyone who dared to spend a long time on the toilet, would be driven out with wild banging on the door or hysterical screaming. An attempt to introduce any form of order was doomed by the irregularity of the shifts. Factions were formed and became irreconcilable. Those who returned home exhausted, from the hard labour that had been allocated to them, and found the kitchen occupied, would scream at the lucky ones who had got there first.[50]

Anna Samuel would have recognised such hardships at once. Her new flat in a *Judenhaus* in Köpenick was dismal. 'It's difficult', she wrote to a friend, 'no running water in the room, only in the hallway, [where] there is always a hubbub.' Though the sixty-eight-year-old pensioner tried to make the best of it, she seemed to be thwarted at every turn. 'How will I create order', she worried, 'out of this chaos, when . . . every kitchen amenity is missing . . . Where will I wash something? There is an electric hot plate in the hallway – but it is always in use . . . To get to the shower, I have to get up between 5 and 6. Then I go back to bed.'[51]

Many *Judenhäuser* were worse still. One of them consisted of a block of properties bordering Katzlerstrasse and Grossgorschenstrasse, close to the railway in Schöneberg. Though it had been earmarked for demolition, as it lay in the path of the proposed North-South Axis, it was instead designated as a 'Jew House' in 1940. It would become home to 220 Jewish families.[52]

Though the raft of legislation had stopped short of a blanket eviction of Jewish residents, Jews were now being corralled into what was in effect, if not in name, a ghetto. By the autumn of 1941, over two thousand Berlin Jews had already committed suicide. Perhaps they had simply had enough of the petty persecution and harassment; perhaps they had suspected that worse was to come. Those they left behind would soon have their darkest fears confirmed. That October, the first transports left the capital, carrying some four thousand Berlin Jews bound for the ghetto at Łódź.[53]

It is sometimes suggested that any analysis of Albert Speer's plans for the rebuilding of Berlin should be restricted to the architectural sphere. Just because the Nazi regime was evil, some have argued, it does not necessarily mean that its architectural output must be damned in turn.

Nazi architecture, some say, should be assessed solely on its architectural merits and demerits: its proportions, its materials, its capitals and its pedestals. Ancient Rome was built on slave labour, yet no one would suggest that the Colosseum should be bracketed in the same heinous category as Hitler's projected 'Great Hall'.

This is a specious argument. Speer's plans for Berlin are indeed fascinating. Architecturally, they are if nothing else a potent display of the astonishing extremes that can be reached by megalomaniacal designers. Yet, those plans cannot simply be viewed from this perspective alone: in examining them, one is morally bound to consider not only the designs themselves, but also the brutal methods by which they were to be realised.

The Germania project perfectly reflected the dark, misanthropic heart of Nazism, and in realising that project Speer's office was not a passive, innocent bystander. Rather, it emerges as a prime mover: a motor of policy, not only in its own narrow 'artistic' sphere, but also in areas as diverse – and nefarious – as the concentration camps and the preparations for the Holocaust. Speer's influence, therefore, was clearly not confined to the artistic and the aesthetic. Speer was not, as he later protested, merely an architect.

Hitler intended his new Berlin to stand as a monument to his rule. Appropriately enough, none of his grand designs ever saw the light of day. Today, only the *Schwerbelastungskörper* – the mushroom – still stands. High on an embankment in the south of the city, it is now stained and weather-worn and weeds crowd around its base. It served its purpose. Its gauges recorded that the earth below it *did* shift, sinking between 11 and 18 centimetres across the six measuring points – a little beyond the criteria deemed acceptable by Speer – but whether this might have curbed the architect's enthusiasm, or reined in his designs, is anyone's guess.

The mushroom was supposed to have been pulled down after the measurements had been completed, yet the worsening situation of the war intervened and its demolition was repeatedly postponed and then finally abandoned. To generations of post-war Berliners, it was a conundrum, an eyesore that should not be permitted to remain, but which could not feasibly be demolished. It stands now as architectural curiosity, a silent witness to one man's megalomania.

6

Unwelcome Strangers

They would arrive at any time of day or night. Their train would inch down the siding in a cacophony of hissing and the screeching of brakes. Many of them had travelled in relative comfort, in third-class passenger carriages, with simple wooden seats and luggage racks. Others had been packed unceremoniously into goods trucks, without seats, toilets or any creature comforts at all. All of them would be hungry and exhausted upon arrival. Their journey, whatever its starting point, would have been long and arduous, with much time spent idling in sidings, while military transports and civilian traffic were given priority. Very few of the new arrivals had any inkling of what awaited them. Many had no idea of precisely where they had been taken, even of which country they now found themselves in.

Emerging from the train onto a small platform, the arrivals were confronted by ranks of soldiers, police and rail personnel. There, under barked instructions, they collected themselves and formed into a column to march through a gate and off down a track, leading into a birch wood. After about 100 yards, they would have glimpsed barbed-wire fences and, in a clearing beyond, a cluster of sturdy wooden barrack blocks. Frenchman Albert Flammant arrived there in the summer of 1944:

> It was a terrible sight. The high gate was made with wooden beams interlaced with barbed wire. To the left and right of the gate, there were watchtowers made with rough-cut branches; above a single searchlight. Two parallel barbed wire fences, separated by about 2 metres, marked off a closed area, where there were numerous barracks.[1]

There, deep in a wood known to its inhabitants as 'the Forest of Tears', was his destination: the *Durchgangslager*, or 'Transit camp', of Wilhelmshagen.

The new arrivals were labourers. They would come to be known as *Zwangsarbeiter*, 'forced labourers' or even 'slave labourers', though they were officially known as *Ausländische Arbeitskräfte*, or *Fremdarbeiter* – 'foreign workers'. Millions of them were brought in to feed the Nazi military-industrial complex and replace those German workers who had been drafted for military service. It is estimated that over six million[2] foreign workers laboured within Germany during the war. They served in every capacity imaginable, from helping to gather the harvest in rural communities, to working as servants in private homes and labouring within the flagships of German industry.

It was not the first foreign worker programme in Nazi Germany. A voluntary labour scheme had been rolled out across occupied Europe in 1940, seeking to attract workers by promising adequate food, good conditions and regular leave for visits home. However, the wartime needs of German industry quickly outstripped the available volunteers. Soon, more coercive measures were being employed.

By the time Wilhelmshagen opened for business, in the autumn of 1942, workers were being 'recruited' across occupied Europe by means of raids on church congregations, mass arrests, forced conscription and intimidation. Those who arrived at the camp came from all corners of the continent, from rural France to the western republics of the Soviet Union. In total, it is estimated that as many as 150,000 labourers made their way down the ramp and through the barbed-wire gates of Wilhelmshagen.

Their new home was certainly in a picturesque area. Located at the south-easternmost limit of Berlin's suburbs, Wilhelmshagen was a quiet settlement of villas and detached houses, surrounded by beech woods. There were also lakes: the Müggelsee to the west, the Dämeritzsee to the south, and the River Spree linking the two before meandering off into the city centre. The logic of placing a transit camp there was simple: not only did the semi-rural location allow a great deal of space, it also assured a degree of privacy. Moreover, the camp was located off a main rail line, with its own siding, on the eastern approaches to the city – the direction from which most of its inhabitants would be arriving.

Broadly rectangular, with a total area of over 100,000 square metres, the camp at Wilhelmshagen was conceived as two mirror-image enclosures, divided by the roadway linking the rail siding with a nearby road. Each side of the camp would consist of ten single-storey wooden barrack blocks – each for around 240 inhabitants – as well as administrative buildings, a hospital block and sanitary facilities. It housed around five thousand people.[3]

Arriving at the camp, it is likely that some of the labourers initially felt relief. Many of them had been en route for days, with stops at other transit camps along the way. For some, especially those from Poland or the Soviet Union who tended to be transported in goods wagons, the camp at least offered the possibility of a wash and some brief rest. This was certainly the attitude expressed by one labourer, Kazimiera Czarnecka, who recalled that in the barrack blocks, 'there were wooden bunk beds, no mattress, but clean. We lay down, still in the same clothes that we had arrived in . . . Finally, we could wash our sticky hands and faces.'[4]

Any tentative optimism quickly vanished, however, when the labourers were processed. The procedure was one that few of them would ever forget. Some are sober in their recollections. 'We were led to a large clearing', recalled young Polish labourer Irena Pawlak, 'all around us stood many trees and large barrack blocks. There we had to parade and photographs were taken of us for the *Arbeitskarten* [identity cards]. Everyone was given a number on their chest. I was number 3379.'[5] Others found the experience more difficult. Aleksandra Reniszewska described it in the following uncompromising terms:

> The worst part was when all the women were herded together in a barrack. Our clothes and underwear were taken to be deloused, and we had to stand, naked, on the concrete floor. Photographs were taken of us and numbers were distributed, which were necessary for registration in the office. Then we had to stand, legs apart with heads lowered, over a drain, whilst the male guards . . . poured a stinking, greasy liquid on all parts of our bodies with hair; allegedly it was to protect against lice. Then they poured cold and hot water over us and laughed at us.

It was, she said, the most 'humiliating and degrading' experience of her life.[6]

There were other privations to follow. One Polish labourer complained that the guards at the camp were all Ukrainians and that they would beat the workers with whips. Others protested that they were treated 'worse than dogs'.[7] Overcrowding was endemic. Though the camp was designed to house and process nearly five thousand inmates, it was quickly operating well beyond that capacity. The lucky, or more forceful, inmates could find themselves a place in the barracks, but the remainder had to make do with whatever space they could find. 'We were like cattle in a paddock', one recalled; 'you couldn't escape, you didn't know where to go. Day and night we sat on our cases, on the ground, or leant on trees. There was no room to move.'[8]

Food, too, was limited, primarily for the simple reason that the rationing system for labourers was dependent upon the type and the severity of the work that they had been assigned, and, as the labourers at Wilhelmshagen had not yet been assigned a job, they technically did not 'qualify' for any rations. Some inmates recalled a regular – if insufficient – distribution of bread, ersatz coffee and watery soup; others found any sort of nourishment extremely hard to come by. Czech Vojtěch Fiala complained that he spent two days and three nights at Wilhelmshagen 'without any food at all . . . and without even the opportunity to quench [his] thirst'.[9]

Thankfully, therefore, the average stay for a labourer in Wilhelmshagen was less than a week. According to official instructions, the camp was intended to enable a 'swift and orderly registration of arriving labourers' in which each transport would be dealt with within 2–4 days.[10] Once passed fit for work and registered, new arrivals would quickly be allocated a workplace and another camp elsewhere in the city. If a labourer had a particular skill – welding, perhaps, or carpentry – this would be taken into account. Heavy labour, meanwhile, would usually be assigned to young men, but beyond that the selections were made more or less at random.

Every morning at roll-call, lists of names were read out and those called up were ordered to present themselves, with their belongings, for transfer. Generally a representative of the employer would then arrive to accompany them to their new place of work. Larger groups would be accompanied by a detachment of police or gendarmes.

Businesses of all sizes could avail themselves of Wilhelmshagen's

labour pool. Smaller businesses and tradesmen were often invited to
come to the camp in person to make a selection. The circumstances
were akin to a slave market. One coal merchant who needed help
after one of his employees had been called up for the Wehrmacht was
informed by the authorities that a transport from Poland was arriving
the following day. 'If you can use a Pole', he was told, 'come and
choose one.'[11]

Whether individually, or in long, bedraggled columns, the labourers
that passed out through the gates of Wilhelmshagen were entering a
new and frightening world. The vast majority of them had never been
away from their home country before; many had never even ventured
beyond their own home town. Berlin – with its wide boulevards, public
transport systems, its huge factories, parks and architecture – must
have made both a fascinating and terrifying impression.

Moreover, most *Zwangsarbeiter* came from countries recently defeated
and occupied by German forces. Some might have lost their fathers,
husbands or brothers in the fighting, or been forcibly torn from their
friends, their families and their home communities. Even those who had
come to Germany voluntarily tended to do so for reasons of economic
necessity rather than ideological sympathy. All foreign labourers, therefore, tended to view themselves as 'working for the enemy'. As one of
them commented: 'for us Germany was always something evil, and now
we had arrived in the centre of it . . . Little wonder then, that it was a
shock for which we were scarcely prepared.'[12]

For all their fears and antipathy, foreign labourers were to become the
very cornerstone of the German wartime economy. They served
almost every business in Berlin, from the largest industrial concerns
– such as Daimler-Benz, AEG and Bosch – down to the smallest independent tradesman or shopkeeper. In the summer of 1943, the number
of foreign and forced labourers in Berlin topped 400,000, comprising
one in five of the capital's total workforce.[13] Siemens, for instance,
employed nearly 15,000 foreign labourers in the capital, housed in over
100 camps. German Railways employed a further 13,000, Speer's Berlin
Building Inspectorate 10,000 and AEG, 9,000.[14]

The workers themselves came to the capital from across Europe.
Figures for the summer of 1944 show that about a quarter of them –
100,000 individuals – came from the areas of the USSR occupied or

formerly occupied by German troops. A further 65,000 came from occupied France, with over 30,000 coming from Belgium, and the same number from Holland and Poland. Thus, one-third of all the foreign labourers in the German capital came from western Europe. One-third of them, too, were women.[15]

The quarters in which these workers were housed varied enormously. A minority – those who were employed in small family businesses – might find lodging within a family home (until this practice was forbidden in 1942), or on business premises. The majority, however, were housed in purpose-built barracks or converted warehouses. The largest camp in the Berlin area – housing over 2,500 labourers – was that attached to the Fritz Werner factory in Tempelhof, which manufactured the Wehrmacht standard-issue K-98k rifle. Only three other camps, however, housed over two thousand labourers and the vast majority held barely a couple of hundred. Thus the total number of barracks, camps and hostels for foreign workers in the Berlin district was enormous; recent estimates have pushed the total figure up close to 3,000.[16] As the French former forced labourer François Cavanna recalled:

> At that time, Berlin was covered with wooden barracks. In even the tiniest space in the capital, there were rows of brown, wooden blocks, covered in roofing felt. Greater Berlin resembled a single camp, which had been scattered between the sturdy buildings, the monuments, the office blocks, the rail stations and the factories.[17]

Given the sheer variety of camps, conditions within them also varied enormously, but there were at least some overarching guidelines from which generalisations can be drawn. Foreign and forced labourers were not treated equally in Nazi Germany: crucial racial distinctions affected the working and living conditions of the labourers concerned. As a general rule, labourers from western Europe and the Czech lands tended to be treated as employees rather than prisoners. In 1943, the German government even produced a lavishly illustrated book on the foreign labourers entitled *Europa arbeitet in Deutschland*, – 'Europe is working in Germany' – which contained photographs of cheerful workers enjoying their free time in writing letters, playing cards, eating and drinking in clean, bright, well-appointed accommodation.[18]

Surprisingly, perhaps, they were scenes that some labourers would have recognised. One French worker who came to Berlin in the spring of 1943 had initially been concerned that he would be interned in one of the notorious concentration camps:

> But we were soon reassured. It was not armed military personnel that awaited us. We were welcomed by very polite civilians, and calmly stepped off the train. There was nothing there that one could compare to [. . .] the concentration camps. We were taken to whitewashed buildings that had obviously not yet been occupied. Nothing but cleanliness; everything tipp topp! The sanitary facilities were brand new, and there were showers with warm water.[19]

Though this experience may well have been exceptional, conditions for many of the 'westerners' were nonetheless quite favourable. In the average barracks, they were given a bunk and a wardrobe as well as blankets, mess tins and cutlery. They worked a twelve-hour day, but had free time at weekends and even a little money to spend. Many enjoyed the sights of the city, or went to the cinema, the opera or attended concerts.[20] Some firms organised football tournaments with teams made up from 'their' Czech or Dutch labourers.[21] Under the auspices of the German Labour Front and the social 'Strength through Joy' organisation, cultural and educational programmes were also offered and newspapers were produced in numerous languages, including Croat, Dutch, Czech and French.[22]

Western labourers were also to be paid, according to a published scale, and normally received a proportion of the regular wage offered to their German equivalents. One Czech labourer, for instance, recalled earning a third of the amount paid to his German colleagues.[23] In addition, western labourers were required to contribute to the German social insurance system, which rendered them eligible for unemployment, sickness and accident benefits.[24] Most important, however, they were permitted ration allowances that were broadly equivalent to those of a German labourer, with a 'normal' consumer receiving 2,400 calories per day, while a 'heavy labourer' would be allocated 3,600.[25]

Many of these rights and benefits were at best theoretical. Official commitments to medical treatment and social security benefits for foreign labourers were rarely honoured, while rationing allowances and pay often did not reach the stipulated levels. And it is doubtful whether many foreign labourers had the energy, or the inclination, to see the capital's cultural offerings, engage in educational programmes or play sport. Nonetheless, it is important to recognise that the experience for many of them was far removed from the horrors they might have expected. Theirs was not necessarily a happy lot; it certainly had its privations and its petty humiliations, but it was a long way from the experience of the inmates of the concentration camp at Sachsenhausen, just a few miles away to the north. As one labourer concluded:

> There were no disputes or conflicts . . . I can't remember any serious incidents. No one was bothered what we did in our free time, we could come and go when we wanted; no one told us what we could and couldn't do. The most important thing was, to turn up for work in the morning, and to do what was demanded of you . . . The behaviour of the Germans towards us was, in general, good.[26]

The same would not have been said by one of his eastern counterparts. Although all labourers were vital to the German economy, the mere presence of those from eastern Europe in Hitler's Germany was considered an affront to the more racially and ideologically minded Nazis. Therefore, some restrictions were deemed necessary. Workers from the Soviet Union – the so-called *Ostarbeiter*, or 'eastern workers' – as well as those from Poland, were subject to a raft of legislation, limiting their movement, rations, pay and conditions. One Ukrainian labourer summed up the differences: 'All the other foreigners that were [in Berlin] were also in camps, but they had completely different rights to us . . . For us, everything was forbidden.'[27]

This summary is not far from the truth. *Ostarbeiter* and Poles endured a status similar to that of POWs. They lived in fenced-off, guarded barracks from which they would be marched to and from work in columns, accompanied by a guard detail. They were also obliged to sew a cloth badge, bearing the letter 'P' for Poles, or 'OST' for *Ostarbeiter*, onto their clothing. Unlike their 'western' fellows, they were forbidden to visit the city in their spare time. Even if they had sufficient funds, restaurants, bars, theatres, cinemas, even public baths, were out of bounds to them.[28] Personal contact with German civilians was also strictly forbidden: 'we avoided each other like the plague', one Polish forced labourer recalled.[29]

Pay for *Ostarbeiter* was also restricted. 'It was like a slave trade', one remembered: 'I worked from 6 in the morning to 4 in the afternoon and I received between 20 and 40 Marks every two weeks . . . two years without leave.' 'Our wages were ridiculous', another recalled, 'deductions were made for everything; for the blankets, mattresses, for the badge with the latter "P", for the soup, for insurance and for other things.' There was, as a Ukrainian labourer complained, little left over: 'We were paid a little bit, we got a few Marks. But it was impossible for us to buy food or clothes.'[30]

Poor sanitary conditions, combined with hard labour, malnourishment and persistent infestations of lice, often made for horrific living conditions, yet few of the *Ostarbeiter* camps offered even the most rudimentary medical treatment. While a few of the larger factories had on-site infirmaries, as many as three hundred camps had no duty doctor at all; in one instance, a single doctor from the central district of Friedrichshain was supposedly responsible for nearly five thousand labourers spread right across the city.[31]

For this reason, medical care for 'eastern workers' in some instances rarely stretched beyond crude gynaecological inspections for women and piecemeal measures undertaken against tuberculosis. Even the latter was not forthcoming at times. A German observer noted that it was forbidden for camp doctors to prescribe medicines to the *Ostarbeiter*, and that those infected with tuberculosis 'were not even isolated from the others'; indeed, they 'were beaten and forced to continue their work, as the camp authorities doubted the competence of the doctors'.[32] Trained medical staff were also rare. As one 'patient' recalled: 'In our camp, there was a sick bay and a nurse called Tamara. She arrived with me in the camp and understood as much about medicine as I did about ballet.'[33] For an *Ostarbeiter* to register as sick, therefore, was often akin to writing a suicide note.

There were exceptions, however. The lucky ones might have found themselves referred to one of the dedicated clinics for foreign labourers, such as that at Malchow, which was largely staffed by Russian and eastern European doctors and had a capacity of about eight hundred beds. Although conditions there were predictably poor, patients at least stood a chance of receiving competent medical treatment.

One nineteen-year-old Russian male, for example, was admitted to the facility on 9 February 1944 with an inflamed appendix. He was operated on and released three weeks later. Another young Russian male, admitted with a suspected fractured skull in May 1943, spent a month in the clinic under observation.[34]

A few *Ostarbeiter* had the rare good fortune to gain admission to a regular civilian hospital. But they, too, would have had profound cause for concern and would have been made acutely aware that all men were not treated equally in the Third Reich. In one such instance, a foreign labourer was rather surprised to see that he was the only person on the ward who was not evacuated to the cellar during an air raid. It seems that though he could make no complaints about the standard of medical care he received, he evidently did not 'qualify' for even the most elementary protection during an air raid. 'Luckily', he recalled, 'the bombs missed.'[35]

For many sick *Ostarbeiter* – especially those diagnosed with terminal diseases or chronic debilitating conditions – the final stage of the journey was a transfer to the transit camp at Pankow, from where they would supposedly be returned to their home countries. Given the logistical complexities of such a move, however, most were never transferred out of the capital at all; the 'transit camp' became, in effect, a 'death camp'.[36] In some instances, the long-term sick would even be sent to one of the Third Reich's sinister euthanasia 'hospitals'.

Food was the greatest source of discontent and many 'eastern workers' complained bitterly about the starvation rations that they were forced to endure. Most of them were fed in a factory canteen, and so were guaranteed at least some nourishment each day, but it was hardly appealing. As Kazimiera Czarnecka remembered:

We received the weekly ration cards for the kitchen, where we collected the food. It was 250 grams per day of greasy, black bread, a smear of margarine and a ladle of soup, usually from carrots. Sometimes one found a piece of horsemeat in the soup, with skin or other pieces of carcass. We learnt to make the most of our allowances, so that we would eat the soup straight after work and would save the bread for breakfast the next day.

In the canteen, one could buy a cup of bitter malt coffee for 5 pfennigs. Occasionally, on Sundays, there was a quarter of a baguette instead of bread, and goulash for lunch with a few small potatoes. The problem was, however, that they were often rotten, so we went hungry.[37]

The observations of a German Foreign Office official, on an inspection tour of labour camps in the capital, confirmed that this was not an isolated example:

In spite of the official ration allocated to *Ostarbeiter*, it can be concluded that the situation regarding food supply in the camps is as follows: mornings – a half-litre of turnip soup. Midday, at work, a litre of turnip soup. Evening, a litre of turnip soup. The *Ostarbeiter* also receives 300g of bread each day. In addition, there is a weekly allocation of 50–75g margarine [and] 25g meat or meat products, which is distributed according to the whim of the camp commandant.[38]

This lack of sufficient and regular food had a profound effect on the behaviour of the *Ostarbeiter* themselves. In a minority it inspired an entrepreneurial spirit, whereby the workers would make wooden toys or ornaments, which they would then exchange for bread with their German colleagues. One Czech labourer in Berlin recalled producing wooden trolleys and crates, which 'were of great value to [the Berliners] when they had to rescue their belongings during the air raids'.[39]

This was not the reaction of the majority, however. Increasingly, solidarity in the camps broke down and was replaced by a dog-eat-dog mentality, in which intimidation, begging, theft, prostitution and petty criminality became commonplace. Pushed to the very margins of society, forced labourers had to survive as best they could.

Not all foreign and forced labourers, 'easterners' or 'westerners', were confined to camps and forced to work in industrial concerns. A proportion of them were allocated to small businesses and even to private houses, where a sympathetic employer might extend exemplary hospitality and welcome 'their' labourer as a part of the family. Teenager Erich Neumann recalled the arrival of two labourers at his mother's café in the western district of Charlottenburg. When business flourished, he remembered, his mother had applied for two foreign labourers from the local *Arbeitsamt*, or 'employment office'. She duly received:

One pretty, German-speaking waitress, late twenties, and a young girl
in her early twenties as a kitchen help. Both of them came from Belgium
and spoke amongst themselves predominantly in French. My mother
didn't like this at all, so she took private lessons in French and paid for
German lessons for the [younger] girl, [who] very quickly, could speak
German. Mother, however, in spite of all her efforts, never spoke French
. . . The two very quickly became part of the family and enjoyed coming
to work.[40]

In rare examples, that hospitality could take a more intimate form.
Frenchman Marcel Elola arrived in Berlin in 1943. A trained butcher,
he was allocated to a small business in Schöneberg, whose owner had
been called up for military service, and which was now being run by
the man's wife. 'The serving girls smiled at me', Elola reported. 'My
first impression was that here was a good atmosphere.'[41] On the evening
of that first day, however, events took an unexpected turn. Over dinner,
in the half-light of the blackout, he felt a hand reaching for his own:
'In that moment, there was nothing for me to do but collaborate.
I was twenty-one years old and in good shape. I didn't understand
what she was saying to me, but that gesture spoke volumes . . .
That night, she offered me the hospitality of her bed.' It was a
bed that he would share for the following five months, until the
return of the woman's husband put paid both to Elola's employment and to his nocturnal adventures. 'I thought I was going to
Hell', he wrote, 'but found myself in paradise.'[42]

Had he been discovered, Elola would not have enjoyed 'paradise'
for long. Since such fraternisation was strictly forbidden, those who
transgressed would swiftly have found themselves exposed to the
full fury of the Gestapo and the SS. Few foreign labourers, however,
would have had the opportunity to follow in Elola's amorous footsteps. The most common offence among them was a 'breach of
contract', which could cover a multitude of sins, from sloppy
working practices to persistent absences and perceived 'laziness'.
Beyond that, there were a number of more serious offences, such
as sabotage, black-marketeering, prostitution and theft. If offenders
were not caught red-handed, a thriving culture of denunciation
within the camps was bound to bring their activities to the ears of
the authorities.

Discipline for foreign and forced labourers was enforced, in the first instance, within the camp or workplace itself. Minor misdemeanours would be punished via a system of forfeits; a verbal warning would be followed by withdrawal of privileges, of pay or even rations. Continued ill discipline would then result in the withdrawal of a prisoner's bedding and the allocation of 'special' work assignments. Finally, criminal activity, or persistent minor transgressions, would be met with a complaint to the Gestapo, which would usually result in arrest and interrogation.[43]

Those forced labourers who fell foul of the regime in this way would generally be sent to an *Arbeitserziehungslager* (AEL) – or 'Work Education Camp'. Conditions here were often extremely harsh, as the Nazi security chief Ernst Kaltenbrunner explained with remarkable candour in 1944: 'the working and living conditions for the inmates [in an AEL] are in general harder than in a concentration camp. This is necessary to achieve the desired results.'[44] As well as being harder, it should also be remembered that there were more AELs in the Third Reich than there were concentration camps.

The Berlin district had a number of AELs: one at Grossbeeren, to the south of the city, and one for women at Fehrbellin, to the northwest. The best known, however, was that at Wuhlheide. Set up in April 1940 in the south-eastern suburbs of the capital – not far from the transit camp at Wilhelmshagen – Wuhlheide had been one of the very first AELs established in Nazi Germany. The five hundred or so prisoners held there – who were primarily employed repairing Berlin's railways – were generally sent for a twenty-one-day sentence, but could face a maximum of eight weeks.

Dutchman Willem de Wit was barely eighteen when he came to Wuhlheide, following a fourteen-day interrogation by the Gestapo. After a savage beating on his arrival, all his belongings were taken from him. He was then allocated a number and a 'uniform' that consisted of old, patched clothes. He would soon learn that there was a strict hierarchy among the prisoners:

In the barrack . . . there were three steel beds on top of one another. New arrivals slept on the floor for a week, then one was promoted and could sleep on a wooden bench. Next, one could sleep on the bunk. In the barrack, I was beaten again by the guard, as he thought I had

brought lice in . . . Sometimes we were beaten up at night, when the
guards were drunk.[45]

Such violence was all-pervasive. A German inmate recalled seeing a
Polish prisoner who had made a number of escape attempts singled
out for especially hard treatment: 'he received numerous brutal blows.
And later . . . he was beaten further with a rubber truncheon. The
next day, he was dead.'[46]

The other AELs in the Berlin district were no less brutal. Another
Dutchman remembered when one of his fellow labourers returned
from a stint in AEL Grossbeeren, after an escape attempt: 'the little
lad became so thin that he looked like a skeleton. For six weeks, they
had mistreated and beaten him. He had become completely
apathetic.'[47]

Fortunately, the stay was limited. At the end of their sentence,
inmates were released and returned to their regular place of work,
but not before being required to sign a form stating that they had
been well treated and being warned that the next time they mis-
behaved they would end up in a concentration camp.[48] For most, the
experience was enough. Word of the AELs at Wuhlheide, Grossbeeren
and Fehrbellin quickly spread among the foreign labourers.[49] One
Dutch labourer recalled that, at her factory, workers who stepped out
of line were threatened with the single word 'Wuhlheide'.[50] Wuhlheide
is estimated to have seen some 30,000 prisoners pass through its
gates over the course of the war. Of these, it is thought that one
in ten perished.[51]

Although they were rarely mentioned by diarists and contemporaries,
forced labourers were ubiquitous in wartime Berlin. Every district of
the capital – from Adlershof to Zehlendorf – would have seen barrack
blocks, barbed wire and columns of sullen, ill-nourished labourers. At
their peak in 1944, Berlin's 400,000 forced labourers made up over one
in ten of the population of the German capital. Though they were
largely concealed from public view, they would nonetheless have been
hard to miss.

Moreover, as the war turned against Germany from the end of 1943,
and the Allied bombing of the capital intensified, forced labourers increasingly found their barracks and places of work damaged or destroyed.

As a result, some were forced to live rough on the capital's streets, surviving from barter, begging and the black market. For ordinary Berliners, therefore, their presence was increasingly difficult to ignore. The writer Felix Hartlaub wrote to his father in the autumn of 1944, describing the effect of 'the foreign element' in the capital:

> In some streets and districts one really hears not a single word of German and so has the feeling of strolling through a peculiar Babylon; a Babel of rubble, and labour and tremendous expectation . . . In some areas, in which hardly any of the street signs are still standing, one gets a whiff of the atmosphere of the Parisian *banlieue*, the Italian piazza, or the Ukrainian village square.[52]

When Ursula von Kardorff was forced into the bowels of the Friedrichstrasse Station during an air raid that winter, she was astonished by the multinational underworld that seemed to inhabit the tunnels:

> Down there, it's like I imagine Shanghai to be. Tattered figures in padded jackets with the high cheekbones of the Slavs, between them, white blonde Danes and Norwegians, coquettishly dressed Frenchwomen, Poles with hate in their eyes, pale, freezing Italians – a mixture of peoples such as has probably never been seen in a German city.[53]

And yet, for all that apparent omnipresence, Berlin's foreign labourers existed in a curious legal, political and social demi-monde between toleration and persecution, between the strictures of Nazi racial policy and the necessities of the German economy.

It should not be forgotten that German civilians had been exposed to years of highly effective propaganda, which constantly told them that most foreigners were racially inferior to them. In some cases, and especially where the *Ostarbeiter* were concerned, such inequality could take extreme forms. As one Berliner recalled, 'To us, the Russians were not people.'[54] While such attitudes may indeed have been a response to Nazi propaganda, they also stemmed from witnessing the brutal treatment meted out to those deemed 'subhuman': the worse such individuals were treated, the less they resembled human beings. Thus the propaganda became a self-fulfilling prophecy.

With forced labourers living and working in their midst, the Berlin public seems to have developed a curiously myopic indifference; a desire to avert their gaze, ask no questions, keep their heads down. This attitude was summed up by another Berliner, living close to the transit camp at Wilhelmshagen, who recalled that the local inhabitants advised 'that one should make a detour around it'.[55] On one level, Berlin civilians facing rationing, the blackout and air raids had little energy left to worry about the fate of foreign labourers. Moreover, they were living under a dictatorship, and most were well aware of the perils of stepping out of line and of asking difficult questions. Hence the myopia was often tactical.

For many, this indifference was tinged with mistrust and resentment. It was relatively easy to conflate foreign labourers – even those who had volunteered – with prisoners of war and concentration camp inmates. After all, in many cases they looked the same, and could sometimes be seen working alongside one another. The assumption was reinforced by the Nazi habit of referring to all such individuals as 'criminals', regardless of their precise origin.[56] This attitude is well illustrated by the recollections of one Berliner, who remembered the female prisoners of the AEL at Fehrbellin, close to his home, north-west of Berlin: 'it was very well known that there was a camp there', he said, 'but the population had been told that it was a work camp and that the women were work-shy and prostitutes. So no one was bothered by it.'[57]

At the most basic level, this prejudice was made manifest by blaming any theft, burglary or misdemeanour in the local area on 'those in the camp'. In the later period of the war, Wehrmacht mood reports were full of complaints from the Berlin public about the behaviour of 'foreigners': concerns were aired about foreigners hanging around in the suburbs, black-marketeering – 'while German men and women have to work hard' – or that foreigners 'received larger ration allocations than Germans'.[58] In one report it was claimed that the renowned Café Kranzler on the Kurfürstendamm had become such a hub for the forced labourers that it was known locally as the 'Gangsters' Rendezvous'.[59]

Upstanding Germans, it seems, were also much distressed by the apparent attraction that foreign workers held for Berlin's womenfolk. One report from January 1945 noted how 'regrettable' it was that

'German women sold their honour for a cigarette' and how they 'paid no attention to their fellow Germans' and instead 'sit only with the mostly well-dressed foreigners and later take them home'.[60] More comically, perhaps, one informant noted that foreigners showed disrespect during the newsreel show at a cinema close to Alexanderplatz: '[they] didn't watch the newsreel at all', he fumed. '[They] behaved as if they were in a bar, some went, others arrived. References to serious events in the newsreel were met with laughter.'[61]

More seriously, wild rumours began to circulate that foreign labourers gave 'light signals' to the bombers during air raids, telling the crews where to drop their bombs.[62] In truth, there were numerous genuine cases of theft, prostitution and petty crime that were attributed to the forced labourers in the capital. In early 1944, a Czech labourer was convicted of stealing twenty-one pairs of shoes during a night-time break-in on a shoe shop in the Potsdamer Strasse; he was sentenced to three years' hard labour.[63] Three Frenchmen, meanwhile, were arrested in December 1942 after they had stolen 20 kilos of butter and twenty bottles of brandy. Though they claimed to have carried out the robbery only to satisfy their own hunger, their pleas fell on deaf ears: all three were sentenced to death.[64]

There were also more serious crimes. In 1943 two young foreign labourers were executed in Plötzensee after being found guilty of the murder of a young German woman. Under interrogation, it emerged that the pair – a Belgian and a Frenchman – had intended to threaten the woman and rob her, but had inadvertently killed her with their first blow. They then threw her body from a train to make the death look like a suicide or an accident.[65] Cases such as this were widely reported in the press, with the inevitable result that German Berliners became ever more suspicious of the foreign labourers as unpredictable and potentially violent 'others'. Such sentiments could swiftly boil over into violence and confrontation. One Dutchman recalled that Berlin civilians, waiting on the city's rail platforms, frequently 'swore and spat' at foreign labourers working on the nearby tracks.[66]

Not everyone succumbed to the indifference, however, or to the xenophobia. Some German civilians sought, where possible, to make life a little easier for the forced labourers among them. One woman, for instance, chose the rather perilous method of distributing bread and water through the wire of a nearby camp to newly arrived prisoners.[67]

Another example is that of Otto Langrock, a master-craftsman working in the Volta factory in the north of the capital, who came to blows with the factory's director after a guard dog was let loose on a group of Russian forced labourers. Though such an action would normally have had serious consequences, Langrock was saved by his colleagues, all of whom testified to his good character.[68]

Other Berliners understandably chose the less obvious and less risky approach of attempting to improve the conditions of those who were in their own employ, or whose lives they could directly influence. Memoirs and diaries contain many examples. One woman living close to Wilhelmshagen was allocated a French labourer from the camp to come and chop wood for her. She paid him in food, which she divided up from her own ration allocation.[69]

Even strangers sometimes extended kindness to the workers. The Ukrainian *Zwangsarbeiter* Larissa Safjanik recalled how, while clearing rubble after a bombing raid, she had begged a passer-by for some bread: 'She waved us aside and carried on. But after a few steps, she stopped and bent down as if she was tying her shoelace. In fact, however, she was placing a ration coupon under a stone. So, that day, I got a piece of bread.'[70] In another instance, Lidia Affanasjewna tried to sneak away from the column of workers returning to their camp, so that she and a friend could try to find some food. Finding a bakery, the two 'asked – with hearts beating in our chests – for a piece of bread. Behind us, an elderly man and a woman entered the shop and closed the door behind them. We were given food, and even a few rolls to take with us.'[71] It could be upon such small interventions that the lives of Berlin's forced labourers depended.

As the war ground on to its conclusion, a new emotion began to overtake all others – fear. The presence of many thousands of foreigners in the German capital – the vast majority of whom came from those lands with whom Germany was at war – became cause for considerable concern. German civilians seem to have conflated the millions of foreign labourers with the many millions more prisoners of war to form an enormous would-be enemy army, which was described by one commentator as 'a bomb hanging in the air, which threatens to crash down in a devastating detonation'.[72]

Many Germans sincerely believed this idea. The otherwise quite sensible Ursula von Kardorff, for example, believed that the foreign labourers' 'army' was already in existence: '[They] are apparently very well organised', she wrote in her diary. 'It is said that there are agents among them; officers, emissaries from the various underground groups that are well supplied with weapons and with radios . . . Some people call them the Trojan Horse of this war.'[73] Another commentator warned ominously that 'if we do not change this situation, then the foreigners will stab us in the back'.[74]

The truth was more mundane. The vast majority of forced labourers in Germany were not minded to avenge themselves on their German captors. A few were even keen to stay. Close to the end of the war, for instance, a Serbian labourer was recalled stating in his best broken German that 'If officer come today, and say, you can home. I not go, I stay here.'[75] He was one of the countless thousands who were fearful of being received as traitors if they dared to return to Tito's Yugoslavia or Stalin's Soviet Union, and were hopeful that they might be able to forge a better life for themselves in the German capital.

For all such concerns, the majority wanted nothing more than to go home. As the verse of a female Czech labourer betrayed, homesickness proved in most cases to be a far stronger emotion than revenge:

> We have got used a little
> to life in Berlin,
> that our stomachs will never be full here
> and we will not sleep through the night.
> Perhaps the day will come,
> when we will see our homeland again,
> perhaps the day will come
> when we will hear our mother's voice.[76]

7

A Taste of Things to Come

The night of Wednesday 28 August 1940 was cool for the time of year. Those making their way out of the city centre, or wearily heading home after a day's work, would have turned their collars up against the breeze, or else cursed their optimism of that morning, when they had decided not to take a coat.

Yet despite the unseasonal chill, the public mood in Berlin was buoyant. The victories of the first half of 1940 had made for a heady atmosphere in the capital. As the Wehrmacht marched from success to success, many Berliners had considered that the war was as good as won: Versailles had finally been smashed, France had been routed and Germany now stood as the dominant power in Europe. The British had been defeated in France and many reasoned that they too would soon be forced to come to terms. But for all their justified optimism, a good many Berliners hurrying home that evening would have cast a nervy eye skywards.

The previous Monday, Berlin had been raided by the RAF. It had been a fairly minor affair. A force of around thirty twin-engine Hampdens and Whitleys had found the German capital shrouded in thick cloud and consequently had dropped their bombs over a wide area – some in the northern suburbs and some beyond the city limits to the south. The official German reaction to this first raid on Berlin was surprisingly muted. Despite the outrage that would soon become common currency, the event appears to have warranted only six lines in the newspapers the following morning and military communiqués noted only that a few incendiaries had fallen on the northern suburb of Rosenthal, where a garden shed was set on fire. There were no casualties reported and it was asserted that no bombs had been dropped on the city itself.[1]

The American reporter Fred Oechsner recalled that the authorities 'laughed off [the raid] as a fluke' and assured the press that such a 'nuisance would not occur again'.[2] Given that a number of farms and allotments had suffered in the attack, some Berliners even joked that the RAF was now trying to starve the city into submission.[3]

Confidential SD reports were a little more forthcoming, recording that the raid had come in a number of waves, causing the alarm to be sounded for over three hours, with the all-clear being given only at 3.30 a.m. The total damage caused by the 150 or so 'small incendiaries' dropped was estimated at a mere 3,000 Reichsmarks. Though the capital had certainly sustained 'its first heavy air attack', the report concluded that the results of the raid were 'extremely small'.[4]

While the material damage inflicted was minimal, the shock to Berlin morale was rather more substantial – not least by virtue of the simple fact that a night's sleep had been lost. As Helmuth James von Moltke noted to his wife, 'it is no joke to lie awake from 12 to 4'.[5] In addition, many simply had to adjust to the new procedures demanded by the air war. It was not an easy task. A Swedish newspaper correspondent reported that Berliners had initially taken little notice of the siren, and had only taken the raid seriously – and sought shelter – when they had heard the sound of the anti-aircraft fire.[6] However, those early raids also posed a deeper and more intangible challenge. Many had believed the official propaganda and could not imagine that the war would be played out as much in the skies above their city as in the skies over London. They found it hard to believe that the British would have the temerity to attack the German capital, especially as Britain was itself under threat of invasion. And, after all, hadn't Göring joked that if a single enemy bomber reached the German capital, then his name was not Göring, it was Meyer?* As William Shirer noted:

> The Berliners are stunned. They did not think it could happen. When this war began, Göring assured them it couldn't. He boasted that no enemy planes could ever break through the outer and inner rings of the capital's anti-aircraft defence. The Berliners are a naïve and simple people. They believed him. Their disillusionment today therefore is all the greater. You have to see their faces to measure it.[7]

* A phrase broadly equivalent to the English saying ' . . . then I'm a Dutchman'.

Berliners would have read the news reports of the German raids on Warsaw, Rotterdam and London; they had probably also seen the graphic images in the newsreels. Now, they were no longer the perpetrators, they had become the victims. This was their 'baptism of fire' as one journalist put it, 'the first-hand taste of aerial warfare'.[8]

Until then Berliners had had little experience of the new threat that they faced. The first 'raids' over the capital the previous autumn had barely been worthy of the name. The alarm that sounded on the evening of 1 September 1939 had evidently been caused by a single plane straying too close to the city; some considered it all to be a propaganda exercise. The alarm on the night of 9 September, meanwhile, would have troubled quite a few Berliners, not least as it was sounded at four o'clock in the morning. But even then, no planes were seen and no bombs were dropped. William Shirer recalled a peculiar episode in mid-October 1939: 'Last night the inhabitants had a scare', he wrote; 'the anti-aircraft batteries around Berlin started going off and searchlights scanned the skies. That was the first time the people of Berlin had heard any gun actually firing in this war, and many of them went out into the streets to listen. Some expected an air-raid alarm, but none was given.'[9] It later emerged that a German plane had got lost and flown over the capital.

Yet, false alarms soon gave way to real alerts. While the German armies were racing across northern France in the spring of 1940, the RAF was carrying out offensives of its own. The first German city to be raided was Mönchengladbach in the Rhineland, which was targeted on the night of 11 May, the day after the French campaign began. Thereafter, the German public slowly grew accustomed to sporadic enemy air raids: numerous cities, from Hamburg in the north to Koblenz in the south, experienced the new horror of aerial bombing. Though the material damage tended to be minimal, lives were lost. On 1 July, four civilians were killed in Düsseldorf and eight in Kiel. Three days later, Hamburg was raided at the cost of sixteen lives, twelve of those children. The official German reaction was one of outrage and the Nazi press embarked on a campaign of vilification of the RAF, routinely denouncing British air crews as 'pirates of the air' or 'terror flyers'.

Leafleting raids were also common. Throughout that summer, the RAF dropped batches of propaganda leaflets across northern and western Germany. They frequently mocked the Nazi press or official announcements, by using the same bureaucratic 'tone' as the genuine article, as in the following example from early August 1940: 'In order to avert the dangers to the Party (and the people) that would result from a continuation of the war, the Führer and Reich Chancellor has invited the English people to sue for peace.'[10] Others were altogether darker, presenting stark statistics or outlining the grim fate that awaited Germany if Hitler were not removed. The following extract is from a leaflet that was dropped over the southern suburb of Lankwitz in the late summer of 1940:

> Berliners! Have you lost your minds? When they tell you that only England now stands against the Axis powers; 47 million against 200 million, do you believe them? Have you forgotten that there is a British Empire, in which 492 million are united against Hitler? Have you forgotten that of the 200 million of Hitler's slaves, 80 million are conquered peoples, who despise their oppressors and are waiting for their moment; and that 44 million are only Italians?! Have you forgotten that the entire industrial and agricultural production of North and South America is being mobilised against you?
>
> . . .
>
> The war that Hitler started goes on!'[11]

All such leaflets were required to be handed in to the authorities for safe disposal. Officially at least, the regime was fairly relaxed about their possible effect on the morale of the German public. An SD report from late July 1940 claimed that the leaflets were generally 'dismissed as ridiculous' and expressed the opinion that 'such antics could not unsettle the German people'.[12] Nonetheless, the regime took few chances. Those who chose to keep the leaflets did so at their peril; if they were discovered they might be charged with the dissemination of enemy propaganda or undermining the German war effort. Either of these offences carried a mandatory death sentence.

Thus the German public had grown accustomed to increased enemy activity in the skies over Germany in the summer of 1940. And now even Berlin, though far from the western and northern borderlands that were most often targeted, had witnessed its first raid. For many Berliners, the previous Monday's raid would have been an ominous

sign and those returning home on the night of 28 August would have
had good reason to anxiously scan the skies above them. They were
right to do so. The RAF was already on its way.

Shortly after midnight, British planes once again appeared over Berlin.
After breaching the outer ring of flak defences to the north and north-
west of the city, a small squadron of aircraft – mainly Wellingtons
and Whitleys – proceeded to the southern suburb of Kreuzberg, one
of the most densely populated districts of the capital, and released
their payloads. Unencumbered by heavy flak fire, their pilots were
able to hit their targets with a degree of accuracy. One of them even
claimed that 'it was just like a bit of practice bombing'.[13]
    The results on the ground were devastating. The area around
Kottbusser Strasse, Skalitzer Strasse and the Görlitzer Station was the
worst hit. A stick of bombs fell down the middle of the main street,
leaving four-foot craters in the thoroughfare, and twisting and buckling the tram lines. A high-explosive bomb also destroyed two floors
of a large house on Kottbusser Strasse, sending shattered glass, window
frames and rubble tumbling into the courtyard below. One eyewitness
noted 'the worst fires were caused . . . where the Görlitzer railway
goods yard near the Wiener Strasse was set on fire'.[14]
    According to government records, over nine hundred Berliners
were rendered homeless by the raid.[15] Many of them congregated
beneath the raised railway line that cut thorough the district, along
Skalitzer Strasse, or else made their way to a local school, where a
makeshift soup kitchen and first-aid station had been established.
There they received food, ration cards and sympathy. The official
Wehrmacht report, released the following day, summed up the events:
'In the night, British aircraft systematically attacked residential areas
of the Reich capital. High-explosive bombs and incendiaries brought
death and injury to numerous civilians and properties sustained roof
fires and damage.'[16]
    Hidden within that report was a key admission: Berlin had witnessed
its first civilian deaths from aerial bombardment. In fact, as well as
the thirty or so who were injured, ten Berliners lost their lives that
night, with two more dying of their injuries in the following days.[17]
Four men and two women were killed on the street by flying debris.
Tragically, a young mother lost both her children after her home took

a direct hit. She had gone down to the cellar alone, and had left the children in their beds as she had not wanted to wake them.[18]

The German press was outraged, denouncing the RAF as 'bandits',[19] and attacking Churchill for such a 'dastardly act of cowardice'.[20] Most of their ire was directed at the fact that the British, while claiming to have attacked military targets, had succeeded only in bombing a residential district. 'The battle in France was too dangerous for [the RAF]', one newspaper editorial mocked, 'so they flew to Germany and chose non-military targets. Their bombs fell on hospitals and clinics, on residential suburbs, on farms, on cemeteries and churches, on Goethe's summer house in Weimar and on Bismarck's mausoleum.' It went on to pillory the RAF for its 'one-sided war' on the German civilian population, and its 'cowardly and outrageous methods' of dropping its bombs 'blindly' on 'women and children'.[21] As the raids continued, this theme would be one that the press would return to almost on a daily basis. Ironically, perhaps, every news report that denounced such actions by the RAF was surrounded by other articles listing which 'military installations' across Britain that the Luftwaffe had apparently succeeded in hitting.

The political fallout was substantial, especially when the RAF returned over three consecutive nights the following week. Hitler was outraged, perceiving the raids as a calculated insult.[22] In early September, he took the opportunity of a speech at the Berlin Sportpalast, where he had been scheduled to talk about the annual winter charity collection, to rage about British actions and threaten the most blood-curdling revenge:

> And should the Royal Air Force drop two thousand, or three thousand, or four thousand kilograms of bombs, then we will now drop 150,000; 180,000; 230,000; 300,000; 400,000; yes one million kilograms in a single night. And should they declare they will greatly increase their attacks on our cities, then we will erase their cities!
>
> We will put these night-time pirates out of business, so help us God! The hour will come that one of us will break, and it will not be National Socialist Germany.[23]

The day before this speech, in a quiet corner of the southern suburb of Neukölln, four of the casualties from the Kottbusser Strasse raid had been laid to rest. In the St Jakobi Cemetery a ceremony was held with both the Lord Mayor of Berlin, Julius Lippert, and the deputy Gauleiter of Berlin, Artur Görlitzer, in attendance. An SA military band was also present, along with honour guards from the police and the Hitler Youth and the cemetery was bedecked with Nazi flags, wreaths and flaming pylons.[24] Defiant speeches were made and sombre faces were fixed.

For all the politicking and outrage, it would have been clear to many Berliners that week that the war had entered a new phase. Not only had British aircraft demonstrated their ability to reach the city, but they had shown themselves able to bomb almost at will and take the lives of Berlin's civilians. The myth of the capital's inviolability – which had been shared by all sections of the city's society – had been irrevocably shattered.

William Shirer reported that the raids had made a considerable impact:

> The main effect of a week of constant British night bombings has been to spread great disillusionment among the people here and sow doubt in their minds. One said to me today: 'I'll never believe another thing they say. If they've lied about the raids on the rest of Germany as they have about the ones on Berlin, then it must have been pretty bad there.'[25]

The official mood report of the SD arrived at essentially the same conclusion:

> The attacks on Berlin have aroused considerable interest across the Reich, as people were wholly convinced that not a single aeroplane could reach the city centre. The population is thereby reminded of announcements, which claimed that enemy aircraft would be unable to attack Berlin. However, as it has recently been shown that it is possible for the English even to linger over the capital and drop their bombs, without suffering appreciable losses, the expectations for the capital's defence have clearly not been fulfilled.[26]

Almost exactly a year into the conflict that Hitler had unleashed, the war had come home to the German capital.

★   ★   ★

After that debut, the raids continued into the autumn of 1940 and quickly became a regular occurrence. The city was raided on average four nights per week, but air raid alarms sounded almost nightly. Few of its districts escaped attention. Many prominent sites were damaged, including the Reichstag, Goebbels' Propaganda Ministry, the criminal courts at Moabit and the Palace at Charlottenburg. Industrial targets hit included the Henschel works at Schönefeld, the Arado aircraft factory at Babelsberg, Rheinmetall-Borsig at Tegel and Daimler-Benz at Genshagen. Berlin Zoo also took a number of hits and, despite the large letters 'USA' that had been painted across its roof, even the American Embassy found itself under fire when a number of incendiaries fell in its gardens.

That September, the German capital was bombed nineteen times. On the night of the 23rd, for example, over eighty RAF bombers subjected Berlin to a four-hour alarm, which was only lifted shortly after 3.00 a.m. Two days later, the bombers returned, this time confining Berliners to their shelters for five hours. The attack, which was concentrated on the city centre as well as Schöneberg and Kreuzberg, damaged a hospital and numerous residential streets.

The bombing continued into October, with the city being hit fourteen times that month. On the night of the 7th, the RAF arrived so early over the German capital – soon after 10.00 p.m. – that the Berlin public was in many cases caught out in the open, leaving the cinema or returning late from work. According to one eyewitness, many Berliners simply stood in the street, necks craned towards the sky, where the searchlights had begun scanning the heavens and the distant rumble of aero-engines could already be heard. 'Look at that', they said in astonishment, 'they are already here.'[27]

The raid that followed was one of the heaviest experienced so far, with two hundred high explosives dropped as well as a huge number of incendiaries. Among the targets hit were the Lehrter and Stettiner stations, as well as the Robert Koch Hospital, the Lazarus Hospital, a maternity clinic, a children's hospital and a cemetery chapel.[28] The Propaganda Ministry had a field day.

Later that month, Goebbels himself toured those districts of southern Berlin, mainly Schöneberg, Wilmersdorf and Steglitz, that had been most grievously affected. Among his uniformed entourage, the Propaganda Minister stood out in his white overcoat and matching fedora, as he spoke earnestly with officials and consoled civilians. Yet for all his smiles, his encouragement and his sympathy for those bombed out, Goebbels was worried. As he confided to his diary a few days later, on 26 October: 'Report on morale from the [Sicherheitsdienst] . . . things are none too rosy. We absolutely must do more to keep morale high. The continual air raid alerts are making the people nervous. We must be careful.'[29]

In November, the frequency of the raids fell again, with the capital being hit on only eight occasions, although a number of those raids were substantial and the lengthening nights allowed the RAF to arrive ever earlier over the city. On one occasion, 14 November, the raid began before 9.00 p.m. and lasted for over four hours, damaging the Schlesischer railway station as well as marshalling yards at Tempelhof and Grunewald.[30] As Goebbels noted in his diary, the destruction wrought was 'more serious than hitherto'.[31] British losses were also high and a number of aircraft were reported as crashing in the city and its immediate hinterland.

The last raid of 1940 – on the night of 20–21 December – was also a peculiarity. Where the British usually arrived over the city at around midnight, on this occasion they surprised many by appearing shortly before 5.00 a.m. Then, after the all-clear had been given, a second wave of planes arrived – soon before 7.00 a.m. – thereby sending bleary-eyed Berliners scuttling down into their cellars once again. The raids concentrated on the area of Alexanderplatz, as well as Wedding and the Lustgarten. In the process, the Arsenal, the Protestant cathedral and a number of museums were damaged.[32]

After a short hiatus in the early months of 1941, the raids resumed in March with sporadic attacks over the central areas of the city, which continued into the summer, but without the intensity or frequency that had been experienced in the autumn and winter of 1940. Indeed, in the second half of that year, RAF activity over the German capital dwindled almost to nothing. Though Berlin was occasionally over-flown, and leaflets were still dropped, it was subjected to only a handful of serious raids.

The precise numbers of Berliners killed during the opening phase of the air war cannot be ascertained precisely, but some salient events can nonetheless be sketched out. On 4 September, for example, 10 civilians were killed in a raid on the Görlitzer Station.[33] Three weeks later, on 23–24 September, 22 Berliners were killed and 83 injured.[34]

Adolf Hitler's fiftieth birthday parade, 20 April 1939:
'It was a feast for the eyes and the applause never seemed to end.'

'We have now been returning fire since 5.45 a.m.': Hitler announces the invasion of Poland
to the Reichstag inside the Kroll Opera House, 1 September 1939.

Whitewashing the kerbstones
in preparation for the blackout.

Another novelty from the early days
of the war: a sign directs Berliners to
a public air-raid shelter.

Camouflage netting close to the Brandenburg
Gate. 'We absolutely must do more to keep
morale high', Goebbels wrote in his diary.
'The continual air-raid alerts are making the
people nervous. We must be careful.'

A Berlin street scene: Unter den Linden in the summer of 1940 – normality reigns.

Girls of the BdM spread flowers across the road to welcome Hitler back to the capital after the fall of France.

Crowds gather to watch a parade of victorious troops in July 1940: 'They yelled and yelled until they were hoarse.'

The dream:
Speer's plans for the
Great Hall, which
would have dwarfed
the Brandenburg
Gate (*left*) and the
Reichstag (*centre*).

The reality:
the lawns of the elegant
Gendarmenmarkt in
the heart of Berlin
being ploughed up
for cultivation, 1942.

'Radio must reach all or it will reach none': passers-by pause on a Berlin street to listen to the latest announcements broadcast via loudspeaker.

Flag-waving children leave Anhalter Station in the autumn of 1940 en route to the KLV camps. Not all of their fellows were so enthusiastic.

Berlin Jews wearing the *Judenstern*: at a stroke, their public humiliation was complete.

The Levetzowstrasse synagogue: used as a transit camp from October 1941, it was the last stop for many Berlin Jews en route to their deaths.

'Radio must reach all or it will reach none': passers-by pause on a Berlin street to listen to the latest announcements broadcast via loudspeaker.

Flag-waving children leave Anhalter Station in the autumn of 1940 en route to the KLV camps. Not all of their fellows were so enthusiastic.

Berlin Jews wearing the *Judenstern*: at a stroke, their public humiliation was complete.

The Levetzowstrasse synagogue: used as a transit camp from October 1941, it was the last stop for many Berlin Jews en route to their deaths.

Working for the enemy: French forced labourers at Siemens in 1943.

A fourteen-year-old Ukrainian forced labourer in a Berlin factory in 1945. He would have endured far harsher conditions than his Western European counterparts.

Schutzraum 2
50 Personen
Ruhe bewahren!
Rauchen verboten!

A public shelter in the capital in 1942: 'Nobody said a word, but we could feel the fear.'

The calm before the storm: a Berlin cellar in September 1940, complete with reinforcing beams, placards and wooden benches.

Twelve of them died in a single incident, when a bomb penetrated the entrance to an air raid shelter on Lüneburgerstrasse in Moabit before exploding.[35]

The heavy raid of 7–8 October, meanwhile, brought the highest death toll recorded in the capital up to that point, when 31 Berliners were killed and 91 were injured. Eight of the dead were discovered in the south-eastern suburb of Köpenick, where an air raid shelter collapsed.[36] William Shirer recorded the luck of one of the city's civilians that night:

> One young woman I know owes her life to the fact that she missed her suburban train by about twenty feet. She caught a second one about fifteen minutes later, but it did not run very far. The first had been hit square on by a British bomb and blown to pieces, fifteen passengers perishing![37]

Two weeks later a second air raid shelter collapsed, this time in Carmerstrasse in Charlottenburg; fifteen civilians were killed.

It was not only civilians who found themselves in the line of fire. The following month, 10 Polish labourers were killed when a bomb penetrated a section of train tunnel near the Stettiner Station, which was being used as a shelter.[38] Later, on the night of 14–15 November, 33 workers were killed when a British bomber was shot down over the southern district of Marienfelde, where it crashed into a *Reichsarbeitsfront* barrack.[39]

The official reaction of the Nazi state, in the early phase of the air war, alternated between righteous indignation and mockery of the perceived shortcomings of the RAF. The Propaganda Ministry worked hard to push its twofold agenda, stressing how ineffectual the bombing raids were on the one hand, and complaining on the other that civilian targets were being hit. It also organised tours of every fresh bomb-site, encouraging all foreign correspondents still in the capital to join officials in inspecting the damage, so as to better 'manage' the unfolding news stories.

The American journalist Fred Oechsner was one of those who was often invited along on what he called the 'dawn bombing-inspection junkets'. Initially, he recalled: 'the Propaganda Ministry did its best to pooh-pooh the significance of the raids', but gradually, as the autumn

nights closed in and the bombing grew more serious, Goebbels' officials found it increasingly difficult to dismiss them so easily. They also
began to complain about 'unfair reporting' and even suggested that
the journalists were providing information to Germany's enemies about
military targets in the capital. By mid-September 1940, barely two
weeks after they had started, the bombing tours were officially
cancelled. As Oechsner recalled:

> I went on the last of these bomb tours on September 11th. As usual,
> we traipsed from hospital to hospital, none of which had sustained any
> damage worth mentioning, and when we found bomb craters in the
> streets we were promptly informed of the existence of some unsus-
> pected hospital or children's home a hundred or so yards away, 'which
> without a doubt this bomb was meant to hit'.[40]

The real story that day was in what the Propaganda Ministry decided
not to show – the damage sustained in the Wilhelmstrasse, in the
administrative heart of the Nazi state. 'What the Nazis had originally
tried to laugh off as a joke', Oechsner wrote, 'had now become a
serious matter.'[41]

Already in that autumn of 1940, the government had revealed plans
for a massive public works programme to build air raid shelters and
to overhaul air defence provisions across northern Germany. Hitler's
Sofortprogramm, or 'Emergency Programme', envisaged a network of
public bunkers in Berlin, Hamburg and other major cities, which would
provide protection for the civilian population. In addition, existing
shelters and cellars were to be reinforced and brought up to a minimum
safety standard. Finally, three enormous flak towers were to be built
in the capital, which would not only each provide safe shelter for eight
thousand civilians, but also serve as the cornerstones of a reorganised
and strengthened air defence system. Berlin would emerge as the best-
defended and best-protected city of the war. Never, in the field of
human conflict, would so much concrete be poured in response to so
few incendiaries.

Until those plans were realised, however, Berliners got on with their
lives and made the best of the facilities that they had. Though the
raids were not yet especially heavy or concentrated, Berliners were
nonetheless well prepared. The original Air Protection Law had, after

all, been in force since 1935 and most households would have received at least rudimentary training in air raid procedure.

Responsibility for ensuring the public's adherence to such procedures fell to the *Luftschutzwart*, or 'air raid warden', who was in charge of each block or group of houses. His role was a vital one, encompassing the maintenance and provision of each cellar, as well as ensuring the cooperation and compliance of those civilians under his authority. He supplied leaflets advising each household on procedures and requirements and, in those first months of the war, was primarily concerned with bringing 'his' cellar up to the required safety standard. To this end, he allocated tasks to the various households under his supervision: sandbags had to be sewed, filled and stacked, placards had to be made, signs had to be painted and cellar windows had to be boarded and sealed.

Inside the cellar, benches and sometimes bunk beds were supplied as well as all the essentials required for self-defence: first-aid kits, buckets of water for fighting fires, sand for extinguishing incendiaries, shovels for clearing debris, and axes and picks in case a cellar should be blocked in by rubble. Structural alterations were sometimes required. Ceilings, for instance, had to be reinforced with wooden beams and stays. Partition walls to neighbouring cellars also had to be furnished with a 'breakthrough', an area of deliberately weakened brickwork, which could be smashed down to effect an escape to the neighbouring cellar in the event that the entrance should be blocked or otherwise rendered impassable.

Lastly, there was the protocol for the raid itself. Those who had paid attention to the instructions they had been given would have known that, when the alarm sounded, they were required to turn off the water, gas and electricity and open the windows and doors, while observing blackout discipline. Then they were to proceed, briskly but calmly, to the cellar, taking with them only a small, prepared suitcase containing essentials, such as a gas mask, a change of clothes and any important documentation. There they were to sit out the raid, maintaining order and calm, and wait for the all-clear to sound.

So much for the theory. For many, the reality could be rather different. Berlin's growing complement of foreign and forced labourers, for example, often faced a difficult task getting into air raid shelters at all, and those who succeeded could face insults and prejudice from the Germans already there. Fred Oechsner recalled the sometimes highly charged atmosphere. 'I ceased going down to the cellar of my apartment house altogether, partly because of the boredom of having to sit around in the cold for four or five hours at a stretch . . . and partly because the neighbours made rather pointed remarks about "your British friends up there".' This difficulty was echoed by another American journalist, Henry Flannery, who recalled the following exchange in an air raid shelter:

I was standing by a pillar when one of the young soldiers staggered up.
    'I heard you talking English', he said . . . 'I used to be in England', the soldier continued. 'I was there for a year – played a piano in an orchestra. I liked it, liked the people, had a grand time.' Then he stiffened, leaned towards me, shook his finger in my face. 'But now,' he cried, 'it's war, and I hate the English. I don't want to do anything with them, except kill them.'
    The conditions, in an air raid shelter surrounded by drunken Storm Troopers, were not the best in which to defend the English. I merely answered that I could understand his feelings, and tried to determine which wall to move to.[42]

Berlin's Jews also faced considerable difficulties. In most cases, they were not permitted to enter the communal air raid shelters at all, and were obliged to congregate in the hallways of their buildings, where they were at much greater risk. Occasionally, however, and especially where a building had numerous cellars, one room might be given over for their use. However, the extent to which ordinary Berliners enforced, or even knew about these measures, is questionable. In one instance, a woman explained to her air raid warden that her building had two cellars: one was always crowded and the other was comparatively empty, so she usually took the quieter one, which in any case had a 'more cheerful' atmosphere. 'But don't you know?' the air raid warden replied. 'Those are for Jews.'[43]

For many, the sound of the air raid siren, wailing across the city, was something to which they would never grow accustomed. In fact, the signal consisted of three separate sounds. The first – three long tones, of a constant pitch – served as a warning, while a single, long, constant tone served as the all-clear. The main siren, meanwhile, was a 'menacing howl', which would emanate from countless locations dotted around the city. It was a sound that one eyewitness described as 'a cacophony of loud and quiet sirens . . . an asynchronous concert. A nasty sound, up and down from too high to too low. It fairly chased one out of bed.'[44] Christa Becker recalled how 'The siren seemed much louder at night. When they had tested in the daytime, it felt less threatening and was muffled by the noise of the city. But at night its angry howl echoed terror from house to house.'[45]

Some took the siren as the signal to begin their well-rehearsed routine, preparing their property for the possibility of being bombed. One Berliner recalled how well-drilled his household was:

When the siren began its warlike howl, we flung ourselves out of bed, as though the devil himself were after us, and hurried, half-asleep to our allotted tasks: wake Puppi from the sleep of the innocent, open the curtains, up with the blackout roll, window open, shutters folded back, doors open, mains fuse out, mains water off . . .[46]

For others, just the experience of being woken and of stumbling down into the cellar in the early hours was distressing. Gisela Richter was one of those who found that the worst aspect of the air raids was the lack of sleep: 'I would never have thought that sleep could be so sweet, and how the whole body suffers when you don't get enough of it.' Consequently, Gisela sought to stay for as long as possible in her bed, sometimes until the flak was already firing, before finally conceding to go down into the cellar. There she would be received by her nemesis – the *Luftschutzwart*, Frau Schumm – with a withering look. In time, her sleep deprivation grew so bad that Frau Schumm was forced to adopt new tactics:

she would stamp up the steps and ring our doorbell. I would answer that I was coming, and . . . would go back to sleep. Finally, Frau Schumm was given a key, and she would come right up to my bed, shake me awake, and then stand there for as long as it took for me to get up . . . In those days, my nerves were so shot that sometimes I didn't care what would become of me, I just wanted to sleep![47]

The cellars themselves could be surprisingly well appointed, with cots and bunk beds and space for their inhabitants to read, play chess or do their knitting. In time, themed board games were even developed to keep children occupied, while simultaneously reinforcing the principles of air raid procedure. Some cellars, however, though functional, were often damp and offered few creature comforts. One Berliner described his in the most unflattering terms as 'a gloomy and unstable-looking construction, supported on crooked beams, where people perched on ramshackle seats, wrapped up against the cold, and listened anxiously to events outside'.[48] The prospect of spending any length of time in such places was one that few greeted with any enthusiasm.

Others complained of the boredom. One young Berliner detested the cellar of his block with such a passion that often neither his mother nor the local air raid warden was able to persuade him to go down there. 'It stank', he recalled,

> it was damp, cold and dark with a pile of mouldering potatoes in the corner. Worst of all, there was nothing that we could do. We were so bored. We children could not run around, we had to sit still. I hated it, and just wanted to stay in my bed in our apartment. I made such a scene when the siren sounded that my mother had to practically drag me down the stairs.[49]

The boredom and the stench of potatoes were the least of most people's worries. The experience of a raid could really shred one's nerves. As one Berliner recalled: 'it was calm in the cellar, nobody said a word, but we could feel the fear'.[50] Christa Becker described one raid in the autumn of 1940:

> People looked different that night. Faces were grey. The sparse light from the bulb allowed no colour. Some people were in their night clothes, wrapped in robes or coats hastily thrown over bed-warm bodies . . .
> A violent shudder convulsed our building. The walls of our shelter shook. A few boxes fell from their shelves . . . A fearful silence followed. Sentences stopped in mid-stream. Instinctively we ducked . . . 'Varroom!' the walls shook.[51]

Despite the hardships, however, most Berliners got on with life and in some cases a new spirit of friendship and community grew directly from the shared experiences: it was, as one Berliner summed up, 'a difficult time, we had to stick together, we had to help each other'.[52] For some, the air raids provided an opportunity to meet one's neighbours, to chat or to gossip; advice could be sought or given, assistance requested. Others made more intimate contacts. An increase in promiscuity certainly accompanied the air raids, and many a relationship had its first seed sown in the damp, sweaty environment of a shelter or cellar.

That autumn William Shirer made a new acquaintance when he found himself seated next to William Joyce, alias 'Lord Haw-Haw', in the cellar beneath the Berlin radio headquarters. Joyce, a renowned fascist and senior member of Mosley's British Union of Fascists (BUF), had fled Britain as war loomed in 1939 and had surfaced in the German capital where he was immediately set to work making English-language propaganda broadcasts. As neither Shirer nor Joyce had any particular desire to see out the raid in the cramped shelter, the two stole past the guards and proceeded to Joyce's room. Shirer described his companion in curiously ambivalent terms, mentioning both the twinkle in his 'Irish eyes' and his 'nasal voice', and branding him as a 'hard-fisted, scar-faced Fascist rabble-rouser'. Yet, he conceded that 'if you can get over your revulsion at his being a traitor, you find him an interesting and amusing fellow'. In Joyce's company, lubricated by a bottle of schnapps, Shirer 'watched the fireworks' as the flak hammered away over the south of the city, lighting up the sky.[53]

Though often cramped and uncomfortable, the cellars repeatedly proved their worth as the bombing intensified that autumn. Newspaper reports after many of the raids noted that the casualties recorded were among those people who had 'failed to follow instructions' and had remained above ground.[54] The subtext was clear: if you neglected to proceed to the nearest cellar or air raid shelter as soon as the siren sounded, you did so at your own peril.

Consequently, those caught away from home during a raid faced the sometimes ignominious prospect of being shooed into the nearest shelter by an often brusque policeman or air raid warden. Henry Flannery was on the Friedrichstrasse in central Berlin when the sirens sounded in late November 1940. He noted that the pedestrians picked up their pace, hurrying hither and thither, as calls and shouts echoed through the darkened streets. Soon after, he was stopped by a policeman: 'Get in a shelter', he was ordered. He protested that his hotel was only two blocks away, but the policeman was unmoved. 'Doesn't make any difference', he said. 'Get into a shelter.' After asking directions, Flannery found himself in the doorway of a house with a young German, watching the searchlights and 'pandemonium' as the raid began in earnest. This time, it was the air raid warden who admonished him and ordered him to go down into the cellar. '"You'll have to go below", he said. "I'm responsible for this place and no one can stand outside. Someone might see you and report me."' Finally, Flannery was forced to make his way down into the cellar.[55]

Though the activity was frowned upon and actively discouraged, remaining above ground to watch the raids was a common sport that autumn. Those who managed to evade the air raid wardens and policemen and witness the raids first-hand were often impressed by the tremendous light show that unfolded. Searchlight beams raked across the sky, while the flak shells flashed between them and tracer bullets slashed through the darkness. Above it all, the coloured marker flares drifted down, spreading a pale light amid the gloom. Missie Vassiltchikov observed from the western suburb of Grunewald as flares fell on the city during a raid. 'We stood in the garden', she wrote, 'watching the many green and red "Christmas trees" that were dropped.' It was, she recalled with considerable understatement, 'quite a to-do'.[56] Another eyewitness recalled British parachute flares falling over the very heart of the city: 'Once a tangle of four flares swung down vertically over the centre of Berlin, and sank with a blinding light onto Unter den Linden.'[57]

For all the deadly beauty of the light show, it was the awful concerto of sounds that many recalled most clearly, probably because it could be heard even by those who dutifully remained in their shelters and cellars. First came the wailing of the siren, which was followed by the din of a rushed evacuation and the hushed chatter in the cellar. In time, the distant hum of aero-engines could be discerned, growing louder and more distinct with every passing minute. 'The noise was ghastly', Missie Vassiltchikov wrote, 'the planes flew so low that one could hear them distinctly . . . they seemed just above our heads.'[58] Finally, the climax of the performance would be reached, as the noise of the aero-engines, flak fire and detonating bombs coincided. It was a cacophony to which some would become hardened and immune, a combination of sounds that one learned to filter and block out. Helmuth James von Moltke described the various – almost musical – components of a raid in September 1940:

> I had slept through the starting sirens again but woke when the heavy anti-aircraft artillery . . . began firing like mad. The windows were rattling and the explosions of the guns created lightning effects. Quite soon I was wide awake . . . From time to time a little hail of shrapnel fell in the garden, some splinters so close to the window that they made a whistling noise.

For many, such sounds were genuinely terrifying. One eyewitness described how an acquaintance of hers reacted when the flak began to fire during a raid: 'The shooting was very loud and poor Mäxchen Kieckebusch, whose nerves have gone to pieces since he was injured in the spine in France, rolled on the floor moaning *"Ich kann das nicht mehr hören"* ["I cannot listen to this any more"] over and over again.'[59]

Much of the sound and light generated during a raid came from the flak batteries positioned around the capital. Goebbels described the flak barrage as 'a majestic spectacle',[60] and Missie Vassiltchikov found her room brightly illuminated by its intensity. William Shirer was no less impressed. 'The concentration of anti-aircraft fire', he wrote, 'was the greatest I've ever witnessed. It provided a magnificent, a terrible sight.'[61]

The anti-aircraft defences around Berlin were indeed substantial, consisting of searchlight units, barrage balloons and some isolated squadrons of fighters. Their mainstay, however, was flak artillery, especially the formidable 88mm anti-aircraft gun. These guns would provide the backbone of Berlin's air defence network in 1940, being arranged in 29 batteries, alongside 14 batteries of lesser calibres and 11 searchlight units. These detachments were situated across the city, primarily located in the suburbs to the north and north-west, but also perched on high buildings and dotted around the parks and open spaces. In addition, four squadrons of night-fighters were posted around the capital and a railway-mounted anti-aircraft battery was positioned in the sidings close to Sundgauerstrasse Station in the south-western suburbs.[62]

Because of the sheer intensity of the barrage they fired, the Berlin flak batteries inspired great confidence in the population. One young Berliner spoke for many when he expressed the optimistic belief that 'as long as the flak was firing, we were in no danger.'[63] As many neutral observers noted, however, for all its impressive firepower the flak actually appeared to be rather ineffectual at bringing down enemy planes.[64]

Yet Berlin's anti-aircraft gunners were certainly effective enough, especially if one considers that the flak barrage was intended not only to shoot enemy aircraft down, but also to force them to increase their altitude or to abandon their bombing runs altogether. Another American journalist, Percival Knauth, observed many raids, often from a rooftop close to his office. In late September, he recalled a particularly dramatic incident:

> For more than quarter of an hour, the silvery shape [of a British plane] flashed in and out of the spiderweb of white beams stabbing upward from various parts of the city, while anti-aircraft batteries poured a veritable hail of fire directly around it. It was a scene of the highest intensity. Once the plane was caught, the searchlights were inexorable, moving slowly around from the north to northwest as the flier attempted to escape from the trap . . . If that plane got away, it must have been riddled with shell punctures.[65]

Whatever shortcomings there were in the air defences, they were at least partially rectified in late autumn, when the flak targeting system was overhauled. Whereas flak crews traditionally aimed by ready reckoning and a fair amount of guesswork, by the winter of 1940 a new, automated targeting system was brought into service, which would greatly improve the accuracy of anti-aircraft fire. In addition, an Air Raid Warning Centre was established in Berlin to coordinate air defence. Visited by Goebbels in November 1940, it was described by the Propaganda Minister as 'a miracle of system and organisation'.[66]

As a result of such advances, a number of British raids were very hard hit. German successes were naturally trumpeted in the press and often accompanied by ghoulish pictures of the wreckage. One report from mid-October 1940 was accompanied by a graphic image of a British bomber that had crashed in a leafy suburban street in the west of Berlin. The raid of 14 November was especially disastrous for the British. Of the twenty-five or so bombers that actually reached the city, ten were recorded as being shot down – the heaviest nightly loss of the war to date for the RAF.[67] True to form, Goebbels claimed that the losses were greater, insisting that twelve bombers had been downed, but he was certainly correct in attributing the success to the new targeting techniques that were being employed.[68]

For all the elaborate measures designed to thwart them, British bombers caused comparatively little material damage in the German capital that autumn. This was only partly a result of the efficiency of the flak. For one thing, the numbers of aircraft available were very limited. Though the RAF would boast of its 'thousand-bomber raids' later in the war, in the autumn and winter of 1940 only a handful of raids consisted of more than a hundred aircraft, and it was not unusual for only half of any force dispatched actually to reach the target area. Meanwhile, the payloads offered by the British planes of the period – mostly twin-engine medium bombers such as Hampdens, Wellingtons and Whitleys – simply did not compare to those that would later become available with the advent of the Avro Lancaster in 1942.

The result was that the tonnage and the numbers of bombs dropped were never sufficient to cause the mayhem that was desired. Incendiaries, therefore, though dreaded on the ground, could not be dropped in sufficient concentrations to cause widespread fires. And even though a stick of high explosives might destroy a single house, or even two, it would scarcely dent a residential block, let alone an entire street. In fact, the most disruption was often caused by bombs with 'delay fuses', which could cause roads to be closed, factory work suspended and residents evacuated, sometimes for days on end, until the peril had been defused and removed. In 1940, therefore, the bomber could certainly 'get through', but whether it could have much effect once it had got there was rather more debatable.

Ironically, then, one of the primary risks to the Berlin public during that early phase of the air war came not from the bombs themselves, but from the German flak splinters falling back to earth. Given that each of the approximately fifty flak guns around Berlin fired up to fifteen 16-pound shrapnel shells per minute – each of which burst into around a thousand jagged fragments – it is not hard to understand why those on the ground sometimes got the impression that it was raining metal. William Shirer recalled the experience in August 1940:

> As I stepped out of the building at five minutes to one . . . I heard a softer but much more ominous sound. It was like hail hitting a tin roof. You could hear it dropping through the trees and on the roofs of the sheds. It was shrapnel from the anti-aircraft guns. For the first time in my life, I wished I had a steel helmet. There had always been something repellent to me about a German helmet, something symbolic of brute German force . . . Now I rather thought I could overcome my prejudice.[69]

The damage inflicted by flak splinters on Berlin's roofs was such that the task of checking for missing or cracked roof tiles was added to the already substantial remit of the air raid wardens. In addition, serious material damage was regularly caused by unexploded flak shells. During a raid in late October 1940, thirteen faulty flak shells exploded on returning to earth, causing extensive damage. The following month brought similar chaos, with thirty-six exploding on the night of 14 November alone.[70]

There were also serious injuries and deaths. In October 1940, a railway worker was killed by a flak shell in Rummelsburg.[71] The following month, twelve soldiers were injured in a single night by falling flak splinters.[72] In the suburb of Reinickendorf, meanwhile, a forty-two-year old man was killed when a flak shell exploded after falling into his bedroom.[73] From reading such reports, one could almost conclude that Berliners were as much at risk from their own flak guns as they were from the bombs of the RAF.

Nonetheless, for all the danger that they caused, the flak splinters were a great source of excitement to Berlin's children. As many commentators record, already the morning after a raid few of these metal fragments would be found as they had all been collected up by eager schoolchildren. In general, the larger, more jagged or more twisted the fragment was, the better; others preferred those fragments that had a threaded section of the screw-in fuse still visible, or those that were still warm from being fired. Such splinters – often up to 10 centimetres in length – would then be taken into school to be shown off or exchanged in the playground.[74]

The pretence of invulnerability in Berlin was enhanced by the speed with which the authorities set about repairing what little damage had been done. Very soon after a raid, 'roof and window gangs' began making good all the damage in the capital. Groups of workmen began to clear the more serious bombsites, boarding them off to escape the gaze of the inquisitive. Harry Flannery particularly admired the extraordinary effort that was made after bombs were dropped on the Tauentzienstrasse, one of the main shopping streets in the fashionable west end of Berlin:

> Early the next day a monster crew was on the job, working in an amazing fashion. There were men down in the stricken subway between the important stations of Wittenbergplatz and the Zoo, others busy fixing water mains, gas lines, and other public utilities in the street, and gangs of men up and down the street restoring store fronts and installing new shop-window glass. In a few days, no one could tell that any bombs had fallen on the Tauentzienstrasse.[75]

Perhaps because it was tidied away and repaired so swiftly, bomb damage became a real novelty in the autumn of 1940 and countless Berliners flocked to view the aftermath of each British raid. Though this was, in part at least, a result of a ghoulish fascination with death and destruction, it is also tempting to see it as a symptom of a more serious malaise – namely the dawning sense that the Nazi authorities were not telling the truth about the scale or seriousness of the attacks.

Kurt Radener witnessed the extraordinary popular response after the house opposite his in Tempelhof was destroyed by a bomb in one of the earliest raids on Berlin in August 1940. He recalled that it was 'a sensation' and that a 'mass migration began with all of Berlin coming to Tempelhof to see a bombed-out house'.[76]

Young Dieter Zimmer recalled that the excitement was also tinged with the chilling realisation of the fragility of life:

> That afternoon, my parents and I went to the affected streets to have a look at the damage . . . Two houses had been wrecked by high explosives. On one, the whole front had been torn away and lay as a pile of rubble in the front garden. The furnished rooms were laid bare, like the rooms in a doll's house. The middle-class living room, now

inaccessible and exposed to prying eyes, gave me a profound shock. I couldn't sleep for a couple of nights afterwards. Everything could now be turned inside-out and collapse in on itself. The world had lost its former solidity.[77]

As the attacks multiplied, the destruction wrought increasingly became a part of Berliners' everyday lives, but this curiosity took rather longer to fade. Ruth Andreas-Friedrich noted in October 1940: 'After each raid, the populace turns out, curious and sensation hungry, to view the so-called "damage". They gape at a burned attic here, a few paving stones dug up there, a half-collapsed house over yonder.'[78]

The phenomenon was even worse when the city centre was hit. On the morning of 11 September, for instance, one American newspaper correspondent reported: 'The downtown district of Berlin, especially near the Brandenburg Gate, was jammed today with pedestrians who had come to view the damage inflicted in last night's raid. Unter den Linden and the other streets . . . were a mass of curious Berliners.'[79] In reality, there was precious little to see, but that did not serve to keep the crowds away. Instead, they milled around the government district, congregating many deep at each of the locations where a bomb had hit. At one site – an eight-foot crater in the East-West Axis – a constant stream of Berliners peered solemnly into the hole in the roadway, as if seeking revelation.

Yet, whatever the material damage inflicted in that early phase of the bombing, the effect on the civilian population – both in terms of sleep deprivation and the wider impact on morale – was substantial. Goebbels summed up the problem in his diary when he complained that: 'Late in the night comes the usual air-raid warning. Two aircraft scuttle over Berlin. And for that, a city of 4½ million people must take to the shelters.' 'Berlin', he complained, 'is a tired town.'[80]

Later that autumn, the Italian Foreign Minister Count Galeazzo Ciano noted the 'depressed spirit' in the German capital, which he attributed to the constant air raids. 'Every night citizens spend from four to five hours in the cellar. They lack sleep, there is promiscuity between men and women, cold, and these things do not create a good mood. The number of people with colds is incredible. Bomb damage is slight; nervousness is very high.'[81]

William Shirer suggested that the effect the bombing was having on morale in the German capital, far more than the damage inflicted, should be the primary rationale for the British. He explained his reasoning in a diary entry on 26 September: 'We had the longest air-raid of the war last night, from eleven p.m. to four o'clock this morning. If you had a job to get to at seven or eight a.m., as hundreds of thousands of people had, you got very little sleep. The British ought to do this every night. No matter if not much is destroyed . . . the psychological effect is tremendous.'[82]

By the winter of 1940–41, the air raids – which had been unthinkable only a few months before – had already become a part of everyday life in the German capital. As in Britain, 'business as usual' was the order of the day; Berlin society endured the hardships and privations and got on with life. Yet, for all the pride and stoicism on display, there was, for many, a profound underlying disquiet; an unspoken fear of what horrors the coming years might bring. As Ruth Andreas-Friedrich noted on 16 December:

> Now, we are all emerging together from the basement after the fifty-second alarm. The firing was heavier than usual tonight. 'They're getting in practice' says Frank pointing to the red glow that stains the western sky. We join him at the window. The siren of the fire brigade is screeching in the distance . . . 'They're getting in practice' says Frank again. His words bring a cold shiver to our hearts.[83]

8

Into Oblivion

On 1 October 1941, Berlin's Jews gathered to celebrate the holiday of Yom Kippur. One of the holiest festivals of the Jewish calendar, it was a time for reflection, prayer and fasting; a time when man repented of his sins and asked for God's forgiveness.

That October day, many hundreds of Berlin Jews squeezed into the large synagogue on Levetzowstrasse, in the suburb of Moabit. There they prayed, perhaps with special fervour, for those family and friends, who had managed to leave Germany – but also for themselves. There were many reasons for prayer in the autumn of 1941. Life for most German Jews had deteriorated markedly in the past year. Already subjected to a programme of persecution, they had been systematically expropriated, demonised and marginalised. Prohibited from state employment and removed from most of the professions, the areas of legitimate activity open to them had dwindled to nothing. And new legislation now sought to remove what few comforts remained to them: radios were to be confiscated, and the keeping of pets was to be forbidden.

Perhaps the most visible sign of this process of ostracism and persecution was the introduction of the *Judenstern*, or 'Jewish star'. From 18 September that year, all Jews over the age of six were obliged to wear a yellow cloth star when out in public. According to the legislation that accompanied the measure, the star, which bore the word *Jude*, or 'Jew', in black Hebrew-esque lettering within a yellow Star of David, was to be worn firmly stitched to the left breast and had to be visible.[1] Those who dared to contravene the order, or who covered the star in any way, would receive a fine or imprisonment.

While most ordinary Berliners reacted with indifference or occasional sympathy,[2] the effect of the new measure on the city's Jews was profound. At a stroke, any anonymity that they could have enjoyed was taken from them; their public humiliation was complete. As the philologist Victor Klemperer noted, the day of the *Judenstern*'s introduction was 'the worst day for the Jews during those 12 years of hell'.[3]

For all the uncertainty of the times, however, there was much about Yom Kippur that October that had the comforting ring of familiarity about it. For one thing, the service was led by the well-known rabbi Leo Baeck. Born in Posen in 1873, Baeck had studied in Berlin and Breslau and had emerged as an eminent Jewish intellectual in Germany. After service as an army chaplain during the First World War, he had returned to Berlin to serve as a rabbi and had become one of the pillars of the Jewish community there. As head of the *Reichvereinigung der Juden*, the 'Reich Organisation of Jews', he was a respected authority on Jewish affairs. His white hair and kindly, bespectacled face were reassuringly familiar to many in the congregation that evening.

The location, too, was held in special regard. Built during the First World War, the synagogue on Levetzowstrasse was one of the largest of the thirty-four synagogues in the German capital, capable of accommodating over two thousand worshippers. Built in the classical style, it was an elegant construction, presenting clean lines in sandstone, a high, saddle roof and little of the architectural complexity and exoticism of conventional orthodox synagogues. Those entering the building would pass through a high pillared portico, with a Hebrew inscription from the Book of Isaiah emblazoned above: 'O house of Jacob, come ye, and let us walk in the light of the Lord.'[4] Inside, there was a large main hall, almost square in outline, flanked on three sides by raised galleries, all of which were laid out with elegant wooden pews. At the eastern end of the hall, beneath a decorated Risalit, was the 'Holy of Holies', where the Torah scrolls were kept.

Though it had been damaged in the *Kristallnacht* pogrom of November 1938 – in which most of Berlin's synagogues had been seriously damaged, desecrated or destroyed – the building in Levetzowstrasse was the only large synagogue in the German capital to have survived more or less unscathed. Where many of Berlin's Jewish community were thus forced to congregate in the remaining private prayer houses, or in their own homes, the Levetzowstrasse synagogue offered its congregation a familiar refuge from an outside world which had turned decidedly hostile.

The services and rituals held for Yom Kippur that day took the traditional and familiar form. It had begun with the moving *Kol Nidrei* service, the previous night, in which the Talmudic Scrolls were held aloft and the congregation had prayed to be released from the vows that they had made during the previous year. The day of Yom Kippur itself was taken up almost exclusively with prayer and fasting. One highlight was the *Minchah* service in the afternoon, which included the reading, in its entirety, of the Book of Jonah with its well-known parable of the prophet and the whale. The story's message was clear: it is impossible for man to escape God's will. The day closed with the evening service of *Ne'ila*, when the final prayers of repentance were offered. Thereafter, the *shofar* horn was sounded and the faithful were sent out into the dusk – with joy in their hearts – to end their fast.

But even as the congregation was leaving the Levetzowstrasse that evening, events were taking a sinister turn. At that very moment, Gestapo officials appeared at the synagogue, demanding the keys to the building. Jewish community elders were then ordered to go to the Gestapo office on the Burgstrasse, where they were informed that the 'resettlement' of the Berlin Jews was soon to begin. They were told that the Jewish community itself was required to cooperate fully in the resettlement and that the synagogue on Levetzowstrasse was to be used as a transit camp for those selected for deportation.[5]

With the help of the Berlin Jewish officials, therefore, lists of those Jews scheduled for 'resettlement' were compiled and, in the following days, the first notifications to would-be deportees were sent out. These notifications, on the headed paper of the Berlin Jewish Organisation, used a correct, unthreatening tone. Recipients were informed of the date scheduled for their 'emigration' and were advised of the procedures that were to be followed. Baggage, they were told, could be deposited at the collection point on Levetzowstrasse two days prior to departure. On the day before departure, the recipient's apartment would be sealed by the Gestapo and the recipient, along with his or her spouse and any unmarried children, would have to proceed to the collection point.[6]

An instruction leaflet was also enclosed, giving precise details of what evacuees were permitted to take with them. Lists of necessities were given, including warm clothing, underwear, umbrellas and bedding. Medicines, matches, shaving equipment and scissors were also permitted. Importantly, all documents – including birth, marriage and death certificates, but with the exception of passports – were to be handed to the authorities. Similarly, all cash, jewellery, savings books, bonds and financial papers had to be surrendered. Evacuees were reminded that all bags were to be labelled with the transport number and the name and address of the owner, and they had to ensure that the *Judenstern* was clearly visible on any jacket or overcoat.[7]

The evacuation notice ended with a plea for evacuees 'to follow these instructions very precisely and to remain calm and collected while preparing for the transport'. It concluded:

> Those of our members affected by the evacuation must be aware that their own behaviour and the orderly fulfilment of all instructions can make a decisive contribution to the smooth conclusion of this evacuation. Obviously, so far as is permitted, we will do everything we can to stand by our members and afford them every possible assistance.[8]

As with each previous imposition, this new order was met with a combination of fear, stoicism and impotent rage. Yet, perhaps because of the involvement of their own community officials, the majority of those affected complied with the order, collected their things and prepared themselves and their families for a journey into the unknown.

The packing itself was an agonising process for many, as items of sentimental value often had to be discarded in favour of more practical additions. Evacuees, therefore, inevitably spent many of those remaining hours packing and repacking the few possessions and mementoes that they wished to take with them. Food would be prepared, and carefully packaged for the journey. Jewellery and cash – though forbidden – would be sewn into the hems of coats, so as to provide hidden reserves for barter or exchange.

In addition, all evacuees were obliged to compile an inventory of all those possessions and household items – furniture, fittings, kitchenware and other belongings – that they intended to leave behind. One such inventory is that of Marion Samuel, who lived with her daughter on Rhinowerstrasse in the working-class district of Prenzlauer Berg. It gives a glimpse into a doomed world:

1 wardrobe	5 [Reichsmarks]
1 cabinet	5 -
1 table	15 -
5 chairs	10 -
1 bed frame	15 -
1 couch	30 -
1 mattress	5 -
2 side tables	2 -
3 suitcases	10 -
1 carpet	worthless
1 lamp	5 -
1 pair curtains	10 -
1 child's chair	worthless
clothing	40 - . . . [9]

Marion's possessions were valued at a total of 220 Reichsmarks: about a month's wages to the average Berliner.

In time, a final balance sheet would be drawn up, upon which the proceeds from a deported individual's estate would be set against various charges and demands made by the authorities – such as the cost of their deportation. Utility companies were also permitted to deduct any sums owed to them. All remaining monies automatically fell into the coffers of the Reich.

After such formalities were completed, the time came for departure. Inge Deutschkron described how her neighbour, a sixty-five-year-old widow, was collected by the Gestapo:

Shortly after 8 a.m. the doorbell rang loudly and insistently. My mother sat there as though paralysed. Almost soundlessly, she whispered only: 'For God's sake!' As there was no doubt who was demanding entrance, I put on my coat, with the 'Star of David', and opened the door. Before me stood two tall men in grey leather coats. 'Does Klara Sara Hohenstein live here?' they asked. I pointed to the door to her room, and went back to my mother. . . .

We heard virtually nothing, apart from the footsteps in Frau Hohenstein's room. Then we heard her voice. She called to Aunt Olga, who, trembling with fear, stood up and haltingly went to the door. She stopped on the threshold and called out 'Yes, what do you want?'

Frau Hohenstein said, quite calmly, that she was being taken away.
She did not know any more. As soon as she could, she would be in
touch, she said. As if to interrupt any further speculation, one of the
men added that the room would be sealed and that it was an offence
to break the seal or to remove anything from the room. Then they led
Frau Hohenstein to the door. We heard it slam and then listened to
the men's footsteps, and the quiet patter of Frau Hohenstein, as they
reverberated in the stairwell. Then we heard nothing more. Once again,
it was as quiet as the grave.[10]

As this testimony suggests, the 'evacuations' to the transit camp, though
harrowing for all concerned, were usually carried out in an orderly
fashion. At the time given in the deportation notice, the evacuees would
be collected by the Gestapo, and be transferred to the camp by truck or
car. When it became clear that the authorities were encountering little
resistance in their round-ups of evacuees, the Jewish community itself
was permitted to supply its own personnel – *Ordner*, or auxiliaries – to
carry out that first stage of the evacuation, supposedly with a little more
consideration than the Gestapo.

For the auxiliaries, this proved a most difficult task. They found
themselves caught between the wrath of their own community and
that of the Gestapo. Held responsible by the authorities for the smooth
running of the deportation process, they were threatened with deportation themselves when things went wrong. Two such auxiliaries were
summarily sent on the transports that they had helped to organise,
after it transpired that they had allowed a young girl to escape.[11] At
the same time, they were viewed with little sympathy by their own
people. As one eyewitness recalled:

[They] were mostly young men. They were doing their duty.
Sometimes they seemed to be inhuman. Driving their victims
on: 'Quick, quick, you not ready yet?' But perhaps delaying the
inevitable would just have been crueller. They overpowered our old
landlady from Bamberger Strasse 22, who fought against her deportation with her hands and feet and with terrible screams. They carried
her down the stairs to the truck waiting below, complete with the
chair in which she sat as though nailed down. They had their quota
to fill.'[12]

Though their initial 'collection' might be civil, most evacuees found that conditions altered rapidly once they arrived at the transit camp on Levetzowstrasse. Here, they would be registered and ticked off the 'Deportation List'. Then they would have to wait for the transfer to their allotted train, which in most instances would leave at least twenty-four hours after its 'passengers' had been processed.

The Jewish community did its best to make the assembly camp as comfortable for the deportees as possible. One of its representatives was Hildegard Henschel, the wife of the organisation's head, Moritz Henschel, who was intimately involved in the community effort:

> Food supplies, medicines, sanitary materials, underwear, clothes, shoes . . . everything was brought to the Levetzowstrasse and, within a few hours, separate kitchens for adults and for children were up and running [as well as] a section of the Jewish hospital, with doctors and nurses, for accidents and first aid. There was a separate children's room for toddlers with nursery nurses and teachers, a store of mattresses for the old and weak . . . a baggage porter service was organised by members of the community and in a nearby kitchen packages of supplies were prepared for everyone.[13]

Despite such noble efforts, however, the long wait in the former synagogue was a harrowing time. For those that remembered the synagogue as a house of worship, it would have made a shocking sight. Now little more than a bare hall, all of its fittings, pews, and sacred paraphernalia had been removed and destroyed; in their place rough hessian sacks filled with straw provided the only creature comforts. Here the deportees were constantly exposed to the barked orders and abuse of the Gestapo. 'Everything was confiscated', wrote the Berlin Jew Hermann Samter:

> At Levetzow street they first took all the money from the people, then all metal belongings (including razors if they were metal), all documents [were taken] with the exception of the identity card which was stamped 'evacuated to Litzmannstadt' . . . No one except the community workers was permitted to enter the camp.[14]

Such confiscations, it seems, were an established part of the process. 'The Gestapo "filtered" all baggage', one evacuee recalled,

> searching through and removing anything that seemed desirable ...
> Fortunately the Jewish community people almost always managed to
> replace those important items of clothing that had been 'filtered' from
> their supplies. The items that were confiscated varied from day to day,
> as each Gestapo officer had his own preferences and his own require-
> ments. It was an open secret that when Commissar Stubbs was on
> duty, no mouthwash, after-shave or eau de cologne would get through.
> Anything with even a small alcohol content would be removed and
> drunk on the spot.[15]

Quite apart from the depredations of the authorities, the evacuees
would have been profoundly unnerved by the simple lack of knowledge about where they were being taken. Though very few of them
had any inkling of their true fate, they were still being torn from their
homes and their loved ones and were taking a step into the unknown.
For some, it was step that they would do anything to avoid. 'I will never
forget the nights that I spent there', recalled Siegmund Weltlinger, who
worked for the Jewish community at the camp, 'heartbreaking scenes
would be played out. There were always suicides or suicide attempts.
Some women threw themselves down from the balcony onto the marble
floor below.'[16]

Even when a destination was given for a transport, it brought the
deportees little clarity or comfort. Though they might have been dimly
aware of Riga, Minsk, Warsaw or Kaunas, they had little idea of conditions in those cities. 'Litzmannstadt', meanwhile – the destination of the
first four transports to leave the capital – was almost completely unknown.
Only a few of the deportees would have known that Litzmannstadt was
the former Łódź, the western Polish city which had been rechristened
by the occupying Germans the previous autumn. Fewer still would have
known that – since the previous year – it was home to one of the largest
Jewish ghettos in occupied Europe.

In the absence of hard facts, the Berlin rumour mill ran riot. It was
suggested, for instance, that a kibbutz was to be established 'on the
Palestinian model' in the former Latvian capital, Riga.[17] Though few
dared to ask questions, the official story was that Berlin's Jews were

being sent to labour camps where, it was insinuated, they would 'finally be taught the meaning of hard work'. This fiction was believed by many of those deported from the capital. Others, however, suspected the truth: that the unfortunates were being sent to concentration camps, or even to certain death.

Two days after the initial round-up, on the morning of Saturday 18 October 1941, the first one thousand Jews were taken from the collection camp in the Levetzowstrasse synagogue and marched to the railway station at Grunewald in the western suburbs of the capital. Despite the pouring rain, only the very young and the infirm were permitted to use the open trucks supplied by the authorities; the remainder made the six-kilometre journey through the city on foot, most of them carrying the 50 kilograms of luggage allotted to each of them. Upon arrival at Grunewald Station, they were calmly loaded into passenger carriages, according to a system worked out by the community elders. 'Once everyone had taken their place', one eyewitness recalled, 'warm food and hot drinks were distributed, and the prepared packages of supplies were handed out to each evacuee.'[18] In the early afternoon, their train departed. It would reach Litzmannstadt, some 250 miles to the east, sometime during the following day.

More transports quickly followed. On 24 October, a further 1,000 or so Berlin Jews were sent to the same destination, on the 28th another 1,000 and on 2 November yet another 1,000 were dispatched. Arriving in the Łódź ghetto, the 'evacuees' were descending into a world they would barely have recognised as human. In the autumn of 1941, the ghetto was home to approximately 200,000 individuals, crowded into an area of barely two and a half square kilometres. The squalor, malnutrition and disease would challenge all but the most robust. It was a nightmarish world where the emaciated wandered the streets dressed in rags and the dead lay untended where they fell. Within just a few weeks, the Berlin Jews who left Grunewald Station that rainy Saturday in October 1941 would be dying. Within a year, the majority of them would already be dead.

This was only the beginning. In the next phase, new destinations were found for Berlin's Jews, including the ghettos at Minsk, Kaunas and Riga. While there was little change in the procedure followed, there were two minor yet significant differences from the way in which the early transports had been processed. The first was that the Jewish deportees were now marched to the Grunewald Station at night, thereby giving fewer 'Aryan' Berliners the opportunity to witness events. The second change was to the demographic make-up of the transports. In an effort to speed the removal of those Jews who were unable to perform manual labour, the authorities now targeted old people's homes and hospitals in making up the new transport lists. The tenth Berlin transport, for instance, which left for Riga on 25 January 1942, had an average age of 58; fully 500 of its complement of 1,044 were over 61, 103 were over 71.[19]

On boarding the trains, passengers on these transports would have noticed other differences too. The veneer of civility – paper-thin at best – was slipping. Though much of the processing of evacuees was still done by members of the Berlin Jewish community, the real power – the Gestapo – was making its malicious presence felt. Casual brutality increasingly became the order of the day. Moreover, where the early transports had used the comparative comfort of passenger carriages, now the deportees – especially those who were disabled or bed-ridden – tended to be packed into goods wagons, or cattle trucks covered with a simple tarpaulin. Lacking even the most basic amenities, such elderly or frail deportees would often not survive the five-day journey, through the depths of a northern European winter, to distant Riga.

For those who survived the ordeal, arrival at their destination was scarcely more comforting. One deportee from Berlin, Heinz Bernhardt, arrived at the ghetto in Minsk in December 1941. There he and his fellows were marched to a collection of shabby wooden huts, all strangely deserted. 'The wrecked houses looked as if a pogrom had taken place there', Bernhardt remembered. 'Pillow feathers everywhere. Hanukah lamps and candlesticks laying around in every corner . . . Later we were informed that this was the Russian ghetto, whose Jewish residents were shot in early November 1941.' Those victims were still nearby and were shown to them by an SD man, who 'pointed and said: "There, in front of you, a heap of bodies." And in fact we saw a hillock with parts of human bodies sticking out.'[20]

Those deportees who found their way into the ghetto at all might be counted among the lucky ones. All of the 1,006 Jews from the sixth Berlin transport, for instance, which reached Kaunas in occupied Lithuania on 21 November 1941, would be murdered four days after their arrival. The 1,053 Berlin Jews on the very next train, arriving in Riga on the last day of November, did not even have four days in which to collect themselves. After their arrival, they were marched straight off the train and into the nearby forest of Rumbula, where they were shot en masse in freshly dug pits. Thirty-eight of them were children under ten years old. They were the first of an estimated 13,000 Jews murdered at Rumbula that day, the first of 25,000 in total.[21]

The killing of that Berlin transport at Rumbula was to prove controversial. The officer in charge of the operation, SS-*Obergruppenführer* Friedrich Jeckeln, had initially received instructions to murder the inhabitants of the Riga ghetto so as to make room for arriving 'Reich' Jews. While 'eastern' Jews were viewed as thoroughly expendable, the attitude then current in Berlin was that Reich Jews were not to be exterminated out of hand and were, initially at least, to be housed in the ghetto and put to work. The reasoning behind this distinction is unclear. It is most unlikely that Himmler was moved by any residual humanitarian scruples or feelings of sympathy for those people who might have previously been his neighbours. Rather, it is most plausible that he was concerned about the effect on public opinion at home, should the true fate of Reich Jews get out.[22]

As senior SS officer in the Baltic, Jeckeln would have been well aware of this policy when he opted to include the Berlin Jews in the 'liquidation operation' that was planned for the Riga ghetto. Himmler was not best pleased, especially after his personal intervention, explicitly ordering that the Berlin Jews were not to be liquidated, arrived too late. He forcefully reminded Jeckeln that Jews were to be dealt with according to the guidelines given and that 'unilateral acts and violations' would be punished.[23] Nonetheless, for all his apparent displeasure, he promoted Jeckeln to Head of SS Upper Section *Ostland* ten days later.

Though deportations from the Reich continued into January 1942 – including three transports from Berlin, each of over a thousand Jews, bound for Riga – thereafter the process slowed. Between then and June 1942, only two more transports left the capital; one in March bound for the ghetto at Piaski in south-eastern Poland, and the other in April bound for Warsaw. One of the factors behind that slow-down, one must surmise, is that the authorities were struggling to find suitable locations for the many Reich Jews that were still awaiting 'evacuation'. It would take until that summer before new destinations could be found and for the deportations from Berlin and elsewhere to begin once again.

One of those new destinations was Theresienstadt in northern Bohemia. Formerly a Habsburg fortress, Theresienstadt had initially been established as a camp for Jews from the Czech lands, but was later transformed into a ghetto for elderly Jews from the Reich, as well as those designated as 'privileged', such as veterans who had received a combat decoration in the First World War. Theresienstadt played primarily a propaganda role, serving as the quasi-acceptable face of the deportation of the Jews from the Reich, a place whose comparatively tolerable conditions could be trumpeted so as to assuage the concerns of the international community and the Red Cross.

The first transport from Berlin to Theresienstadt departed in the early morning of 2 June 1942. It contained fifty elderly Berlin Jews, almost all of whom were former inhabitants of the Jewish old people's home on Grosse Hamburger Strasse, which – like the Levetzowstrasse synagogue – had now been transformed into a transit camp. The deportees were taken by tram to the Anhalter Station – one of Berlin's busiest rail termini – where they were loaded into closed passenger cars, which were coupled to the scheduled service towards Dresden and Karlsbad. Departing early in the morning, usually around 5.00 a.m., the deportees would generally reach Theresienstadt by evening, and, as one eyewitness recalled, the journey was carried out 'under quite tolerable conditions'.[24]

This process continued into the autumn and winter of 1942. Every few days another transport was formed taking between 50 or 100 individuals to Theresienstadt. By the end of that year, 82 such transports had departed from the capital, carrying over 9,000 elderly, infirm and juvenile Berlin Jews to the camp.[25] Those deportees from the capital had little inkling of their fate. Even if they had believed the propaganda about Theresienstadt, they had no idea that, for the vast majority of them, that camp would not be their final destination. Theresienstadt was not all that it seemed. Though it would be periodically buffed and polished for the benefit of press photographers or outside

observers, it was little more than a transit camp, briefly accommodating its inmates prior to a second deportation to other locations
further east.

In June 1942, for instance, as the first transports were arriving from
the capital, another transport with over 1,000 unfortunates on board
was departing from Theresienstadt for the newly built extermination
camp at Sobibór. In July, 1,000 more were sent to the ghetto in Minsk,
and another 1,000 to Baranowitschi, both in former Byelorussia. The
following month, another 1,000 were dispatched to Riga. Clearly, whatever scruples had conspired to stay the hands of German executioners
the previous winter had now been overcome. In the majority of such
cases, arriving Jews would be marched by the thousand into the nearby
forest and murdered. Their bodies, limed to speed decomposition,
would be left to rot beneath a thin layer of soil.

In time, new techniques were developed. At Treblinka – a small,
unassuming town on the rail line north-east of Warsaw – gas chambers were installed that autumn, using carbon monoxide from diesel
engines, which could 'process' over 300 individuals in one hour. In
September, 10,000 Jews in five transports left Theresienstadt bound
for this then-unknown destination; 8,000 more followed in October.
By the time the camp that has become synonymous with the Holocaust
– Auschwitz-Birkenau – was brought on-stream as an extermination
centre that winter, the vast majority of the 29,000 Jews already deported
from the German capital were dead. In the following months and
years, a similar number would follow them to a similar fate.

In June 1943, Joseph Goebbels declared that the German capital was
now *judenrein* – 'cleansed of Jews'. It was a rather premature announcement, for many thousands of Jews remained in the city, either in
hiding, or in mixed marriages, or in the remaining Jewish hospital.
Yet, though the factual basis of the announcement was misleading,
its 'tone', its sentiment and its fundamental message were absolutely
correct. Berlin's Jewish community – one of the most numerous and
vibrant of all Germany – had been destroyed.

How much did ordinary Berliners – and, indeed, Berlin Jews – know
about the Holocaust?

There *were* rumours. Despite being top secret, any event of the
scope and emotional magnitude of the destruction of the Jews was

bound to find an echo in the domestic rumour mill. Soldiers in the east heard rumours of the mass killings and, in some instances, these would be relayed to friends and family back in Germany. A few of them might have seen proof – in the form of grainy photographs of mass shootings and the like – or perhaps even themselves been witness to 'actions', round-ups or massacres. The experience of the later resistance member Philipp von Boeselager was perhaps typical. He heard news of the Holocaust after a fellow officer shared a train carriage with some drunken SD men, who had boasted that they had murdered 250,000 Jews in the rear areas of Army Group South on the Eastern Front in 1941.[26]

Surprisingly perhaps, some information about what was going on was transmitted by post. Given that limited communication was possible between those incarcerated in the ghettos and those back home in Berlin and elsewhere, news of the awful conditions and hardships experienced by deported Jews was occasionally able to seep back to friends and family. Ruth Andreas-Friedrich received a letter from her friend Margot Rosenthal, who had been deported, in December 1941, to a camp at Landshut in Bavaria. 'Send us something to eat, we are starving', her friend implored, before closing with 'Don't forget me, I cry all day.'[27] However bad the conditions may have been at Landshut, the ghettos in the east were infinitely worse.

In time, the trickle of desperate letters and cards home stopped entirely. Thanks to the efficiency of the German postal service, letters sent out to the ghettos would also go unanswered and be returned to the senders, with the words 'addressee deceased' or 'address unknown' written across them.[28] Hermann Samter recorded this worrying turn of events. 'Since the beginning of the year', he wrote in late January 1942, 'no news has been heard from Litzmannstadt. Post sent there, is returned with the note that no postal deliveries are being made in this or that street. It is suspected that Typhus is the reason.'[29] When the transports bound for Treblinka, or the death pits of Maly Trostinets, left Berlin later that year, no correspondence was received from the deportees at all. Samter again voiced the fears of many: 'Of the thousand people who were supposedly taken to Kaunas on 17 November, not one of them has written. As a result, the widespread rumour has emerged that these people have been shot en route, or otherwise murdered.'[30]

As a result the domestic grapevine was alive with tales of the atrocities and horrors perpetrated against the Jews. Ruth Andreas-Friedrich heard the darkest stories in the winter of 1942. That December she wrote that 'ghastly rumours are current about the fate of the evacuees – mass shootings and death by starvation, tortures and gassings'.[31] On the basis of such evidence, some historians have argued that reports of the mass killings abounded and that the German civilian population was under no illusions about the fate of the deported Jews.[32] This seems to be an exaggeration, however. A recent study has concluded that around one-third of the German population 'knew in some form or another about the mass murder' of the Jews; the figure for Berlin is estimated at 28 per cent.[33]

The rumours and the stories, therefore, were certainly not heard by everyone. Interestingly, as late as January 1944, the Berlin journalist Ursula von Kardorff confessed her ignorance of the ongoing slaughter. 'If only one knew', she wrote in her diary, 'what was happening to the deported Jews.'[34] It would seem that the majority of Berliners – Jew and Aryan alike – simply had no idea of the fate of their neighbours, friends and loved ones. In the absence of any contradicting information, they were obliged to accept the official fiction that the deportees had been 'resettled' to camps and ghettos in the east, where they would be engaged in a programme of hard labour for the benefit of Germany. One evacuee was informed by a German colleague in January 1943 that he was: 'now . . . going to break rocks in Russia'. Lacking information to the contrary, he believed what he was told.[35]

Yet, even the estimate that 28 per cent of Berliners knew about the grim fate of the Jews requires qualification: hearing a rumour is not the same thing as believing that rumour to be fact. It was all too easy for Germans to dismiss such horror stories as enemy-inspired propaganda, designed to undermine the regime and the wider war effort. Though the Nazis never publicly responded to rumours about the Holocaust, there were enough instances of Allied propaganda stories being supposedly disproved by Goebbels' ministry that the seed of doubt would have been sown, even without the active intervention of the authorities.

More importantly, however, there was an 'imagination gap' with regard to the Holocaust. Most Berliners would have found it hard to believe the grim truth of the Holocaust, even had they known it. And those, on both sides, who had an inkling of what was going on were often unwilling to believe that their darkest suspicions could possibly be true. The idea that an entire race of people could systematically be killed on an industrial scale was beyond the imagination of most people.

This disbelief was widespread. Holocaust survivor Primo Levi recorded the profound and gnawing fear that many Jews had – even when inside Auschwitz – that, should they survive to tell their stories, their sufferings would not be considered credible. The enormity of the Holocaust was such, he realised, that it simply defied belief.[36] The same phenomenon was witnessed when the Polish underground courier Jan Karski travelled to Washington, DC, in the summer of 1943, to present his evidence of the Holocaust to a group of American Jewish leaders. After he had finished his testimony – which included his own eyewitness account of life in the Warsaw ghetto and the murders taking place at the Izbica transit camp – Karski was addressed by Justice Felix Frankfurter of the US Supreme Court: 'Mr Karski', he said, 'I am unable to believe you.' When a Polish diplomat then interjected and asked whether Mr Frankfurter was calling Mr Karski a liar, Justice Frankfurter clarified his response, replying: 'I did not say this young man is lying. I said I am unable to believe him. There is a difference.'[37]

If the world at large found it impossible to believe the truth of the Holocaust, even when provided with incontrovertible proof, Berliners presented with piecemeal evidence, rumour and hearsay were bound to dismiss such talk as enemy propaganda, or perverted fantasy. As Ursula von Kardorff recalled after the war: 'we were realistic and pessimistic. But Auschwitz?'[38]

This reaction was bolstered by a profound belief in the fundamentally 'civilised' nature of the German state and society. Not only could the majority simply not conceive of mass killing on the scale of the Holocaust, they could also not see how – legally and administratively – such atrocities could be permitted to occur at all. Germany was a *Rechtsstaat*, a state governed by the rule of law, and even the recent racial legislation had the backing of law and was written into the legal framework. The order confiscating the property of those Jews about to be deported, for instance, cited in its preamble the six pieces of legislation on which the authority was based.[39] Even in Nazi Germany, therefore, the law was paramount; nobody would have believed that it could permit state-sponsored mass murder. As one German Jew recalled, his reaction to the rumours of the Holocaust was: 'That can't be so . . . it's the twentieth century and we're German.'[40]

For all these reasons, one has to assume that the vast majority of both Aryan and Jewish Berliners either knew nothing of the Holocaust or else were unable to believe and accept what little they might have heard. It is in this light that the spectrum of contemporary reactions to the deportations must be viewed.

For Jewish Berliners impotent stoicism was still the dominant reaction to the rumours and to the events that were engulfing them. They had seen their fellows deported to an unknown fate and would have felt that the persecution they had suffered in recent years was coming to a head. In the early months of 1942, for instance, Berlin Jews had to cope with a flurry of new restrictions and prohibitions. They were banned from all public baths in January; the following month, they were forbidden to buy firewood, newspapers and periodicals. In May, Jews were banned from many areas of the centre of the capital, including Unter den Linden and Kurfürstendamm. The following month, all optical and electronic items – such as cameras, typewriters and binoculars – in Jewish possession had to be surrendered to the state.[41]

If such measures appear petty, it is important to realise that other legislation passed at the same time was much more serious. In a series of decrees, the isolation and expropriation of German Jewry – a process begun in 1933 – was finally brought to its conclusion. Jews were forbidden to sell, loan or trade their belongings and the sale of non-rationed items to Jews was prohibited. Jewish schools were closed, and the fit and healthy amongst the community were sent to forced labour camps, where conditions often mirrored those of the concentration camps. In such circumstances, it is easy to appreciate how those Jews that remained often found little time and little energy to worry about their fellows.

Such hardships quickly became the new everyday norm, as can be gleaned from the poetry composed by a young Berlin Jewish girl, Ruth Schwersenz. In a leather-bound volume, Ruth collected short ditties and rhymes, sometimes accompanied by a photograph, written by each of her school friends as they were deported in the winter of 1941–2. The entries are not maudlin or sad, rather they are bright, often optimistic

– 'Where there's a will, there's a way', one of them wrote, or 'Tomorrow
is another day'. Some are rather more profound. Jutta Pickardt, for
instance, quoted Goethe: 'You will never stray from the right path /
Just act according to your heart and your conscience.' Ilse Baer, meanwhile, advised her fellow students: 'Bring your parents joy / make them
happy through your hard work / Then, with age, you will reap the best
prize of all.' Though it is too much to expect eleven-year-olds to have
knowledge of the hideous fate awaiting them or their friends, it is still
instructive to see the sheer normality of their verses, composed as if
they were leaving the school, or simply moving away.[42]

Adults found such optimism more difficult to maintain.
Nonetheless, many reacted with admirable pragmatism, offering help
to deportees as far as they could and seeking to make both the time
spent in the transit camp in the capital and the 'evacuation' itself as
comfortable as was possible. Bertha Falkenberg, though herself of
pensionable age, set up a group to help 'evacuees' by supplying them
with extra provisions – sandwiches, coffee, water and soup – at the
railheads.[43] Some Berlin Jews sought to help the deportees further,
even after they had reached their destination. As Elisabeth Siegel
recalled: 'When the first letters, or rather postcards arrived from
addresses in Warsaw or Litzmannstadt . . . we collected money, flour,
sugar and tea. This was then wrapped into small packages and
addressed. Then a group of schoolchildren went from district to
district to post the packages in letterboxes.'[44]

Others – mindful perhaps of the horrific rumours or merely
unwilling to accept the latest impositions – were prepared to fight for
their destiny in any way they could. One approach was to effectively
deny one's Jewishness. Petitioners would apply to the Reich Race
Research Office in Berlin to claim that they were not actually the
biological child of Jewish parents, but the illegitimate offspring of an
Aryan father. Family photographs would be produced as supporting
evidence, and the testimony of family members would be recorded.
'Never before', wrote Ruth Andreas-Friedrich, 'have there been so
many marital infidelities, and so many daughters and sons ready under
oath to assert their mothers' vagaries.'[45]

For all the imagined infidelities, fraudulent testimonies and carefully
constructed genealogies, the Reich Race Research Office operated on
a strictly scientific – or pseudo-scientific – basis. Photographs would

be minutely studied, and living relatives would be invited for 'interview'. Then, precise measurements would be taken, comparing the
features of the applicant to those of his or her putative father – the shape
of the nose, the eye and the ear, as well as the relationship of the jaw
to the nose, the nose to the eyes, and the hairline to the forehead. In
addition, phrenological measurements would be made of the shape of
the skull. The Office's judgements not only carried the weight of law,
they also meant the difference between deportation and the chance to
remain in Berlin and ultimately between life and death. Few applicants,
however, succeeded in their endeavour. All too often the reply would
come back stating that a family resemblance was discernible and that
the application was dismissed.

For some Jews, such legal gymnastics were beyond the pale and,
weary of the barrage of legislation and persecution that they had been
forced to endure, they simply resigned themselves to their fate and
opted to take their own lives when the notice of their deportation
from the capital arrived. For many such cases, the method of choice
was to take an overdose of the barbiturate Veronal, which was relatively easily obtained and promised a swift death.

Ursula von Kardorff recorded one such suicide in the spring of 1943.
'Mrs Liebermann is dead', she wrote in her diary, 'they actually came
with a stretcher to collect the 85-year-old for the transport to Poland.
At the last moment, she took Veronal and died a day later in the Jewish
hospital without regaining consciousness.' The agonising final hours
of Hans Michaelis, a retired lawyer living in Charlottenburg, were
recorded by his niece, Maria:

I hear from Uncle Hans and hurry to say farewell. He is grateful. He
looks at me and asks – glancing at the clock before him –

'Maria, I don't have much time. What should I do? What is easiest,
what's the most dignified? To live or to die? To suffer a terrible fate,
or to end one's own life, to kill oneself as quickly as possible before
the horde of swastika-wearing SS fetch me? And – my friends say – this
will be in the next day or two!'

We speak. We examine both possibilities. We ask ourselves what his
late wife – my dear Aunt Gertrud – would have advised. Again he grabs
the clock.

'I have 50 hours left here, at most! . . . Thank God that my Gertrud died a normal death, before Hitler. What would I give for that! In bed, surrounded by a doctor and nurses. Or a soldier's death, amongst my former comrades. . . . Maria, see how the time flies!'

My heart is racing. Racing and hammering. I'm racking my brains for the right words. Can't God inspire me? It seems not. We are both hot and we have to escape the room. We go down in the lift to get some air at the front door. There, we somehow say our farewells. 'Uncle Hans, you will know the right thing to do. Farewell.'[46]

Two days later, Maria heard that her Uncle Hans had taken his own life.

In some cases, a suicide pact was agreed. Helmuth James von Moltke related an example in a letter to his wife. 'Yesterday', he wrote, 'I said goodbye to a once famous Jewish lawyer who has the Iron Cross First and Second Class, the Order of the House of Hohenzollern, the Golden Badge for the Wounded, and who will kill himself with his wife today, because he is to be picked up tonight.'[47] Another Berlin diarist recorded the heart-rending case of a young half-Jewish girl, who administered poison to her Jewish mother, when notice of her deportation came through. 'I loved my mother so much', the girl said, 'that I have killed her.'[48] The total number of suicides among Berlin Jews is unknown, but some estimates suggest that fully one in four Jewish deaths in Berlin at this time were suicides, and that around 10 per cent of those who received their deportation notices opted to meet their fate in this way.[49]

Other Berlin Jews – especially the young – sought a different form of escape: they went underground. Though a drastic move, it was one that in many instances would have developed gradually, evolving from the common practice of avoiding the authorities by staying temporarily with friends or relations. In time, some decided to make such arrangements rather more permanent. Sympathetic friends would be sounded out; possible hiding places – lofts, garden sheds or eaves cupboards – would be investigated.

For others, the transition to a life 'underground' could be rather more precipitate. Twenty-year-old Joel König was virtually pushed out of the door of his home in August 1942, when his family's deportation notice came through. 'The last thing we need is for the Gestapo to find you here', his mother told him. 'Get on your way . . . make sure you get to Switzerland!' With that, he recalled, 'she ushered me out of the door without a kiss or a shake of the hand'. He would never see his parents again.[50]

Those who took the plunge were generally known as *Taucher*, 'divers', or, more colloquially 'U-boats' – because they slipped beneath the surface of Hitler's Reich into the invisible depths of wartime society. Unlike their namesakes, however, these human U-Boats were not self-sufficient and were almost always entirely reliant on the help and support of their Aryan neighbours and friends. In one example, a Jewish doctor named Arthur Arndt approached his old gentile friend Max Gehre to ask for help. He had been unsure of what response he would get, but after tentatively asking whether his friend might be able to help him find somewhere to hide, he was relieved to hear the reply 'You will stay with us'. Gehre offered Dr Arndt and his wife and two teenage children his daughter's bedroom. It was the first step on an underground odyssey that would ultimately save all four of them and would involve at least fifty Berliners risking their own lives to help.[51]

For all their bravery and sacrifice, however, the number of those who actively helped Berlin Jews was rather small. The majority would have been ignorant of the true fate of the Jews who disappeared from their midst. Other factors served to inhibit Aryan acceptance of the truth of the Holocaust. The first was self-censorship. Given that Nazi Germany was a dictatorship, one was profoundly ill advised to ask searching questions regarding the fate of the deported Jews. Ordinary Berliners, even if they broadly supported the Nazis, would have known very well that that regime had teeth, and so tended to avoid behaviour that might bring them into conflict with the authorities. Self-censorship, therefore, and an element of political and social conditioning, played an important role for the civilian. Even those who heard the rumours of the Holocaust would instinctively have blocked them out, and turned a blind eye, so as not to compromise themselves or their loved ones. As one historian has pithily summarised, 'they knew enough to know that it was better not to know'.[52] Tellingly, in this regard, one Berliner recalled: 'My husband told me about [the killing of the Jews], but I wasn't allowed to tell anybody else. Had I done this, my husband would have been put up against the wall, I would have been sent to a concentration camp, and I would never have seen the children again. One had to keep quiet.'⁵³ Far from being cowardly, such reactions were all too human.

Anti-Semitism also played a vital role, and there were undoubtedly some Berliners who openly celebrated the removal of the Jews from the city. One such example occurred as a group of Jews was being assembled for deportation; 'Unfortunately', one German woman recalled, 'I must also report that many people stood in their doorways and in the face of this procession of misery, gave expression to their joy. "Look at the impudent Jews!" shouted one. "Now they are still laughing, but their final short hour has rung."'⁵⁴ In another instance, a young Jewish woman noted events at a transit camp for Berlin Jews in the northern district of Wedding, where 'a hateful crowd of people . . . had gathered in front of the building and were gloating over the misery that had befallen their fellow citizens – the Jews.'⁵⁵

Such reactions were primarily the result of the anti-Semitic climate in Nazi Germany, but in some cases were also stoked by greed. As has recently been argued, there was a peculiarly 'kleptocratic character'⁵⁶ to Nazi Germany, in which the public was encouraged to become complicit in the expropriation of the property of the Jews. Anything formerly belonging to them was minutely listed and inventoried and everything – from the building itself to the crockery and carpets – would pass to the state, where it would then be used to supply those who had been bombed out.

Dieter Borkowski witnessed the clearance of Jewish properties in the spring of 1943. The fourteen-year-old used occasionally to accompany his uncle on his driving jobs, but one day the pair were joined by a Nazi Party functionary, brandishing a list. As Dieter recalled, his normally talkative uncle was strangely quiet. They made their first stop at the corner of Bülowstrasse and Potsdamer Strasse in the district of Schöneberg. 'It was strange', he recalled:

> there was no one in the flat, no one to hand the furniture over to us, and the household items had not been packed into crates. The flat appeared as though the owners had just gone shopping and would be back soon. I thought it had to be a mistake, but the Party man had a list in his hand. He ordered that Uncle Alfred was to clear the flat. I was amazed when he took some large crystal vases and silver candlesticks for himself and put them in the van in a special crate. Some oil

paintings disappeared into there too. It was a magnificently furnished apartment, perhaps belonging to a lawyer or a doctor . . . Then we drove to the next flat, and to my astonishment it was the same as before. . . . Again no owner there to meet us, and it appeared as though the people there had got out of bed and had had to leave the flat in a tremendous hurry.[57]

Aside from those treasures squirrelled away by the Party functionary, most other items would pass to the regime and would, in due course, be used to the benefit of the Aryan victims of the war. It was a policy that Joseph Goebbels, as Gauleiter of Berlin, had made plain in 1942. Jewish property, he noted, was to be kept 'for the purpose of supplying [our] ethnic comrades who suffered damage in bombing raids and as a reserve supply against possible future damage'.[58]

Some of that Jewish property also went for auction. There, as one commentator put it, 'good Aryans fought like jackals over a carcass to buy shabby objects [that] the Russian war had made scarce'.[59] Notices in the newspapers would alert the public to upcoming sales. As the American Howard Smith recalled, such auctions could even be carried out in the abandoned homes themselves, and in one instance 'one could see on the table inside two tea-cups still half filled with brownish water. The two old women had been having a night-cap of ersatz tea when the Gestapo arrived, and were not given time to finish it.'[60] Those Berliners who participated in such auctions would clearly have been under few illusions that they were bidding for the property of Jewish deportees. Whether out of greed or necessity, they were being made complicit in a crime whose true extent they could barely have imagined.

In some instances, Jewish properties passed directly into the hands of Party members or SS men. In one example, a Jewish doctor was obliged to show a Nazi official around his family's apartment on the very day his mother and sister had been deported. The official, obviously pleased by what he saw, grew increasingly excited as they moved from room to room. Finally, he burst out: 'All my life I have always dreamt of furniture like this!'[61] With that, it became abundantly clear who the next inhabitant of the apartment was destined to be.

Yet, both those who helped Jews and those who revelled in their deportation constituted a minority of the Berlin population at large;

the vast majority of Berliners reacted towards the Jews in their midst
with indifference.[62] It seems that the barrage of anti-Semitic legislation
in Nazi Germany had so marginalised the Jews from German public
life that they were effectively erased from the consciousness – and
indeed the conscience – of most ordinary Germans. Their physical
destruction had been prefaced by a lingering social death.[63]

Many years after the demise of Hitler's Third Reich, a memorial book
for the Jews of Berlin was published. The *Gedenkbuch Berlins* drew on
the available documentary sources to list as many as possible of those
Jews deported from the German capital between 1941 and 1945, who
subsequently died at the hands of the Nazis and their accomplices.
Each entry begins with the victim's name in bold, followed by a date
and place of birth, a date and destination of 'evacuation' and finally
a date of death. The very first entry is that of Jutta Aal, born in
November 1860 in Bavaria and deported to Theresienstadt in the
autumn of 1942. Already eighty-one at the time of her deportation,
Jutta survived in the ghetto for barely two weeks.

From that entry, the victims proceed – around forty per page – for
nearly 1,400 pages. Entire extended families are listed; children alongside parents and grandparents, the great and the good alongside the
unremarkable and unexceptional. Some are listed simply as 'declared
dead' or as '*Schicksal ungeklärt*', 'fate unknown'. Most entries, however,
just state that the individual is '*verschollen*', 'missing'. There are 6 pages
of Abrahams, 11 pages of Hirsches, 12 pages of Levys and 13 pages of
Wolffs. The final entry is that of Leo Zyzman, who was just sixteen
when he was sent to Auschwitz in the autumn of 1942. The total
number of victims listed is 55,696.[64]

9

An Evil Cradling

Berlin's Anhalter Station was one of the most potent symbols of the German capital. Unlike the Brandenburg Gate, the Victory Column or the Reichstag, it spoke not of military victory, nationalist bombast or the grubby business of politics; rather, it was a symbol of civic pride, of German industrial prowess and of the astonishingly rapid social and economic developments of the nineteenth century.

When it first opened in 1841, it had been a rather modest affair, with a three-storey frontage, resembling a suburban mansion block, and a small platform area behind. As its trains passed through the district of Anhalt, to the south-west of the capital, it became known as the Anhalter Station. This modest terminus soon proved insufficient for the growing city's needs, and in the 1870s a radical rebuild was carried out. When it reopened in 1880, the Anhalter Station was the largest rail terminus in continental Europe. Its new façade, constructed in yellow Greppiner brick, was over 100 metres wide and embellished with Romanesque arches and elaborate terracotta detailing. Behind that impressive frontage was the enormous locomotive shed. Constructed in iron and glass, its curved roof measured over 60 metres in width and 171 metres in length. Beneath it, six platforms were laid out, which, it was claimed, could accommodate 40,000 passengers.[1]

The rebuilt Anhalter Station served rail traffic to the south, initially in the direction of Leipzig, Frankfurt and Munich, but by the early decades of the twentieth century it was also serving destinations as far afield as Athens, Rome and Naples. By the 1930s it was handling over 40,000 passengers a day, with trains leaving, on average, every four minutes. It soon became known as Berlin's 'Gateway to the World'.[2]

With the outbreak of war in 1939, the Anhalter Station retained its high profile. It was there that Stalin's Foreign Minister Vyacheslav Molotov arrived for talks in November 1940, when a Wehrmacht military band greeted him with an intentionally fast rendition of The Internationale. The Anhalter was also the station of choice for Hitler's train, a grand locomotive codenamed *Amerika*, and it was there that crowds would gather to welcome the Führer back to Berlin. Most famously, it was there that Hitler returned after the victorious French campaign in July 1940. The station's halls and platforms were adorned with swastika banners and celebratory laurel wreaths and crammed with people, ranging from the excited children of the Hitler Youth to high-ranking generals and ambitious Party functionaries.

As the war progressed, the Anhalter Station would not only be associated with flag waving and grand ceremonial, it would witness countless tearful farewells as soldiers left their loved ones to travel to the front. In time, some nine thousand Berlin Jews also passed through the station, en route to the camp at Theresienstadt in Bohemia. Above all, however, the Anhalter Station would become synonymous with the evacuation of children from the capital.

Though still minimal in their material effect, by late September 1940 the British air raids on Berlin were beginning to have a substantial social and political impact. On 26 September, in a week in which Berlin had been raided on four consecutive nights, Hitler had a meeting with Baldur von Schirach, the Reich Youth leader, at which he was persuaded of the possible benefits of an evacuation of the city's most vulnerable citizens. The following day, he instructed his Party secretary, Martin Bormann, to send a secret circular to all higher Party and state officials, ordering that 'young people who live in areas which are subject to repeated air raid alarms' were to be sent 'to other areas of the Reich'.[3] The programme was to be known as the *Kinderlandverschickung*, or – as so many titles were abbreviated in Nazi Germany – the KLV.

The KLV represented a recognition of the new realities that Germany faced in the winter of 1940–41. Up until that point, the Nazi regime had persistently downplayed the domestic effects of the war, in an attempt to perpetuate the fiction that it could be prosecuted without undue impact on German society. The RAF offensive now demonstrated that the war was entering a new phase and the harsh realities of this situation had to be acknowledged – if not in public, then at least among the leadership of the Party and the Reich.

The planning of the evacuation, therefore, contained two significant, yet silent, admissions. Firstly, it implied that the air raid defences of the capital and the other major urban centres were insufficient for the task of protecting the civilian population – a deficiency that was to be rectified in the coming months (see Chapter 15). Secondly, and more importantly, it acknowledged that Britain would not be easily defeated – and that the war was destined to last for some considerable time to come.

Yet though these realities might have been acknowledged at government and Party level, they could not be permitted to penetrate the public mind. Therefore the regime did its best to disguise the evacuation as a precautionary exercise: a measure voluntarily entered into rather than forced upon the German people by an adverse turn of events. To this end, Bormann stressed in his circular that public participation in the operation was to be voluntary. He also emphasised that 'by order of the Führer [. . .] there is to be no use of the word "evacuation", but rather the action was to be described as a "despatch to the countryside" of children from the big cities'.[4]

It had been common practice in Germany's urban centres, from the end of the nineteenth century, for the churches and the labour movement to send their youngest and poorest inhabitants to the countryside to recover from the stresses and strains of city life. Thus, when the evacuation was ordered in 1940, it was dressed up to draw on that beneficial tradition; while the word *Evakuierung* – 'evacuation' – was avoided, the clumsy compound *Kinderlandverschickung* – 'sending children to the countryside' – took its place.

The German people were not fooled, however. Within days of the secret circular, the capital was alive with speculation. As the SS mood report for 30 September noted:

In all of Berlin the most varied rumours are circulating about an evacuation of children. The reports say that the rumours are causing serious and growing disquiet among the population. From almost all districts, it is being reported that employees of the NSV [the Nazi welfare association] are going from house to house to discuss the evacuation with parents.[5]

The following day, Goebbels complained in his diary about the

> serious problems of evacuation of children from Berlin. The NSV has
> proceeded very clumsily in this area and has created enormous dis-
> content . . . Unfortunately, we cannot clear matters up through the
> press. But I hope things will work out, even so.[6]

For all his anger, on one issue at least Goebbels really could not
complain. The details circulated by the Berlin rumour mill were
absolutely correct.

According to the KLV plan drawn up by Bormann, all children below
the age of fourteen living in the threatened cities were to be eligible for
a six-month stay in the rural areas of the Reich, such as the Sudetenland,
Brandenburg, Saxony or Silesia. Those below the age of ten were to be
placed with families and could be accompanied by their mothers, while
those above that age would be housed in a wide variety of 'camps',
ranging from commandeered hotels or youth hostels to monasteries and
rural guest houses, all of which were to be run by the Hitler Youth.
Where possible, school classes were to be kept together and their teachers
were to travel with them, so that 'lessons can effectively be resumed in
the new locations'. In accordance with his role as the Reich Youth leader,
Baldur von Schirach was appointed to implement the evacuation, aided
and abetted by the NSV and the Nazi Teachers' League. It was to begin,
it was announced, on Thursday 3 October 1940.[7]

Initially, the plan was to be introduced in Hamburg and Berlin, both
considered to be the most at risk from air attack. Within days, the first
3,000 children from those two cities left for the countryside. By the end
of that first month, over 15,000 had left Berlin and a further 42,000 were
evacuated in November.[8] In early 1941, the industrial centres of western
Germany were incorporated into the KLV programme and the numbers
participating rose proportionately. In January 1941, over 70,000 German
children were sent to the KLV camps and by the following summer over
160,000 children were participating in the scheme.[9] Over the course of
the war, over five million German youngsters would follow in their
footsteps.[10]

In order to qualify, a child would have to undergo an interview and
a short medical examination. Epileptics and those suffering from infectious diseases were excluded; so, too, were chronic bed-wetters, Jews and

those deemed 'anti-social'. Once a child had been accepted, his or her parents would be required to sign and return a pro forma letter of consent.

Berlin schoolboy Heinz Knobloch was adamant that he would not be joining the KLV. He and his friends simply completed the consent letter themselves: 'We three were decided and we wrote the sentence out in the negative: "I am not agreed that my son should participate in the *Kinderlandverschickung*." After all, why should our mothers need to know anything about it?'[12] The ruse worked.

Most children were less inventive, however, and were duly enrolled, whereupon additional information would be received, giving guidelines to the parents and specifying the clothing and personal effects that the child was recommended to take with them:

Clothing
1 warm set of civilian clothes (girls 1 warm winter dress)
1 winter coat (or an additional raincoat or cape)
1 head covering (hat, cap etc)
2 pairs of shoes or boots
at least 3 pairs of socks
1 pullover or woollen jacket
1 pair of gloves
2 or 3 sets of underclothes
2 nightshirts or pyjamas
Sufficient handkerchiefs
Sport kit (gymnastics shirt and shorts)
Tracksuit (if available), swimming trunks or costume
1 pair gym shoes

Wash kit
2 face flannels, soap, toothbrush and toothpaste, comb and brush, nail-
    cleaning kit, clothes brush, shoe-cleaning kit and shoelaces
Sewing kit
Writing equipment
Cutlery
Schoolbooks
(according to the instructions of the teacher)[11]

To help persuade the recalcitrant, the regime mounted a propaganda offensive. In 1941 a documentary about the KLV called *Ausser Gefahr*

('Out of Danger'), was shown along with the newsreels. The following year the feature film *Hände Hoch* ('Hands Up') told the saccharine story of children discovering themselves during the evacuation. Across Germany, meanwhile, posters were displayed featuring happy children waving from train windows, with the chirpy slogan *Kommt mit in die Kinderlandverschickung* – 'Come with us on the evacuation'.[13]

The reality was often rather different. For the vast majority of children, it was a journey into the unknown, and for the younger ones it could be a source of genuine fear and confusion. The parents, too, were often little better prepared. Though they felt they had a duty to be stoical and upbeat, many were worried about being separated from their children in such dangerous times.

Such concerns notwithstanding, participating children were instructed to board one of the special trains departing from the capital's main stations – such as the Anhalter – for the provinces. There they would gather on the platforms, weighed down with luggage and with a brown card label around their necks, giving their name, the date of their departure and their destination. Behind them, their anxious parents looked on. Ten-year-old Jost Hermand, who was evacuated from the capital to Posen late in 1940, recalled the maelstrom of emotions:

> I see myself . . . leaning out of the train compartment window with other boys; with my right hand I wave to my mother, who is standing below on the railway platform, fighting to keep back the tears . . . the bewildered ten-year-old and his seemingly calm and collected mother, trying not to show her heartache and smiling bravely so that her child won't know she is grieving as he starts out on his journey.[14]

There was little logic applied in the selection of destinations for Berlin's schoolchildren, and the schools themselves certainly did not have any influence on the choices made. Thus, though classes were generally kept together, siblings in different years of the same school could be sent to opposite ends of the country. If one takes the example of the Berlin suburb of Steglitz, the geographical spread of its evacuated children is astonishing. In 1940, many school classes from Steglitz were sent to Carinthia in Austria, although Silesia, Thuringia and occupied Poland were also used. In the following years, East Prussia, Bohemia, Pomerania

and the Sudetenland were all added to the list.[15] Berlin's children could
be sent almost anywhere within the Greater German Reich.

Aside from the logistical challenge, there were other difficulties.
There was often a dramatic difference between the standard of living
in the capital and that in the often primitive hinterlands of Pomerania
or rural Silesia. Gisela Richter recalled her stay in East Prussia:

> the accommodation was extremely primitive, consisting mainly of tied
> cottages and the like . . . Mother was given one of these tiny places,
> without power or running water, and with an outside toilet. Drinking
> water had to be fetched with a bucket from a small hole in the ground,
> which was covered with wire mesh. When I was confronted with it
> one time, it turned my stomach. In my bucket of water, there were
> leaves, spiders and beetles![16]

Younger evacuees often faced rather different circumstances from the
older children. They tended to be quartered individually with a host
family, and so were entirely dependent on their hosts' whim and goodwill. And that goodwill was sometimes a rare commodity. Regional
tensions within Germany could be quick to manifest themselves.
Berliners were often viewed askance in the south of Germany and in
Austria, and would routinely be derided as 'Prussians'. Mothers accompanying small children to the countryside might also be mockingly called
Bombenweiber, or 'bomb wenches'.[17] Those Berliners travelling to rural
East Prussia, meanwhile, were often seen as unwelcome reminders of
a war that had until then barely touched that remote part of the country.
Everywhere, it seems, 'greedy' Berlin children were seen as a burden.[18]

There were also social tensions and jealousies inherent in settling
city children in comparatively primitive rural areas. As one evacuee
recalled of his village school: 'As a Berliner and someone from the
Reich capital, I was a novelty in the village; someone who was asked
a lot of questions and who was keenly listened to. And, as the girls
were interested in me too, I earned myself the enmity of the local
farmers' boys . . . In time, I was no longer able to escape a beating.'[19]

There was moreover a financial aspect to complicate matters. From
1941, hosts were offered compensation for housing an evacuee, which
amounted to about 3 Reichsmarks per child per day.[20] Many host families,
therefore, joined the scheme, not out of altruism but out of a simple

desire for cheap labour. Berliner Gerhard Ritter found himself billeted with an aged tobacco farmer in East Prussia, whom he had to help, not only with the harvest, but also with the sorting and bundling of the crop. Away from the arduous work in the fields, the highlight of his stay was to help in the local pub, while the farmer himself played cards in a back room. 'I drew beer, poured schnapps, cleaned the glasses, selected cigarettes and waited at tables', he recalled, 'the landlord was pleased that I understood how to fill the glasses to his advantage, but without risking complaints from the clientele.'[21] Gerhard was nine years old.

Though the hosting arrangement for the under tens worked tolerably well in many cases, it was also open to abuse. Many children were actively maltreated, housed in abominable conditions or simply left to their own devices. It was not unusual, therefore, for children to be moved – often many times – until their parents were satisfied with the quality of accommodation and care. Dorit Erkner, for instance, was moved seven times in eighteen months, being shunted through a succession of schools and host families, from East Prussia to rural Thuringia.[22]

For the older children at the regular KLV camps, conditions were generally better. In all, there were up to 9,000 KLV camps, ranging from large-scale sites, which could accommodate over 1,000 evacuees, to smaller locations suitable for barely a few dozen children. Geographically, they ranged right across Greater Germany – from Aalen in Württemberg to Zwönitz in the Erzgebirge – and even extended to foreign parts, such as Slovakia, Hungary and occupied Poland.[23]

Conditions for the evacuees varied enormously. The camp buildings themselves could be former monasteries or country houses, luxury hotels, youth hostels or children's homes. Some of the larger camps – those based in requisitioned hotels, for instance – could offer smaller rooms and all modern conveniences. Many others, especially in occupied Poland, could barely muster running water and heating.

In many cases, the arrival of the first batch of evacuees was the most critical time. Especially at the outset, much of the organisation of the KLV programme was improvised, and some of the locations were ill prepared for the immediate accommodation of dozens of children, with the result that the first arrivals were sometimes obliged to sleep on loose straw while their dormitories were being finished off. Others were better prepared. Gisela Stange recalled that upon her arrival at the village of Strobl near Salzburg, her class was greeted by local children with sledges to carry the baggage. When they then reached their destination – a local guest house that had been commandeered for her class of forty children – they were met with plates of warm jam dumplings and custard.[24]

Perhaps the primary challenge facing the evacuees were the pangs of homesickness. Gisela Stange remembered:

> the greatest malady [. . .] was the wretched homesickness, which affected almost all children. Only occasionally was there someone there who had already been away from home for any length of time. We missed home, and especially our mothers and fathers, very much, and some evenings we cried ourselves to sleep.[25]

Renate Bandur wrote to her mother in 1941 from East Prussia: 'Now I have found the bar of chocolate and I felt so homesick that I cried and cried and I can't stop. Please write me a really long letter, which never stops . . .'[26] There were other fears. 'One was always so worried when one heard about the air raid alarms in Berlin', recalled Dorit Erkner. 'When one girl in the dormitory of thirty started crying, then it quickly spread to all of us.'[27]

Such emotions were often assuaged by the evacuees' need to swiftly acquaint themselves with their new routine in the camp. A typical day in a KLV camp was strictly regimented. Reveille was sounded at 6.30 a.m. and was followed by an hour set aside for washing, making beds, tidying and roll call. At 8.00 a.m. all children in the camp had to participate in the flag ceremony, the *Fahnenappel*, when the camp leader would give the children their slogan for the day, usually something snappy and suitably National Socialist, the significance of which would be explained in a few sentences. The children would then be called to attention for the raising of the flag, and would sing perhaps the '*Deutschland Lied*', the '*Horst Wessel Lied*', or the Hitler Youth anthem – the '*Fahnenlied*' – a jaunty ditty composed by Baldur von Schirach himself:

Uns're Fahne flattert uns voran	Our banner flutters before us
Uns're Fahne ist die neue Zeit	Our banner represents the new era
Und die Fahne führt uns in die Ewigkeit	And our banner leads us to eternity
Ja, die Fahne ist mehr als der Tod.	Yes, our banner means more to us than death.

The flag ceremony was a vital part of the day. As the official instructions ran, it was to be 'short, terse and profound, so as not to become a daily burden to the children'. When poor weather prevented the ceremony, it was to be held inside.[28]

After breakfast, classes were given by teachers or representatives of the Hitler Youth from 8.45 a.m. until 1.00 p.m. Following lunch and a short rest period, the afternoon session began at 3.00 p.m. and was given over predominantly to sport, games and singing, with a number of periods set aside each week for homework, laundry, shoe repairs and sewing. After supper at 7.00, an evening session offered more of the same, including a weekly lesson on current affairs and the so-called 'political report'. Weekends were less minutely structured and tended to contain more communal and local activities as well as a weekly 'camp evening', which generally consisted of stories and singing around a campfire. Lights out was at 9.00 p.m.[29]

Even a cursory glance at such a routine demonstrates that conventional education was not especially high on the agenda. Indeed, the official instruction booklet given to all KLV camps devoted fully ten pages to the subject of physical exercise, yet was curiously silent on education, stating vaguely that 'classes are to be carried out according to the teaching plans of the evacuated schools'.[30] In some instances, the teachers went to great lengths to ensure that the children were stimulated and engaged. Yet, in many cases, education came a very poor second to virtually all other subjects. As Gerhard Ritter recalled:

Our teacher's lesson consisted of him dictating, for one subject after another, all sorts of homework for us to do. Then he disappeared. We remained in class for an hour, then marched back to the camp. The afternoons we spent in the yard, sitting on the ground, singing songs or discussing matters. The next morning, we arrived punctually in the classroom. When the teacher arrived, there was absolute silence. He demanded to see our homework. Then, he would become enraged as he realised that no one had anything to show him, in any subject.[31]

Crucially, though the educational responsibilities were theoretically divided between the teachers and the representatives of the Hitler Youth, in practice only the latter held any real power. Any conflict between the two, therefore, would invariably result in a victory for the Hitler

Youth – after all, only they had access to the higher echelons of the Party machine – and led inexorably to a further dilution of any genuine pedagogical content in the daily timetable. In addition, shortfalls in teaching staff were routinely made up by drafting in older students from the Nazi ideological schools, the Napolas, who were sent on three-month tours of duty to the KLV camps, prior to their military service, to organise parades, sports events and entertainment.[32] To a large extent, therefore, the schoolwork component of the timetable was systematically reduced and sacrificed to the paramilitary drill regimen of the Hitler Youth and the Nazi Party.[33] In some cases, education as such was quietly abandoned altogether.

There were, of course, other activities. Writing letters home was encouraged, as was tidying, cleaning and sewing. Much of the timetable was given over to sport, especially boxing and the game of *Völkerball*, a variant of dodgeball, which was very popular during the Third Reich. Yet, in all their activities, KLV children were subjected to an almost militaristic regime, more akin to a boot camp than a school. As one young evacuee enthused in a letter to his parents:

> Yesterday we had a field exercise. We went to Heinzelshof and from there marched into the nearby wood. One group had to defend a flag, which was located on the other side of the river. The defenders stood on a bridge. We attacked in two groups. The first group was to provide a diversion. Then the second group was to attack. The first attack failed. Then the second attempt began. Of course, it was chaotic. Some of them were bleeding, one was half-unconscious. The battle was a draw. How did you spend Easter?[34]

In the KLV camps even everyday matters were infused with a martial spirit. Gerhard Ritter remembered: 'At roll call, extreme military-style tidiness and cleanliness was demanded. Mattresses and blankets had to be smoothed completely flat, and the bed had to be "squarely" made. The clothes in the locker had to be folded and stacked. Not a speck of dust was to be seen.'[35]

Discipline, too, was rigorously enforced. And, though corporal punishment was forbidden, other more imaginative activities were devised for those who dared to transgress. In one instance, an entire dormitory of boys was hauled out of bed and forced to stand to attention in the courtyard in their nightclothes. They were informed that one of their number had evidently urinated in a stairwell, and that they would stand there until the culprit made himself known. 'For hours on end, we stood there, by the flag pole in the freezing cold', remembered Erich Neumann; 'nobody owned up.'[36]

In some ways, Erich might have considered himself fortunate. Gerhard Ritter well remembered the military character of the collective punishments that were meted out to the boys in his camp:

> Punishment exercises were as aggressive and bloody-minded as in the German military . . . Up, up, march, march! Lie down! Up! Down! Crawl! Hop! Form into a column! Repeated hour after hour, regardless of the weather or the conditions. The earth was frozen so solid that one's knees were battered black and blue. Or in the thaw, we had to throw ourselves down in the mud and the puddles. And, at the next roll-call, we had to present ourselves and our muddied clothes, once again, in perfect order.[37]

The political indoctrination could be more subtle, but was nonetheless effective. Numerous everyday activities – from singing around the campfire to organised model building – were laden with political significance, or at the very least intended to strengthen the team spirit and collective identity of the children. As Jost Hermand recollected, 'We participated in rituals such as hoisting the flag, marching drills and roll-calls, calculated to serve the same goals, and intended to wean us from all unboyish, "weak" activities and to engender in us a sense of the grand task that awaited us.'[38]

In some instances, the indoctrination process was made rather more explicit. Erich Neumann recalled that the area surrounding his camp in Lobsens, near Posen, was considered 'enemy territory', because of its predominantly Polish population. It was treated accordingly:

> Breaking open the local tombs and playing football with the bones was supposed to distance us, and harden us towards the 'subhumans' who were living there. Woe betide those who did anything to a German boy, or to those Poles who dared to stand up for themselves and gave one of us a black eye. Then the authorities would avert their gaze, and we would run amok. It got so bad that the Hitler Youth boys would only ever go out in large groups.[39]

The experiences of some evacuees were even darker. Dietrich Schwalbe had been sent from Berlin to a KLV camp outside Łódż in occupied Poland, from where his class would take regular trips not only into the surrounding countryside to witness the squalor in which many Polish peasant families lived,[40] but also into the city, to pass through the Jewish ghetto. Dietrich recalled the scene:

> The tram had to stop in front of the entrance, so that the gate could be opened. Beyond, there was a long fence on both sides of the track . . . The tram was not permitted to stop and had to proceed at a fairly fast pace to prevent people mounting or dismounting the carriage. In the ghetto, one saw children and many older people, mostly wearing black and occasionally pushing two-wheeled handcarts. It all looked pretty grim.[41]

It is highly unlikely that there was anything accidental about the choice of such destinations. It is reasonable to suggest that those KLV camps that were located in the 'hostile' areas of occupied Poland or Bohemia were intended to act not only as the vanguard of German colonial settlement, but also as nurseries of ethnic hatred and bigotry.[42]

Such indoctrination was no random happenstance. The KLV was viewed by the Nazis as a grand socio-political experiment: an opportunity to free German youth from the shackles of their families and forge them into model Aryans. Though the Nazis publicly trumpeted family life as the ideal, many senior ideologists were profoundly suspicious of the old-fashioned, bourgeois beliefs and values – such as Christianity, tolerance and old-style morality – that still prevailed in the German *Volk*. What better way of neutralising those undesirable influences than to effectively remove a generation of German children from the bosom of their families and have them raised in an environment that could be better shaped to suit the 'new' values of the Nazi Party?

Far from being an afterthought, this revolutionary aspect was advocated by the regime from the very start of the evacuation programme. In Hitler's first discussions of the KLV plan, it was stipulated that the measure was to be accompanied by the dismissal of as much as 50 per cent of German school-teaching staff.[43] Thus, at a stroke, both parents and teachers were effectively to be sidelined from the raising of German children.

As a result, many parents felt disquiet about the KLV programme. When in the summer of 1943 the *Sicherheitsdienst* of the SS launched an investigation to try to establish why only around 15 per cent of Berlin's eligible children were placed in KLV camps, the conclusions were clear. Aside from the understandable desire to keep their children close to them, parents were concerned by rumours of poor treatment of the children, who were often placed in 'hostile' environments, and fears that medical care would be insufficient in the event of illness or injury. Parents of girls, meanwhile, feared for the honour of their daughters. The report presciently concluded that 'no trust' was expressed in the Hitler Youth, and suggested that it would be advisable to allow the schools to have more involvement in the KLV.[44]

This lack of trust was not aided by the fact that letters home could be censored, a fact that many parents only appreciated when they received letters from their children with blacked-out sections. One particularly punctilious camp leader even wrote to the parents of the children in her charge to try to explain the policy:

> As you know, the children's letters are subject to inspection. Do not see any malicious intent in this, it is not an attempt to interfere in the trusting relationship between parent and child. It should also not be regarded, as one father has claimed in a complaint to the camp leadership, as a consequence of raising our children in a culture of secrecy. Rather we want to achieve the opposite. What is in the letters is, for us, an official secret. We want to be open with the children. For this reason, I said to the girls on the first day, that rumours and snap judgements about the camp must cease, as such material could be exploited by enemy propaganda.
>
> . . .
>
> So, please do not see my instruction to have outgoing post submitted unsealed, as a form of censorship, but rather view it in an attitude appropriate to the times and the conditions of war.[45]

Parents were not initially permitted to visit their children in the KLV camps. As the information leaflet explained: 'in view of the transport difficulties resulting from the war, a visit by parents to the place of accommodation cannot take place'.[46] Yet, parental contact could not be excluded entirely, and, though it was strongly discouraged, parents were eventually given the right to assuage their fears by inspecting the camps themselves.

Kurt Radener's father chose to visit his son's camp in Elgersburg in Thuringia, in February 1941, where young Kurt had already spent over two months. He stayed for a number of days, inspecting everything he could and spending as much time with his son as possible. He reported back in a letter to his wife that the accommodation – a large guest house – was adequate, though 'awfully' cold, with the temperature in his own room barely reaching 4°C. Sixteen boys – all of Kurt's school class from Tempelhof – were living there in small rooms under the eaves. Kurt's room was simply furnished, with a dresser, a dusty old wardrobe and a bed with grey covers. In the corner was a heating duct, which gave off precious little warmth as the boilers were only fired in the evenings. The children spent their mornings in classes, and in the afternoons they were kept busy with 'Hitler Youth service' and other activities. Kurt, his father noted, spent his free time doing his homework or model-making. The food he found 'modest' but 'palatable', with lentil soup, roast mutton and goulash on the menu during his visit. He concluded, on a most positive note:

> My dear Klärchen
>   You really need not be upset about little Kurt. He is cheerful, chirpy, has young, warm blood and really doesn't understand your concerns. . . . He smiles and is happy. He doesn't look bad, though his face is thin, but he is healthy and has not yet been il. . . .
>   The advantage of the evacuation lies in the comradely contact to one another and the orderly discharge of one's responsibilities. In this regard, I am very pleased with the whole operation. And would therefore like for him to remain in the KLV camp.[47]

It is unlikely that young Kurt was terribly impressed by his father's arrival. Often, such visits could be the trigger for bullying, with the victim immediately, and sometimes indelibly, labelled a mummy's boy or a weakling. Jost Hermand was initially delighted to see his mother, who turned up at his camp in occupied Poland in the spring of 1941. His joy did not last long:

This invasion of our KLV world was very embarrassing for me because it was immediately interpreted by the other boys as a sign of my dependency and weakness. As a result, I fell back at least two rungs on the ladder . . . After a few days, I managed to persuade her to leave so that the other boys would stop making fun of me.[48]

Bullying was endemic in the KLV camps. As Jost Hermand remembered, his dormitory had a firmly established pecking order, which was maintained by brute force. Whatever the teachers knew of this, he is certain that they would have done little to combat it. 'As fascist educators', he recalled, they were 'committed to the principles of "toughening-up" and the selection of the fittest.'[49] Sex, too, appears to have played a role in the maintenance of the hierarchy in the dormitory. Jost Hermand recalled that: 'everybody knew exactly . . . which one of the boys he had to satisfy manually at night and who had to satisfy him'.[50]

In most instances, sexual activity took on a more benign aspect. As one KLV veteran put it, the camp was where he 'made [him]self acquainted with onanism'.[51] Yet, beyond the confines of the dormitory, the evacuation also served to facilitate what for many was the first unsupervised contact with the opposite sex. For some, this sexual awakening was the primary memory of their KLV experience, but it was often not seen in a positive light. Jost Hermand was damning:

> Without any mental or cultural stimulation, without the mediation of a social identity, without instruction in the biological function of the pleasurable physical sensations, we were allowed to regress into a primitive physicality [in which] we were increasingly preoccupied with our bodies: *Völkerball*, field exercises, washing, and the constant manipulation of our genitalia . . .
>
> When we arrived at Lichtenberg station on 10 August, we were not the same boys who – confused and curious – had left for the unknown east nine months earlier. Some of the boys, especially those from the 'good' upper-middle-class families, were belatedly ashamed of the lasciviousness unleashed in the camp, and they resolved from now on to live more ascetic lives. Even the tougher boys had some guilt feelings.[52]

Yet, for many – perhaps the majority – the KLV was, on balance, a positive experience, a healthy blast of independence, adventure and self-reliance. For Werner Lenz, who had grown up in a working-class family in the inner-city district of Friedrichshain, it presented a tremendous opportunity to take part in activities – skiing, hiking and hill walking – that were previously unknown to him.[53] Gerhard Ritter, too, viewed the experience very positively. 'Only a decade or so later', he recalled, 'did I comprehend all the things that the KLV had given me and had taught me: the power of a sense of community, toughening up, self-confidence, one's physical capabilities, stamina, an understanding of one's fellow man and a love of nature.'[54]

For many of that generation, taking part in the KLV would not be the only period that they would spend away from home. Many of them would subsequently be sent on a number of other 'actions' – voluntary and involuntary – ranging from helping with the harvest in the countryside, to performing the year of *Reichsarbeitsdienst*, or 'Reich Labour Service'. For many Berliners, the war was thus passed in a succession of 'camps', as they shifted from one 'action', or 'service', to the next, and were shunted around the German countryside. Werner Lenz, who was twelve in 1939, spent much of the war away from his Berlin home. After an initial stay in a KLV camp near Trautenau in Bohemia in the winter of 1941–2, he was subsequently sent on a number of extended harvest 'actions' in Pomerania and Silesia, before finally serving his period of *Arbeitsdienst* in rural Mecklenburg. In all, he was away from the capital for some two and a half years of the war.[55]

All of this can be interpreted as part and parcel of the totalitarian system and an example of the mobilisation of every sector of society, in which the Nazi regime specialised. It is also easy to see how such programmes fitted neatly with the regime's ideological goals. By removing young people from their parents and homes for long periods of time, such programmes served increasingly as exercises in mass indoctrination. It was this aspect that was responsible for the falling popularity of the KLV programme, despite the increasing threat of air attack. After reaching a peak in that first wave in 1940–41, participation in the capital dropped off rapidly, falling to around 50,000 in November 1941 and remaining at this level for most of the next year. In 1943 a renewed impetus was given to the programme by the escalation in the air war and the resultant decision to close the capital's schools and carry out a partial evacuation. In sharp contrast to many other urban areas of the Reich, Berlin remained stubbornly resistant to the KLV programme. Of the 260,000 eligible children in the German capital, only 40,000 participated; most others were evacuated privately to family or friends in rural districts, and around 80,000 children remained in the city. [56] Even at a time when the German capital was receiving its most serious air raids, therefore, a majority of Berliners continued to shun the state-sponsored evacuation, preferring to make their own arrangements. However successful it might have been as an experiment in mass indoctrination, the KLV had clearly failed as an air defence measure. As one of those who experienced it concluded, it was 'a farce'. [57]

Few of those Berlin children and youths who left the Anhalter Station would return the same boys and girls. For all of them, the KLV evacuation would be one of the most formative experiences of their young lives.

Just as those young passengers had undergone tremendous changes, so too had the city to which they were returning. Christa Becker had spent most of 1941 with her family in rural Pomerania, and upon her return to the capital that autumn it didn't take long for her and her family to notice the impact of the air raids:

'Zorn's Ice Cream Parlor is gone', that was the first thing Peter noticed when we were above ground. In the opposite direction the chimney with the toilet still stood amidst the rubble at Germania Palast. 'Oh my God,' Tante Lenchen and my mother cried out like on cue, 'Leiser's Shoe Store is gone and Bleile Textilien, oh God, oh God.' [. . .] They looked up steep climbing Samariter Strasse to see what else was missing. People went about their business as if nothing had happened. It was September 1941. We had been gone eight months, but it seemed much longer. [58]

The German capital had become, as one returning KLV evacuee recalled, a 'horror city'. [59]

The Anhalter Station, too, was showing signs of considerable damage; the glass arc of its roof was already disfigured with holes from incendiaries and its elegant frontage was sandbagged. In late November 1943, it was so seriously damaged that only local traffic could use the station, and all long-distance trains were redirected to the Silesian Station, or to

Potsdam.[60] After subsequent air attacks, large sections of the roof collapsed, or had to be dismantled. From the autumn of 1944 onwards, rail traffic began to fall away altogether, hampered not only by such structural concerns, but also by wider systemic factors, such as logistical difficulties and the availability of rolling stock.

Where it once proclaimed the grandeur, opulence and confidence of the city that it served, the Anhalter Station was now symbolic of the destruction and dislocation that had become commonplace in Hitler's capital. Passengers on its platforms now found themselves waiting in the open air, the once vast structure above them reduced to a few rickety spans of rusting metal and fractured glass. Christabel Bielenberg passed through the station in the winter of 1944. It was a sobering experience:

> propaganda posters hung unnoticed in red and black tatters from the shrapnel-pitted walls . . . Every day the windowless trains trundled in and out in the few hours left for living between the American mass daylight raids and the sporadic British night attacks; they carried a rudderless crowd of soldiers, civilians, refugees and evacuees along diverse routes to uncertain destinations.[61]

The fate of the Anhalter Station was finally sealed in February 1945, when a daylight raid by the US Air Force wrought havoc in the heart of the city. The Anhalter's platforms were so pitted with craters, and its iron girders so buckled by the heat of countless incendiaries, that the station was considered to be beyond repair and rail traffic was finally suspended. Its cavernous remains would later be demolished, leaving only a small, jagged section of its once elaborate frontage to mark the building through which so many Berliners had travelled to distant parts.

10

The People's Friend

Nazism was in many ways a very modern creed. In the political sphere, the Nazis appeared to offer the country a new alternative; a bright future, far removed from the old, moribund regime that had preceded them. But their embrace of the modern was also evident elsewhere. The building of the motorways in the 1930s, for instance, was an exercise in deficit financing and Keynesian economics, but it was just as much an attempt to harness an emerging technology: the motor car.

Though an impassioned hater of much of the artistic avant-garde, Hitler was keen to embrace some aspects of modernity. During the election campaigns prior to 1933 he had travelled the length and breadth of the country by plane. This radical approach not only served to associate Hitler in the public mind with all the glamour and novel appeal of air travel, it also had the practical benefit that he could reach a large proportion of his electorate, in three or four speaking engagements each day.

The aspect of Nazi Germany that is associated most closely with the 'modern' is its use of radio. From its infancy in the early 1920s, when the first radio stations emerged to utilise the new technology, radio spread swiftly and gained in popularity throughout the world. But its growth – and political exploitation – in Germany was perhaps the most spectacular of all.

The early development of radio in Germany was synonymous with the town of Königs Wusterhausen, barely twenty miles from the heart of Berlin. There, a primitive radio transmitter was established by the German military during the First World War, which was later adapted for civilian use. Its first transmission – a Christmas concert – was broadcast on 22 December 1920 from a makeshift studio and, strangely, the German public was forbidden to tune in.

From this rather inauspicious beginning, the site at Königs Wusterhausen, known as the *Funkerberg*, expanded swiftly. Within a few years, it boasted a main broadcast tower of 243 metres, as well as twelve smaller masts. At its heart were three buildings containing studios, technical installations and an enormous, purpose-built diesel generator, whose 660-litre capacity produced over 1,000 horsepower. With the addition of a new site at nearby Zeesen in 1927, the complex became one of the most advanced radio broadcast facilities in the world.

From here, the *Deutschlandsender* transmitted on long wave all over Germany. In addition, there were regional stations established across the country – from Königsberg to Stuttgart, and Hamburg to Munich – which not only relayed the signal of the *Deutschlandsender*, but also broadcast material with a more local focus. For those living in Berlin, the local station was *Funk-Stunde Berlin*, broadcasting from the 'Vox-Haus' in the Tiergarten.

In its early phase, German radio was avowedly apolitical, with political content being expressly banned. By the late 1920s, political content began to emerge, especially under Brüning's chancellorship from 1930 to 1932. Under his successor, Franz von Papen, this trend accelerated, and radio became virtually the mouthpiece of the state. The only problem was that few Germans seemed to be listening.

The politicisation of radio would reach its apogee after Hitler's rise to power. While they certainly did not invent the technology, the Nazis could well be said to have perfected the use of radio as a political medium. Under the expert guidance of Joseph Goebbels, they would become the greatest exploiters of the political potential of the airwaves. This was achieved not only through the simple application of propaganda, but also by using the immediacy and involvement offered by radio: taking advantage of its unique ability both to penetrate the home and to make the listener feel a part of the programme. In 1933, shortly after the Nazis came to power, Goebbels described radio as 'the eighth Great Power' and 'the most influential and important intermediary' between the Nazi movement and the German people. Hitler's revolution, he said, 'would have been impossible' without radio.[1]

In the years that followed, radio was transformed from a medium that catered largely for a minority audience to an all-embracing method of mass communication. It became the regime's primary tool in transmitting its message to the people, while the people in turn utilised it as their primary source of entertainment and information. The expansion of radio listenership – in line with the maxim 'radio must reach all or it will reach none'[2] – was to be achieved in a number of ways.

The first step was to equip the populace with receivers. Technological advances and improvements in infrastructure meant that reception coverage in Germany was progressively increased throughout the 1930s. But the real advance was achieved through the marketing of affordable receivers, which brought the dream of a radio in every home nearer to reality. Early in 1933, the Nazis decided to subsidise the production of a radio set aimed specifically at those Germans who had not traditionally been able to afford what was still considered a luxury item. The result was the *Volksempfänger*, or 'People's Receiver'. A simple, three-valve, two-band receiver in a Bakelite cabinet, the *Volksempfänger* sold for 'just' 76 Marks, around half the price of the traditional radio set, and roughly equivalent to two weeks' wages for the average German worker.

A roaring success, more than seven million of these simple radios were sold in the following six years. Their connection to the regime was unmistakeable: even the radio's model number – VE 301 – was a reference to the date of Hitler's seizure of power on 30 January. A popular poster of the time showed the radio set superimposed over a crowd scene, with the legend 'All Germany hears the Führer via the *Volksempfänger*'. Another popular image was that of radio-listening as a family occasion, showing a typical German family – father reading the newspaper, mother knitting, children smiling happily – all grouped around a radio set.

In 1938, the *Deutscher Klein Empfänger* ('German Small Receiver'), or DKE, was produced. About two-thirds the size of a *Volksempfänger*, with only two valves and a low-powered receiver, it was marketed for only 35 Marks. It was the cheapest radio set then available anywhere in the world. Fairly crude and primitive, the DKE was nonetheless adequate for receiving strong local signals. Its vital role in the government's ongoing propaganda campaign was acknowledged by its popular nickname, the *Goebbels Schnauze* – 'Goebbels' gob'.

The propaganda aspect of radio was of crucial importance to the Nazis. Indeed, Hitler made a point of speaking live on radio only two days after his appointment as Chancellor in 1933. Thereafter, German

radio schedules were studded with speeches and announcements by
Hitler as well as other Nazi grandees.

Goebbels was well aware of the public's limited appetite for propaganda, however, and ordered that more diverse programming should
be provided. Thus German radio schedules contained both popular
and classical music, sport, poetry recitals and cultural discussions; the
proportion of music transmissions rose from 57 per cent in 1933 to
over 70 per cent in 1938.[3] Goebbels' greatest fear, it seems, was that
the schedules would be so stuffed with propaganda that the German
people would switch off in their droves. He was right to be concerned.
Throughout the war, complaints were rife in the capital about the
content aired on German radio, some decrying the exaggerated propaganda slogans, others demanding more light music.[4] The listening
public of Berlin, it seems, was a difficult audience to please.

More popular, it seems, were the transmission of the Olympic
Games, which were held in Berlin in 1936. The event proved to be a
boon to German radio. A new transmitter was installed at Zeesen to
cope with the expected surge in demand, and a new type of radio
was marketed for the occasion. A portable receiver, running on
batteries, the *Olympiakoffer* – or 'Olympic case' – was larger than the
other popular radios and was rather expensive at 160 Marks, but
nonetheless enabled the listener to tune in out in the open air. The
Olympic Games was a seminal moment in the development of radio;
a moment when many, especially the apolitical and those in rural
areas, were first made aware of the enormous potential of the medium.
Berliner Ernst Schmidt, for instance, who was fifteen in 1936, recalled
that listening to the Games on a neighbour's set was the first time he
had heard radio at all. Soon after, his family bought a set of their
own.[5] They were certainly not alone.

In addition to promoting radio ownership through technological
advances, innovative programming and competitive pricing, the Nazi
regime also encouraged communal listening. To this end, political
broadcasts were often arranged during working hours, and many
factories and offices were obliged to suspend work to allow the workforce to listen in. Similarly, restaurants and cafés were equipped
with radios and loudspeaker pillars were erected in the streets of the
big cities. In this way, German radio probably achieved the largest
listenership in the world.

THE PEOPLE'S FRIEND

Radio ownership expanded rapidly during the Third Reich, tripling from around 4.5 million in 1933 to 12 million in 1939, and then rising to 16 million in 1942.[6] Already by 1939 every second German household boasted a radio set and audience figures, boosted by communal listening, increased almost exponentially.[7] When war was declared in 1939, the vast majority of Germans would have heard the news on the radio.

With the outbreak of war, there was a palpable step change on German radio. For one thing, the Nazi regime used the radio as the primary mouthpiece for the promulgation of its new restrictions and instructions. Hitler, too, was ever present, with both his Reichstag speech of 1 September and the announcement of the Anglo-French declaration of war two days later relayed live and replayed almost continuously, interrupted only by blasts of martial music.

Another innovation was the daily situation report from the High Command, which was transmitted every day following the midday news. Prefaced by an impressive fanfare lifted from one of Liszt's 'Preludes', the broadcast opened with the stock phrase 'Das Oberkommando der Wehrmacht gibt bekannt . . .', 'the Army High Command announces . . .', before launching into an exhaustive overview of military operations, successes, and – in time – 'strategic withdrawals'.

The report of the first day of the war could barely hide the Wehrmacht's glee. 'On all fronts', it crowed,

the expected successes have been scored. Troops advancing from the south, over the mountains, have reached the line of Neumarkt-Sucha. South of Mährisch-Ostrau, the [River] Olsa has been crossed at Teschen. South of the industrial district, our troops are advancing rapidly on Kattowitz. Those forces advancing from Silesia are moving swiftly northwards in the direction of Tschenstochau.

In the [Polish] Corridor, our troops are approaching the [river] Brahe and have reached the [River] Netze at Nakel. There is fighting close to Graudenz.

Forces advancing from East Prussia are in combat deep in Polish territory.[8]

It is easy to see why it quickly became fashionable for schoolchildren to plot the German advance on a large map. Each day, the Wehrmacht's radio report would bring a new list of obscure towns, rivers and geographical features that were excitedly marked with a pin or flag.

For all the excitement, however, there was an altogether darker aspect in evidence. As of the night of 1 September 1939, listening to foreign radio broadcasts became a crime. The preamble to the legislation, drafted by Goebbels himself, outlined the principles upon which the new law was based, betraying in the process a little too much of the Nazis' own attitude towards radio as a propaganda tool. 'In modern war', it began:

> the enemy fights not only with military weapons, but also with methods intended to influence and undermine the morale of the people. One of these methods is the radio. Every word that the enemy sends our way is obviously untrue and intended to cause damage to the German people. The Reich government knows that the German people recognise this danger and expects that every conscientious and decent citizen will refrain from listening to foreign broadcasts.[9]

It was decreed that deliberately listening to foreign broadcasts would be punished by a spell of imprisonment. Aggravated cases, however, such as where a miscreant was caught disseminating the 'lies' of foreign broadcasters and undermining German morale, could be punishable by death.

Though the new law was certainly Draconian, it was difficult to enforce. As it was hard for the authorities to catch a 'radio criminal' red-handed, prosecutions for the offence tended to rely almost exclusively on denunciation. Neighbours informed on one another, wives denounced husbands. One young Berliner even remembered that all members of the Hitler Youth were instructed to help to put a stop to 'radio crime' by reporting such offences at school.[10]

Listeners quickly adapted. William Shirer recalled spending an afternoon with a Berlin family, who were apprehensive about tuning in to the BBC because of the Nazi block warden living in the building. As a result, 'they played the radio so low that I could hardly catch the news, and one of the daughters kept watch by the front door'.[11] A Berlin youth recalled that his uncle Max was a regular BBC listener:

He sat by the radio set, wrapped tightly in blankets, and listened to the 'enemy radio'. The identification sign of BBC London was always a deep 'Bumbumbum, Bumbumbum'. Uncle Max was hard of hearing! After the programme, the dial would immediately be turned back, so that it would not show where it had been tuned to, if the house should be searched.[12]

Every week, the BBC's German-language service, which had started in 1938, offered over thirty hours of news, entertainment and comment, which many Germans valued even more highly than the offerings of their own broadcasters. The precise number of those tuning in to London is unknown, but circumstantial evidence suggests it was very large. By the BBC's own estimate, it was reaching between ten and fifteen million Germans every day.[13] Even the Nazi Security Service – the *Sicherheitsdienst* – acknowledged that Germans were frequent listeners to foreign radio. In a report from April 1943, it was noted that many men and women, who had been busily working in their gardens, mysteriously went inside about five minutes before the regular BBC broadcast.[14]

Contemporary testimony confirms that 'listening to London' was widespread and encompassed all classes and almost all political opinions. One foreign commentator estimated that nearly three-quarters of German adults listened to foreign broadcasts regularly. 'They do not dare to listen openly', he wrote, rather 'they turn the volume down to a whisper, they send their maids out to the picture show in the evening, and they sit on the floor with their ears directly in front of the loud speakers.'[15] This suggestion was borne out by a number of other diarists. One of them, Ruth Andreas-Friedrich, noted on the very first day of the war that 'we have already "sinned" three times, with a blanket over the radio, behind locked doors.'[16]

They tuned in to the BBC primarily as they often doubted the information that they were receiving from their own broadcasters. Andreas-Friedrich was one of the many Berliners who used 'London' to fill in the details that she felt *Deutschlandfunk* was not giving her. When Rudolf Hess flew to Britain in the spring of 1941, for instance, she went straight for the radio: 'Pillows over the set. Tune in. "This is London. This is London" . . .'[17] Lutz Ritter was another. He distrusted German broadcasts because 'German radio presented retreats as being strategically advantageous; a "shortening of the front line" contested by an enemy incurring irreplaceable losses. At best defeats would be conceded as a German sacrifice "to the last bullet".' In contrast, he noted, the BBC kept him 'very well informed, from about 1943, about German military losses and defeats against the Allies, and from the summer of 1944 about the progress of the Normandy Invasion and the situation in the east'.[18]

One evidently did not even have to be politically minded to tune in. Christabel Bielenberg, though certainly an anti-Nazi, liked to listen to the BBC's music programmes. 'Someone had insisted on turning on the radio', she wrote, 'and Ambrose's Orchestra was playing from London. The death penalty? To hell with it, let's have some decent dance music!'[19] She might have been surprised by the company she was keeping. One man from Eberswalde, near Berlin, for example, was an auxiliary policeman and had been an SS guard at Dachau, but he tuned in to London every night and listened through earphones.[20] Another regular BBC listener was Rochus Misch, a member of Hitler's household and decorated member of the SS-*Leibstandarte*, who would be one of the last to leave the Berlin bunker in 1945.[21] The Nazi security service noted that the law was being increasingly broken, not by opponents of the regime necessarily, but by 'good National Socialists', who were politically engaged and unlikely to be negatively influenced by the experience.[22]

Besides being a natural source of comparatively unbiased information, the BBC also used another tactic to expand its audience as the war progressed. To wean German civilians away from the influence of Nazi propaganda, both the BBC and its Soviet equivalent, Radio Moscow, regularly broadcast lists of soldiers taken prisoner in their respective military theatres. The BBC even developed a specific programme for the purpose – with the theme tune of the popular German song '*In der Heimat, In der Heimat, da gibt's ein Wiederseh'n*'. For obvious reasons, many Germans tuned in in the hope of hearing positive news about the fate of missing loved ones, relations or friends.

The problem, however, was that one could not admit openly that one had heard the name of an acquaintance, or family member, on the BBC or on the Soviet German-language station, *Freies Deutschland* ('Free Germany'). Whether due to ideological zeal or reflexive patriotism, there were instances of mothers with missing soldier sons who reported the very people who had given them the good news of their loved ones' survival. Therefore, some method had to be found to communicate the good news without either betraying its source or identifying the messenger.

One way was for a listener to send anonymous letters to the families of those listed in the broadcasts. One Berliner, himself a veteran of the Eastern Front, took to doing just this in 1944, sending up to thirty such letters to prematurely grieving families. One example has been preserved in the archives:

Dear Mrs R.,
On 19 October 1944 at 18.45, the station 'Freies Deutschland' broadcast a message from your husband Lance-Corporal Albert R. sending greetings to your son.
I hope herewith to have brought you good news.
An anonymous comrade.[23]

The letter writer was only caught when he decided to deliver one of his messages by hand so as to witness the joy that he was bringing. Sadly for him, the recipient of his letter – though initially delighted – reported him to the Gestapo, and he was arrested on his way home. Though his precise fate is unknown, it is not unlikely, given the scale of the offence, that he would have faced the death penalty.

Others devised more ingenious methods. One night, the bartender in his local Berlin bar confided to the American William Russell:

'You know everybody around here listens to London,' he wheezed. 'Of course they are afraid to admit it right out loud, but they do listen anyway.' He looked over his shoulder again, expecting to see God knows what. 'Yesterday, old Frau Prause, who's got a son on a submarine, was at home and old Herr Illman came and told her that he had dreamed the night before that her son had been captured by the British – and was safe in a prison camp in England. Frau Prause just thought he was crazy, until four more neighbours came in during the day to tell her that they had dreamed the same thing the night before. She finally believed it was true. Everybody around here heard

her son's name on the London news broadcast in a list of prisoners
they had taken, but they won't admit that they had listened to a
foreign station.

'They just have "dreams" . . . Everybody "dreams" things now.'[24]

If ordinary Berliners found good reasons to listen to broadcasts from
abroad, then the foreign labourers in their midst had even more justi-
fication to tune in. One of these was the Frenchman Marcel Elola,
who lived with a group of fellow forced labourers in a makeshift camp
in Lichtenrade to the south of Berlin. The group's radio became their
primary link to the outside world:

> We had bought the radio from the black market, from the back room
> of a café on Alexanderplatz. The aerial was hidden between the roof
> tiles. We received broadcasts from France, although the signal was
> marred by a clicking sound: klaklakklak, klaklakklak. You had to have
> your ear direct against the speaker, with your head under a blanket,
> and concentrate hard on the voice, to hear and understand without
> turning the volume up.[25]

Of those brought before the Nazi courts for 'radio crimes' around
one in five were foreign labourers.

Faced with a wave of 'radio crime', the regime was obliged to
react. Goebbels began in the first winter of the war by seeking to
publicise the potential punishments that transgressors would incur.
'Foreign radio broadcasts continue to attract an audience amongst
us', he wrote in his diary in December 1939. 'I instruct a few draconian
sentences to be passed and publicised. Perhaps that will help.'[26] Yet,
despite persistently demanding eight- and ten-year prison sentences
for 'radio criminals', Goebbels was dismayed to see the average
sentence handed down for such offences hover stubbornly around
two to three years, a figure he considered so paltry that it was of
little propaganda value.[27]

In response, he tried a different approach. In the spring of 1941,
he ordered that a warning label should be applied to all radios in
German homes. Both new purchases and existing radios were to
have a red card attached to the tuning dial, bearing the following
text:[28]

Denke daran

Das Abhören ausländischer Sender ist ein Verbrechen gegen die nationale Sicherheit unseres Volkes. Es wird auf Befehl des Führers mit schweren Zuchthausstrafen geahndet.

(Remember. Listening to foreign broadcasts is an offence against the national security of our people. By order of the Führer, it will be punished with severe custodial sentences.)

This policy was problematic from the start. It required that the labels were to be distributed to German households by the local Nazi authorities, the most zealous of which even supervised their attachment to the radio in question. As Howard Smith noted:

> in my neighbourhood houses were visited by local Nazi chiefs to make sure that the cards had been fastened to radios and were still there. People who had no radio sets were told to keep the cards anyhow, and to let them be a reminder not to listen to the conversation of people who did have radios and tuned in to foreign stations.[29]

Most civilians found this heavy-handed in the extreme. Else Bittner remembered that her mother was infuriated when the label was delivered to her home in the Berlin suburb of Reinickendorf. 'She was very offended', she recalled, 'she denied ever listening to foreign radio, but they did not want to know. In the end, she refused to hang the label on the tuner dial, and merely tucked it under the set, out of sight.'[30] The SD, too, reported that the measure had found a 'very negative reception' among the people and was seen as 'a form of spying', targeted as it was, not against known offenders, but the entire population.[31] Moreover, many noted with dismay that the name of the Führer was invoked on the label and evidently found it hard to believe that Hitler himself – the leader and father of the nation – had put his name to such an invidious and offensive policy.

For all the propaganda, threats and punishments, 'radio crime'

increased as the war progressed. Though the statistics are patchy and
the numbers committing the offence were much greater than the small
minority convicted of it, it is nonetheless clear that convictions rose
dramatically from 36 in 1939, to 830 in 1940, 721 in 1941, and 1117 in 1942.[32]
Despite Goebbels' repeated calls for stricter sentencing for offenders,
only eleven offenders were ever executed nationwide for the crime of
listening to enemy radio. The most serious radio offences would usually
have included some aggravating circumstances and would therefore
most likely be prosecuted for another more serious misdemeanour,
such as undermining the war effort. But, beyond that, sentences for
straightforward 'radio crimes' tended to be light, with those convicted
generally facing between eighteen months and three years imprisonment.[33] It seems that, for all the bluster and threats, the authorities
were not primarily concerned about the public's listening habits. As
one historian has concluded, were it not for the fact that it was outlawed,
'listening to foreign radio broadcasts was . . . so commonplace that it
could have been considered normal'.[34]

Despite the apparent prevalence of listening to the BBC, German
radio was not all propaganda and drum-beating rhetoric. While there
was a good deal of 'political' content on German radio – Hitler's
speeches, for instance, or headline addresses by the other senior Nazis
– one must resist the assumption that all Nazi radio content was political in nature. It was not. Even in 1943, the proportion of broadcasts
devoted to news and political programming was only 16 per cent.[35]

There was a lot more besides. German radio regularly broadcast
cultural programmes, poetry recitals, plays and 'public information'
advice about the latest legislation, or suggesting ways that housewives
might make the most of their rationing allocation, or economise in
the household. There was also a fair amount of sport. The 1936
Olympics had shown how popular sport on radio could be, and the
airwaves would carry reports of athletics meetings or horse racing at
Hoppegarten. The showpiece of the German football season, the
championship final, held every summer in the Olympic Stadium in
Berlin, never failed to get a large radio audience.

The vast majority of the content transmitted on German radio was
musical in nature. There were numerous restrictions, of course, and
favoured artists. Conventional jazz, for instance, was not tolerated, as
it was perceived to be 'degenerate' and the product of Negro and Jewish

musicians. Only 'German Jazz' – a slower, 'aryanised' version – was permitted. The classical repertoire was also subjected to minute scrutiny. While Hitler's personal record collection contained examples not only of Russian composers like Mussorgsky and Rachmaninov, even of Jewish musicians such as Bronislaw Huberman,[36] the German airwaves were more puritanical. Works by Jewish composers and musicians were not broadcast on German radio, and as the war progressed more 'enemy' composers were added to the list, including Chopin, Tchaikovsky and Ravel. This left a rather stodgy diet of 'Aryan' composers, ranging from Germanic stalwarts such as Wagner and Beethoven to the more avant-garde work of Carl Orff. Even Mozart did not escape controversy; some of his works were slated to be banned from public broadcast as the libretti had been written by a baptised Jew.[37]

Beyond the obvious bans and restrictions, there were also some ingenious efforts made to link particular pieces of music with the progress of the war. Wartime radio communiqués were always prefaced by a bar or two of the 'theme tune' for that particular theatre – the jaunty '*Wir fahren gegen Engeland*' ('We journey against England') for Britain, the '*Wacht am Rhein*' for France, or the '*Balkanlied*' for Greece.[38] The annual commemoration of '*Heldengedenktag*', 'Heroes Memorial Day', meanwhile, was the occasion for an airing of the adagio from Bruckner's mournful Seventh symphony. Hitler himself was always associated with the 'Badenweiler March', a lively piece composed during the First World War. Radio audiences, like those of the newsreels and live events, knew that when the band struck up this particular tune, the Führer was about to make an appearance. From 1939, it was even forbidden to play the march publicly except in Hitler's presence.[39]

The classical repertoire did not make up the lion's share of the music broadcast on German radio, however: that honour went to popular music, which made up nearly half of the playlist. Favourites included the hit songs from stage and screen, as well as conventional dance music. Regional tastes were also catered for, such as the *Volksmusik* so redolent of Bavaria and Austria.

One song that transcended even national boundaries was the famed '*Lili Marleen*'. Originally written during the First World War, the words were set to music in 1938 and recorded the following year by Lale Andersen, a singer at the *Kabarett der Komiker* in Berlin. Though it did not enjoy particular success upon its initial release, the song was made famous in 1941 by its repeated airings on the Wehrmacht station *Soldatensender Belgrad*, which broadcast to the Balkans and across the Mediterranean. Its gentle melancholy – the lively, unsentimental vocals of Andersen telling of a soldier reminiscing about his girl back home, gave it tremendous resonance:

> *Vor der Kaserne, vor dem grossen Tor*
> *Stand eine Laterne und steht sie noch davor*
> *So woll'n wir uns da wieder seh'n*
> *Bei der Laterne wollen wir steh'n*
> *Wie einst Lili Marleen,*
> *Wie einst Lili Marleen.*

Even Hitler, it was said, was a fan, commenting presciently to his adjutant that 'this song will not only inspire German soldiers, it might even outlast us all'.[40] Soon the song became a universal anthem of longing, homesickness and hope, just as popular with British and Allied soldiers as it was with the Wehrmacht. An English version, 'Lilli of the Lamplight' was swiftly penned:

> Underneath the lantern,
> By the barrack gate
> Darling I remember
> The way you used to wait
> T'was there that you whispered tenderly,
> That you loved me,
> You'd always be,
> My Lilli of the Lamplight,
> My own Lilli Marlene.

For all its universal appeal, however, 'Lili Marleen' did not find favour with everyone. Regarding it as 'morbid' and 'unheroic', Goebbels tried to have it banned. Though he had the original master of the recording destroyed, and had Andersen arrested, the flood of requests from troops at the front meant that his demand that the radio stop playing the song had to be overturned.

'Lili Marleen' was a staple on the popular *Wunschkonzert* programme.

More correctly known as the *Wunschkonzert für die Wehrmacht* – 'Request Concert for the Wehrmacht' – the programme was broadcast every Sunday afternoon at 3.00 from a studio in central Berlin. As the name suggests, it played requests from soldiers at the front, and from their families back home, thereby providing a vital channel for messages between the two. Each programme opened with: *Liebe Soldaten, Liebe Hörer in der Heimat, Liebe Freunde jenseits der Grenze* ('Dear soldiers, dear listeners at home, dear friends beyond the frontier'), and then gave a list of those units and individuals who had requested a particular tune. The tone of the programme was upbeat, offering the home front a dose of escapism, and giving soldiers an uplifting vision of 'normality' back home.[41]

The music itself tended to be popular German fare, rather than classical. To this end, so-called *Volksmusik*, or 'people's music' – schmaltzy patriotic tunes, such as '*Glocken der Heimat*' ('Bells of the Homeland') – tended to predominate. Military themes were also ever-present, including the rousing *Panzerlied*, and the song of the Afrika Korps, '*Panzer rollen in Afrika vor*' ('Panzers roll in Africa').

The favourites of German stage and screen also received regular airings, such as Zarah Leander and Marika Rökk. Indeed, one of the most famous songs of the war, after '*Lili Marleen*', was Leander's saccharine '*Ich weiss, es wird einmal ein Wunder gescheh'n*' ('I know a miracle will happen'), which was taken from the hit film *Die Grosse Liebe* ('The Great Love'). Sung in Leander's trademark deep contralto voice, with its extravagantly rolled 'r's, it would become one of the theme tunes of the German home front.

> *Ich weiss, es wird einmal ein Wunder gescheh'n*
> *und dann werden tausend Märchen wahr.*
> *Ich weiss, so schnell kann keine Liebe vergehn,*
> *die so gross ist und so wunderbar.*
>
> I know, one day a miracle will happen
> And then a thousand fairy tales will come true
> I know that a love cannot die so quickly
> That is so great and so wonderful.

Naturally perhaps for a programme that borrowed so much from the silver screen, the *Wunschkonzert* quickly spawned a cinema spin-off of its own. The film *Wunschkonzert* – with Ilse Werner and Carl Raddatz in the leads – told the story of two lovers, separated by the war, who are reunited by the radio request show. After its premiere in Berlin in December 1940, Goebbels noted its 'magnificent reception'[42] and congratulated himself – he had, after all, come up with the idea. *Wunschkonzert* would go on to be one of the most commercially successful films of the Third Reich.

Radio did not only serve as a source of light entertainment and distraction. It could also be a life-saver. *Drahtfunk*, or 'wire radio', had been tested in the 1930s and was later introduced in Berlin and a few other parts of the Reich. It was essentially a forerunner of modern broadband, offering radio signals via the telephone cables, with the advantage that such signals could not be jammed or disrupted and suffered only limited interference.

Drahtfunk could therefore be used as an emergency radio network. From 1943, when the Allied bombing campaign against Germany was reaching a new intensity, conventional *Reichssender* radio was switched off when enemy aircraft were approaching, for fear that their navigators might be able to home in on radio transmissions. On signing off, the *Reichssender* would advise its listeners to switch over to *Drahtfunk*. This was achieved by plugging the radio set into a splitter box on the telephone cable, and tuning to the appropriate frequency.

Drahtfunk did not broadcast programmes or music; rather, it advised solely on the progress of enemy air attacks. As Berliner Gisela Richter remembered: 'The reports went something like this: "Enemy bomber squadrons approaching the territory of the Reich!" After a while: "Enemy bomber squadrons in the grid square Gustav/Heinrich (G/H) flying in the direction of Emil/Nordpol (E/N) and so on." G/H was always dangerous for Berlin. When those letters were given, we knew it was our turn.'[43]

In time, the system would become more sophisticated. When Allied bombers reached the area of Hanover and Braunschweig, the warning siren would be sounded in the capital; and when Stendal and Rathenau – fifty miles to the west of Berlin – were overflown, the air raid siren would wail into life. The longer the war progressed, however, the more unreliable the siren became, sometimes only being sounded when enemy aircraft were already in the skies above the capital. The early warning provided by *Drahtfunk*, therefore, allowed Berliners to get down to their shelters in good time. Ernst Schmidt remembered his father listening in to the 'wire radio' and then ordering the family to leave their home. 'We joined a tide of people flowing down to the shelter', he recalled, 'and father told us that the alarm would not be sounded for another ten minutes.'[44]

Others tuned in to the broadcasts of the local air defence network, the so-called *Flaksender* or *Myosender*, where more thoroughgoing reports of enemy air movements were given. Peter Jung's father was a regular listener:

> My father had got hold of maps, not intended for the public, which showed Germany divided into grid-squares, each one labelled with a letter of the alphabet. Every evening, around six or seven o'clock, the game began anew: the map would be spread out on the table and the radio would be tuned to the frequency of the Berlin control room to hear if enemy planes had entered the Reich's airspace. If the control room was already transmitting, then one heard . . . announcements in the form of grid references with additional geographical locations. . . . In order to follow the individual bomber squadrons, my father gave me the various counters from our game of Ludo, while the direction of flight was marked with matches. . . . When a squadron reached the area of Brandenburg an der Havel, it was clear that Berlin was the target. Then it was time to turn off the radio and go down into the cellar.[45]

Radio enjoyed a chequered career in Hitler's Germany. That which had begun as a propaganda tool of the first order had changed into a source of information and entertainment for the public, before morphing again into a valuable survival tool during the air war. The number of civilian lives saved by this simple technology is unknown, but it must be considered to be substantial. One might conclude that, in this aspect alone, radio truly proved its status as 'the eighth Great Power'.

11

The Watchers and the Watched

In the early hours of 13 June 1942, residents in Kleine Markusstrasse in Friedrichshain were woken by a disturbance on the street outside. It would not have been an unusual occurrence. Friedrichshain was one of the traditional working-class districts of the capital and so would have been alive with all the noise and commotion of urban life. In the 1930s, as one of the hotbeds of 'red Berlin', the district had seen numerous running street battles between communists and 'brownshirts'. It had even been christened 'Horst-Wessel-Stadt' by the Nazis, after their most famous martyr, who was murdered there in 1930.[1]

On that warm June night, the brawling in the street was evidently serious or loud enough for one resident to call the police. When they arrived, order was quickly restored and the miscreants were bundled into a police van. Most of them would duly face a charge of affray, or disorderly conduct, and be fined by a judge before being released. But for one of them, the consequences would be much more serious.

One of those arrested that night was Bruno Wattermann, a Romany. A slightly gaunt man, in his mid-twenties, with a fashionable pencil moustache, Wattermann had been born in Stettin on the Baltic coast and had spent much of his early life on the road, living in a traditional caravan. As a young man, he had then settled in Berlin, where he scraped a living as an occasional horse dealer.

He had been in trouble with the authorities before. In 1938, he had been arrested under the catch-all of 'anti-social behaviour', as he was of no fixed address, and was sent to the concentration camp at Buchenwald, where he had remained for fourteen months. However, as his Gestapo file ominously concluded, this punishment appears to have made 'little impression' on him.[2]

Under interrogation, following the brawl in Friedrichshain, Wattermann told his story. After his release from Buchenwald, he had returned to Berlin and attempted to 'go straight', finding work at a Blaupunkt factory in nearby Kreuzberg. But he had found himself unable to keep to the routine of everyday life and soon was regularly absenting himself from work, claiming illness. After being fired, he found another position at a factory in Neukölln, but the old habits recurred and he was finally hauled before a local court and fined 40 Reichsmarks for his persistent absenteeism. During the year before his arrest, it transpired, Wattermann had been absent from work for twenty weeks.[3]

Aside from his apparent inability to hold down a job, Wattermann also suffered because of his racial background. Nazi Germany viewed the 30,000 or so Sinti and Roma within the German population much as they viewed the Jews – as alien bloodstock that ought to be removed. Thus, most of the racial laws that were applied to German Jews also applied to German gypsies – they were forbidden to intermarry or even have sexual relations with Germans, and were liable to special taxes. Moreover, they could face sterilisation or arbitrary imprisonment.[4]

So the odds were stacked against Bruno Wattermann receiving a fair hearing from the Berlin Gestapo. To make matters worse, Wattermann had been drunk at the time of his arrest, and his interrogators quickly suspected that he was dabbling in the black market, selling textiles and even diamonds. Ordinarily, this combination of minor infractions and unconfirmed suspicions might have sufficed for a suspect to be fined or released with a warning. In Wattermann's case however, the conclusion of the Gestapo was stark and unequivocal. Not only was he a 'gypsy', the report stated, he also 'belonged to those asocial elements which refuse to pursue regular work and persistently seek to lead a carefree life at the expense of the German people'. Many warnings and punishments, it said, had been without effect, and Wattermann had demonstrated that 'he absolutely will not improve himself' and had proved a 'serious disturbance' to the public. The report concluded that it was unacceptable for him to remain 'at liberty'.[5]

Later that summer, two months after his arrest – and without trial – Wattermann was designated an 'asocial' and was sent for indefinite detention with hard labour to the concentration camp at Sachsenhausen near Berlin.[6]

★　　★　　★

The Gestapo, or *Geheime Staatspolizei* – Secret State Police – stood at the very heart of the Nazi regime. Synonymous – along with the SS – with the Nazi 'terror', its origins were rather more mundane. It had been established in 1933, emerging out of the old Prussian political police, and had subsequently taken its place among the constellation of acronyms that populated the German police network. Along with the criminal police, *Kriminalpolizei* (or Kripo), which investigated serious criminal cases, the Gestapo fell under the umbrella of the security police, the *Sicherheitspolizei* (or Sipo). Regular, everyday policing, meanwhile, was handled by the so-called order police, the *Ordnungspolizei* (or Orpo). By 1939, all of these organisations, which operated nationwide, were subordinated to the Reich Main Security Office, the *Reichssicherheitshauptamt* (or RSHA), and ultimately, Heinrich Himmler's SS.

But the Gestapo was not just another police unit. Its primary role was to act as a political police force – to investigate and combat all activities that were deemed dangerous or inimical to the Nazi state. It did not, however, practise the same randomised persecution and killing that had been witnessed in Stalin's Soviet Union. The Gestapo 'terror' was not random. It did not kill by quota, or terrorise its would-be victims by its own unpredictability or caprice. It was very targeted, seeking to weed out political criminals and focus very specifically on those whom the regime decreed to be 'undesirable'. A glance at its internal structure illustrates very well the threats that it perceived. There were sections devoted not only to the 'usual suspects' of socialists, communists, gypsies and Jews, but also to liberalism, Freemasonry, 'Political Catholicism', sabotage and forgery.

In combating these threats, the Gestapo was permitted to operate outside the law if necessary. As a political police force, it served the Nazi regime rather than the established judicial process, and in order to function effectively it had to have free rein to arrest and imprison suspects without recourse to the norms of law, which were seen to be lagging behind the more immediate demands of the Nazi revolution. The Gestapo, therefore, did not derive its authority from the grand traditions of German justice, or even from the narrower requirements of the administrative machine. Rather, its power came from Hitler himself. It answered – ultimately – to no one but the Führer.

In order to better understand how the Gestapo worked, it is essential to grasp the Nazi concept of justice. Unlike the Western legal tradition,

Nazi justice was not blind: prejudice, in the literal sense of the word, as prior judgement, was one of the central tenets of the new legal thinking. When investigating a crime, therefore, the Gestapo would minutely examine not only the circumstances of the offence itself, but also the racial and social background of the suspects. Nazi theory held that supposedly inferior racial groups, such as Jews, gypsies and Slavs, had a natural predilection towards crime. Whereas it was thought that Aryan criminals might possibly be redeemed, rehabilitated or re-educated by a fine or a spell in a concentration camp, non-Aryan suspects were accorded no such leeway. Damned *a priori* by their racial status, they could expect heavier sentences than their Aryan neighbours would receive for the same offence.

Many suspects, however, did not even have the benefit of a formal trial. The Gestapo was quite able to use the courts and the due legal process, but in the majority of cases it used the expedient of *Schutzhaft*, or 'protective custody', thereby circumventing the judicial process entirely. In this way, individuals whom the Gestapo deemed to be a threat to society, or racially undesirable, could be detained even though there was little evidence of serious wrongdoing. Those thus imprisoned had no recourse to the established mechanisms of law, or any right of appeal. They could be interrogated indefinitely and ultimately – whether the evidence demanded it or not – sent to one of the myriad concentration or 're-education' camps, where they would serve whatever sentence was required.[7] For all its simplicity, it was remarkably effective.

Given its apparent omnipotence, it was assumed by many contemporaries that the number of Gestapo operatives and agents in the German capital ran to many thousands. Social Democratic sources, for instance, claimed that Berlin contained what was known as an 'Iron Reserve' of several thousand Gestapo officers and operatives, who lived inconspicuously in apartment blocks across the city and spied on their neighbours.[8] Similarly, the American correspondent Howard Smith was told in the autumn of 1941 by 'a well-informed German source' that 10,000 young Gestapo agents were being sent to Berlin 'fresh from their training institute in Bavaria'.[9] This force, he was told, amounted to a doubling of the complement of agents formerly responsible for the capital. It is easy to see how the popular belief could be engendered that an agent or informer was hiding around every corner, tapping every phone call and eavesdropping on every conversation. It was an assumption that was nurtured by the air of mystery and menace that surrounded the secret police. As SD-Chief Reinhard Heydrich proclaimed to the audience at the German Police Day in 1941: 'The Gestapo, Kripo and SD are enveloped with all the hushed and whispered secrets of the criminal novel.'[10]

In fact, statistics gleaned from official documents and internal memoranda show that the number of Gestapo employees in the German capital was surprisingly modest. Starting from only 391[11] in 1935, the complement of agents responsible for Berlin – as opposed to those based in Berlin but with national or regional responsibilities – rose to 697 by the outbreak of war and to 787[12] by January 1945. Therefore, even at its peak, the Gestapo never exceeded 800 agents and operatives in Berlin. And, in a city of around four and a half million souls, this equated to only one agent for every 5,600 or so Berliners.

So, while the Gestapo was effectively omnipotent – able to bend or break the rules at will in pursuit of the real or perceived enemies of the Reich – it was certainly not omniscient. For all its real or theoretical menace, it had neither the manpower nor the technology to keep the entire German nation under close surveillance and so could not work in isolation. Rather, it tended to rely on two primary sources of information. The first, referrals from the regular police – the method by which Bruno Wattermann was arrested – accounted for around one in ten investigations. The vast majority, however, came via the second route: information supplied by Party functionaries, V-men and civilians.

The first of these sources of information was the Party hierarchy that spread throughout society in Nazi Germany. At its base stood the so-called *Blockwart* ('block warden') who was responsible for the political supervision of between forty and sixty households. Usually a lowly local functionary, the *Blockwart* played a vital dual role in the propagation of Nazi propaganda and the maintenance of order. Not only did he serve as the first point of contact for those individuals who required assistance from the state, such as those bombed out or requiring ration cards and so on, he was also the primary conduit through which the Party's authority penetrated into the social subsoil of every German community, serving as the eyes and ears of the regime. If he suspected that an individual within his block was politically dubious – left-leaning, oppositional or sympathetic towards the Jews

– he would report his suspicions to his Party superiors and in due course the suspect could expect a visit from the Gestapo.[13]

In practice, therefore, the lowly *Blockwart* was generally despised. Burdened with a raft of petty orders and decrees from an ever-watchful government, he was rarely able to exercise sufficient tact in enforcing their implementation among an often apathetic and recalcitrant population. As a result, his dealings with local inhabitants could be fraught with latent conflict; he would be given a wide berth by 'his' people, and earned a number of derogatory nicknames – from 'the stair terrier' to 'the snooper'. In many cases, he was simply referred to as *der Braune*, 'the brown one', in reference to the colour of the SA uniform that many of his number wore.[14]

The second network on which the Gestapo depended was that of its informers, both the so-called V-Men, and its many voluntary, unofficial informers from among the civilian population. The V-Men – from '*Vertrauens-Mann*', meaning a 'person of trust' – were nothing new and had featured in the police networks of both Wilhelmine Germany and the Weimar Republic. However, in Nazi Germany, with its totalitarian pretensions, they were to play an especially important role.

The typical V-Man was someone who was viewed by the Gestapo as politically 'compromised': he might have committed some minor misdemeanour, offered a bribe or been a member of some banned organisation. In many cases, he would have been released early from a concentration camp upon the promise of future 'cooperation'. Importantly, a would-be V-Man was frequently in a position of some authority; perhaps a university lecturer, a small businessman or a factory foreman. There were, of course, a proportion of V-Men who were motivated by greed, or who were simply braggarts and busybodies, but most were citizens upon whom the Gestapo felt a certain pressure could be applied, and from whom information of some value might be gleaned. Expected to report on the activities and political reliability of their neighbours and colleagues, the V-Men occupied a somewhat tragic position, as both victims and collaborators of the Nazi regime.[15]

The precise numbers of V-Men operating in Berlin is unknown. The card indices containing that information were viewed as extremely sensitive and would have been among the first items to be destroyed by the Gestapo as the war came to an end in 1945. Some figures for other German cities have survived, but they offer few clues; Frankfurt for instance, had 1,200 V-Men[16] while Nuremberg had only around 100.[17] Given Berlin's status and size, one would expect its complement of V-Men to be at the top end of that range.

The activities of the V-Men were clearly widely understood. One story serves to demonstrate the degree to which the V-Men had become common currency in the capital. In the summer of 1940, a schoolboy named Erich Vinck was being punished for playing truant from school when he claimed that the real reason for his absences was that he was, in fact, working for the Gestapo. Though he was initially unwilling to explain his connections to the secret police, claiming that he was forbidden to do so, he soon overcame his scruples and told his teachers that he was required to go to clandestine meetings and to spy on workers at an armaments factory. As a reward for his 'work', he said, he had even been given a new bicycle.

Naturally, the teachers suspected otherwise. When the boy's mother confirmed his story, they contacted the Gestapo direct, whereupon young Erich was called in for an interview. Only then did the truth finally emerge: Erich had been missing school to indulge in some petty crime, and the bicycle had been stolen.[18] This episode not only seems to indicate that the existence and role of the V-Men was well known in the capital, but also suggests that their actions were not viewed entirely negatively: Erich would scarcely have chosen as cover a 'profession' that he considered unacceptable or reprehensible.

Perhaps the most controversial component of the Gestapo network, however, was the legion of unofficial, civilian informers. Right from the seizure of power in 1933, senior Nazis had requested the help of the public in keeping their fellows in line. Rudolf Hess, for instance, said in a speech in 1934: 'Every party and fellow comrade impelled by honest concern for the movement and the nation shall have access to the Führer or me without being taken to task.'[19] Similarly, three years later, the Civil Service law had been revised to place the onus of reporting anti-state activities on all civil servants.

Even considering the official encouragement, the German public seems to have informed on its fellows with astonishing alacrity. As one Jewish Berliner would later complain: 'The common people, they were watching you. They were all detectives in civilian clothes.'[20] Informants were motivated not only by a sense of patriotic duty, but also by personal ambition or petty spite – and some Berliners would undoubtedly have used the simple expedient of denunciation to rid themselves of a business rival or an adulterous spouse. Whatever the motivation, they denounced in their droves – so much so that it has been estimated that fully 80 per cent of all Gestapo investigations were started in response to denunciations from ordinary members of the public.[21] Paradoxically, the authorities were often forced to take measures to reduce the sheer volume of denunciations that was flooding in. Some government offices in Berlin even displayed a poster proclaiming that 'Informers receive a cuff around the ear'.[22]

This culture of denunciation seems to have sprung from a general deterioration of civic relations in the capital, resulting in a pernicious spiral of suspicion and accusation. Though this situation was already present in the febrile atmosphere of the 1920s and 1930s, it was naturally exacerbated by the advent of war in 1939. Howard Smith noted how, even comparatively early in the war, Berlin society was already losing its collective bonhomie and solidarity. 'Berliners are ill-humoured', he wrote,

> I can recommend no more effective remedy for a chance fit of good humour than a ten-station ride on a Berlin tube train. If the packed train suddenly lurches forward and pushes your elbow against the back of the man standing in front of you, it is the occasion for a violent ten-minute battle of words, in which the whole coach-load of humanity feels called upon to take part zealously as if their lives depended on the outcome.[23]

It may be that Smith's observations were the result of his being a foreigner, and an American to boot, but he nonetheless made a valid point about the highly charged and accusatory climate of the times. He went on:

> They never fight; they just threaten *'Ich zeige dich an, junger Mann!'* – That's the magic phrase these days: 'I'll have you arrested, you impudent young man', that and 'I have a friend who's high up in the Party and *he* will tell you a thing or two!' They're like children threatening to 'call my Dad, who's bigger than yours.'[24]

This atmosphere contributed to a veritable epidemic of denunciations. One high-profile case was that of the cartoonist Erich Ohser, who worked for the Nazi weekly newspaper *Das Reich*. In 1943, Ohser was bombed out of his house in the centre of Berlin and moved to the

suburb of Kaulsdorf. There, along with his friend and colleague Erich
Knauf, he was reported by a neighbour for his persistent verbal attacks
on the regime, many of which were made during an alert in an air raid
shelter. In his report to the Gestapo, his denouncer complained that
Ohser's 'subversive remarks' had become 'very plain and uninhibited'.
Helpfully, he was able to give a verbatim record of some of the most
scandalous comments. 'Hitler', Ohser was claimed to have said, was
'the stupidest man of all time' and the only solution to 'his insanity'
was 'immediate surrender'. Ohser was arrested in March 1944. He
commited suicide in his cell the following month.[25]

Though Ohser's case may have been justified, many other denunciations were deliberately malicious. Anna Cohn, for instance, was
denounced to the Gestapo seven times for consorting with Jews.
Though her ex-husband was Jewish, he had been forced to emigrate,
so it is most likely that the complaints stemmed either from vindic-
tive neighbours or from an overzealous *Blockwart*. Each time she was
denounced, she had to report to the local Gestapo office to explain
herself.[26] Another Berliner found himself denounced by his stepson
after a family argument. Accused of listening to BBC radio transmissions, he was able to clear his name only after demonstrating in court
that his wireless set was not built to receive foreign broadcasts.[27]

Faced with with what they perceived to be an omniscient force,
Berliners reacted in a number of ways. For a section of Berlin society fear
of arrest and betrayal was very real, not least as the Gestapo was the
primary agent of the Nazi state in rooting out dissent and opposition.
Diarist Ursula von Kardorff spoke for many such dissenters when she
described the Gestapo as 'the eternal pressure under which we stand'.[28]

Others reacted with sarcasm, even humour. Howard Smith noted
that some propaganda posters in Berlin, intended to warn of the
dangers of enemy eavesdroppers, had been doctored:

On one I saw, [. . .] warning, 'Take care with your conversations, the
Enemy is listening', the paper had been scratched away over the word
enemy until only two little paper S's remained, so that the legend read:
'Take care with your conversations, the SS is listening'. Another coloured
placard showed a fine, happy Nordic soldier, talking over a glass of beer
in a tavern to a civilian friend, while near them an evil-looking citizen in
horn-rimmed glasses sat, appearing to read a newspaper, but actually

straining his ear to catch the conversation. The caption ran: 'Take care with conversations, for WHO is the third person?' Some miscreant had scratched away the big WHO and written in its place, in pencil, 'Himmler'.[29]

Berliners also developed some peculiar practices to ensure that their political indiscretions and questionable liaisons were not betrayed. The first such tactic was what came to be known as the 'German glance', a nervous look over both shoulders prior to imparting information to a friend or acquaintance.[30] Some went to greater lengths. The resistance circle around Henning von Tresckow would go for walks in the capital's parks, where they could more easily avoid the supposed attentions of the Gestapo and its informers. Another group of resisters would meet in a Berlin swimming pool, on the logical assumption that any agent tailing them would balk at having to don his swimsuit and join his targets in the water in order to continue his surveillance.[31]

But a large proportion of Berliners did nothing, perceiving that they had little to fear. A recent study has concluded that 83 per cent of Berlin respondents of wartime vintage claim to have had no fear of arrest by the Gestapo.[32] The logic employed was the same as that echoed by later generations threatened by the burgeoning surveillance society: if they had nothing to hide, they had nothing to fear. Those Berliners who did not break the law, resist the regime or consort with Jews or communists genuinely had little reason to fear arrest and imprisonment. Their perception of the Gestapo, therefore, was radically different from that felt by many of their more oppositionally minded contemporaries, or indeed by later generations. The assumption that fear of the Gestapo was a major factor in modulating everyday behaviour and ensuring the compliance of ordinary Germans is clearly one that needs to be revised.

Yet for all the complacency, the fear and the myth-making, the Gestapo was certainly no chimera. For those unfortunate enough to fall into its clutches, it was very real indeed. Those arrested were usually taken to the Police Headquarters, or *Polizeipräsidium*, on Alexanderplatz. Built in the late 1800s, from the same red brick as the nearby *Rathaus*, it was a dark and forbidding place, which was known to Berliners as the *Zwingburg am Alex* – 'the fortress on Alex' – or simply as 'Alex'.[33] After the Nazis came to power, 'Alex' soon became a place into which people began to disappear.

For all its infamy, 'Alex' quickly evolved into a mere holding prison for suspects who were bound for an even more feared location – the Gestapo headquarters on Prinz-Albrecht-Strasse. The Prinz-Albrecht-Strasse itself was an elegant street in the central, administrative sector of the German capital. At its western end, it was adorned with a number of elegant buildings, including the impressive seat of the Prussian legislature and the beautifully ornate Martin Gropius Building, which was home to the Berlin Museum of Prehistory. At its eastern end, however, stood two buildings which came to define the dark heart of Nazi Germany. The first was the former 'Hotel Prinz Albrecht', which became the headquarters of Himmler's SS. The second – at Prinz-Albrecht-Strasse 8 – became the national headquarters of the Gestapo.

Originally an Art & Crafts School, Prinz-Albrecht-Strasse 8 had been constructed in pale sandstone soon after the turn of the century. Spread over five storeys, with an elegant front staircase and two additional wings to the rear surrounding a courtyard, it was a typical Wilhelmine mansion block. When it was taken over by the fledgling Gestapo in the early 1930s, the building was quickly renovated and remodelled, with thirty-eight cells being built into the ground floor, and the remainder being given over to offices and interrogation rooms. It very swiftly came to epitomise the Nazi 'terror'.[34]

For those unfortunates arriving at Prinz-Albrecht-Strasse or at 'Alex', the experience was – initially at least – broadly similar. Typically, they would have been picked up at dawn. According to most accounts, the Gestapo never rang a doorbell or gave a polite knock, but tended to hammer on the door, shouting 'Gestapo! Aufmachen!' – 'Gestapo! Open up!' Dressed in plain clothes, perhaps with their trademark long leather coats and trilby hats, the officers would have introduced themselves by flashing their warrant discs – a metal oval bearing the Nazi eagle on one side and the legend Geheime Staatspolizei ('Secret State Police') on the other. In accordance with their 'secret' role, they were not required to show any personal identification or give their names.

After a brief exchange, the hapless 'suspect' would be informed that he was under arrest, briefly apprised of the charge against him and given a few minutes to dress and prepare himself. He would then be handcuffed and taken away, either in a car, or – if numerous suspects were being apprehended – in a 'Green Minna', the colloquial name for a 'Black Maria'. The suspect's family usually had little idea of his precise destination beyond the supposition that he had been taken either to 'Alex', or to Prinz-Albrecht-Strasse. In many cases, subsequent attempts to visit those held by the Gestapo were rebuffed, so the first contact from a loved one might only come once the individual had been sent to a concentration camp – perhaps some weeks later – at which point he was permitted to write letters home.

Detention was not necessarily a foregone conclusion. The majority of Gestapo officers came to the service via the police force, and in spite of the political pressures under which they operated, they knew how to sift hard evidence from speculation and hearsay. Moreover, given the sheer volume of denunciations and complaints that they received, it was incumbent upon investigating officers not to waste their limited resources investigating what were often trivial offences or unfounded suspicions.

The surprising degree of latitude sometimes employed by the Gestapo is illustrated by the case of the Berlin teenager Anne-Marie Reuss. Gestapo officers visited her home in the suburb of Steglitz in the autumn of 1939, after she had been denounced for publicly singing a song that defamed the head of the Hitler Youth, Baldur von Schirach. The doggerel verse, which had been doing the rounds of Catholic oppositional circles, parodied the Hitler Youth anthem 'Vorwärts'. The original was a stirring call to German youth to rally to the Nazi cause whose refrain proclaimed:

Uns're Fahne flattert uns voran   Our flag flutters before us
In die Zukunft ziehen wir Mann für Mann.   Into the future we go, man for man.

The altered version made less than favourable reference to the rotund physique of the Hitler Youth leader:

Unser Baldur wackelt uns voran   Our Baldur wobbles before us
Unser Baldur ist ein dicker Mann   Our Baldur is a fatty

Harmless fun, one might imagine, but repeating this verse was not only defamatory, it was also considered to be spreading anti-Nazi propaganda, an offence that could be punishable by a stay for 're-education' in a concentration camp.

When the officers arrived at Anne-Marie's apartment, she was not at home and her mother sought to stress her family's bona fides by pointing to the portrait of Hitler that hung in the hallway. 'Look, gentlemen', she said, 'we have a picture of the Führer hanging here.' The Gestapo men simply replied that Anne-Marie should be informed of their visit, then turned on their heels and departed. They did not return.[35]

Another example demonstrates what might be achieved if one went into an interview with the Gestapo with a degree of confidence. Denounced for speaking out in a café, Ruth Andreas-Friedrich was called to Prinz-Albrecht-Strasse to answer for her actions:

> On the principle that attack is the best defence, I expose the assiduous Party Comrade [who had denounced her] as a contemptible informer, weave the names of exalted government authorities into my talk, and juggle big shots, Reich Literature Chamber, complaint to the Press Authority of the Reich government, keeping them all in the air at once like Rastelli the juggler. I make such a frightful fuss that the functionary who is questioning me grows more and more subdued. Finally he almost begs my pardon. What a wretched subaltern mentality it is, turning in a flash from bloodhound to rabbit the moment the name of some superior looms on the horizon![36]

While a proportion of denunciations and complaints would end – for whatever reason – with a single interview such as this, many seem to have resulted in arrests. There are no statistics available for the number of denunciations received by the Berlin Gestapo, but one can safely assume that they ran to many thousands every month. There are, however, some figures available for Gestapo arrests. In both February and March 1942, for instance, the Gestapo in Berlin made over one thousand arrests, a figure far beyond that registered by any other regional office in Germany. By August of that year, the figure had risen further, to 1,478, meaning that, on average, around fifty Berliners were arrested by the Gestapo every single day.[37] One might assume from these figures that the chances of arrest for an offender were greater in the capital than elsewhere. But, in fact, by head of population, Berlin had a Gestapo arrest rate that was broadly similar to those found elsewhere in the Reich.[38]

For those who found themselves under arrest, their first stop would have been the cells at a local station, or at the central police headquarters at 'Alex'. While conditions were generally bad, Prinz-Albrecht-Strasse was described by one memoirist as the 'Gestapo prison de luxe', a place in which its inmates actually feared being sent elsewhere.[39] Yet, with most prisoners there being held in solitary confinement, conditions could hardly be described as comfortable.

The solitude permitted time for often painful reflection. As one inmate wrote, 'Once the cell door closes one has plenty to do pondering the situation and asking oneself "Where will all this lead?", "When are you going to get out of here again?" And the more time passes, the more the question runs through your mind, "Will you ever get back to your family alive?"'[40] For the writer Günther Weisenborn imprisonment in Prinz-Albrecht-Strasse gave rise to some unsettling insights into the human condition. 'When you spend your days', he wrote, 'sitting hand-cuffed on a stool in a wholly unheated basement cell, without a book, hungry, in almost total darkness, you are almost embarrassed by the thought of what humanity has accomplished.'[41] Another inmate summed up his predicament quite succinctly: 'sitting in a cell hour after hour with nothing to do; to see time, which is the very substance of life, as an enemy to be destroyed . . . [this] is an exquisite form of torture.'[42]

While the prisoners at Prinz-Albrecht-Strasse agonised in isolation, those at 'Alex' were faced with different challenges. There, over-crowding was the primary problem, as the cell blocks could contain up to four times the capacity for which they had been designed, some-times holding over two thousand prisoners.[43] There would be no space for them to lie or even sit, they were simply pressed together, bathed in sweat.[44] Food was predictably awful, consisting mainly of a thin, indeterminate soup, served once a day and containing perhaps a single potato or a piece of fatty meat. Some inmates called this soup 'Lorelei': like the mysterious rock from German mythology, no one was entirely sure what it was supposed to be.[45] As one inmate recalled: 'If one was imprisoned by the Gestapo for two weeks, one was lucky. But if one was there for six weeks, it was like a life sentence.'[46]

Those prisoners collected for interrogation each day would have feared for their lives. Dangerous as they were, however, interrogations did not begin with violence and generally proceeded correctly, although repetitiously.[47] The suspect would be interrogated for hours every day; asked the same questions over and over and persistently reminded that the interrogating officer already knew everything about the case anyway. Typical, perhaps, was the experience of one man who had been hauled down to 'Alex' in his nightclothes: 'God knows what [he] had done', a colleague wrote: 'He never found out. No evidence was ever produced. There was no trial. For months he lived within the grey dungeon walls of Alexander Platz. He was questioned for hours each day with no apparent purpose but to exhaust him and drive him mad.'[48] That almost certainly *was* the purpose of such treatment, to see if a suspect would crack and begin to change his story or to divulge the secrets the Gestapo believed him to be hiding. In some cases, it seems the interrogators tired of the chase and released their prisoners: the cell door would simply be opened one day and the prisoner would be informed that he was to collect his effects and leave.

Others were not so fortunate. In those cases where the investigating officers believed vital information was being withheld, they could employ the euphemistically titled *Verschärfte Vernehmung* – 'enhanced interrogation'. Such methods could include comparatively mild procedures, such as sleep deprivation, reduced rations or isolation.

Another Gestapo favourite was the use of bright lights, which would be shone into the faces of suspects or prisoners. When Christabel Bielenberg went to Prinz-Albrecht-Strasse in the winter of 1944, to plead on behalf of her husband who had been arrested in the aftermath of the 20 July Plot, she was called into an interrogation room:

> I came to a dead stop inside the door. For a moment or two I was completely blinded. The room seemed smaller, it was warm and airless and all I could make out was the vague shape of a writing desk in the corner. Arc lights seemed to be fixed behind the desk, somewhere near the ceiling, and they were focused on the door . . . instinct told me I would not be able to stand those lights for very long.[49]

To her surprise, when she asked the officer if the lights could be switched off, he complied. Nonetheless her 'interview' lasted nine hours.

Prisoners would be routinely subjected to much worse treatment, with no such leniency afforded them. Beatings with sticks or rubber truncheons were commonplace. One suspect lodged a formal complaint, claiming that he was thrown against the wall with such force that one of his teeth was knocked out. The official report into the incident cast doubt on the claims, suggesting that the suspect was mistaken, but nonetheless noted that after the application of the 'enhanced interrogation' techniques a full confession was submitted.[50]

Yet the Gestapo had free rein to develop more imaginative techniques, showing a level of brutality that was only matched by their diabolical ingenuity. As one French victim testified, the methods of his interrogators included:

(1) The lash
(2) The bath: the victim was plunged head-first into a tub full of cold water until he was asphyxiated. Then they applied artificial respiration. . . .
(3) Electric current: the terminals were placed on the hands, then on the feet, in the ears, then one in the anus and one on the end of the penis.
(4) Crushing the testicles in a press specially made for the purpose. Twisting the testicles was frequent.
(5) Hanging: the patient's hands were handcuffed together behind his back. A hook was slipped through his handcuffs and the victim was lifted up by a pulley. . . . The arms were often dislocated.
(6) Burning with a soldering-lamp or with matches.[51]

Some of the techniques outlined in the documents from the Gestapo in Berlin, though less immediately spectacular, are no less inventive, especially as it appears that officers at Alexanderplatz often had to make do without specialised torture apparatus. One Gestapo officer, for instance, placed pencils between the fingers of an uncooperative suspect, which were then crushed. Another stabbed the bare chest of a prisoner, again using a pencil.[52] Other methods had a grim, almost comedic quality. One interrogator would simply lock recalcitrant suspects in a small cupboard, with the instruction that they were to knock when they were ready to talk.[53]

The real torture took place at Prinz-Albrecht-Strasse, where not only the specialised hardware, but also the specialist torturers were to be found. One of the most infamous cases of torture in the building was that of Fabian von Schlabrendorff, one of the circle of plotters rounded up in the wake of the failed attempt on Hitler's life in the summer of 1944. In his memoirs, he described his treatment in the interrogation rooms:

This torture was executed in four stages. First, my hands were chained behind my back, and a device which gripped all the fingers separately was fastened to my hands. The inner side of this mechanism was studded with pins whose points pressed against my fingertips. The turning of a screw caused the instrument to contract, thus forcing the pin points into my fingers.

When that did not achieve the desired confession, the second stage followed. I was strapped, face down, on a frame resembling a bedstead, and my head was covered with a blanket. Then cylinders resembling stovepipes studded with nails on their inner surface, were shoved over my bare legs. Here, too, a screw mechanism was used to contract the tubes so that the nails pierced my legs from ankle to thigh.

After these modern variations of the medieval 'iron maiden' failed to produce the required results, Schlabrendorff's torturers resorted to more elaborate techniques.

For the third stage of torture, the 'bedstead' itself was the main instrument. I was strapped down as described above, again with a blanket over my head. With the help of a special mechanism this medieval torture rack was then expanded – either in sudden jerks, or gradually – each time stretching my shackled body.

In the fourth and final stage I was tied in a bent position which did not allow me to move even slightly backwards or sideways. Then the Police Commissioner and the Police sergeant together fell on me from behind and beat me with heavy clubs. Each blow caused me to fall forward, and because my hands were chained behind my back, I crashed with full force on my face.[54]

Eventually, after falling unconscious, Schlabrendorff was returned to his cell; the following day, the thirty-seven-year-old suffered a serious heart attack. He was certainly not alone in his suffering. Even those who had been exposed to less rigorous forms of interrogation often returned to their cells physically broken and mentally scarred.

It is not surprising that some inmates were driven to suicide. Though belts, braces, razors, towels and even spectacles were removed from the prisoners or were strictly controlled, those who were determined or desperate enough could always find a way to take their own lives. One inmate of Prinz-Albrecht-Strasse, the communist John Sieg, managed to hang himself in his cell. A number of others were able to slit their wrists, or to use a momentary distraction during an interrogation to leap from an upper-floor window.[55] In many such cases the authorities were reluctant to release the body of the prisoner to their next of kin, as the corpses often showed the telltale signs of torture and abuse.[56]

Once the interrogation process was complete, a fortunate few were released without charge and returned to their families, exhausted, unshaven and hollow-checked. Many, however, found themselves consigned to one of the myriad camps that dotted the countryside around Berlin, and that formed the very backbone of the Nazi police state.

There were different types of camp for different classes of miscreant. Forced labourers would be sent to one of the *Arbeitserziehungslager*, or 'work education camps', such as those at Wuhlheide, in the south-eastern suburbs, or at Fehrbellin to the north of the capital. Political prisoners, in particular, could find themselves shipped to one of Berlin's regular prisons, such as Moabit, Plötzensee or the notorious women's prison on Barnimstrasse, where the regimes were still harsh but at least inmates might be spared the arbitrary violence and deliberate neglect of Wuhlheide.

Perhaps it was this comparative comfort that meant that Moabit lent its name to a number of literary endeavours that were penned within its walls. It was there, for instance, that the Soviet Tatar poet Musa Dzhalil wrote the poetry cycle that became known as *The Moabit Notebooks*. Though he had his arm broken and his fingers crushed in an earlier interrogation, he was nonetheless able to complete more than one hundred poems before he was executed in August 1944. The notebooks, entrusted to his fellow prisoner and cell mate André Timmermans and smuggled out of Moabit, were published in the Soviet Union in 1953.

Perhaps the best known of Moabit's poets, however, was the geographer Albrecht Haushofer. A professor of geography at the Humboldt University in Berlin, Haushofer had studied with Rudolf Hess in postwar Munich, but had thereafter drifted away from Nazism, before finally joining the conservative opposition and being implicated in the plot to kill Hitler in July 1944. Arrested and imprisoned in Moabit, he spent much of his time between interrogations composing sonnets, through which he contemplated his fate and that which had befallen Germany. The works reflect their author's interests and background perfectly, being full of geographical references and classical allusions.

One of them, which goes to the heart of Haushofer's predicament as an intellectual critic of the Nazi regime, was found in his pocket after he was executed by the SS in the final days of the war:

> GUILT
> I bear lightly that which the court
> Will call my guilt: the planning and concerns.
> A criminal I would be, had I not planned for
> The future of the nation from a sense of my own duty.
>
> Therefore I am guilty, but not in the way you think,
> I should have earlier recognised my duty,
> I should have more sharply called Evil Evil
> I reined in my judgement too long . . .
>
> I indict myself in my own heart:
> I have long betrayed my conscience,
> I have lied to myself and to others –
>
> I knew early on the whole course of the disaster –
> I did warn – but not enough or clearly!
> And today I know what I was guilty of . . .[57]

Plötzensee prison, in the neighbouring suburb of Charlottenburg, also served as a regular jail under the Nazis. As in Moabit, conditions in Plötzensee were hardly comfortable. Inmates were generally confined to a small, damp cell, with only the briefest of exeats permitted, to walk in the prison yard. The lack of food was the greatest torment. On average, inmates received a crust of dried bread and a cup of ersatz coffee for breakfast, followed by potatoes and unidentified vegetable leaves for lunch. In the evening, they would receive a thin soup containing perhaps some scraps of meat or fat. As if such fare was not unappetising enough, one prisoner complained that generally around a third of the food provided was already rotten.[58] Conditions would deteriorate markedly in the second half of the war, with overcrowding and inadequate medical treatment exacerbating an already difficult situation.

But, beyond that, Plötzensee earned itself a much darker reputation.

It was there that the guillotine – first installed in 1937 – put many hundreds of the 'enemies of the state' to death. The execution procedure at Plötzensee was described by the prison chaplain, Harald Poelchau, in his memoirs:

> The bound prisoner was led to the execution room, with his chest bared. After reading out the sentence, before the usual witnesses, the state prosecutor would turn to the executioner with the words 'Executioner, carry out your work.'
>
> Only then did the executioner pull back the black curtain. I will never forget the sound. Then the guillotine was visible in the glow of the electric lights.
>
> The condemned then had to lie against a vertical board. Before he knew what was happening, the board pivoted through 90 degrees and he swiftly found himself with his neck beneath the blade . . . At the same moment, the executioner pressed a button. The blade dropped and the prisoner's head fell into a waiting wicker basket. Now, with similar speed, the executioner pulled the black curtain closed, to hide the terrible scene. Again, that terrible sound that got right under one's skin. Then, in firm military tones, the executioner announced: 'Mr Prosecutor, the sentence has been carried out.'[59]

The killing at Plötzensee did not stop, even after the guillotine was destroyed after an air raid in September 1943. On the contrary, the attempted escape that resulted prompted a review of the policy of keeping large numbers of condemned prisoners on death row, and in response the execution chamber was fitted with a heavy beam, with meat hooks attached along its length, from which prisoners were hanged eight at a time. Over the space of a single week, that September, more than 250 prisoners – mainly Czechs, French and Germans – were hanged. At night, when the power failed, the executioners continued their grizzly work by candlelight. A similar fate would await the many plotters implicated in the Stauffenberg Plot of 20 July 1944. In all, during the course of the war, over 2,500 people were executed at Plötzensee.

Ultimately, Moabit and Plotzensee were mainly restricted to specialised categories of offenders, such as those involved in resistance activity. Most prisoners who passed through the hands of the Berlin Gestapo

would have ended up at Sachsenhausen. Established a few miles to
the north of the capital in 1936, close to the small town of Oranienburg,
Sachsenhausen was seen as a 'model' concentration camp and served
as a training facility for SS guards and officers, many of whom went
on to put their training into practice elsewhere in the Nazi empire.
Among those who passed through the camp in this capacity was the
future commandant of Auschwitz, Rudolf Höss.

In outline, Sachsenhausen was a perfect triangle, with a main gate
– bearing the legend *'Arbeit macht Frei'* – in the centre of one side
opening onto a semicircular assembly area. From there the gable ends
of the wooden barracks radiated out in perfect symmetry, each one
bearing a word inscribed in white gothic script against the dark wood.
Reading along the line, the inscription read: 'There is only one way
to freedom! Through labour, obedience, sobriety, order, cleanliness,
self-sacrifice and patriotism.'[60] If only it were that simple. The majority
of those that would inhabit those barracks were entirely subject to
the whim of the Gestapo and SS; denied any formal trial, they had
been detained under the expedient of 'protective custody'.

Life in Sachsenhausen was predictably harsh. Random acts of cruelty
and humiliation from the guards were commonplace. Often new
arrivals would be targeted in a calculated show of strength. As one
inmate recalled:

> The Jewish prisoner began to explain that his arrest was a mistake and
> that everything could be explained. The SS man listened and then
> suddenly flung a large bunch of keys into the man's face. With blood
> flowing out of his nose, the Jew tried in vain to hold his head up. As
> he saw the SS man coming towards him, he raised his hand in front
> of his face to protect himself. 'What!' screamed the SS man, 'you filthy
> Jew, you dare to raise your hand against the SS? I should kill you on
> the spot.' He began hitting our Jewish comrade, until he collapsed to
> the ground. The SS man then fetched a jug of water, poured it on the
> man and ordered him to get up . . . We stood petrified next to him,
> knowing that this reception was a lesson for all four of us.[61]

On arrival, the prisoners were categorised according to the nature of
their 'offence'. To this end, they were given coloured badges, which
were to be sewn on to the prison uniform over the left breast and on

the seam of the trousers. Political prisoners wore a red triangle, while 'habitual criminals' wore green, forced labourers wore blue and homosexuals, predictably, wore pink. As an 'asocial' Bruno Wattermann would have been given a black triangle. In addition, Jewish inmates wore an inverted yellow triangle superimposed upon the badge denoting their primary offence – thereby creating a Star of David. Further badges could be used to denote repeat offenders or escape suspects, and a capital letter was often superimposed on the triangle to give the nationality of the offender: P for Poles, F for French, N for Norwegian and so on.

The average day at Sachsenhausen began before dawn, at 4.15 in summer, an hour later in winter. Prisoners had forty-five minutes to wash, dress, make their beds and eat a little breakfast – usually a thin ersatz coffee and a piece of bread. Each barrack building generally contained around five hundred prisoners, divided between the two 'wings' of the building, and huddled into three-tiered wooden bunks. At the centre of each block was a latrine with a communal 'fountain' for washing.

Each morning, their ablutions completed, the prisoners gathered on the assembly area – the *Appellplatz* – for roll-call, at which they presented themselves in block order. They would then be counted off into work details and marched out of the camp with a complement of guards and overseers. When they returned in the evening, a second roll-call was held, after which the prisoners could return to their barracks before 'lights out' at 10.00 p.m.

Sachsenhausen was certainly not sealed off from the city on whose fringes it stood. It was an integral part of the local economy, being supplied and maintained by local firms and in turn sending its legions of pyjama-clad inmates to work in local businesses and factories, where they were expected to redeem themselves by their labour. The aircraft manufacturer Heinkel, for example, used many thousands of concentration camp prisoners in its factory at nearby Oranienburg.

But Sachsenhausen was famous for two particularly brutal 'enterprises'. The first of these was the brickworks established close to the camp in 1940, which was intended to produce bricks for the planned rebuilding of Berlin. Because of the dreadful conditions at the site, the brickworks served from the outset as a destination for those prisoners who had been assigned to a *Strafkommando* – a punishment detail. There, prisoners had an average life expectancy of only three months, a figure drastically reduced even from that which was common at

Sachsenhausen itself. One inmate, forty-year old journalist Arnold
Weiss-Rüthel, described conditions:

> Smoke, dust and a dense fog poisoned the air, whilst the deafening
> sound of clanging hammers, clattering chains and wheels, rattling
> machinery and the shrill whistles of the foreman prevailed from
> morning to evening . . . Soon my hands and face were covered in burns,
> breathing became difficult, the scorching heat made every movement
> torturous . . . It still puzzles me how I survived.[62]

As if the heavy labour were not enough, prisoners were also exposed
to the full capricious fury of the SS. Like Sachsenhausen itself, the brickworks complex was surrounded by a cordoned-off perimeter area, which
prisoners were forbidden to enter, and where they could be shot without
warning. This cordon also served a nefarious purpose for the SS guards,
who would deliberately push exhausted prisoners beyond the line, either
for their own sport or as a punishment for insufficiently vigorous labour.
The hapless prisoner, vainly pleading his innocence, would then be
summarily shot. As another former inmate explained:

> The brickworks cost the most blood and the most victims. There was
> not a day that did not bring a death. The record was 28 dead and over
> 50 injured on one day. Many were 'shot whilst attempting to escape'.
> Others were simply flung into the water whilst the bricks were loaded
> onto canal barges; there they either drowned or were used by the SS
> for target practice.[63]

Though many Jews, Poles, gypsies and other prisoners found
themselves working in the brickworks, the site would have a special
significance for the Berlin gay community. Those inmates bearing
the pink triangle – known as '175ers', after the paragraph of the
German legal code that outlawed homosexuality – found themselves
assigned to punishment details with murderous regularity.

The second infamous Sachsenhausen 'enterprise' was the so-called
Schuhprüfstrecke, or 'shoe testing course', a 600-metre track laid out around
the centre of the camp. Here, in a bizarre and little-known example of
Nazi pseudo-science, inmates were forced to test materials for the soles
of Wehrmacht boots. For this purpose, the track itself was divided into

nine different surfaces, ranging from concrete and cobbles to gravel and loose soil. The prisoners selected – again from the *Strafkommando* – were forced to march up to 40 kilometres per day, carrying 15-kilogram sandbags, often in ill-fitting boots. They would march, in many cases, until they collapsed. One of those who experienced the 'shoe testing course' at first hand was Kurt Bachner:

> Already on the first day my feet were so raw that the material that I had wrapped around them was soaked through with blood. On the second day, I was in the most excruciating pain, right from the first moment. My shoes were so big that my blisters and wounds were rubbed with every step. After roll call the next day, my block senior managed to have me taken to the medical barrack. But after some ointment was applied, my feet were packed back in the filthy rags and I was sent back to the column of marching men. I cannot tell you how I got through that day.[64]

In fact, Bachner was fortunate to have received even the perfunctory medical treatment that he did. One of those who were denied treatment was a Dutch resistance fighter by the name of Graafland. As one of his fellow prisoners recalled:

> The Dutchman [. . .] came into the medical barrack as his feet were completely frozen and inflamed [but] on the orders of Dr Baumkötter [the SS camp doctor] he was not allowed to be treated. He had no blanket and lay on the bunk only in his shirt. His feet were not bandaged. The skin was falling off them. In places the muscles were already decomposing and the flies fed on his wounds. He lay there for a few weeks. Then, one day, he was taken away to the crematorium.[65]

Many more did not survive the ordeal. One Jewish inmate testified in a post-war trial that only 24 of his 60 comrades survived a three-day assignment to the shoe testing facility. As one historian has summarised, transfer to the 'shoe testing course' was 'practically a death sentence'.[66]

Sachsenhausen is also synonymous with an altogether different enterprise – 'Operation Bernhard'. Beginning in 1942, the Nazis began the large-scale forgery of British banknotes, with the intention of undermining not only the British economy, but also global confidence in sterling. Using 142 Jewish prisoners, labouring in workshops within the camp, the SS began what would become the largest forgery operation in history. At their peak, the forgers of Blocks 18 and 19 were producing over 600,000 banknotes per month, with a total yield of over £130 million. To cap it all, the forgeries were not mere pale imitations; they were regarded by the Bank of England itself as the most perfect counterfeits ever produced.

Though the forgers had successfully produced millions of pounds worth of excellent forgeries, their work was never put into circulation in the way that had been foreseen. The Nazis appear to have balked at their original plan of dropping the forged notes over Britain from the air. Instead, it seems the notes were used to pay off German spies – one of whom even sued as a result – and to purchase raw materials and currency in neutral countries.[67]

The project did at least save the lives of many of the forgers involved. Given the importance and delicacy of their task, they lived in comparatively luxurious conditions, with clean cotton sheets, improved rations and a modicum of leisure time. One of them spent much of his free time playing table tennis with his SS guards – being careful not to win.[68] At a Christmas revue the forgers sang and danced to entertain their SS overlords. Moreover, given the importance of the forgery programme, requests for the delivery of the Jewish forgers to Auschwitz were persistently refused.[69] Sachsenhausen thereby became a perverse sort of refuge for the forgers, but few of them were under any illusions. As one of their number would pithily summarise, they saw themselves as 'dead men on holiday'.[70]

Another challenge for the inmates was the lack of food. With the outbreak of war, rations for concentration camp prisoners had been halved and would continue to deteriorate as the conflict progressed. But such stipulations – though far from generous – often proved to be theoretical, and prisoners found themselves forced to subsist on much less. Some supplemented their diet by scavenging for food, raiding the bins of the kitchen block or even eating grass.[71] Those that were responsible for the camp's pigsties, for example, stole the animals' food.[72]

All concentration camp prisoners suffered from gnawing hunger, but there was real danger for those who didn't take drastic action. Those who were more squeamish, or lacked the imagination or opportunity to find additional sources of food, ran the very real risk of starvation and physical collapse. As one inmate of Sachsenhausen recalled, the physical effects could be shocking: 'What I see before me does not even look like a human body; these ghostly figures don't even look like skeletons . . . the skin hangs on their bones in loose folds, as though there is no flesh left beneath. Every bone sticks out and is visible, whether it be the collarbone, the vertebrae, a rib or a knee-cap.'[73]

Violence, too, was ever-present. Like all concentration camps, Sachsenhausen was a place where caprice and the vagaries of fate were as likely to decide one's destiny as anything else. Human life, it seemed, really did hang by a thread. Prisoners were not even safe from physical abuse within their barracks. There they were exposed to the arbitrary brutality of the *Kapos* or 'senior prisoners', who were held responsible by the SS for each barrack and were quite adept at dishing out their own brand of sadism. Armed with cudgels and clubs, the *Kapos* and their henchmen would routinely beat prisoners who crossed their path – and sometimes they went further. In one instance, three brothers were murdered in the latrine of a barrack block at Sachsenhausen. As a witness would later testify:

> After the brothers had been in the camp for about 8 days, they were drowned by the room senior of block 11 in one of the basins . . . I personally saw how the arms of the second prisoner were held behind his back. The first two brothers defended themselves and yelled out for help . . . The third of the three brothers, who was left standing outside in front of the block, had to listen to his brothers' call for help and soon started crying out for help himself. He was . . . hanged in the washroom during the following night.[74]

It is not clear what the brothers had done to so displease their block leader.

Sachsenhausen had the usual instruments for dealing with those who dared resist the harsh regimen of the camp. On the eastern side of the site was the punishment block, where prisoners would be held in isolation, interrogated and tortured. Just outside it stood a wooden pillory, where public punishments – such as the strappado, or 'reverse hanging' – would be carried out.

On the opposite edge of the camp was an even more sinister installation. 'Station Z' was a purpose-built execution site. Initially consisting simply of a deep, sloping trench, lined with logs, it would grow more sophisticated in time, with the addition of a room where prisoners could be surreptitiously shot in the back of the neck, while undergoing a medical 'examination'. In 1943, the site was augmented by the building of a crematorium and a small gas chamber, disguised as a shower room, which was used primarily for the execution of those prisoners no longer able to work.[75] The numbers killed there are unknown.

Aside from such targeted killings, Sachsenhausen also claimed a large number of lives through hunger and abuse. Stories of the misery endured by inmates in the camp are legion, but one incident stands as an example of the casual everyday brutality. In January 1940, as the prisoners returned from the work details and gathered on the *Appellplatz* for the evening roll-call, the guards found that a prisoner was missing. As was usual, all the inmates were then obliged to stand as a collective punishment, until the matter was cleared up. To maximise the punishment, the SS guards demanded that the prisoners also do some physical exercises. It took ten hours for the escapee to be captured; ten hours in which the exhausted prisoners stood in the snow, 'exercising'. The following morning, over four hundred of them were carried away for cremation. The remainder were sent straight out again to work.[76]

It is thought that around 30,000 people died at Sachsenhausen. Bruno Wattermann, whose story opened this chapter, was not one of them. Transferred to Sachsenhausen in the late summer of 1942, he was given the prisoner number 46434. There are only sparse details of Wattermann's presence in the camp. We know that he was consigned initially to Block 37 and that he was twice sent to the medical barrack, in August and October 1943.[77] Then, in February 1945, Wattermann was transferred from Sachsenhausen to the infamous concentration camp at Mauthausen in Austria.[78] Thereafter, he disappears from the record. His ultimate fate is unknown.

12

The Persistent Shadow

Berlin's Invaliden cemetery was the city's most prominent burial ground. First laid out to the north of the city centre in the mid-eighteenth century – at a time when much of the area was fields and allotments – the cemetery was initially intended to provide a final resting place for those killed in the War of the Austrian Succession. By the early nineteenth century, it was dedicated as the burial ground for prominent members of the Prussian military and, in this capacity, it would soon develop into one of the most impressive cemeteries in the capital, a veritable who's who of German military history. A publication from 1925, entitled *The Berlin Invaliden Cemetery: A Site of Prussian-German Glory*, listed its 'residents' as including 11 field marshals and colonel generals, 7 ministers of war, 9 admirals, 67 generals, 104 lieutenant generals and 93 major generals.[1] Among the most celebrated of these were General Gerhard von Scharnhorst, the hero of the Napoleonic Wars, Field Marshal Alfred von Schlieffen, author of the eponymous offensive plan employed during the First World War and the pioneer airman Manfred von Richthofen, the famous 'Red Baron'.

Bounded to its western edge by the Hohenzollern canal, and shaded by a generous smattering of linden trees, the Invaliden cemetery was a riot of grandiose sarcophagi, sombre bronze statuary and earnest inscriptions. Among the statues, angels predominated. Some perched atop lofty pillars, while others sat pensively upon individual graves. Eagles, too, were common, either in the traditional Prussian form, or in the grander type preferred by Imperial Germany and the Third Reich. The tomb of General Hans von Seeckt, for instance, featured stone eagles at each corner with wings outstretched, almost caressing the sarcophagus itself.

Variations on the theme of 'the Spoils of War' included empty suits of armour, elaborate plumed helmets, or sheaves of surrendered weapons.

The inscriptions were generally short and to the point: 'He was the embodiment of honour!' proclaimed the grave of General Eduard von Wedel; while the tomb of the crashed pioneer aviatrix Marga von Etzdorf suggested poignantly that 'Flight is worth Life'.[2] The grave of the 'Red Baron', meanwhile, took that brevity to the extreme. Set in grey granite close to the canal side, it bore the single word 'RICHTHOFEN'.

The outbreak of the war in 1939 promised a new intake for Berlin's cemeteries. The first to be laid to rest in the Invaliden cemetery was General Werner von Fritsch. As supreme commander of the Wehrmacht in the mid-1930s, Fritsch had been a prominent, if discreet, critic of the Nazis and as a result had been eased out of his post in 1938, when an elaborate intrigue engineered by Göring had smeared him as a homosexual. Condemned to an ignominious retirement, Fritsch had returned to the army on the outbreak of war and had taken command of the unit in which he himself had served during the Great War, the 12th Artillery Regiment. He was killed in battle, outside Warsaw, on 22 September – the most prominent German casualty of the Polish campaign. Among both those who knew von Fritsch and those who had fought alongside him, it was widely suspected that he had committed suicide by deliberately exposing himself to Polish gunfire close to the front line.[3] William Shirer was told by an 'unimpeachable source' that Fritsch had refused the pleas of his adjutant to let himself be carried to the rear and had subsequently bled to death.[4]

Whatever the exact circumstances of his life and death, Fritsch was lavishly and spectacularly rehabilitated. In an elaborate state funeral, his coffin – draped in the swastika flag and topped with the general's own steel helmet and dagger – was borne aloft by eight officers of his regiment. Placed upon a black-draped catafalque, it was then symbolically guarded by four fellow generals with their side arms drawn. In the pouring rain, and before thousands of spectators, speeches were made and two battalions of the elite *Grossdeutschland* Division paraded solemnly on Unter den Linden.

All the senior figures of the military and the Nazi Party were in attendance: Goebbels, Hess, Göring and Rosenberg rubbing shoulders with admirals, generals and field marshals.[5] Only Hitler was absent, pointedly visiting the front near Warsaw, close to where the general had met his end. Göring himself laid a wreath before Fritsch was finally interred in the Invaliden cemetery. His tomb, a flat oblong of polished granite, bore the general's arms beneath a simple cross. At its foot, a quote from the Book of Revelation: 'Be thou faithful unto death, and I will give thee a crown of life'.

In time, new graves would be added. On 22 November 1941, the funeral was held of the charismatic Luftwaffe general Ernst Udet. As a member of Richthofen's 'flying circus', Udet had been the highest scoring surviving air ace from the First World War. He had gone on to work as a stunt flyer and test pilot before joining the Luftwaffe, where he had been instrumental in developing the tactics of dive-bombing. Disillusioned by the progress of the war, however, and scapegoated by Göring for the shortcomings of the Luftwaffe, Udet committed suicide in his Berlin apartment.

Despite this rather ignominious end, a state funeral was ordered and the fiction was proclaimed that Udet had been killed testing a new weapon. On the very morning of Udet's funeral, however, another prominent life was lost. General Werner Mölders was one of the most successful airmen of the Second World War: the first fighter pilot to be credited with a hundred 'kills' and the first German serviceman to be awarded the prestigious Diamonds to the Knight's Cross. On the morning of 22 November, Mölders was a passenger in a Heinkel He-111 flying to Berlin for Udet's funeral when the plane crashed in bad weather near Breslau in Silesia. A few days later, Mölders too was buried in the Invaliden cemetery alongside his friend and superior.

All such state funerals followed a similar formula, but the event reached its apogee with the death of SS-*Obergruppenführer* Reinhard Heydrich, the Reich protector of Bohemia and Moravia and the most prominent Nazi to fall victim to assassination during the Second World War. Heydrich's funeral, in June 1942, was a protracted affair. His coffin was laid in state, first in the Hradčany castle in Prague and then in the Mosaic Room of the Reich Chancellery in Berlin, flanked by flaming torches and an SS flag. An elaborate funeral ceremony was held, with Hitler himself inspecting Heydrich's orders and decorations, before paying tribute to him as 'one of the best National Socialists, one of the strongest defenders of the German Reich' and – most famously – as 'the man with the iron heart'.[6]

Broadcast live over *Grossdeutscher Rundfunk*, the service featured the German state orchestra playing the '*Horst Wessel Lied*', the funeral march from Wagner's *Götterdämmerung*, and the soldier's hymn '*Ich hatt' einen*

Kameraden'. The latter, originally penned during the Napoleonic Wars, was a staple at countless military funerals, and was the only song – apart from the national anthem – for which soldiers were required to salute. It was a moving soldier's tribute to a fallen comrade:

Ich hatt' einen Kameraden,	I had a comrade,
Einen bessern findst du nit.	you won't find a better one.
Die Trommel schlug zum Streite,	The drum was rolling for battle,
Er ging an meiner Seite	he marched at my side
In gleichem Schritt und Tritt.	in the same step and stride.
Eine Kugel kam geflogen:	A bullet flew towards us
Gilt's mir oder gilt es dir?	is it meant for me or meant for you?
Ihn hat es weggerissen,	It tore him away,
Er liegt vor meinen Füssen	he lies beneath my feet
Als wär's ein Stück von mir	like a piece of myself.
Will mir die Hand noch reichen,	He wants to give me his hand,
Derweil ich eben lad'.	while I reload.
'Kann dir die Hand nicht geben,	'I can't give you my hand,
bleib du im ew'gen Leben	rest in eternal life
Mein guter Kamerad!'	my good comrade!'[7]

As Heydrich's coffin was finally borne from the Reich Chancellery to be taken to the Invaliden cemetery, Beethoven's *Eroica* was played in tribute, and a long line of mourners filed out in silence to follow the honour guard. Then, to the accompaniment of muffled drums, the procession – with the coffin mounted on a gun carriage and draped with the swastika flag – filed through the streets of the capital, past a silent crowd of Berliners.

On arrival at the Invaliden cemetery, the solemn commemorations continued. Among a sea of pressed uniforms and elaborate wreaths, Heydrich's coffin was buried alongside that of General Tauentzien, a Prussian hero of the Napoleonic Wars, its position indicated by a simple wooden grave marker, noting Heydrich's name and dates beneath an outline of the Iron Cross. It was intended that the spot should be the site of another impressive sarcophagus, designed by two Nazi favourites, the architect Wilhelm Kreis and the sculptor Arno Breker. It has also been suggested that Heydrich's remains were only to stay in the Invaliden cemetery for a short time, as they were apparently to be removed to a dedicated cemetery for SS personnel – a *Totenhain,* or 'death grove'.[8]

For all the elaborate ceremonial, in one respect Heydrich was ultimately to share the fate of the humblest infantryman. As the pressures of war mounted, neither his sarcophagus nor the bespoke SS 'death grove' was ever built. Finally, in the chaos of the German collapse in 1945, his wooden grave marker disappeared as well.

Death was ever present in wartime Berlin. There was scarcely a family in the capital – just as elsewhere in Germany – that did not lose a loved one during the war years, yet ordinary Berliners were rarely accorded even a fraction of the ceremonial, the fanfares or the solemn pantomime of a state funeral. Of the five million or so German servicemen killed during the Second World War, few were ever brought back to their homeland for burial. Most of them were never formally buried at all.

As was usual in many armies, only senior officers could expect to be repatriated after death in the field; ordinary soldiers and lower ranks would generally remain more or less where they fell. In some cases, a casualty would be buried, temporarily, by his fellows, with a simple wooden cross bearing his name, unit and date of death, topped perhaps with his 'coal-scuttle' helmet. Those same comrades would also register the death, by snapping off half of the victim's *Erkennungsmarke,* or dog tag – a tin disc worn around the neck, bearing the holder's serial number, unit and blood group – and handing it in to headquarters. In due course, and if the military situation allowed, the body would later be disinterred and reburied nearby in a formal war cemetery.

Word of a soldier's death would in time be passed to the bereaved at home. In some cases, news of the death would be brought personally by troops on leave or by letter from a fellow soldier. Ursula von Kardorff recalled receiving the news of the death of her brother Jürgen in a letter from his comrade in the spring of 1943. 'I sit on night watch in our regimental command post', it began, 'and don't know how to tell you . . .'[9]

In the majority of cases, however, the victim's next of kin would receive notification of the death from the relevant authorities – the *Wehrmachtsauskunftstelle,* or 'Army Information Centre', in Berlin, known colloquially as the 'WASt' – usually in the form of a letter forwarded from a superior officer or regimental chaplain.[10] Such letters, though they could incorporate a personal note, were nonetheless rather formulaic, bearing many of the same phrases: 'painful duty to inform', 'died in our nation's struggle for freedom', 'the ultimate sacrifice for Greater Germany'. Details would also be given, where possible, of the location of the soldier's grave. Such notifications became so common that they were known simply as 'the letter'. One Berliner recalled her neighbour getting 'the letter' in the summer of 1942:

> I saw Frau Müller who lived in the building next door. Her black-clad figure was shrouded to her waist in the sombre sad veil of mourning. I curtsied in homage to her grief and hurried home. Death in our midst, my heart pounded. 'Who died?' 'Tsk, tsk,' Mutti and Oma clucked their tongues in unison. 'Such handsome boys, both of them. So young.' . . . 'The mail carrier brought the second letter only a few days ago.'
>
> I had heard about letters like that. 'She got a letter' women would say, meaning the one that they all dreaded. 'The one with the black border on the envelope and the military markings.' . . . The mail carrier had tossed the letter into the mailbox in the door and raced down the steps so she would not hear Frau Müller's screams. She was not fast enough though . . .
>
> The list was getting longer. On the streets I saw too many people with black crepe bands on their sleeves, black robed women who got 'the letter' and not a body to lay to rest.[11]

Some families would also receive the personal effects of the deceased – a diary, watch or wedding ring and perhaps a medal. Ursula von Kardorff recalled the arrival of her brother's belongings, after his death:

> Yesterday, the remainder of Jürgen's things arrived. 'Fallen for Greater Germany' was written on the package. The sight of it brought it all back. His books: Luther, Rilke, Kant, Spengler, Tolstoy's 'War and Peace', a frivolous French novel and the Bible. Typical of him. In addition, both Iron Crosses. His signet ring wasn't there . . .[12]

In a few instances, the bereaved would also receive an official scroll to commemorate the death. Under a gilt German eagle and swastika, the text read that the deceased had fallen, 'True to his Oath in the struggle for the Freedom of Greater Germany'. Beneath his name, rank and unit was appended the sentence: 'A Hero's Death for Führer, People and Fatherland.'[13] Such mementoes would often find pride of place on a mantelpiece or in a quiet corner, carefully sited alongside a black-edged photograph of the deceased.

In most cases, however, no personal effects were passed back to the family. One Berlin woman, who lost all three of her brothers in the war – one in the Battle of Britain, one in the Battle of the Atlantic and one in Stalingrad – recalled that her family received no personal effects whatsoever.[14] This lack not only of a body, but also of any mementoes and possessions of the deceased, can only have compounded her family's mourning.

Some soldiers took extraordinary measures to assuage the anguish of a loved one left in a simple grave close to the front line. Wehrmacht officer Philipp von Boeselager went to remarkable lengths in an attempt to bring the body of his friend Wendt back to Germany. As he explained after the war:

> I had seen during my previous leave, how much it affected my mother that my brother's grave was [at the front]. Then, the following year, my comrade Wendt died and I [. . .] had a wooden crate made with a zinc lining. Then I dug him up, which was complicated as it was freezing and one had to light a fire to thaw the earth, and people came along and wanted to put it out. [Finally] we got him in the crate and I took him with me . . . I thought, 'one day we will go home.' He was with me for a year and a half . . . No one was bothered by it.[15]

Despite his efforts, Boeselager was unable to return his friend's remains to his family. Transferred to the High Command, he was eventually forced to entrust the crate to a friend, with the instruction that the body should be buried and a sketch of the site made, so that it might be found after the war. It seems unlikely that the body was ever retrieved.

Most were much more modest in their endeavours. From the very first days of the Polish campaign, grieving families posted sombre black-lined death notices, mourning those lost in the conflict, in German newspapers. The notices spanned the confessional divide, and in some instances were even placed by the deceased's employers as well as his family. Most of them carried similar wording. Beneath a facsimile of the Iron Cross, the heavy gothic text would tell of a 'Hero's death' 'for Führer and Fatherland' on the 'Field of Honour'. A typical example is this notice from the autumn of 1939:

My dear son gave his young life
for his Führer and Fatherland

Josef Schreiber
Lieutenant in a cavalry regiment

Fell on 8 September on the Narew
Johanne Schreiber, and her children
18 September 1939[16]

The SS newspaper *Das Schwarze Korps*, meanwhile, followed a rather different tack. While early SS death notices tended to be short, containing little more than the name and rank of the soldier, as the war went on they became more effusive and ideologically loaded. One such notice carried the 'Nordic' runes for birth and death, and was posted by a grieving family from the Berlin suburb of Britz in the autumn of 1942:

For the Führer and the Reich,
our dearest only son, fell, in the East,
at the head of his platoon,
in the struggle against Bolshevism

⚡⚡ Unterscharführer in ⚡⚡ Sturm 3/75
Hans Niebauer
Lieutenant
Platoon commander in a motorcycle infantry battalion

Recipient of the Iron Cross 2nd Class, the Tank Close Combat Badge,
the Tank Combat Badge in Bronze and other awards

ᛉ 7. 12. 1916   ᛦ 12. 9. 1942

In the name of those left behind [17]

Whatever their circumstances, such notices could be heart-rending. One particularly poignant example was posted in August 1941 by the family of the renowned photographer Theodor von Lüpke, from Zehlendorf in south-western Berlin. That summer, Lüpke's third-eldest son, Burkhard – a lieutenant in an infantry regiment – had died of wounds sustained in the attack on the Soviet Union. The notice, however, also commemorated Burkhard's two brothers, Hans von Lüpke, a pilot who had been killed the previous August during the Battle of Britain, and Günther von Lüpke, a private, who had fallen in the opening days of the Battle for France.[18]

Given the prevalence of death notices, the system was open to abuse, potentially exposing grieving families to the attentions of fraudsters and criminals. In one such case, a man named Max Wilke defrauded a woman from the Berlin suburb of Köpenick, who had lost her only son in the Polish campaign. After reading the son's death notice in the newspaper, Wilke had presented himself at the woman's home claiming to have served with the man and even to have fought alongside him in the action that had cost him his life. He had come, he told the woman, with the sad task of bringing her son's last greetings. Over time, Wilke made numerous visits to the house and succeeded not only in appropriating the dead man's belongings, but also in stealing cigarettes and money.

At his trial, the state prosecutor took a very dim view of Wilke's actions, describing the case as 'the most repellent crime that a man could commit'. Given the 'especially base exploitation of the war' exhibited by Wilke, he requested that the defendant should face the additional charge of 'defiling the race', which carried the death penalty. Found guilty, Wilke was sentenced to death and executed.[19]

More seriously for the regime, however, death notices quickly became extremely politicised, an arena in which loyalties could be covertly expressed and subtle criticisms aired. At the most basic level, the Nazi regime feared that the publication of large numbers of death notices might adversely affect public morale and so decreed that the placing of numerous notices for the same individual – from family, business and professional organisations – would be forbidden. To the same end, Goebbels also announced, early on in the war, that each newspaper could only print a maximum of ten death notices per day.[20] Neither order, it seems, was followed very scrupulously.

The regime's concerns about death notices went much deeper. The SD security service, for instance, was much exercised by those notices that stressed the personal pain of the bereaved, rather than concentrating on the wider issue of the sacrifice given for the German people. Complaints were also raised about the 'tastelessness' of some of the verses that accompanied the notices. An SD report from 1940 quoted the following example:

> Now we stand with a sorry look,
> and know our Otto will never come back.
> Rest, oh dear departed one,
> you have freedom, we have pain.[21]

In time, it would not be the stylistic merit that agitated the SD, however, but the growing lack of loyalty to the regime that the death notices appeared to betray. In the early months and years of the war, the standard formula was that death notices would contain the phrase *'für Führer und Vaterland'* – 'for Führer and Fatherland' – which was itself a variation of the traditional *'für König und Vaterland'*, 'for King and Country'. Some of the bereaved, meanwhile, expressed their enthusiasm for National Socialism and for Hitler with more personalised wording, such as *'Er fiel für seinen Führer'* – 'He died for his Führer'.

But, increasingly, the death notice presented an opportunity to make a subtle criticism of the regime. This phenomenon was recognised by the contemporary chronicler Victor Klemperer, who analysed the linguistic peculiarities of the Third Reich: 'If someone is not at all in agreement with National Socialism', he wrote,

> if they want to vent their antipathy or perhaps even hatred without, however, showing any demonstrable signs of opposition, because their courage doesn't quite stretch that far, then the appropriate formulation [for a death notice] is 'our only son died for the Fatherland' without any mention of the Führer . . . It appears to me that as the number of victims increased, and the hope of victory diminished, the expressions of devotion to the Führer became correspondingly less frequent.[22]

Klemperer's suspicions were correct. Mention of Hitler in death notices fell from a high of over 82 per cent in 1940, to 40 per cent in 1942, 25 per cent in 1943 and 16 per cent in 1944. Consequently, in September 1944, the free choice of text was abolished. From then on, a single phrase was to be used: 'Für Führer, Volk und Reich' – 'For Führer, People and Reich'.[23]

In the vast majority of cases, however, even the scant comforts offered by a memorial service or a death notice were denied to the bereaved. As the intensity of the war escalated, and especially after the tide of battle on the Eastern Front turned in 1943, it became increasingly difficult for casualties to be registered and retrieved for burial. Some of them would be collected together by the Soviets to be interred, unmarked and unremembered, in a mass grave. Many would simply lie where they fell, only to be disturbed in later years by a farmer's plough or by battle-field archaeologists. Of the 3.1 million German soldiers thought to have perished in the war against the USSR, only around 200,000 have a grave, and about half of those are actually named.[24]

In many cases, therefore, families would simply be informed that a loved one was *vermisst*, 'missing in action'. The wording of the notice – a pro forma with large spaces for the insertion of the soldier's name and unit – would give the last known location of the soldier with the note that additional information on his whereabouts was unavailable. The investigations into his fate, it promised, would be continued 'with the greatest possible urgency'. The sentence that followed betrayed a note of desperation, however, for it requested that any information received by the family from other sources on the whereabouts of the soldier were to be passed on to the military authorities without delay. The notice closed with the hope that further information would be available soon.[25]

From 1944, the numbers of 'missing' easily exceeded those confirmed as dead.[26] While some families receiving word that a relative was missing hung on to hope, others feared that it was little more than confirmation of death. The poet Agnes Miegel sought to put the pained stoicism of those waiting for news – many of whom had lost loved ones in the First World War – into verse:

> But then the heart aches and knows again the great, bitter word
> and knows, he went as his father went before him!
> And we are brave, just like we were then,
> And ready again, to wait patiently for news.[27]

Though it left open the possibility of capture, internment and an eventual return, the status of 'missing' also suggested the horror of receiving no further word at all.

It was all rather different from the Nazi 'ideal'. Hitler's Germany had a highly developed sense both of the blood sacrifice paid by German soldiers and of the political martyrdom suffered by individual Nazis; so highly developed, in fact, that some commentators have described it as a 'cult of death'.

At its most benign level, this commemoration of military dead mirrored that witnessed elsewhere. In Berlin, the elegant *Neue Wache* on Unter den Linden served as a national monument to the fallen of the Great War, and every town and city across the Reich erected monuments to commemorate the estimated two million German casualties of that conflict.

In addition, the annual *Heldengedenktag*, or 'Heroes Memorial Day', commemorations – traditionally held in March – gave expression to similar sentiments. In its original form, the event was known as *Volkstrauertag*, or 'Day of National Mourning', expressing dignified solemnity in the same way as Remembrance Sunday in the UK or Memorial Day in the United States. Yet, after Hitler came to power, that sombre character was changed. Nazi ceremonial placed death much to the fore in public life and the tone of the event now changed to emphasise national pride in the soldier's sacrifice and the glorification of military heroism. The day itself was renamed accordingly.[28]

Beyond such traditional acts of commemoration, there were darker aspects of Nazi Germany's public ceremonial that hinted at a fascination with death. In common with many of the fascist organisations of the inter-war years, the Nazi 'cult of death' preached the constructive value of martyrdom – the political and symbolic usefulness of a glorious death for the cause. But it went far beyond any woolly sense of '*Dulce et decorum est . . .*'. Death was not merely to be welcomed when it came, it was to be actively sought. According to the inter-war commentator and pacifist Hermann Keyserling:

> Death is a fundamental trait of the German nation . . . [a nation] in love with death. . . . Only in this situation do the Germans feel entirely German: they admire and desire death without a purpose, self-

sacrifice. . . . The French or English want victory, the Germans always only want to die.[29]

This may be overstated, but the concepts of death and martyrdom clearly had a powerful political echo in the Nazi movement. The best example of it was the *Sturmabteilung*, or SA, the squads of brownshirts formed in the earliest days of the movement to protect Nazi meetings and to disrupt those of its rivals. Many SA units had their own 'blood flag', embroidered with the names of their fellows who had fallen in the movement's struggle, and in imitation of the '*Blutfahne*', the swastika flag stained with the blood of those killed in the Munich Putsch of 1923, which became Nazi Germany's holiest relic.

The SA's most famous 'martyr' was Horst Wessel. As the leader of an SA troop in the eastern Berlin district of Friedrichshain, in 1930, Wessel was targeted by his political opponents, not least because of his alleged involvement in the murder of a communist activist and an ongoing rent dispute with his left-wing landlady. Shot in the face by an assailant, he took fully six weeks to succumb to his injuries. His lavish funeral drew an emotional eulogy from Goebbels, in which the streetfighter was hailed as a martyr. The event climaxed with the singing of Wessel's own composition, 'Raise High the Flag', which contained the dark refrain:

> *Kamraden, die Rotfront und Reaktion erschossen,*
> *Marschier'n im Geist in uns'ren Reihen mit.*

> Comrades shot by the Red Front and reaction,
> march in spirit with us in our ranks.[30]

Wessel went on to become the Nazi martyr *par excellence*. Raised almost to the status of a saint, he became the subject of more than 250 biographies, plays and novels during the Third Reich, including a big-screen outing as the lightly fictionalised *Hans Westmar*. His 'hymn' was adopted as the official anthem of the Nazi movement.

The Hitler Youth, too, had its precious martyr. In January 1932, a twelve-year-old *Hitlerjugend* boy, Herbert Norkus, was distributing leaflets in the Berlin suburb of Moabit when he was set upon by a gang of young communists. After suffering numerous stab wounds, he bled to

death in a stairwell. Like Horst Wessel, Norkus was raised to the Nazi
pantheon; his grave became a place of Nazi pilgrimage, and his 'sacrifice' was held up as an example for the youth of Germany. His story
was popularised still further when the fictionalised adaptation of his
story, *Der Hitlerjunge Quex*, appeared in German cinemas in 1933. Norkus
was one of twenty-three Hitler Youths to die for the Nazi cause. All of
them were a gift to the Party's propaganda machine, but they also
served a more sinister function. As the Hitler Youth's leader Baldur von
Schirach declared: 'The more who die for the movement, the more
immortal it becomes.'[31]

With such a rich culture of death within its ideology, one would have
expected the Nazi regime to seek to exploit every military and civilian
casualty to further its cause and reinforce its message. Early in the war,
this was certainly the case; the first civilian deaths registered in Berlin,
for instance, in August 1940, were accorded grand funerals, with honour
guards, speeches and sombre ceremonial. The *Heldengedenktag* commemorations, too, always took great pains to make honourable mention of
contemporary casualties.[32] In this way, it was thought, bereaved civilians could be drawn into the ceremony, personally and emotionally,
thereby inoculating them against politically damaging sentiments of
anger or futility.

Some still sought to apply the ideological gloss. In an essay from
1942, for instance, Goebbels gave expression to the pseudo-religious
sentiments concerning military losses that were evidently then circulating in Nazi minds. He likened the military struggle to climbing a
towering mountain, and it was the dead who marked the way to
the summit: 'We bury them along the edges of the steep path', he
wrote.

> They fell in the first ranks, and all who march after them must pass
> by them. Like silent directional markers, they point toward the peak
> . . . In this way, our fallen enter the mythology of our *Volk* for all time:
> they are no longer what they were among us, but instead the eternal
> models of our epoch. . . . They are the fulfilled.[33]

As the war progressed and the casualties mounted, deaths became
less an opportunity for the regime's propagandists and more a liability.
By 1943, the Nazi Party was evidently so concerned about the impact of

bereavement that it increasingly took on the role of informing bereaved families of soldiers' deaths itself, thereby ensuring that the right political 'message' could be imparted along with the death notification.[34] As this memo makes clear, the regime was well aware of the potential difficulties that it might encounter as the death toll rose: 'The survivors should find strength and refuge in our community. We want to give them fresh heart, as they should never have even the most fleeting thought that the sacrifice of their fathers, husbands, sons and brothers had been for nothing.'[35]

Such measures evidently met with some success, dovetailing, as they did, with the natural desire among the bereaved to see the death as serving some higher purpose. Even the rising death toll on the Eastern Front failed to spark any widespread civilian opposition and resistance to the Nazis; on the contrary, it engendered a sense of apathy and depression.[36] Nonetheless, as the war ground on to its conclusion, the patience and stoicism of the Berlin public would be tested to destruction.

If the commemoration of German dead was fraught with difficulties, that of the capital's remaining Jews was infinitely more trying. Where the city once had a number of Jewish cemeteries, by the middle years of the war only the largest and most prominent of them – Weissensee – was still functioning in any meaningful sense.

Founded in 1880, the Jewish cemetery at Weissensee, to the northeast of Berlin, had swiftly grown into one of the largest in Europe, covering an enormous area of over 40 hectares and containing over 100,000 graves. Not only its sheer size – equivalent to about fifty football pitches – was impressive: Weissensee also displayed a huge variety of gravestones, statues and sarcophagi – ranging from the modest to the opulent, from classicism to Bauhaus. The large red granite mausoleum of the Ashrott family, for instance, was designed by the same architect who created Leipzig's impressive monument to the *Völkerschlacht*, the Battle of the Nations against Napoleon in 1813.

The writer Kurt Tucholsky, meanwhile, was more struck by the Prussian precision of the place, the strictly ordered system of plots by which the graves were arranged. A regular visitor to the cemetery in the 1920s, where he paid his respects at his father's grave, Tucholsky penned the affectionate but gently satirical poem 'In Weissensee':

Each one here meets his lot:
A plot.
And such a plot is named somehow:
'I' or 'U'

. . .

There, where I have often been, in mourning,
there you will come, there I will come, when it's all over
You love. You travel. You enjoy yourself. You –
Plot U.
It waits in absentia
Plot A
The clock is ticking. Your grave has time,
Three metres long, one metre wide
You'll see another foreign land,
You'll get another Gretchen manned,
The winter's snow you'll often see –
And then:
Plot P – in Weissensee
in Weissensee.[37]

Weissensee was associated with the more assimilated, 'reformed' Jewish community in the capital: those Jews who felt their 'Germanness' just as keenly as they did their 'Jewishness'. The vast majority of its graves and sarcophagi, therefore, bore German inscriptions, and the dates given were almost always according to the Christian, rather than the Jewish, calendar. In addition, the cemetery contained a small section where the four hundred or so fallen of Berlin's Jewish community from the Great War were laid to rest.

Weissensee would have reminded the visitor of the Invaliden cemetery, just a few miles away down the Greifswalderstrasse. Both contained those perceived by their fellows as the brightest and the best; both stood as testament to communities at the very peak of their power and influence. That is where any similarity ends. From 1939, the fates of the two cemeteries could scarcely be more different. While the Invaliden cemetery became the scene of state funerals and grand ceremonial, Weissensee became a last refuge for the desperate.

Because of its large size, Weissensee quickly became overgrown as Berlin's Jewish community was decimated, and the manpower required to maintain it dwindled. Rachel Becker, who worked there during the war, recalled the transformation:

> In the years before, hundreds of workmen, gardeners, guards, in addition to the administrative, clerical, funeral and burial staffs, had been employed to maintain the many thousands of graves and the grounds ... even during the war, right until [1943] the modern nursery had still worked full speed and a few dozen gardeners had tried, in vain of course, to take care of ... the graves that were still being visited.[38]

After the last Jews had been deported from the capital, however, 'the huge place was suddenly "dead" ... the vast grounds were empty of human life ... the offices, the telephone exchange, the kind old Rabbi Levy's flat on the premises – all deserted.'[39] Except that they were not quite so deserted as Becker imagined. Given that it swiftly became overgrown, Weissensee had become a favoured hiding place for those Jews who went underground to escape deportation. One grave site in particular offered sanctuary: the mausoleum of the opera singer Joseph Schwarz featured a small classical-style temple with a glass hatch in the roof, through which one could climb to snatch a few hours of undisturbed rest. The temple carried a prophetic inscription from Psalm 90: 'Lord, You have been our refuge through all generations'.[40]

In the increasingly difficult circumstances, the cemetery at Weissensee struggled on as best it could, chiefly under the remarkable leadership of Martin Riesenburger. Riesenburger owed his own survival to his gentile wife, who, though a convert to Judaism, was viewed by the Nazis as an Aryan. He had worked as the chaplain of the nearby Jewish old people's home and, when it was closed by the Gestapo and the last rabbi deported late in 1942, he emerged as the *de facto* head of the fast-dwindling and increasingly desperate Jewish community of Berlin.

It is unclear precisely what the Gestapo had in mind for Riesenburger. His own memoir sheds little light on the subject, stating merely that, after his arrest, he was called into an interview with a senior SS officer, Alois Brunner, who instructed him simply to go back to work.[41] It may be that the Gestapo were seeking to use Riesenburger as a 'lightning rod' to attract fugitive Jews, who could then be captured. However,

it is also possible that they sought, by leaving him in place, to maintain a façade of normality. Perhaps – at the very basest level – they
just wanted a Jew to bury the last remaining Jews.

Whatever his precise capacity, Riesenburger attempted to create
some semblance of normal Judaic life in the very heart of the Third
Reich. Existing in a no-man's-land between indifference and persecution, he continued to lead weekly prayer services and ceremonies,
albeit necessarily brief and surreptitious. His last wedding, for instance,
was conducted in June 1943, between a forty-year-old Jewish man and
his thirty-seven-year-old bride. A few days later, the newlyweds were
deported to a concentration camp.[42]

The vast majority of services carried out by Riesenburger were
funerals. In 1942 he held over three thousand – on average nearly sixty
every week. Most of these were carried out at night in a quiet corner
of the cemetery, with few mourners, makeshift headstones and no
official registration. Increasingly, too, he had to bury those who had
taken their own lives, individuals whose actions, though strictly
anathema under Jewish law, could be overlooked *in extremis*. By his
own estimate, Riesenburger buried nearly two thousand such cases.[43]

In addition, he sometimes received urns of ashes, supposedly from
individuals who had perished in Sachsenhausen or Buchenwald, which
he was required to inter. Wherever possible, he prepared the remains
for burial and ensured that dignity was maintained, even in the most
trying of circumstances. As Rachel Becker recalled: 'until the very end'
Jewish dead 'were decently buried in wooden coffins, blacked with
tar-paint'.[44] Though his sermons and eulogies were always short, simple
and eschewed any reference to the wider Jewish plight, Riesenburger's
words could still be very moving. As one eyewitness recalled: 'He
wouldn't stop talking until the last person had his handkerchief out.
He could really squeeze the tear ducts.'[45]

The survival of Weissensee is all the more remarkable when one
considers what befell the other Jewish cemeteries in the German capital.
The one on Schönhauser Allee was desecrated in the spring of 1945.
Its prayer rooms and mortuary were destroyed, and its gravestones
were uprooted to be used to build barricades and anti-tank obstacles.
And, when a group of Wehrmacht deserters was discovered there by
the Gestapo, they were summarily hanged, to a man, from the boughs
of nearby trees.[46] The cemetery on the Grosse Hamburger Strasse,

meanwhile, was bulldozed in 1943. When a slit trench was subsequently dug across the site, the remaining gravestones were used to shore up the trench walls, while the bones of the dead were casually tossed aside. In April 1945, the site was used for sixteen mass graves, containing nearly 2,500 civilian and military casualties from the battle for Berlin.[47]

In his post-war memoir, Riesenburger proudly claimed that 'every Jew who died, up to the hour of liberation in 1945, was buried precisely according to the prescriptions of our Jewish religion'.[48] As the 'Last Rabbi of Berlin',[49] he had ensured that, at Weissensee at least, some semblance of dignity in death was maintained.

At the Invaliden cemetery, meanwhile, life – and death – continued rather as they had before. After the highpoint of Reinhard Heydrich's burial in the summer of 1942, the number of state funerals held there tailed off, but the prominent and worthy of the Third Reich still found their final resting place beneath its trees, close to the Hohenzollern canal.

Carl August von Gablenz was buried there in the late summer of 1942. A pioneer flier in the First World War, he had gone on to become a co-founder of Lufthansa, a senior official in Göring's Air Ministry, and had been one of the first to fly from Berlin to Peking. He was killed in a plane crash. Another addition was Lieutenant Hans Fuss, a fighter ace from the Eastern Front, who had seventy-one victories to his name and had received the Knight's Cross only a few weeks before his death.

Later additions included Wehrmacht General Hans-Valentin Hube, who died when the plane bringing him back to the Reich from the Eastern Front crashed near Salzburg in the spring of 1944. A veteran of the French campaign, Stalingrad and the defence of Sicily, he was Germany's only one-armed senior officer, having been maimed at Verdun in the First World War. Highly respected by his men, he was known simply as *Der Mensch* – 'The Man'.[50]

In the autumn of 1944, a new candidate for the Invaliden cemetery's hallowed turf foreshadowed a very tangible change in Germany's fortunes. Lieutenant General Rudolf Schmundt was a career soldier. Having served with distinction in the First World War, he had progressed into the elite 9th Infantry Regiment of the post-war Reichswehr and had excelled in a succession of staff positions. A convinced National

Socialist, Schmundt was appointed as Hitler's Wehrmacht adjutant in 1938, a position which naturally secured him entry into the Führer's entourage.

It was in this capacity that Schmundt was to meet his fate. As a participant in a situation conference on 20 July 1944, he was present when Colonel Claus von Stauffenberg made his famous attempt on Hitler's life. Though Hitler survived the bomb blast virtually unscathed, four of those present in the room were killed: the stenographer Heinrich Berger bore the brunt of the explosion and died at the scene, while two other senior officers – General Günther Korten and Colonel Heinz Brandt died of their wounds within days. Schmundt, meanwhile, lost an eye and both legs. Though he initially made a promising recovery and was well enough to be visited in hospital by the Führer, he deteriorated in early October and finally succumbed to blood poisoning and organ failure.

Schmundt was accorded a state funeral, held in the imposing surroundings of the Tannenberg Memorial in East Prussia, with Göring in attendance, on 6 October 1944. The following day, his coffin was taken to Berlin's Invaliden cemetery, where it was buried after a graveside eulogy from General Heinz Guderian. Alongside the generals, the field marshals and the ministers of war, he would not have appeared out of place, but his presence there spoke volumes about the spirit of the age. Rudolf Schmundt was the first resident of the Invalidenfriedhof to have been murdered by his fellow German officers in an attempted *coup d'état*.

13

Enemies of the State

The Lustgarten, or 'Pleasure Gardens', in the very heart of the German capital, was well known to every Berliner. Located on one of the islands in the River Spree, in the shadow of Berlin's impressive Protestant cathedral, it was an open area of parkland that had long been the location for parades and public events. It had been there that a large crowd had gathered to hear the Kaiser speak on the outbreak of war in 1914, and where an even larger crowd had assembled to witness the declaration of the German Republic four years later.

In the 1920s, the Lustgarten had hosted not only boxing matches, Christmas markets and May Day festivities, but also communist, socialist and Nazi rallies. It had also earned a reputation as a place of protest. It had been there that tens of thousands had gathered for an anti-war demonstration in 1929; and four years later, 200,000 Berliners had assembled on the Lustgarten to protest about the appointment of Adolf Hitler as German Chancellor.[1]

In May 1942, the tradition of protest returned. That summer, the Lustgarten was the location of an important exhibition. Sarcastically entitled 'The Soviet Paradise', it was intended to highlight all the 'poverty, misery, depravity and need' of life in the Soviet Union. Inside a long, single-storey building, which had been specially constructed on the Lustgarten in the stark neo-classical style, various dioramas and exhibits were intended to bring home to Berliners the full horror of life under the Bolsheviks: the miserable hovel inhabited by a poor cobbler, for instance, or the grim surroundings of a worker's flat.

The displays were accompanied by a fifteen-minute film, which juxtaposed the positive images of Soviet propaganda with some of the gruesome discoveries supposedly made by invading German troops: starving, neglected orphans, desecrated churches and massacred civilians. 'Where once stood prospering villages', the film began, 'the grey misery of the collective farm predominates today. This is where the Soviet peasant lives as a slave.'[2] For those who were still confused as to why Nazi Germany had declared war on its erstwhile ally in June 1941, the propaganda offensive of the 'Soviet Paradise' was intended to provide some conclusive answers.

Not everyone was convinced, however. One communist resistance group distributed stickers across the capital, which parodied the exhibition:

> Permanent Exhibition
> THE NAZI-PARADISE
> War Hunger Lies Gestapo
> How much longer?[3]

Others resorted to more extreme methods. One night in mid-May, some ten days after the exhibition had opened, the police were called to the site after it emerged that an arson attempt had been made. Damage to the exhibition was minimal and it opened, as usual, the following day, but the fact that it had been attacked at all was enough for the matter to be taken seriously. As the Gestapo report noted:

> At about 8 p.m. on May 18, 1942, as yet unidentified perpetrators attempted to set fire to the exhibition. A wad of cotton soaked in phosphorous and placed on a wooden post covered with cloth was set aflame at the site of the first fire. An incendiary device with two bottles of phosphorous carbon disulphide exploded in the farmhouse. . . . A sabotage committee of the State Police office in Berlin has begun necessary investigations without delay.[4]

Those investigations quickly bore fruit.[5] Just four days after the arson attempt, the perpetrators were rounded up in dawn raids at a number of locations across the city. Joseph Goebbels recorded the arrests in his diary entry of 24 May:

> We have now discovered a club of saboteurs and assassins in Berlin. Among them are also the groups who undertook the bombing of the anti-Soviet exhibit. Significantly, among those arrested are five Jews, three

half-Jews and four Aryans. An engineer at Siemens is even among them.
The bombs were manufactured partly at the Kaiser Wilhelm Institute.[6]

That 'Siemens engineer' was Herbert Baum, the leader of the group.
Born in 1912, Baum had grown up in Berlin and trained as an electri-
cian. Already active in left-wing circles prior to 1933, he began to
organise a Jewish, pro-communist youth group after the Nazi seizure
of power, hosting clandestine discussion evenings and cultural events
in the capital, or arranging outings and walking expeditions to the
countryside.

Soon, his activity grew more overtly political, including attempting
sabotage actions at Siemens and assisting those Jewish colleagues who
wanted to escape deportation by going underground. Among other
activities, he printed and distributed anti-Nazi flyers, especially after
the attack on the Soviet Union in the summer of 1941. One of these
flyers was sent to Berlin's doctors and surgeons, reminding them that
the military casualties acknowledged by the regime on the Eastern
Front were but a fraction of the true figure. Other campaigns targeted
German housewives or soldiers. One of the latter proclaimed: 'point
your weapons at the grave-diggers of the German people! Death to
Hitler!'[7]

In the spring of 1942, however, Baum seems to have sensed an
opportunity to step up his activity. Given that the Nazi war against
the Soviet Union was now entering its second year, and increasingly
aware of murmurings of discontent on the home front, he decided
on decisive action. It was not an entirely popular move, as some within
the group were wary of provoking the Nazi regime unnecessarily,
but Baum had won his opponents round. By targeting the anti-
communist 'Soviet Paradise' exhibition, he wanted not only to strike
a symbolic blow against the Nazi propaganda campaign; he also
hoped that his action would provide the spark that would foment
revolution in the capital.[8]

In this wider ambition, Baum would fail, frustrated not only by the
rather puny results of his arson attempt, but also by the news blackout,
which kept his efforts from the attention of the Berlin public. His action
would not be without consequence, however. For one thing, given that
the majority of those arrested with Baum were both Jews and communists, the incident appeared to confirm the Nazi world view that

270   BERLIN AT WAR

conflated those two enemies into one all-encompassing conspiracy. Moreover, coming as it did only a few days before the assassination of SS-*Obergruppenführer* Reinhard Heydrich in Prague, the Lustgarten sabotage was seen in Berlin as a profoundly worrying precedent. As Goebbels wrote in his diary, the remaining Jews in the German capital represented 'an invitation to assassinations'; and the Minister for Propaganda, for one, did not want 'to be shot in the belly by some 22-year-old *Ostjude* like one of those types who are among the perpetrators of the attack against the anti-Soviet exhibition'.[9]

Thus Nazi revenge was swift to materialise. Goebbels pressed Hitler to speed up the deportation of the remaining Jews in Berlin, and five hundred Jewish men were rounded up immediately. Half of them were shot out of hand in Sachsenhausen, the remainder were sent to the concentration camps.[10] In addition, their families were deported to an unknown fate 'in the east'.

The fate of Baum and his fellow conspirators was similarly grim. Arrested a few days after the arson attempt along with his wife Marianne, Baum was subjected to a ferocious and prolonged 'interrogation', and died three weeks later in the cells of the Gestapo headquarters.[11] It is not known whether he took his own life or succumbed to torture. His fellow arsonists, meanwhile – including his wife – were tried for high treason on 16 July. Found guilty, they were executed by guillotine in Plötzensee prison on 18 August.

As the interrogations implicated an ever-wider circle of conspirators, four subsequent trials were held. No quarter was shown to the defendants. The most tragic of them all, Sala Kochmann, had tried to escape the clutches of the Gestapo by jumping from the window of the police station. Despite breaking her back in the fall, she was tried and sentenced to death with the others, and was carried to her execution on a stretcher.[12] In all, thirty-three people were executed for the Lustgarten arson attempt.

The story of the Herbert Baum Group is rightly lauded as one of the few examples of Jewish resistance against the tyranny of Nazism. Yet that narrow affiliation does not tell the whole story. It should not be forgotten, for instance, that not all members of the Baum Group were Jewish and that they had extensive contacts with other non-Jewish dissident groupings in the German capital, on which they relied for material assistance in everything from typing their flyers to manufacturing their bombs.[13] Seen in this light, the Herbert Baum Group should also be interpreted as one of the few examples of *German* resistance to Nazism.

Berlin was the focal point of the domestic resistance against the Third Reich. With its liberal-cosmopolitan character, its large Jewish population and its tradition as a bastion of the left, the city had never been a natural constituency for the Nazis and had consistently returned below average votes for Hitler. Even as the Nazis made their electoral breakthrough after 1930, and in some places gained as much as half of the popular vote, Berlin's Nazi return never amounted to more than a third of the total.[14] The American diplomat George Kennan noted that this attitude was still current in 1939: 'Most of the people', he wrote, 'had nothing to do with the regime . . . The Berliners themselves – the simple people, that is – were, of all the major urban or regional elements among the German population, the least Nazified in their outlook.'[15]

The reasons for the city's comparative resistance to Hitler's charms were twofold. Firstly, Berlin's left-wing heritage was hugely influential. Its working-class suburbs, such as Wedding and Friedrichshain, developed very strong socialist and communist affiliations and were the scene of violent clashes between left and right during the 1920s. Indeed, when Goebbels was sent as Nazi Party Gauleiter to the capital in 1927, his mission was described in the Nazi press as that of conquering 'Red Berlin'.

Alongside this left-wing tradition, Berlin's position as the German capital also helped to provide a partial immunisation against Nazi ideas. As the seat of government, the city was the natural home of the nation's elite and attracted a large number of intellectuals, lawyers and politicians, many of whom opposed the Nazi regime. Their opposition was in part political, but it was primarily based on higher ideals; on a fundamental objection to the regime's habit of riding roughshod over established legal and moral principles. As a result of these factors, Berlin gained a deserved reputation as a hotbed of resistance against the Nazi regime, with as many as 12,000 individuals involved in organised opposition.[16]

Among the most principled and determined opponents of Nazism in Berlin were the communists. For much of the 1930s the left had appeared an increasingly moribund force in German politics. Officially outlawed, riven by internal divisions and persecuted by the regime, its adherents had in many cases shed their allegiances, or headed into an embittered 'internal emigration', in which they sought desperately to keep the hostile outside world at bay. Others were seduced by the Nazi successes of those early years and managed to convince themselves that their working-class duty was to support Hitler, aided by a belief in the 'socialist' component of 'National Socialism'. Yet, there were many more in Berlin who resisted Hitler's appeal and remained ferociously loyal to the political left throughout the Third Reich.

The war did not start well for German communists. Though their socialist brethren were largely drawn in by the reflexive patriotism common in wartime, communists faced a more difficult situation. Hitler's alliance with Stalin of August 1939 proved profoundly disconcerting and the sudden shift in propaganda on both sides – from hatred to mutual admiration – meant that a new round of ideological compromises and contortions were forced upon the faithful. Some remained unbowed, however.

One of the most effective proponents of the communist cause in the capital was Robert Uhrig. Born in Berlin in 1903, Uhrig had been a communist almost all his life, joining the party in 1920 and forming workplace cells wherever he worked. First arrested in 1934, he had been released two years later, but had returned to his old ways, quickly heading a network of over twenty underground communist cells in Berlin. By the outbreak of war, he had emerged – alongside the remarkable Josef 'Beppo' Römer – as one of the leaders of the communist resistance in the German capital.

Römer was of a quite different stamp to Uhrig. Around ten years older, and born in Munich, Römer's early career had perfectly mirrored those of many senior Nazis. Service in the First World War had been followed by a seamless segue into the right-wing paramilitary Freikorps, in whose ranks Römer had even participated in the suppression of the Munich Soviet Republic in 1919 and the crushing of the communist revolt in the Ruhr the following year. Yet the expected graduation to right-wing politics did not follow, and in the mid-1920s Römer began moving in the opposite direction, soon developing close ties to the German Communist Party (KPD). An embittered opponent of the Nazis right from the outset of the Third Reich, he spent much of the 1930s in prison.[17]

Berliners inspect a bomb crater on the East–West Axis late in 1940:
'The world had lost its former solidity.'

Civilians help with the clear-up after a raid on the northern suburbs in October 1940.

Gestapo Headquarters on Prinz-Albrecht-Strasse.

Some of those who passed through the building (*clockwise from left*): Communist resistance fighter Beppo Römer; Otto Weidt, who saved Jews by employing them in his factory; Johanna Solf, who ran a 'salon' of oppositionally minded Berliners; and Jewish *Greifer* Stella Goldschlag, who betrayed hundreds of fugitive Jews to the Gestapo.

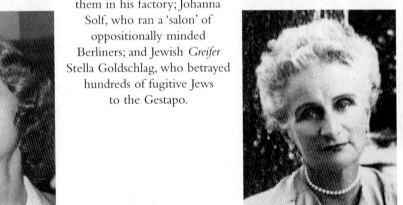

The beautiful surroundings of the Invaliden Cemetery, where the myth of the 'heroic death for the Fatherland' was most effectively propagated.

The grim reality: the corpses of Berliners killed in air raids laid out in a sports hall ready for burial, autumn 1944.

Central Berlin burning fiercely: Jerusalem Strasse, July 1944.

Berliners struggle through the rubble-field that had once been their street:
Stallschreiberstrasse in Kreuzberg, February 1945.

Distributing soup and sympathy to those bombed out,
August 1943.

The Zoo flak tower:
'like a fantastic monstrosity from a lost world'.

Barricades being constructed in March 1945: few of them offered any real obstacle to the Soviets.

'A terrifying sight': Red Army soldiers advance across a Berlin street, April 1945.

'What will become of us?' Civilians nervously watch the arrival of Soviet T-34 tanks: Mehringdamm in Kreuzberg, April 1945.

German soldiers captured trying to evade the Red Army by disguising themselves.

A feast for the unfussy: Berliners butcher a dead horse.

The end of the Thousand Year Reich: contemplation, recrimination and hope.

The Nazi invasion of the Soviet Union in the summer of 1941 galvanised the communists anew. Whereas they had previously been restricted to spouting rather weak and unconvincing slogans about Nazi excesses and the rights of sovereign nations, now they were being called upon to defend the very homeland of the proletarian revolution. With the period of ideological limbo at an end, Römer and Uhrig were among the first to call the faithful to arms.

Their primary weapon in the struggle was the monthly 'Information Service' pamphlet, which they produced in Berlin for distribution to communist cells in the city, as well as across Germany and abroad. Intended to inform its readers about the military and political situation, and inoculate them against Nazi propaganda, the pamphlet also called for sabotage actions against industrial and military targets. Its December 1941 issue, for instance, made the following demands of its readers:

> Every intervention that we can make in the economy, however modest, must lead to an effective blow against the imperialist, anti-proletarian war of the Hitler-Bourgeoisie.
>
> . . .
>
> Hitler's Achilles Heel is the fuel supply. Any action that destroys fuel, weakens his military capacity.
> Rubber is rarer still. Its destruction will ground German bombers.
>
> . . .
>
> Above all, give your full backing to every slowing of the work-rate to weaken productivity. In this way, the proletarian revolution will break forth, and will be victorious.[18]

Both Uhrig and Römer were reasonably adept at avoiding the attentions of the Gestapo, but they could not escape detection for long. Early in 1942, a wave of arrests across Germany signalled an end to the conspiracy. In Berlin alone, more than 150 individuals were arrested, Römer and Uhrig among them. Charged as 'enemies of the state', and members of an 'illegal organisation', they would spend over two years under interrogation, being shunted between some of the most odious camps and prisons of the Berlin area, including Sachsenhausen and Wuhlheide. Brought to trial for high treason in the summer of 1944, both men were sentenced to death and guillotined. Over seventy of their fellow conspirators faced the same fate, while many more were sentenced to lengthy periods of hard labour.[19]

With the demise of Römer and Uhrig, the baton passed initially to Anton Saefkow, a trained machinist, who sought to gather all those who had not been arrested. Under his leadership, acts of sabotage, distribution of flyers and help to fugitives continued. Like his predecessors, however, Saefkow could not escape the Gestapo and was arrested in the summer of 1944. Along with another sixty members of his group, he was sentenced to death and executed that autumn.

A similar fate awaited the most famous communist resistance group in wartime Berlin – the so-called 'Red Orchestra'. Founded by Air Ministry officer Harro Schulze-Boysen and the economist Arvid Harnack, it too was active in producing fly-posters and aiding fugitives in the capital, but its primary activity was espionage – it was one of the many sources that warned Moscow of the looming German attack in the early summer of 1941. The group – which is known by the name given it by Gestapo counter-intelligence – was large and eclectic, and unlike the Uhrig–Römer and Saefkow groups comprised not only communists, but also left-leaning intellectuals, artists and pacifists, including the playwright Adam Kuckhoff and the writer Günther Weisenborn. Despite this more elitist complexion, however, the 'Red Orchestra' fared little better than its more working-class fellows, and was rounded up in the autumn of 1942. The vast majority of its members – including Schulze-Boysen and Harnack – paid for their actions with their lives. Among them was Harnack's wife, Mildred Fish-Harnack, the only American woman executed during the Second World War as an underground conspirator. As she was led to the guillotine, her last words were 'And I have loved Germany so much'.[20]

Berlin's Christians were also active. Most notable among them were those of the Confessing Church, which had emerged in protest at the Nazification of the established Protestant Church. One of the movement's founders was Martin Niemöller, a parish pastor in the Berlin suburb of Dahlem. A former U-boat captain from the First World War, Niemöller had been an early supporter of Hitler who was spurred to resistance by his objection to Nazi racial policies and the regime's interference in religious affairs. Arrested for his public criticisms in 1937, he would spend the entire war in a succession of concentration camps. The post-war poem attributed to him eloquently summed up the humanitarian case for resistance against Nazism:

> First they came for the communists,
> and I did not speak out – because I was not a communist;
> Then they came for the trade unionists,
> and I did not speak out – because I was not a trade unionist;
> Then they came for the Jews,
> and I did not speak out – because I was not a Jew;
> Then they came for me,
> and there was no one left to speak out for me.[21]

The Provost of Berlin's St Hedwig's cathedral, Bernhard Lichtenberg, was another outspoken critic of the Nazis, often fulminating against the regime's excesses from his pulpit. Most famously, he wrote to the Chief Physician of the Reich in August 1941 in protest at the 'T4' euthanasia programme. 'As a human being, a Christian and a German', he wrote, 'I demand of you . . . that you answer for the crimes that have been perpetrated at your bidding and with your consent, and which will call forth the vengeance of the Lord on the heads of the German people.'[22] In the autumn of 1941, Lichtenberg was denounced for concluding his evensong sermon by saying: 'Now let us pray for the Jews and for the poor prisoners in the concentration camps.'[23] Arrested soon after, he perished en route to Dachau.

Churchmen were also well represented in the resistance groups that were formed among Berlin's elites. The first such group was the Solf Circle, which was established in the capital in 1936 as a traditional 'salon', where intellectuals would gather to discuss the pressing matters of the day. Meeting initially in the Wannsee home of Johanna Solf, the widow of the former German ambassador to Tokyo, the group contained a number of prominent and well-connected members, including minor aristocrats, diplomats and senior civil servants. Though it was not primarily involved with subversion or active resistance against the Nazi regime – despite Solf and her daughter personally assisting many fugitive Jews – it was intended to provide a forum for like-minded individuals, where they could exchange opinions and keep the concept of intellectual and political liberty alive. Yet, even these rather modest ambitions were too much for the authorities, and in the autumn of 1943 the circle was infiltrated by a Gestapo informant, a doctor by the name of Paul Reckzeh. Though the members were warned about the infiltration by Helmuth James von Moltke, they were rounded up for questioning the following January. Only a few of them would survive the end of the Third Reich.[24]

Moltke himself was typical of this type of non-violent, intellectual opposition to the Nazis, and was the focus of perhaps the most famous opposition group in Nazi Germany, the Kreisau Circle. Named by its Gestapo investigators after Moltke's Silesian estate, where the group had first come together, the circle held most of its meetings in Moltke's Berlin flat on Derfflingerstrasse, close to the Tiergarten.

Moltke was a dynamic and genial host. Born in rural Silesia, the scion of an old Prussian military family but with a South African mother, he was self-consciously cosmopolitan. Educated in Berlin, he had travelled widely and had completed his legal training in Britain, before returning to the German capital with the outbreak of war in 1939. It was there that he began to gather like-minded individuals, who would meet for largely theoretical discussions on topics such as international law and the nature of the state and society that might succeed the Nazis. It was an eclectic group – socialists, aristocrats and churchmen – but one whose resistance was primarily a cerebral one, influenced by Christian morality and by Moltke's strict advocacy of non-violence. Indeed, when they were finally tried, Moltke quipped that he and his fellows were to be hanged 'because we thought together'.[25]

The uncomfortable truth for all of the organised resistance groups in the capital, however, was that ordinary Berliners were not generally minded to risk their lives to oppose the Nazi regime. Most were not minded to resist at all. It should be remembered that the regime ruled primarily by consent. It was very effective, not only at co-opting those who might have opposed it – through the promise of work, for instance – but also at maintaining at least nominal popular support through its social policies and the expert use of propaganda. It had also been astonishingly successful, not only in restoring the nation's fortunes before 1939, but also in the early phase of the war that followed. These successes convinced vast numbers of ordinary Germans that the Nazi regime deserved their support. For the majority, therefore, 'resistance' to the Nazis never went beyond a raised eyebrow.

Importantly, even those who might have thought otherwise were often silenced. Would-be opponents of the regime often had their rebellious impulses curbed by the reflexive patriotism engendered in a nation at war. They were also dissuaded from voicing their dissent by knowledge of the dark role played by the Gestapo in preserving the consensus. And the fact that almost every one of the capital's resistance groups – of whatever hue – had been infiltrated, betrayed and judicially murdered would have done nothing to embolden them. Ruth Andreas-Friedrich, herself a member of the 'Uncle Emil' resistance group, outlined the difficulties in her diary: 'If we talk, plan, and recruit allies, we are hanged; among ten people there is always at least one who is treacherous or loose-mouthed.'[26] For many ordinary Berliners, therefore, engaging in formal organised resistance must have seemed like something akin to suicide.

Yet, there was still much that determined and principled individuals could do on a personal level to express their opposition. It was a course of action that was certainly not without its perils and could easily result in a visit from the Gestapo or a spell in a concentration camp, if betrayed. But it was nonetheless a relatively common occurrence in wartime Berlin; more common indeed, than anywhere else in the Reich.[27]

One method was simply to refuse to give the Nazi greeting. George Kennan noted that this was already common in the capital early in the war. Berliners, he recalled, 'could never be induced to give the Nazi salute. They continued to greet each other with the usual *"Guten Morgen"* in place of the obligatory *"Heil Hitler"*.'[28] Maria Nickel was one of those who chose this route and taught her two young sons not to use the new 'German Greeting'. In retrospect, she recalled, it was her first revolt against Hitler and the Nazis.[29]

Other protests were more overtly political. The reports of the SS security service attest to a spate of incidents of politically motivated vandalism and graffiti, beginning in the autumn and winter of 1939. Anti-Nazi leafleting also flourished. One of the most remarkable cases was that of Otto and Elise Hampel, an ordinary couple from Wedding, who began leafleting in the autumn of 1940 after Elise's brother was killed in France. Beyond a vague, working-class solidarity, the couple were largely apolitical and their protest was as much spurred by the slaughter of Germany's young men in war as anything else. Centred on their home district of Wedding, they distributed postcards and leaflets – which were often crudely printed, with disjointed, misspelt text – calling for civil disobedience and decrying the Nazi 'Winter Aid' scheme as fraudulent. One of their cards implored the German people simply to 'wake up', while another urged that 'we need to believe in ourselves'. For over two years, the Hampels evaded detection and distributed countless postcards and leaflets across the German capital. Denounced and arrested in the autumn of 1942, they were sentenced to death and executed the following spring.[30]

The Hampels were not alone. Many others followed suit. Most commonly, leaflets would be fly-posted on street signs and postboxes in the centre of the city, where they would be visible to the largest number of citizens. In content, they ranged widely from simple slogans – 'Down with Hitler!' – to subversive ditties such as:

> Great are the times
> But the portions are small
> What good does it do us
> When Hitler's flags stand tall!
> If under those flags
> There is no freedom at all.[31]

Only a few contained serious political comment. One distributed in Charlottenburg, for example, predicted that the war would lead to the emancipation of mankind, an end to exploitation and the demise of 'the class rule of the bourgeoisie'. 'The air', it concluded, 'would be cleared once and for all.'[32]

There were also a number of instances of communist agents leafleting in the capital in broad daylight. In one example, a group in Wilmersdorf enlisted the aid of a traditional schoolboy jape. After engaging passers-by in conversation, they would give their unwitting victims a valedictory pat on the back. Only later did the passers-by discover that they had leaflets stuck to them and that they had – in effect – been used as a communist sandwich board.[33]

Other Berliners sought to provide ideological sustenance only to their fellow communists. Alfred Hoernle, from the northern suburb of Hermsdorf, was known by the pseudonym 'Black Carl' and distributed communist propaganda to the like-minded citizens of the area. As one of his 'customers' explained:

> I worked in those days in my father's firm as a barber. 'Black Carl' always came at the same time, there was a very specific rhythm. He would enter the shop, remove his rucksack from his shoulders and hang it on a hook. He behaved just like a regular customer, as I cut his hair, except that he always 'forgot' to take his rucksack with him when he left. Inside it there was printed material for us to distribute. It wasn't much . . . but it was the only 'spiritual nourishment' that we received.[34]

Another Berliner who made small gestures of dissent was Josepha von Koskull. A housewife in her mid-forties, she recalled how in the spring of 1943 she had seen the date '1918' daubed on a nearby house. The significance of that date would have been immediately obvious to any German of the wartime era: 1918 was the year Germany was defeated in the First World War, the year the country was plunged into civic unrest, economic collapse and revolution. Impressed by the simplicity and effectiveness of this warning from the past, Koskull began writing the date on notices and posters, 'usually early in the morning, around half past seven, going down the Nürnberger Strasse'. Each time she returned to the site of her 'protest' some days later, she noticed that the number had been covered with thick black paint. Though she was well aware of the dangers of her actions, Koskull wanted to send those of a like mind 'a sign of life'.[35]

Some were less immediately political. Manfred Omankowsky belonged to the 'Swing Kids' movement, which disdained the Spartan, militaristic nature of Nazi ideology and defined itself primarily through its adherents' passion for swing music. Omankowsky was a typical 'Swing Boy'. Coming from a Social Democratic household in Reinickendorf, he grew his hair long and was an avid fan of jazz, collecting records sold illegally on the black market and attending underground dance clubs. Though he had not initially been motivated by political concerns – instead expressing what he described as a 'natural protest against the authority of the state' – he soon found himself in open conflict with the Nazis. One of his favourite haunts was the notorious Pharus Hall in the northern suburb of Wedding.

Once a hotbed of communist agitation and the scene of a brutal 'battle' with the SA in 1927, it was still a site of protest:

> That's where it was all going on. Within a radius of 200 metres there were sometimes whole crowds of youths hanging around. There were hundreds of us. There were lots of Swing Kids in the neighbourhood. We danced – or as we put it 'scrubbed' – to our banned music especially in the side rooms and in the toilets of the Pharus Hall. When the Hitler Youth turned up, we fought with them.[36]

It is perhaps inevitable that the attention of history should traditionally have been focused on the headline acts; on those who actively sought to bring down Hitler, such as Stauffenberg and the Red Orchestra. They, after all, were playing for the highest stakes and running the greatest risks. But it is also high time that recognition was given to those whose ambitions were much more modest; to those who sought to preserve a modicum of normality, of freedom of thought and expression; to those who – like Josepha von Koskull – merely sought to give their fellow Berliners 'a sign of life'.

One hot afternoon in the summer of 1944, fifteen-year-old Dieter Borkowski was enjoying a few days' leave from a Berlin flak battery. He had spent the day strolling along the banks of the Havel River in the south-west of the city with a young Ukrainian forced labourer, Marussja, on whom he had developed something of a crush. The two had caught the tram from the city centre out to the suburbs and had whiled away the afternoon picnicking and chatting in the sunshine. 'One could almost believe', he wrote in his diary, 'that we were at peace.'[37]

Later that afternoon, that sense of tranquillity was rudely interrupted. Walking back towards the city along the river, the pair were suddenly confronted by a barbed-wire cordon erected on the Glienicke Bridge and patrolled by soldiers. For a split second Borkowski wondered if it might have been put there to catch him – he had, after all, broken the law by spending the day with a Soviet forced labourer – but he quickly dismissed the idea as ridiculous. However, when he and Marussja passed through the checkpoint unhindered, his confusion deepened. He had no idea that he was witnessing part of Operation Valkyrie.[38]

Operation Valkyrie was the brainchild of a Wehrmacht colonel, Claus Schenck von Stauffenberg. Born into an aristocratic south German family, Stauffenberg was a career soldier who had participated in the Polish, French and North African campaigns before being seriously wounded in April 1943 in Tunisia. Returning to Germany, his convalescence coincided with a growing disgust at the Nazi regime, particularly its racial policies and its foolhardy prosecution of the war.

Rather than passively plan for some putative post-Nazi government, Stauffenberg intended nothing less than to bring about the demise of the Nazis. Allying himself with others of like mind – politicians and military men – he used his position within the army reserve to help develop a plan for a military coup against Hitler. The result, Operation Valkyrie, was the single most important episode in the story of the German resistance to Nazism, combining both the most serious attempt to assassinate Hitler and the only attempted coup in the history of the Third Reich.

Operation Valkyrie was set in motion on 20 July 1944, when Stauffenberg planted a time bomb in a situation conference at Hitler's East Prussian headquarters at Rastenburg. The bomb duly exploded, killing three of those present outright and mortally wounding one other, and Stauffenberg – believing that Hitler was among the dead – hurried to Berlin to take charge of the wider coup against Nazi rule.

In the capital, Stauffenberg's co-conspirators were busy attempting to seize power. They hoped to achieve this by a ruse. By activating an official contingency plan, designed to suppress unrest on the home front, they hoped to bring sufficient troops out onto the streets that they could seize temporary control of key strategic points in the capital and thereby dislodge the Nazis from power. Crucially, however, those troops would not be let into the secret of the coup attempt; they would be acting in unwitting support of the conspiracy.

While secrecy was an essential component of the plot, it is obvious that the military and political elites that made up the backbone of the 20 July conspiracy were profoundly dubious about permitting any sort of 'popular' involvement in the action. To some degree, they rightly doubted the level of popular support that any such coup might enjoy.[39] But it is also clear that many of the conspirators – and especially the military men among them – were simply not thinking of 'the people' as players in the drama at all. As conspirator Hans Gisevius complained, they were aiming at little more than a straightforward military takeover: 'Stauffenberg', he wrote, 'wanted to drop no more ballast than was absolutely necessary, then he would paint the ship of state a military grey and set it afloat again.'[40] 'Valkyrie', it seems, was to be an old-fashioned military coup, not a full-blown revolution, and it was designed to take place well above the heads of ordinary Berliners.

Thus, when the coup was launched in Berlin that afternoon in the summer of 1944, the people of the capital – regardless of their political affiliations and loyalties – were kept well and truly out of the loop. A few diarists knew what was going on, but this was primarily because they had contacts with the circle of conspirators. Ruth Andreas-Friedrich, for instance, rashly claimed to have been 'right in the midst of it',[41] while Missie Vassiltchikov was genuinely well informed, having first learned of the conspiracy nearly a year before.[42]

The reaction of most ordinary Berliners, however, was one of utter bewilderment. 'The general confusion is indescribable', wrote one diarist. 'Everyone seems to have lost their head.'[43] Countless rumours swirled around the capital that day – that Hitler was dead, that the SS had carried out the coup, or that Goebbels was now in charge – and, to add to the chaos, the city echoed with the sounds of marching troops, shouted orders and rattling tanks. As Ursula von Kardorff noted, pickets were erected on many streets in the government district, but few of those watching events from their apartments or workplaces had any idea why the soldiers were there, or indeed which 'side' they served.[44]

The only clarity, it seems, was provided by the radio. Ruth Andreas-Friedrich recalled hearing that afternoon that Hitler was dead: 'As if at a signal we reach for the switch of the radio. Music – the lively *Badenweiler March*, Hitler's favourite tune . . . That doesn't sound like death', she thought, 'it sounds damnably like he's alive.'[45] Shortly after 6.00 that evening, a radio announcement was finally made confirming that an attempt had been made on Hitler's life, but that he was unhurt and had received Mussolini for talks. A later bulletin announced that Hitler himself would speak to the nation that night.

It was shortly after midnight when Hitler was ushered into the simple, pine-panelled tea house at his eastern headquarters, the *Wolfsschanze*. Dressed in a black tunic, standing before a modest white podium with three microphones, he showed little outward evidence of the drama of that day. But for those countless Germans listening at home, his voice seemed to lack the fortitude of earlier years; his delivery was slow, halting even. 'My fellow Germans', he began:

> Yet another of the countless attempts on my life has been planned and carried out. I am speaking to you for two reasons: 1. So that you can hear my voice and know that I myself am not injured and well. 2. So that you can hear the details of a crime without parallel in German history.

He went on to castigate what he described as the 'very small clique of ambitious, unscrupulous, criminal and stupid officers' that had spawned the conspiracy. 'The claim by these usurpers that I am no longer alive, is at this very moment proven false, for here I am talking to you, my dear fellow countrymen.'[46]

For many of Hitler's listeners, the burning question was whether it was really him. But the voice was unmistakeable. 'From the first word', Theo Findahl wrote, 'we realise that it is Hitler and not one of his imitators. His voice is extremely agitated . . . It is easy to hear that it is not an act.'[47] With that broadcast, all lingering doubts about Hitler's survival were banished. For the masses of ordinary Germans huddled that night around their crackling radio sets, clarity was finally restored. Whether they had secretly welcomed the assassination attempt or not, they now at least knew where they stood; the war would go on, the Nazi regime was to be obeyed as before.

In the days that followed, Berlin presented the impression of normality. Theo Findahl wrote: 'the attempted coup of yesterday has not left the slightest trace on Berlin's outward life. Everything is taking its usual course – trams, underground trains are again running to their timetables, shops and offices are open as before, on the streets and in the market places people are behaving just like on any other workday.'[48]

That veneer of normality concealed an oppressive atmosphere. The SS and Gestapo had begun to round up all those connected to the plotters, dragging in families and acquaintances as the net was cast ever wider and ever more individuals were implicated by the interrogation of their fellows. As a result, people were nervous, lips were sealed and faces adopted an inscrutable mask. One diarist wrote in the aftermath: 'It is dangerous to show a sorry expression. Many have already been arrested, just because they said "shame".'[49] Berliners with contacts, however tenuous, to those involved in the conspiracy soon began to fear the inevitable Gestapo dragnet, the knock at the door. Ruth Andreas-Friedrich wondered who had already been arrested, and prepared herself not to 'so much as think' of the names of those she knew who might be involved.[50] Ursula von Kardorff, meanwhile, who had also had contact with some of the plotters, wrote: 'one day they will come for me too. Every time the doorbell rings, I think that the time has come.'[51]

For the majority, however, the dominant reaction was one of indifference, even relief. Theo Findahl described Berliners as 'apathetic', an assessment borne out by contemporary SD mood reports, which evinced little popular sympathy for the plotters around Stauffenberg and even claimed to discern an improvement in public morale and a 'deepening' of the faith in the Führer.[52] Diarist Hans-Georg von Studnitz explained the reflexive display of loyalty:

The public reaction to the plot is less violent than one would have expected, although July 20 brought home to the masses the crisis in our national leadership, it has not reduced their readiness to follow that leadership. Since no one has a comprehensive view of the situation that has arisen or can see any way out, and since everyone fears that any display of disloyalty might well contribute to a deterioration of the situation, the regime can continue to rely on the further support of the people ... The morale of the nation is unimpaired.[53]

Whatever reservations the people of Berlin may have had about the Nazi regime, they were clearly even less enamoured with the prospect of a palace coup by the old elites, a process in which they had played no part and had been permitted no voice.

14

Against All Odds

The first arrivals came alone or in pairs. With collars turned against the chill of a February afternoon, they converged outside a nondescript building in the very heart of Berlin. They were mainly women, predominantly middle-aged, though a few brought with them their young children and older siblings. They all wore the determined frowns of those who had endured much and had learned self-reliance. They did not, at first, converse too much with their fellows, except for a few whispered exchanges to confirm what most of them already suspected. A few dared to approach the solitary guard, in a vain attempt to elicit some precious information. In time, that afternoon, their number grew to over one hundred individuals. It would continue to grow.

Unremarkable though it was, Rosenstrasse 2–4 was a building that would have been familiar to many of those congregating outside it that cold afternoon. A solid Wilhelmine-era block of four storeys, with a fifth squeezed beneath a saddle roof, it had formerly been a welfare office for the Berlin Jewish community. It had been there that Berlin Jews 'had clothed their destitute, fed their hungry, healed their sick'.[1] It was there that the relations of the deported had gathered to find information and solace, where medical care had been provided and where the bereaved had been comforted. Yet, for that week at least, Rosenstrasse would assume a much wider importance; indeed, it would be pushed to the very forefront of events.

That morning – Saturday 27 February 1943 – had witnessed the final round-up of the capital's remaining Jews. In the so-called *Fabrik-Aktion*, or 'Factory Action', Gestapo and SS personnel had raided a number of factories across Berlin arresting Jewish labourers. Others were picked up off the street or at their homes. Those arrested – around 10,000 in

all – were taken by lorry to a number of locations across the city, where
they were processed and held prior to their planned deportation.

The prisoners in most of those makeshift camps – such as the 'Clou'
concert hall or the Levetzowstrasse synagogue – were all so-called
Voll-Juden, 'Full Jews', those who constituted the last remaining Jews
in the city, and who would, in due course, be deported to Auschwitz.
The 1,800 prisoners now huddled within the building on Rosenstrasse
were rather different. One of them, Hans Grossmann, quickly realised
when he was picked up that morning that he was being singled out
for special treatment:

> The SS were very precise. Everyone had to enter an office and was
> questioned on his name, birth date and address. The information was
> evidently compared with a card, because in my case, the Gestapo-man
> called out 'Mischling of the first degree!' – 'Any Aryan relatives?' he
> then asked me. I nodded. 'Off to Rosenstrasse!'[2]

Siegfried Cohn had also been picked up that morning. After a brief
interview at his place of work – the Osram factory in Wilmersdorf –
he had been taken to a barracks in Moabit, where the prisoners were
sorted. As the husband of an Aryan spouse, he was separated from
the others, and a white pass was hung around his neck. He was then
taken to Rosenstrasse.[3]

Rather than *Voll-Juden*, therefore, the Jews taken to Rosenstrasse
that day were those who fell into various marginal categories; those
who were *Mischlinge* (part-Jewish), or were living in a *Mischehe* (a racially
mixed marriage), as well as 'privileged' Jews, such as decorated veterans
of the first World War and so-called *Geltungsjuden*, those cases – such
as Christian converts – who were legally deemed Jewish, even if they
did not consider themselves so. The women who had converged on
the pavement outside, therefore, were predominantly the Aryan wives
of Jewish husbands. And they had come to show support for their
captured menfolk.

Conditions inside the building were unpleasant but not intolerable.
'It was not a concentration camp', wrote one of those held there. 'There
were doors that opened and closed. Occasionally someone shouted down
"Hey, can't we get some water in here!" There were people moving
about. One should not imagine it as just Nazis standing around with

whips . . . It was peaceful.'⁴ Even so, violence was not altogether absent. Another prisoner, Hans Bloch, recalled that the SS personnel there 'worked on him with their fists' in the basement of the building, in an attempt to glean information about a fellow Jew, who had escaped into the Berlin underground. Bloch told them nothing.⁵

Even for those who did not directly experience physical abuse at the hands of the SS, conditions were far from agreeable, with count-less men – they were mostly men – crammed into rooms that were entirely lacking in creature comforts. Siegfried Cohn was allocated to a room containing about fifty or sixty others 'packed together like canned sardines'. 'There are maybe ten straw sacks', he wrote, 'so that most of the inmates have to lie on the bare ground.'⁶ Toilet facilities too were quite inadequate. 'If one has the need to relieve himself', Cohn complained, 'he has to wait in line for about three hours, and the most degrading part is that the men and women have to use the same toilet, without it being possible to close the door to the room.'⁷

The few women in the building were generally kept together, but conditions for them were not much better. Inge Unikower remem-bered that 'the small, empty office rooms were packed so full that those imprisoned had to stand and could only squat down for a short time, with their backs to the wall and their knees pulled in tight'.⁸ Another female inmate, Erika Lewine, remembered that the sanitary conditions left much to be desired. Her room did not have a toilet, she recalled, 'only a bucket, in a sort of closet'. To make matters worse, the extreme stress of the day had caused many of the women to menstruate. 'We couldn't wash ourselves', she wrote, 'we had nothing there; we were totally covered with dirt.'⁹

The food supply in the building was similarly insufficient, amounting to little more than an occasional ration of boiled cabbage, sausage and a little bread, which was supplied by the Jewish Hospital. Ruth Bileski remembered the meagre fare: 'Nothing to eat. They served . . . one meal a day. I remember the sauerkraut. No spoon, nothing. We still had an old ticket from the streetcar. It was made from cardboard. My sister and I used it as a spoon.'¹⁰ Most of the prisoners at Rosenstrasse, therefore, depended on food supplied by their families outside.

In the street, meanwhile, the crowd continued to grow and the event began to take on the characteristics of a spontaneous yet largely passive protest. Hans Grossmann, who arrived there as a prisoner that afternoon, recalled:

> As we turned onto Rosenstrasse, I couldn't believe my eyes! I saw so many people, many women. A real gathering. I saw policemen. But not that many. I saw SS men.
>
>   The truck couldn't even be driven up to the office building. It was immediately surrounded by women. We had to climb down and the SS men cleared us a path through the crowd.[11]

The women outside were initially most concerned to get basic information – to ascertain whether their menfolk were indeed being held in the building, and enquire after their condition. With increasing desperation, they demanded to know what was going on, why their husbands were being held and what would happen to them. As the afternoon wore on, the crowd grew larger. Some of them had been alerted by the Berlin grapevine – the so-called 'mouth radio', or *Mundfunk*, a pun on the German for radio, *Rundfunk* – others had been alarmed when their husbands and sons had failed to return home that afternoon, had made enquiries and had managed to track them down. They tended to have little luck demanding information of the guards posted at the entrance, who simply told them to move on. Charlotte Friedmann, who was looking for her husband Julius, resorted to a simple ruse:

> Through a trick I determined that my husband was there . . . I asked the guard for the potato ration cards, which Julius had. Then I received them. On the back he had written very lightly, so that I could read it when I held it up to the light, 'I'm fine!' Other women demanded a house key, or food rations cards, to confirm that their husbands were there.[12]

Later arrivals came with food, toiletries and other essentials that they hoped to be able to pass on. Ruth Gross brought food for her father. Each time she visited, she handed a small package of bread to a civilian orderly, giving her father's name. She initially doubted whether it was getting through to him, until she glimpsed him at an upper window. 'He saw me too', she recalled, 'and waved with the little note from the package we had sent him. So he had received it!'[13]

Despite such minor successes, the mood of the crowd grew increasingly agitated as time wore on and the guards at the door were reinforced by additional SS men. Though the women were repeatedly warned to move away, they began to articulate their demands more vociferously, chanting: *'Gebt uns unsere Männer wieder!'* – 'Give us our husbands back!' The chant would soon grow to a cacophonous din. When Annie Radlauer arrived at the nearby railway station the following morning, she could hear the noise of the Rosenstrasse protest from fully three blocks away.[14]

The stand-off continued for the rest of that week. The numbers outside on the pavement grew steadily. Though some contemporary accounts were prone to hyperbole – one diarist, for instance, estimated the number of protesters at 6,000 – the real numbers were comparatively modest, being reckoned at around 600 at any one time, and about 1,000 in total. Yet the women were determined. And, as rumours reached them of the deportation of the other Jews seized at the same time and held elsewhere, their determination grew. Day after day they returned and stood arm in arm in small groups outside the building, chanting and shouting. Others paced the pavement, or craned their necks in an effort to catch a glimpse of a loved one at an upper window. Occasionally, the chanting was interrupted when the barked orders of the SS guards and threats to shoot sent the women scurrying into the nearby side streets and alleyways for cover. Within minutes, they would be back on the pavement, continuing their noisy protest. As Ruth Andreas-Friedrich put it, the women at Rosenstrasse 'called for their husbands, screamed for their husbands, howled for their husbands, and stood like a wall, hour after hour, night after night'.[15]

Then, after around a week, there was a change in fortunes. Slowly at first, some of those imprisoned began to be released. On Friday 5 March, the first inmates – primarily those 'privileged' Jews in mixed marriages – were sent home. Over the subsequent days, others followed, with the last of them being released up to two weeks after their initial arrest.[16] Each of them was given a certificate, detailing their name, address and occupation, and stating the date of their release from the 'Rosenstrasse collection camp'. Even the twenty-five 'privileged' individuals who had already been deported to Auschwitz – apparently 'mistakenly' – were swiftly returned to the capital.

The prisoners released from Rosenstrasse couldn't believe their luck.

Most of them would have expected to be deported and, though they were ignorant of the precise workings of the Holocaust, they would have known or suspected enough to have been profoundly concerned for their lives. As one of the prisoners, Ernst Bukofzer, recalled:

> When I left that house, equipped with my official release note . . . my wife and both daughters were there, expecting me. They had already been there for hours, patiently sticking it out, and led me home, glowing with happiness. I was exhausted, as if a heavy burden had fallen from my shoulders. There had indeed been hours when I had not expected to return once again to the circle of my family.[17]

For many, however, the release must have seemed less a liberation than a stay of execution. Ruth Gross's father arrived home 'exhausted, hungry, tired and stubbly' in the early morning of 6 March. But already at 4.00 p.m. that same day, he had to attend an interview with the local police and the following day he was obliged to report for his next stint of forced labour – this time clearing buildings containing unexploded bombs.[18]

The Rosenstrasse protest has been much discussed by historians in recent years and has spawned two rival interpretations.[19] Some argue that the women's protest on Rosenstrasse was instrumental in securing the release of the prisoners and in saving them from certain death in the gas chambers of Auschwitz. They believe that Goebbels, the SS and the Nazi hierarchy 'blinked' when faced with the determined opposition of the Rosenstrasse women. Unable to risk such open dissent, they stayed their hand, thereby halting – albeit on a small scale – the apparently unstoppable progress of the Holocaust.

Others take a rather more nuanced, if less romantic view. They argue that the Rosenstrasse revolt, though heroic in itself, actually had little effect on the progress of the Holocaust. They hold that the inmates of Rosenstrasse were never actually scheduled for deportation, rather they were separated out from the remaining 'full-Jews' in the capital, while their identities and precise racial status were checked. They were then to be used to replace the staff of the remaining Jewish organisations in Berlin, who were almost all scheduled for imminent deportation.[20] Thus one might see the Rosenstrasse protest as a side show: a distraction from the more serious – and more deadly – operations then going on elsewhere. After all, while the 1,800 at Rosenstrasse were freed, the 8,000 or so held elsewhere that week were all deported to Auschwitz, and the majority of those were murdered immediately upon arrival.[21]

Whichever way one interprets the events on Rosenstrasse, it is clear that it *was* a remarkable episode. But, while historians argue over archival minutiae and precise chronologies, the most extraordinary fact of all seems to be that mass, popular resistance erupted in 1943, in the very heart of the Third Reich. The fact that many hundreds of Berlin women dared to demonstrate openly against the deportation of their Jewish sons, husbands and fathers – the only protest of its kind in Nazi Germany – is little short of astonishing.

Yet another important consequence of the *Fabrik-Aktion* and the Rosenstrasse revolt has traditionally been overlooked. Prior to that final round-up of late February 1943, the remaining Jews in the German capital could still convince themselves that the work they were doing in the munitions factories and elsewhere was so vital to Nazi Germany that they would effectively be spared the horrors of deportation. They had bought their lives, they would have reasoned, by their hard labour.

For those Berlin Jews who had dared to entertain this opinion, the *Fabrik-Aktion* would have come as a shock. It would have become immediately and brutally clear that they were not indispensable; their places would be taken by Poles, French and Dutchmen, as well as by the more 'privileged' of their fellows, and they would be sent to meet their fate. For Rachel Becker, whose father had been held in Rosenstrasse, it was a sobering realisation: 'All those who did not even want to believe the strange rumours according to which the Jews, being ostensibly deported for "resettlement" somewhere in the east . . . were not put to work but [were put] to death, were suddenly shaken out of their complacency and faced, at last, with the whole and cruel truth.'[22] For some, there was now only one alternative to boarding the cattle trucks bound for Auschwitz: to 'go underground' and take their chances as fugitives beneath the Aryan surface of Hitler's capital.

It is easy to underestimate the enormity of the decision to 'go underground' in wartime Berlin. For one thing, the so-called Jewish *Taucher* or 'U-boats', had no idea how long their underground odyssey would last, or if it would ever end at all. Modern readers with the benefit

of hindsight should not forget that the Third Reich was in the ascend-
ancy at least until the winter of 1942–3 and even after that point those
on the German home front often had little idea of the war's progress.
For a Jew deciding to 'dive' in 1943, therefore, it was very much a leap
into an unknown and very forbidding future.

First of all, going underground in Nazi Germany was to break the
law. Becoming a fugitive involved removing the *Judenstern* and
discarding one's papers; it implied a life on the run – lying, stealing,
cheating, doing anything to survive. And, despite everything they
had already endured, the majority of Jews – especially the older generation – found this an unnerving prospect. Like their Aryan fellows,
they were to a large degree wedded to the principles of civic obedience, and the implicit belief in the authority of the state and its organs.
In this regard, one must not forget that the deportation of German
Jewry bore the legitimate stamp of Nazi officialdom and was backed
by the necessary paragraphs of German law. Thus, many Berlin Jews
could not contemplate such a radical course of action and preferred
to comply with their deportation. After all, deportation was the only
certainty that many of them had left.

There were other factors that would complicate the decision to
flee. For a Jew, to become a 'non-person' was to leave behind one's
own past. Previous residences – even whole areas of the capital –
would have to be routinely avoided. And though a few trusted friends
might be called upon to provide shelter, most former neighbours and
acquaintances would also have to be actively shunned by a *Taucher* for
fear that any contact might lead to betrayal and arrest.

In addition, the decision to go underground effectively meant giving
up on those friends and family who had already been deported. Though
many Jews had heard the rumours and feared the worst, they still
hoped that their direst imaginings might prove to be wide of the mark.
Making the leap into a life in the underground, therefore, often meant
a simultaneous acceptance that the rumours were true and that loved
ones would not be returning. It meant abandoning all that they held
dear.

Nonetheless, despite the drastic nature of the move, many went into
hiding, especially after the *Fabrik-Aktion* of spring 1943. It has been estimated that around 10–12,000 Jews went underground in Germany over
the course of the war. Of these, the vast majority hid in the big cities,

where anonymity was easier to maintain. Berlin, with its left-liberal traditions and history of Jewish settlement, offered perhaps the greatest opportunity for survival. Consequently, about half of all those Jews braving the 'dive' into the underground – some 5–7,000 – are thought to have done so in the capital.[23]

For those taking the plunge, there were a number of essential survival tactics. The first step for any would-be fugitive was to remove the hated *Judenstern* stitched to their clothing. For some, this act alone was something of a liberation, a way of celebrating their new identity. Yitzhak Schwersenz went underground in the late summer of 1942. Escaping his scheduled deportation, he travelled with a friend to the semi-rural area of Pichelsberg, close to the Olympic Stadium. There, the two of them removed the Jewish star and replaced it with the insignia of the Nazi labour service, the *Deutsche Arbeitsfront*. As Schwersenz recalled: 'I left Berlin with the *Judenstern* and came back with the swastika . . . After dark, I returned to Berlin alone and made my first wander through the streets of the city, to get used to my new "role" as a free, ordinary citizen.'[24]

For many it was imperative to change their appearance. For those who were 'blessed' with Aryan looks – blue eyes and blond hair – this was not an issue, but for the majority of Jews, some visual sleight of hand was usually necessary, altering their looks, their hair colour, even their style of dress.

Some went to greater lengths to forget, deny and expunge all traces of their Jewishness, and to live as far as was possible as 'Aryans'. One young woman hiding in Pankow was advised by her aunt to 'forget that she was a Jew'.[25] On the most basic level, this would involve altering one's whole demeanour, learning to walk tall once again, and shaking off the hunted, mistrustful look that the years of persecution had brought. One *Taucher* noted that one of the golden rules for underground life was 'never to look unkempt. An unshaven face or dirty collar would always attract attention.'[26] Regardless of the difficulties of their predicament, therefore, fugitive Jews had to adopt a confident, 'normal' bearing in order to survive.

While there were many within the Jewish community of Berlin who were willing to help fellow Jews, the scope of their activity was severely limited. Nonetheless, some self-help organisations were formed, such as *Chug Chaluzi* – the 'Pioneer Circle' – which was established in 1943 in response to the *Fabrik-Aktion*. On one level, the Circle sought to maintain some semblance of Jewish spiritual and cultural life, by visiting theatres and concerts, or celebrating Rosh Hashanah and Yom Kippur.[27] Beyond that, it also offered practical help to fugitive Jews by exchanging information and organising meals and lodgings. For the Circle's founders, its actions were a form of resistance: 'We're combating Hitler', they said, 'with every life we save.'[28]

A few tried to be as independent as possible, seeking out abandoned houses or garden sheds, frequenting the railway stations, or riding the trains for as long as they could. The houseboats on Berlin's lakes – the Havelsee, Wannsee and Müggelsee – were also favourite hideouts – and, as we have seen, so were some of the more elaborate tombs of the capital's cemeteries. Yet for all their valiant efforts at self-help, Jewish *Taucher* were, in most cases, entirely reliant on Aryan helpers. Indeed, it has been estimated that, on average, it took the cooperation of seven Germans to help each fugitive Jew.[29]

Quite a number of Aryans in Berlin were willing to help Jews – even to run the ultimate risk and hide Jewish refugees in their own homes. Often, such assistance consisted of very modest gestures: the sharing of ration coupons, for instance, or the donation of clothes. One evening, two fugitive Jews arrived at Ursula von Kardorff's door:

> Yesterday at dusk the doorbell rang. Outside two figures, who haltingly enter. In the light of the hall, I see that they are wearing the Jewish star. They are relatives of a Breslau merchant, who owned one of Papa's pictures, which they now want to sell, because they need the money. We give them some food and slowly they thaw out. It is indescribable what these people are going through. They want to go underground, before they get picked up, take off the star and live as bombed-out refugees from the Rhineland. Of course, Papa buys the picture from them. I think they not only wanted material help, they also sought a certain comfort.[30]

For many, such small-scale acts would be the start of much wider and more risky involvement. Most immediately, Jewish *Taucher* needed to find safe accommodation. For some, this most pressing requirement was solved by serendipity, by a stroke of fortune or a chance meeting. Irma Simon, for instance, had little idea where she would go when she left her apartment to avoid deportation in the *Fabrik-Aktion*. Carrying a heavy suitcase, she paused to rest on Lehrterstrasse in Moabit, where she found her saviour – a young shoemaker and communist sympathiser who offered her shelter. 'A person whom I had never seen in my life', she later recalled, 'calmly promised something that anyone in this city of millions, Berlin, would have considered insane.'[31] The man, August Kossmann, hid Irma, her husband and her son in his modest apartment for the remaining two years of the war.

In most cases, however, *Taucher* first approached those they believed they could trust. Erich Neumann was a teenager when his mother took in a Jewish friend at her café in Charlottenburg in the winter of 1944:

> Suddenly, that October, Wolfgang S., our accountant and a friend of the family, stood at the door, saying, 'Klärchen, please help me, they are after me!' Warned by friends, Wolfgang had been able to leave his refuge in the Drakestrasse in Lichterfelde. Now he stood, with a small suitcase in his hand in our back room, shaking. The usual yellow star on his jacket and coat were missing, but the marks where they had been were still noticeable.[32]

Wolfgang was washed and clothed, and a small room was set aside behind the café for him. He was supplied with food and would spend twenty-three hours a day in his room, only venturing out after dark to walk the family dog in a nearby park. He stayed for the following five months. Erich recalled that his mother knew very well that such behaviour risked the wrath of the Gestapo, if discovered, 'but she simply suppressed the thought. She had never left someone in the lurch, when her help was required . . . For her, it was only natural.'[33]

Taucher often preferred not to risk all with one location and one host, preferring instead a peripatetic existence, sometimes involving the assistance of dozens of Aryan sympathisers. Max Krakauer, for instance, compiled a list at the end of the war of all of those Berliners who had provided him with refuge, accommodation, work and false papers. He counted sixty-six names.[34] Alfred Bornholmer went underground in the autumn of 1942 to escape his deportation, and though he initially stayed hidden with his aunt, the continued attentions of the

Gestapo forced him to seek accommodation further afield. He would travel right across the capital, even to outlying towns such as Beelitz and Luckenwalde, rarely staying in the same place twice. Though all of his close family – mother, brother and sister-in-law – were deported to their deaths, Alfred would survive the war.[35]

Another example was Salomon Striem, a friend of the Knirsch family. He often visited them at their home in the suburb of Pankow, where he was known to the children as 'Uncle Fritz'. 'He was blond', recalled Rita Knirsch:

> lived illegally in Berlin and did not wear the *Judenstern*. Day by day, he would travel with the railway right across the city, as he had no fixed address. He would ask: 'Let me stay with you awhile, but wake me if there's an air raid alarm, I don't want anyone to see me with you!' Our mother always let him stay, and reminded me: 'Rita, you must tell nobody about this!' . . . she explained 'I cannot just turn this poor hunted man away.'[36]

In this way, 'Uncle Fritz' evaded the Nazi authorities for over eighteen months, before he was finally caught in a round-up at Alexanderplatz in the autumn of 1944 and deported.

Those Aryan Berliners who sought to help fugitive Jews could have any number of motivations – from the political and ideological to the venal. Otto Weidt was one of those who were more ideologically inspired. A convinced pacifist and former anarchist, Weidt was manager of a workshop on Rosenthaler Strasse, which manufactured brushes and brooms, and was assigned around thirty deaf and dumb employees from the local Jewish Home for the Blind. When the deportations began in 1941, he fought for the life of every one of his employees, visiting the Gestapo offices to argue – in many cases successfully – that his workers were essential for the war effort and should be taken off the deportation lists. In time, he became bolder. He bribed Gestapo officials, hid as many as eight Jews on his factory premises and even secured the release of one of his workers who had already been deported to Auschwitz.[37] Otto Weidt is thought to have directly aided fifty-six Jews, half of whom survived the war.[38]

Other Aryan 'helpers' had no specific political affiliation beyond a sense of shared humanity. Foremost among them were the churches, particularly the oppositionally minded *Bekennende Kirche*, or 'Confessing Church', a few of whose members collected passbooks and identity cards, which would be modified by forgers and then passed on to fugitive Jews.[39] Catholic chaplain Harald Poelchau was also active in this regard. As chaplain of Berlin's prisons, he was able not only to provide spiritual succour to those in direst need, he also supplied a number of fugitive Jews with accommodation and false papers.[40]

Another remarkable case is that of Otto Jodmin, who was a caretaker in an apartment block in Wielandstrasse in Charlottenburg. Exploiting his position of not inconsiderable influence, where he was responsible for much of the administration of the building, he allowed individuals or small groups of refugees to use the cellars – to which only he had access – until they could find more permanent and secure shelter elsewhere. In addition, he falsely registered Jews as Aryan residents, or bombing victims, thereby enabling them to get access to identity papers and ration cards. He did all this, he said, because he had been brought up to show compassion to others. 'I simply had to do it', he later recalled, 'there was nothing else for it, there was no other way. I did not even think long about it, not at all . . . I just couldn't act in any other way.'[41]

Housewife Maria Nickel, meanwhile, was moved to act by her opposition to Hitler. Appalled by the rise of the Nazis and their 'intolerable' anti-Semitism, she had made a vow in the autumn of 1942 that she would attempt to save 'at least one Jewish life'. She began rather modestly, befriending a Jewish woman, Ruth Abraham, and supplying her with groceries. As the friendship progressed, however, Nickel was inexorably drawn into the task of saving Abraham's family from deportation, supplying false documents and helping them disappear into the underground. In the end, she helped to save, not one, but three lives.[42]

Others hid Jews for love. Gerda Wiener moved in with her Aryan lover, Gerhard, in the spring of 1943, and would remain with him, hiding under the bed or in the wardrobe whenever guests came, for the remainder of the war. The greatest peril, however, was having to hide her Jewishness and fugitive status from Gerhard's mother, who lived with them. 'We had to come across carefree and happy with her', she wrote, 'as she would most certainly have informed the Gestapo if she had had any idea of our double life.'[43]

The most famous example of this sort in Berlin, however, is the wartime affair between Berlin housewife Lilly Wust and the feisty Jewish fugitive Felice Schragenheim. Though Wust was a Nazi sympathiser, with four children and a husband fighting on the Eastern Front, she fell for Schragenheim when the two first met in a Berlin café in November 1942. By that time, Schragenheim was already living as a *Taucher*, having faked her own suicide when her deportation notice had arrived and subsequently resurfaced under false papers. The two began a lesbian relationship, evidently made all the more passionate by Wust's desire for adventure and Schragenheim's need for protection. Captured by the Gestapo in the autumn of 1943, Schragenheim would ultimately meet her end on a death march in the final days of 1944, despite Wust's desperate efforts to secure her release. 'She was my other half', Wust said shortly before her death in 2006, 'literally my reflection, my mirror image . . . I have never stopped loving her.'[44]

Though the primary and most deadly risk was certainly run by the *Taucher* in wartime Berlin, the tribulations endured by their Aryan helpers should not be forgotten. While it is not realistic to blithely assume that any Aryan Berliner caught hiding or assisting a Jew would automatically face the death penalty, neither is it accurate to claim that most of those caught helping *Taucher* would receive nothing more than a ticking-off from the Gestapo.

It is true that there was no specific crime in Nazi Germany which approximated to 'aiding Jews', hence there was no automatic penalty. However, there were a number of offences – ranging from 'racial defilement' to 'rationing irregularities' to 'undermining the war effort' – with which Aryan helpers could be charged if they were caught. In the majority of examples, discovery by the authorities would mean at the very least an interrogation and a temporary imprisonment. In repeat cases, meanwhile, or those with aggravating circumstances, a stay in a concentration camp could be the result, which could mean – *de facto* if not *de jure* – a death sentence.

For this reason, perhaps, some of those Berliners who aided Jews preferred not to know the identity and racial status of those they were helping; after all, ignorance could at least be some token defence in the event of capture. They were often happy to assume – whether they really believed it or not – that their temporary residents were simply refugees, deserters or those bombed out and waiting for new accommodation and paperwork. Similarly, Jewish fugitives were often content to collude in the deception. Though the majority of *Taucher* tended to reveal their Jewishness when they initially went underground, they soon learned that such candour was not always beneficial. In time, it seems, many of them pretended to be Christians.[45]

In addition to the ever-present fear of detection or betrayal, there were everyday practical concerns to consider. Once underground, those Jews who did not manage to find a new identity and new papers would not receive any ration allocation, meaning that they had to be fed from the already meagre food supplies of their hosts. As a result, some of those Berliners who hid Jews did so – in the first instance at least – for material or financial reward, thereby rather denting the altruistic ideal. In many such cases, the financial aspect served only as a sweetener, soon to be replaced with genuine concern for the fate of the unfortunate *Taucher*. But, in a few examples, it remained the primary motivation, and if the Jews could not pay, they would be betrayed to the Gestapo. In one instance, a woman in Schöneberg informed the local Gestapo about the mother and daughter she had been hiding in her flat.[46] Her motivation for doing so is unclear, but it is possible that her Jewish 'guests' had simply run out of money.

Whatever their precise motivation, the Aryan helpers of fugitive Jews were making a hard choice. Ruth Andreas-Friedrich, who was herself active in assisting Jews in the Berlin underground, claimed in 1944 that 'No one who has not seen it himself can imagine how difficult even the simplest act of assistance may be.' Nonetheless, she went on:

If ever anyone risked his life for his Jewish brothers, it has been the German Aryans – hundreds, thousands, tens of thousands, risking their necks every day and every hour for a few wretched bread stamps, a lodging for a night or two. A little bit here, a little bit there, and still a little bit, scraped together out of their own need, fought for amongst bombs, forced labour, failing communications, and personal hardship, gained by defying every prohibition, law, and propaganda decree.[47]

There were myriad additional concerns. As Erich Neumann discovered, if a Jewish refugee died under Aryan care, it was extremely difficult to dispose of the body. A conventional burial for an anonymous corpse with no documentation was out of the question; likewise, simply dumping a corpse often raised profound ethical concerns. In Erich's case, a solution to the problem of what to do with the body of Wolfgang – the refugee he and his mother had been hiding – was eventually forthcoming. A regular at his mother's café, who was often required to collect air raid dead, was prevailed upon to take Wolfgang's body and dispose of it in the local cemetery, along with other air raid casualties, at the next opportunity.[48]

Correct documentation, therefore, was vital. Forged or stolen documents could afford a fugitive a certain degree of independence, enabling him or her to receive ration cards, medical care, even legitimate accommodation. Yet, they were fairly hard to come by. Though there was a roaring black market trade in original documents or in forgeries, the prices were prohibitively high. In 1941, one forger was charging over 400 Marks for identification documents, but in subsequent years his fee would rise to as much as 4,000 Marks.[49]

There were, however, other sources. The lucky few were able to persuade Berlin's oppositionally minded citizens to part with their documents, which they could then report as lost. In some cases, no persuasion was necessary. In one peculiar instance in 1941, a young Jewish woman working in a factory noticed that she was attracting the close attention of one of her colleagues. Leaving the factory one evening, she found herself following her Aryan colleague, who deliberately dropped her identity papers on the pavement, before walking on. Though no words were ever exchanged between the two, this single act of selflessness enabled the young Jewish Berliner to survive the war.[50]

In later years, as the air raids increased in intensity, there were other opportunities. The daring could simply present themselves to the authorities as refugees from the bombing, whose homes and records had all been destroyed, and demand new documentation. As Charlotte Joseph recalled:

I chose a district in which not only the Police Station, but also the Rationing Office had been destroyed . . . Schöneberg . . . there I told them that I had lived in that area and had been bombed out. As my details could not be checked, I received a so-called 'Bomb Certificate' as a refugee . . . with the name Elsa Hohberg.[51]

Later, Charlotte – or Elsa – presented herself at a state-run shelter for refugees at Rüdnitz, just outside the capital, where she was housed and supplied with ration cards. While her worries were far from over, she would at least survive the war.

For those *Taucher* who did not choose this method, there was always the chance of finding a fresh corpse – preferably one with some physical similarity to themselves – from which identity documents and ration cards could be 'liberated'. Hanna Sohst was one of the lucky ones:

> When the all-clear was given, I saw that there were people lying dead on the street. Then I got the idea, check if they have an identity card on them. Everywhere, at all times, and at every opportunity I kept my eyes peeled for papers, day and night . . . like a man dying of thirst looking for a mirage. And then . . . I struck gold![52]

In their desperation to source documents, some Jews fell into the clutches of criminals and swindlers. Early in 1942, three individuals – one of whom was a Berlin lawyer – were arrested in the capital for running a scam in which wealthy Jews were persuaded to pay 5,000 Reichsmarks on the understanding that strings would be pulled with the authorities to provide them with Aryan identities.[53] The three men were successfully prosecuted for fraud, while their 'victims' – who had testified at the trial – were deported.

Life in the underground put enormous mental strains on Jewish refugees. In addition to the normal difficulties of living in a city at war – the bombing, rationing and so on – they had to cope with isolation, exhaustion and the constant fear of capture. In response, some abandoned the pretence of a 'normal life' altogether and found a refuge of sorts in crime and prostitution.[54] In the netherworld of Berlin's bordellos, they were often free to rent rooms with no questions asked, and could come and go without attracting attention to themselves.[55]

The young in particular seemed to have exulted in the sudden freedom of life as a fugitive, relishing the thrill of being on the run and living on their wits. In one case, two female *Taucher* found accommodation with a fanatical Nazi woman by telling her that they were agents engaged on a secret mission for the Führer. They only abandoned their refuge when the woman suggested that they might like to meet her son, an officer in the SS.[56] Cioma Schönhaus, meanwhile, liked to spend the profits from his forgery business by dining in the best Berlin restaurants, often surrounded by Nazi functionaries. His logic, it seems, was that the best place to hide was in plain sight.[57]

Another such daredevil was Margot Linczyk, a sixteen-year-old Berliner, living with her mother under false papers:

> I thought our life was a great adventure. I got us hiding places. I could steal, I could lie – it was fun! I think it was a reaction to my Germanic upbringing, always having to sit up straight and so on. I got my identity card from the post office by yelling 'Heil Hitler!' so loud that they got scared I might report them for not responding fast enough.[58]

The remarkable memoir by Larry Orbach testifies to this paradoxical 'liberation'. Orbach had just turned eighteen when he went underground in the winter of 1942. Under the Aryan identity of 'Gerhard Peters', he robbed, cheated, lied and fornicated his way through Nazi Berlin, demonstrating by turns tremendous courage and astonishing nerve. In one instance, he and a friend hatched a plan whereby they would team up to swindle rich Aryan men. His friend would pose as a rent boy, while Orbach would play the role of the Gestapo man who caught the two *in flagrante*, only to be bribed into silence. For all the undoubted perils that Orbach endured in surviving wartime Berlin, his memoir has a thoroughly uplifting, even optimistic tone. For him there were 'flashes of light and warmth' in the darkness; there was 'romance, friendship, delight and adventure in the midst of murderous oppression'.[59]

The vast majority of *Taucher*, however, found it extremely hard to meet the challenge of a life on the run, an existence one of them described as 'like living in a mousetrap'.[60] As one young Jewish woman noted in 1943, 'We live . . . only from day to day, worrying about our sheer survival doesn't give a moment's respite.'[61] After a series of near misses with the Gestapo, one *Taucher* confided to a friend: 'I can't go on; I'm too tired', before adding in grim resignation: 'They'll catch me and kill me.'[62] She disappeared soon after.

The authorities were certainly not tardy in tracking down fugitives. As well as encouraging denunciations from Aryan Berliners, the

Gestapo organised blitz raids in an effort to find *Taucher*. Most no-toriously, they sought the assistance of Jewish *agents provocateurs* or *Greifer* ('catchers'), who would betray fugitive Jews in return for payment, or immunity from deportation.

The most infamous of these *Greifer* was Stella Kübler. Born Stella Goldschlag in 1922 and raised in a middle-class, thoroughly assimilated household in Berlin's western suburbs, Stella was one of those Jews who would benefit from the blond hair and blue eyes that the Nazis considered to be typically 'Aryan'. Initially, Stella's existence mirrored that of her fellow Jews; she wore the *Judenstern* and worked in an armaments factory. Like others, too, she went underground after the *Fabrik-Aktion* in the spring of 1943. However, her capture by the Gestapo later that year, along with that of her parents, compelled her to take a rather different path.

Betrayed by a Gestapo 'catcher', Stella was brutally tortured as her interrogators sought – in vain – to beat out of her the identity of the man who had supplied her with false documents. Psychologically broken by the experience, she agreed to use her Aryan looks and inside knowledge of the underground community to identify other Jewish fugitives. In return, she was given Aryan papers and a room, and was paid 200 Marks for each *Taucher* she turned in. Furthermore, she was assured that in return for her cooperation her parents would be spared deportation to Auschwitz.

Stella soon turned out to be a model 'catcher'. Having already impressed the Gestapo with her ingenuity, after two escape attempts, she would not disappoint them once in their employ, using her memory for names, dates and addresses and her naturally flirtatious nature to devastating effect. The first Jew she denounced was her own husband. Quickly earning herself the nickname 'the blonde poison', she was feared in the Berlin underground, where a photograph of her was circulated by way of a warning. One *Taucher*, Ernst Goldstein, recalled seeing her sauntering into a café on the elegant Kurfürstendamm, coolly surveying the clientele, looking for fugitive Jews. Fortunately for Goldstein, he had the presence of mind to react swiftly. Whispering to his wife that the 'head-hunters' had arrived, he quickly but incon-spicuously paid his bill and left.[63]

Stella Goldschlag remained active as a 'catcher' right to the very end of the war. The total number of her victims is not known, but is thought to range between many hundreds and a few thousand. In one single weekend, she was said to have led her Gestapo handlers to sixty-two fugitive Jews.[64] She herself became a victim of sorts, when the Gestapo reneged upon its agreement with her and sent her parents to Auschwitz. Goldschlag escaped with her life, but little more. Imprisoned after the war, she committed suicide in 1994, at the age of seventy-two.

Bizarrely, it seems that, apart from going underground, the only other chance Jewish Berliners had of avoiding the deportations was to become seriously ill. Though every other Jewish institution across the Reich was shut down by the Nazis, the Jewish Hospital in Berlin, located on the Iranische Strasse in Wedding, was permitted to exist right through to the end of the war.[65] The precise logic applied by the Gestapo in allowing the hospital to remain open is unclear, but it may well have been similar to that which allowed the Jewish cemetery in Weissensee to survive – the principle being that Jews should deal with Jews. So, while there were Jews remaining in Germany, who were forbidden to be treated in Aryan hospitals, it was necessary to have a Jewish hospital to treat them.

Whatever the reasons, the decision did not go uncontested. In the immediate aftermath of the *Fabrik-Aktion*, the hospital was almost shut down and in the remaining years of the war would be exposed to the full capricious and murderous fury of the Gestapo. Its medical and nursing staff were routinely required to accompany each of the transports taking Berlin Jews to their fate 'in the east', a trip from which none of them would return. In due course, the hospital was itself targeted to make up the numbers in the deportations, with its director – Dr Lustig – having to draw up a list of those employees that would be sent to their deaths.

Consequently, experienced and qualified staff had to be replaced by individuals much like those who had been held at the Rosenstrasse – people of mixed race, those in mixed marriages, those Jews who were 'privileged' and 'tolerated' by the Nazi regime. As a result, medical care at the hospital became increasingly perfunctory, more and more conspicuous by its absence.

In such circumstances, merely being ill was no guarantee of survival; one also had to be lucky. Countless patients at the hospital were deported once they had recovered sufficiently to be moved. The hospital also received those Jews who had attempted suicide upon hearing of their scheduled deportation. Many of them – perversely – would be nursed back to health and then deported to their deaths. Other patients were removed as a matter of routine; the entire psychiatric ward, for instance, was deported en masse to Theresienstadt in November 1943.

One of the most remarkable stories to emerge from the Jewish Hospital is that of Ursula Finke, a young Berlin Jew who was living underground. In August 1944, Ursula was caught by a *Greifer* while standing on the platform at Gesundbrunnen S-Bahn station. As she was being arrested, she managed to escape her captors and jumped in front of an oncoming train. When she came to, she was being pulled from beneath the train by railway personnel, with her lower leg and foot mangled almost beyond recognition. She was then put into an ambulance and driven to the Jewish Hospital, where she was taken straight into surgery. Ordinarily, the foot would have been amputated, and Ursula would have been deported to Auschwitz as soon as was possible. But the hospital director sought to save Ursula's foot by a series of time-consuming and excruciatingly painful operations. If it *was* a reprieve, it certainly didn't feel like it. As Ursula recalled:

I remained incarcerated . . . behind barbed wire in the [hospital], chained to the bed, the foot for months in traction, with the most intense pain. At night the surveillance personnel came through the rooms, stuck flashlights into beds to see that everybody was there, and constantly people were transported away, even on stretchers, so that I ended up having screaming fits out of fear of being transported away in this condition.[66]

In spite of everything, however, Ursula survived to the end of the war.

By 1945, the hospital resembled a Jewish ghetto, with a secure block for fugitives, a permanent Gestapo presence and a *Sammellager*, or 'collection camp', for those former patients who were waiting to be deported. The deportations, though much more infrequent than they had been, nonetheless continued with the same grim efficiency to the end of the war. Fugitive Jews would be collected from across the city by the Gestapo and kept at a number of secure collection centres –

like the former hospital – until enough had been gathered to fill a 'transport'. These transports continued on average at monthly intervals, carrying fifty or so unfortunates each time. The final one – carrying forty-two Jewish deportees – was sent to Theresienstadt on 27 March 1945.[67]

Less than a month after that last transport, Wedding, and with it the former Jewish Hospital, was overrun by the Soviets. On the morning of 24 April 1945, as the Red Army closed in, some eight hundred Jews remained – many bedridden and close to death – in the squalor of those once pristine wards. Alongside the 1,400 or so fugitives who were estimated to have survived illegally in the Berlin underground, they were the last representatives of a community annihilated.[68] But when those Jewish survivors emerged to greet their liberators, they were met with consternation. One Russian soldier stated categorically that it was 'not possible' that they were Jews. In his best broken German, he explained his reasoning, '*Nichts Juden. Juden kaput.*' 'You can't be Jews', he said. 'The Jews are all dead.'[69]

15

Reaping the Whirlwind

By early 1943, Berliners had grown accustomed to the calm. After the first spate of bombings through late 1940 into the spring of 1941, there had followed a period of almost two years in which RAF raids on the capital became fewer and farther between. For the second half of 1941, the few nightly visits that there were had consisted mainly of leafleting and low-intensity nuisance raiding. The whole of 1942 had seen only a single British raid on the German capital. Berliners were beginning to feel secure, even optimistic.

So, when the RAF reappeared in the skies over Berlin on the night of 1 March, it came as a shock. Dieter Borkowski spoke for many when he recorded in his diary that no one had expected the return of the bombers after such a long absence.[1] What surprised Berliners most, however, was the sheer intensity of the raid. Official reports gave little away, but eyewitness accounts were rather more loquacious. Secretary Helene Braun sent a breathless account to her nephew, describing the destruction around her home in Kreuzberg:

> The night of 1/2 March was the worst air raid that we have experienced in our area. All around us, to north, south, east and west, the sky burned red, and the black branches of the trees were clearly visible against the fiery glow. The danger was very close. The property at no. 21 in our street, with two courtyards and side buildings, has been badly hit and the fires there could only be extinguished at about 5 o'clock this morning. Numerous houses in Grossbeerenstrasse are a sea of flames. The big corner house on Hagelbergerstrasse and Möckernstrasse is almost completely destroyed. The goods yard on Yorckstrasse is still burning![2]

It was soon apparent that the destruction wrought across Berlin that night was greater than had been seen before. A Swedish source claimed that fires burned in the city for fully three days and that the destruction caused by the raid was 'at least ten times that of all . . . previous raids'.[3] Another eyewitness noted that the fires that night seemed to burn with an 'unusual intensity'. They were correct. Though the people of Berlin would not have known it, they had endured the largest tonnage of high explosives that had yet been dropped in the air war – a payload of over 900 tons that was twice the amount the Luftwaffe had dropped on London in their largest raids of the Blitz in 1941.[4] As well as the countless incendiaries, one novelty was the first appearance of the 'cookie' or 'blockbuster' – a 1,800-kilogram high-explosive bomb capable of destroying entire blocks. One eyewitness experienced the blast of one of these weapons that night in the south-western suburbs: 'a powerful, thunderous explosion', he wrote, 'with a pressure wave that I had never experienced before, and which made me feel as insignificant as a tiny ant . . . In the darkness, I felt myself all over, and realised that I was still alive.'[5]

The havoc wrought that night is testament to the severity of the raid. Most spectacularly, the Catholic cathedral of St Hedwig – on the Opernplatz, in the very heart of the capital – was severely hit, with the large, domed roof collapsing into the building's interior, which subsequently burnt out. Nearby Unter den Linden suffered a number of hits, as did the prestigious Wilhelmstrasse and Friedrichstrasse. The elegant Prager Platz in Wilmersdorf was reduced to rubble. The former American Embassy building – the Blücher Palais – on Pariser Platz was also damaged, as was Göring's Air Ministry building, where more than two hundred rooms were wrecked.[6]

Berliners witnessed destruction on an unprecedented scale. As Ruth Andreas-Friedrich noted in her diary the following day: 'The city and all the western and southern suburbs are on fire. The air is smoky, sulphur-yellow. Terrified people are stumbling through the streets with bundles, bags, household goods, tripping over fragments and ruins.'[7] Even in those buildings that were not destroyed outright, the damage incurred could be substantial. One young flak helper recalled seeing the destruction in a home close to his. 'Everything that was not nailed down', he wrote, 'had been hurled to the floor. Between the smashed windows there were chandeliers, the remains of vases and crystal bowls and piles of smashed porcelain. Everywhere, glass fragments crunched beneath our feet.'[8]

The human cost was also considerable. Estimates of those killed and injured varied, but contemporary accounts concluded that nearly 500 civilians were killed in the raid, with a further 2,000 or so being injured. In addition, over 100,000 Berliners were thought to have been rendered homeless. It was the deadliest raid Berlin had yet suffered.

Equally damaging perhaps was the effect on morale. As the SS mood reports conceded, the raid of 1 March 1943 profoundly dented the faith of ordinary Germans in the ability of the state – and particularly the Luftwaffe – to protect them.[9] It did not escape Berliners' attention, for instance, that the raid had come on the night of the annual 'Day of the Luftwaffe', in which there had been marches and grand ceremonial in the city.[10] With this humiliation, the Luftwaffe began to lose the sympathy of the German public.[11]

Returning to the capital on the train from Munich on the morning after the raid, Goebbels had been informed that Berlin had suffered a serious attack, but its full severity did not become clear to him until he approached the station and realised that the rail tracks themselves had been uprooted. After his arrival, he set about touring the affected areas. The city centre, he noted, 'looked a mess', and the suburbs 'were an even less comforting sight'. He consoled himself with the positive attitude of those Berliners he met. 'One must not believe', he wrote in his diary, 'that the population of Berlin are not capable of withstanding such massive raids.'[12] His optimism would soon be put to the test.

Berliners had been repeatedly told that theirs was the best-defended city in the world. And, for once, Nazi propagandists were telling the unglossed truth: Berlin's air defences really were state-of-the-art.

The centrepiece of the hugely impressive network of defences in the city was the three Berlin flak towers. The first of these concrete behemoths appeared on the capital's skyline in April 1941, in the heart of the Zoo, to the west of the city centre. It rose some 39 metres into the sky – taller than the nearby railway station at Bahnhof Zoo, taller even than the tallest trees in the nearby Tiergarten. In the rather flat, low-rise landscape of Berlin, it would have been hard to miss.

Broadly square in plan, the tower's side walls – over 3 metres thick and over 70 metres across – were rendered in raw concrete and studded with small windows. Resembling a huge medieval fortress, it was adorned at each corner with a squat, octagonal tower, and beneath the roof were five floors of storage rooms and air raid shelters, even a hospital ward. Designed to accommodate eight thousand civilians, it also provided an air-conditioned home to many of the valuables from Berlin's museums, including the golden treasures of Priam and the bust of Nefertiti.

The building's sheer size was not only the result of the Nazis' passion for monumental architecture. It was in essence an enormous static gun platform – and it fairly bristled with weaponry. At each of its four corners, there was a heavy-calibre anti-aircraft gun. The 128mm 'Dora' flak gun was one of the largest produced during the war, and weighing in at over 25 tonnes – with a further 25-tonne recoil force – it required a substantial structure to support it. In addition, guns of lesser calibres, such as the 20mm *Vierling*, or four-barrelled 'quad' weapon, were located elsewhere on the roof.[13]

Apart from the Zoo flak tower, two identical towers were erected to form an arc around the centre of Berlin, one at Humboldthain to the north and the other at Friedrichshain to the east. Each flak tower – known as the *G-Turm*, or 'battery tower' – was accompanied by a nearby *L-Turm*, or 'command tower', which was of a similar size and equipped with searchlights, listening equipment and radar installations.

The flak towers were meant to intimidate Germany's enemies, but they also served to convince Berliners that they could be protected from the RAF. They certainly made an impression on the American journalist Howard Smith. The Zoo tower, he wrote,

> looks like a fantastic monstrosity from a lost world, or another planet. It is huge and positively frightening just to look at. . . . It is an enormous, square clod of cement a hundred feet high, about five or six storeys. It is painted green so as not to be too visible among the trees from above. On each of its corners is a long, powerful gun, pointed at the sky.[14]

Living nearby, Missie Vassiltchikov noted the new addition to the skyline in her diary in April 1941: 'Our flat is very near the Zoo bunker',

she wrote, 'which has just been built of heavy concrete. It is very high
and sprouting with flak guns, and is considered the safest air-raid shelter
in this part of the town. When the guns start firing the earth trem-
bles, and even in our flat the noise is ear-splitting.'[15]

Despite their size and grim grandeur, the flak towers were only the
most visible part of an enormous and highly sophisticated ring of
defences around the German capital. Since 1940 Berlin's air defences
had been systematically upgraded, with a central command centre,
located within the Zoo tower. They were remarkably complex,
consisting of two primary rings of defences surrounding the city – an
outer searchlight ring approximately 50 kilometres from the city centre
and an inner flak ring around 30 kilometres out. Interspersed between
them were smoke generators, which could send a pall of thick, grey
smoke many miles across the city, obscuring large parts of it from
view.[16] Within Berlin itself, many main streets, boulevards and military installations were strung with camouflage netting, so as to make
them difficult to identify from the air. This tactic was also applied to
some of the city's waterways, which could otherwise serve as a vital
point of reference for enemy pilots. The Lietzen Lake in Charlottenburg,
for instance, was disguised to make it look like a suburban landscape.

The mainstay of the city's defences, however, was its flak crews.
By 1943, there were around 100 batteries in and around the capital,
each containing searchlight units, radio telemetry, and on average,
between 16 and 24 individual artillery pieces.[17] Though a variety of
weapons were used, at the heart of each battery was the venerable
88mm gun, known as the *acht-acht*, or 'eight-eight'. Developed during
the First World War, and combat-tested during the Spanish Civil War,
the 'eight-eight' was arguably the most famous artillery piece of the
Second World War. With its distinctive outline of recoil tubes framing
a long, tapering barrel, it saw action in every branch of the German
military and in every theatre – from the high seas to the Russian steppe
and the deserts of North Africa. Mounted on a tank chassis or pulled
on a wheeled carriage, it would earn a fearsome reputation as a 'tank-
killer', but it was designed to serve primarily as an anti-aircraft weapon.

Usually operated by a crew of eleven, the 'eight-eight' boasted a
360° traverse and could fire up to fifteen rounds per minute – one
every four seconds. Its range, too, was impressive, reaching nearly
15 kilometres in the horizontal plane, and almost 10 kilometres when

fully elevated.[18] In its anti-aircraft role, it fired a 16-pound shrapnel shell, which could be timed to explode at a specific altitude, where-upon anything within around 200 metres of the detonation risked significant structural damage.

Given the sheer size of the capital's air defences, the system required large numbers of personnel to operate the guns and searchlights. Though there was a core of trained cadres from the Luftwaffe, and some ancillary units – such as Italians and Soviet POWs – drafted in from elsewhere, many were so-called *Luftwaffenhelfer* or *Flakhelfer* – 'flak helpers' – fifteen- to sixteen-year-old boys, often plucked straight out of school and thrust into the front line of the air war. One of their number, Hans-Detlef Heller, described the composition of an average battery crew:

> A gun detachment consisted of nine men: the gun commander and three layers, who aimed the gun and set the fuses in the shells; two soldiers to load and fire the weapon; and four people who brought up the ammunition. The layers were *Luftwaffenhelfer*. The loading and firing of the gun was done by proper soldiers. And the job of carrying the shells up from the bunker was done by Russian POWs.[19]

These distinctions became increasingly elastic, especially as the war progressed, and by its later stages many a flak gun was being operated almost exclusively by young *Luftwaffenhelfer* and POWs. Training for the crews was rather perfunctory, consisting of little more than a couple of weeks practising on site with the battery that they would later serve. One of those called up to a flak battery recalled his first day on the job: 'Since 8 o'clock this morning', he wrote in his diary,

> I am a *Luftwaffenhelfer* . . . a loader in battery No. 1, Flak Tower section 123 . . . We are all fifteen or sixteen years old, only the platoon leader, Corporal Ullrich, is an experienced artilleryman . . . He takes photos of us for our passes. In the afternoon the battery commander, Lieutenant Küttner, addresses us . . . [and] we receive our uniforms from the quar-termaster . . . In the evening, we swear an oath to the Führer, Adolf Hitler and to Greater Germany. The swastika flutters in the breeze, as we gaze to the east and swear loyalty until death.[20]

Such young men would form the backbone of the capital's defences against air attack.

Beyond this offensive capacity, however, most of the emergency public building work begun in the autumn of 1940 had been defensive in nature, consisting of protective bunkers and shelters for the civilian population. The plans, which were contained in the so-called *Sofortprogramm* issued by Hitler on 10 October 1940, had been rather vague, stating merely that 'protection measures' were to be undertaken in those residential areas with insufficient provision of shelters, and that ongoing public works projects, such as road-building, were to be exploited for the creation of secure underground installations.[21] However, in private meetings and briefings over that autumn, the sheer enormity of Hitler's vision became clear. In Berlin alone, he declared, between 1,000 and 2,000 bunkers were to be built, each one capable of housing a minimum of 100 civilians. In addition, further bunkers were to be constructed for the use of the government's 'essential' personnel, as well as for schools, museums and administrative buildings. Bunkers were also to be constructed for the capital's hospitals, main railway stations, diplomatic buildings and large industrial concerns. Prominent hotels such as the Adlon and the Kaiserhof were to follow suit.

The *Sofortprogramm* lacked nothing in ambition. It identified some 92 cities and towns as potential targets and aimed to protect over 35 million civilians in more than 6,000 bunkers. In total, it was estimated that the programme would consume 200 million cubic metres of reinforced concrete, a figure that would correspond to around twenty years' normal supply to the German construction industry.[22] It would become the largest public works project in history.

The types of bunkers and shelters constructed under the *Sofortprogramm* spanned the spectrum. In Berlin, however, because of the sandy soil and the prohibitive cost of excavation, the majority of the bunkers built were *Hochbunker*, built above ground level, rather than below it. The 'Railway Bunker' close to the Friedrichstrasse Station in central Berlin was typical of this sort; standing over 18 metres tall with small windows set in bare concrete, it was faintly reminiscent of a Mesopotamian ziggurat. Its five storeys were divided into more than a hundred rooms and were designed to offer shelter for up to 2,500 civilians, although the number using it in the later years of the war would be significantly greater.

To accommodate Hitler's vision there were also a number of short cuts that could be taken. As in wartime London and Moscow, the platforms of the underground system provided a ready shelter for many Berliners. Yet in addition, a number of air raid shelters were also built into the network of tunnels, voids and shafts that are integral to underground and subway stations. The best example of this type of shelter – preserved to this day as a museum – is that at Gesundbrunnen U-Bahn Station to the north of the city. Accessed via the platform or through a door in the station concourse, the shelter is a ramshackle warren of different-sized rooms, with interconnecting stairwells and passageways. Due to its rather improvised construction, and the fact that it did not have the requisite thickness of concrete in the roof, the shelter could not technically be called a bunker, but its forty or so rooms gave protection for around 1,500 Berliners.[23]

Some Nazi engineers were more imaginative still. The *Achsenkreuz* tunnel network constructed beneath the Tiergarten as part of Speer's 'Germania' project provided a ready shelter for thousands of Berliners. Many more found refuge in the city's gasometers, which were converted by the addition of reinforced walls, a three-metre thick concrete roof, ventilation equipment and an independent generator. Each one could safely house six thousand civilians spread across six floors.

The ambitious plans of the *Sofortprogramm* inevitably fell victim to the icy blast of reality. When the more pressing military need of the construction of the Atlantic Wall laid claim to Germany's finite supply of concrete, the number of bunkers initially foreseen for Berlin was halved to one thousand; of these, just under half were actually constructed.[24] As a result of such cuts, the official provision of space in purpose-built bunkers for civilians in Berlin never exceeded a total of 60,000 spaces, corresponding to only a tiny percentage of the population.[25] It would be easy to imagine, therefore, that for the majority of Berliners the *Sofortprogramm* was rather a dead letter. But this was not the case.

While it is true that the majority of Berliners endured the most intensive period of Allied bombing from the 'comfort' of their own cellars, it would be wrong to assume that the city's purpose-built bunkers were only used by a minuscule minority. For one thing, the stated capacities of bunkers were generally ignored – especially as the air war intensified – and many of them were found to accommodate up to four or five times their designated capacity. Moreover, many public bunkers and shelters were erected around the city centre, to be used by those passing through the capital or working nearby. A stay in a *Sofortprogramm* bunker, therefore, even if only for a few hours, was an experience that very many Berliners would have endured.

The bunkers were well equipped. Of necessity, they were fitted with gas-proof doors, not only as protection against chemical attack, but also because of the concern that other noxious gases and smoke could be drawn into the shelter during an air raid. In addition, bunkers required sophisticated ventilation systems with their own independent power supply, as well as hand-operated air pumps. Those built into the underground train system, meanwhile, often had vents that would utilise the air pressure from the trains passing below to circulate fresh air around the site. An easy method of checking air quality in the bunkers was by using three small 'tea lights' – known as 'Hindenburg lights' – which would be lit and placed at head height, waist height and floor level. If the uppermost candle went out, it was a signal to those in the room to man the air pumps.

Beyond such necessities, bunkers tended to be rather Spartan. Peculiarly, all bunkers – even those that were purpose-built – were divided up into small rooms. In this way, it was thought, outbreaks of panic could be contained during a raid, as each 'compartment' would contain someone able to keep their fellows calm. There were few creature comforts. The rooms were fitted out with simple wooden benches, perhaps some bunks for children, and the odd slogan painted onto the bare concrete walls reminding Berliners to obey the rules. Electric lighting was usually provided, and when it failed candles, tea lights and the liberal use of phosphorescent paint ensured that people could find their way about. In some locations, entire walls would be painted in this way, and it was said that one could even read a newspaper in the eerie half-light.

Medical and sanitary facilities were basic. Most larger bunkers had toilets and those that did not have a mains water connection could be supplied with 'turf toilets', in which a 'flush' of peat would absorb odours and maintain some semblance of hygiene. Medical rooms were also common in larger bunkers, usually consisting of little more than a couple of drop-down bunks, a medicine cabinet and a resident nurse.

A few bunkers had more elaborate healthcare provision, especially those attached to Berlin's hospitals, or the seventy or so 'mother-and-child' bunkers that were specifically reserved for those with infants and small children.

Initially, access to the bunkers was controlled by the distribution of passes to the most deserving cases, such as those without adequate shelter in their own cellars. In time – and especially with the renewed RAF attacks from 1943 – such restrictions were ignored, but some regulations were still applied. Foreign labourers, prisoners of war and Jews were not generally permitted to enter the bunkers and the presence of service-age men was often frowned upon, as it was popularly considered that they should be out fighting the enemy, rather than huddling among the women and children.[26] However, the degree to which such selections could be effectively carried out – with the sirens wailing and a throng of civilians all pressing for entry – is open to question. In any case, there were often ways around the checks. Frenchman Marcel Elola perfected the art of gaining entry into Berlin bunkers simply by looking for a woman struggling with a couple of children, whom he would then assist. With a child on his hip, or in his arms, and a German housewife at his shoulder, he was rarely questioned.[27]

Most of his fellows, meanwhile, would hope to get into one of the U-Bahn stations, where one might at least find a secure spot on a platform or a stairway on which to sit out the raids. Many foreigners in the capital did not even have that luxury. Those who were considered racially 'undesirable', such as Soviet POWs and Poles, had to make do with simple slit trenches, dug in whatever patch of open ground they could get access to.

The majority of Berliners simply made for their cellars. They were all well drilled. Though they had only faced minimal bombing since 1941, everybody in a block had a task to fulfil and the cellars were often very well equipped, in sharp contrast to the often rather makeshift provisions of the earlier period of the war. Though still a child, Lore Kastler had already been taught first aid, how to use a gas mask and how to extinguish incendiaries. The shelter beneath her parents' home in Pankow was similarly well prepared:

> the ceiling was strengthened with planed tree branches. There were
> benches, chairs, a covered billiard table for the bags and cases. There was

shelving with provisions and bottles of water, and a large metal bath tub full of shimmering water. Furthermore, there was a bucket of sand, gloves, towels, blankets, candles, matches, bandages, gas masks, steel helmets and torches with batteries. Outside on the fence, there was a sign 'Air Raid Shelter'.[28]

So, when the bombers returned to Berlin in the early months of 1943, the city could rightly claim not only to be the best defended capital of the belligerent nations, but also to have made the most comprehensive provision for the protection of its citizens. It remained to be seen how well those defences would stand up to the renewed attentions of the RAF.

In the event, after the shock of the raid on 1 March, the air war once again settled down into something like the routine of the earlier phase of the conflict. There was the novelty of nuisance raiding by RAF Mosquitoes, whereby a couple of speedy fighter-bombers would either select a specific target or would attack at random, in the process causing panic on the ground and sending thousands of Berliners scrambling for shelter, but beyond that Berlin saw only a couple of major raids that spring and summer.

For all the apparent calm, however, there were reasons for disquiet. Most importantly, it would not have escaped the attention of some Berliners that the numbers of aircraft involved in the early raids of 1943 far exceeded those that had been seen in the opening phase of the war. Whereas previously Berlin had been attacked by barely a couple of dozen aircraft at the most, now RAF forces over the city numbered well into the hundreds. Moreover, the advent of the remarkable Avro Lancaster heavy bomber provided a marked increase in both the range and the capacity available to RAF crews. Some Berliners must have feared that it was only a matter of time before the capital would be exposed to a truly catastrophic raid.

Events further west that summer would have done little to calm Berlin nerves. In late July 1943, Hamburg was hit by a series of concentrated day and night raids, while German defences were paralysed by the first operational use of 'Window' radar jamming. With ambient temperatures already high due to a spell of fine, dry weather, and the city's narrow streets of wooden buildings bearing the brunt of the bombing, the resulting firestorm tore through the city, consuming everything in its path. In the aftermath, about half of Hamburg was laid waste with more than 40,000 civilians killed.[29]

The shock in Germany was almost palpable. As an SD mood report noted glumly: 'the fact that one city after the next can be attacked and razed to the ground weighs like a nightmare on the people and makes a considerable contribution to a general feeling of insecurity and helplessness'.[30] Such sentiments were made all the more immediate for Berliners by the realisation that they were a certain target for a similar attack. Hans-Georg von Studnitz summed up the feeling of looming inevitability:

Hamburg was heavily bombed the night before last and again last night. Twenty-four hours previously Hanover was attacked in broad daylight. This morning a hundred and twenty four-engined American bombers were flying on Berlin, but later turned away to Magdeburg . . . we are at the mercy of our enemies.[31]

The sense of foreboding was only heightened when Hamburg's thousands of evacuees and refugees were sent, via Berlin, to the comparative safety of the east. On the way, they inevitably shared their horror stories with anyone who would listen. Ursula von Kardorff noted the stories then doing the rounds in the capital: 'entire districts of Hamburg are said to have been engulfed in a sea of flames', she wrote, 'people stuck in melting asphalt, asphyxiated by the firestorm'.[32] She also noted the paranoia that often resulted. A nurse on the ward where she was recuperating after an operation kept running up to the hospital's roof, from where she claimed to be able to see the dim orange glow of Hamburg burning in the distance. Each time she returned, she would mention darkly that the hospital's cellar was hardly equipped to serve as a shelter.[33]

The official reaction also betrayed a sense of fear. An immediate evacuation was ordered of all the capital's most vulnerable inhabitants: children under fourteen and those women not employed in war-related work. Even Goebbels was brutally honest in his assessment of the situation, writing in his diary on 1 August 1943:

As a result of the experiences of Hamburg, a whole host of decisive measures must be taken in Berlin. . . . The population is requested to dig protective trenches, new orders are being published in the press regarding civil air raid protection, the evacuation has already been set in train. It is clear that these measures will cause tremendous nervousness in the capital, but there's nothing we can do. We must take these necessary steps, regardless of the popular mood.[34]

The result – temporarily, at least, was chaos. Not only were the railheads jammed with traumatised refugees from Hamburg, but their numbers were swollen by Berliners desperate to get out of the city before the bombers returned. Helmuth James von Moltke described the situation in Berlin in a letter to his wife:

I have come back to a madhouse. . . . Everything is in a process of total dissolution . . . Yesterday morning Dr Goebbels favoured his subjects with [a] leaflet, which expresses sheer panic. Not a word of confidence, of comfort, no call for calm and composure . . . no intimation that the authorities have made arrangements to protect the population and to provide for those who have suffered. Nothing but fear and panic.[35]

The Hamburg Raid had come at the end of a catastrophic month for Germany, in which defeat in the Battle of Kursk on the Eastern Front had coincided with the collapse of Italy, her closest ally, and the resignation of Mussolini. Unsurprisingly, therefore, SD reports that summer confirm the profound damage done to German confidence:

The air raid on Hamburg is generally regarded as a catastrophe, far exceeding previous attacks in western Germany in its harshness and extent, [and] in combination with the sudden evacuation of women and children from Berlin . . . has strengthened the feeling of heading towards an annihilation, which only a section of the population will be able to avoid.

In response, some called for revenge attacks, by the Luftwaffe or via the much-rumoured 'secret weapons' that were thought to signify a restoration of German fortunes. Others concluded that the evacuation measures amounted to an 'official admission of powerlessness against air attack'. Many, it seems, laid the blame directly on the Nazi regime, which they accused of 'negligence', 'bragging' and 'fobbing the people off with promises'.[36]

A few managed to resist the ensuing hysteria. Ruth Andreas-Friedrich heard the broadcast ordering the evacuation early one morning that August:

> a hoarse voice rattles out . . . 'Men and Women of Berlin! . . . The enemy is ruthlessly continuing his aerial terror against the German civilian population. It is urgently desired, and is in the interest of every individual who is not obligated for professional or other reasons to stay in Berlin – women, children, pensioners, and those who have retired from active life – that such persons move to regions less subject to air attack.

Still groggy with sleep, Andreas-Friedrich asked her partner, Andrik, if he had heard it too. He had. 'I'll stay here', she declared firmly. 'So will I', Andrik replied, rolling over with a yawn.[37]

Dieter Borkowski, meanwhile, saw it all as a great adventure. '[The evacuation] doesn't affect me', he wrote in his diary. 'As I am almost 15, I count as a grown-up.' He was keen to stay in Berlin. 'Mother will be happy', he added, 'as at least she will have one of us at home. After all, soon I'll be a real man and can look after her during the raids. . . . This "air war" seems to be getting exciting.'[38]

It certainly was. It took a couple of months for the feared attacks to materialise – that autumn saw only nuisance raiding by small numbers of Mosquitoes and a couple of unsuccessful larger-scale raids – but by November the RAF had returned. In fact, something rather audacious was in store. Arthur Harris, the Commander-in-Chief of RAF Bomber Command, was planning something that had never been attempted before: to bomb an opponent into submission through the use of air power alone. Mindful of the RAF's improved capacity, and its various tactical and technological advantages that had been in evidence over Hamburg and elsewhere that year, Harris planned a knockout blow on the German capital – to cause such chaos and destruction that the Nazi regime itself would collapse. As he explained in a letter to Winston Churchill that November: 'We can wreck Berlin from end to end. It will cost us 400–500 aircraft. It will cost Germany the war.'[39]

The RAF offensive began on the night of 18 November 1943, when over four hundred Lancasters launched a largely ineffectual raid on the capital, hampered by poor visibility. Four nights later, however, on the 22nd, they returned. This time, more than 750 planes hit Berlin, concentrating their attacks on the western districts of the city from the Tiergarten and Charlottenburg out to Spandau. The following night, they were back again; then again three nights later, when the north-western suburbs of Reinickendorf, Siemensstadt and Tegel were especially badly hit.

The 'Battle for Berlin' had begun. Within just over a week, the German capital had been subjected to four major RAF raids, each one of which was larger, more concentrated and more deadly than anything the city had experienced before. In that week alone, about half a million Berliners were left homeless and nearly 10,000 were injured. The fact that only 3,758 were killed was testament to the extent and quality of the city's civilian air defences.[40]

Eyewitnesses were astonished by the sheer extent of the destruction wrought in the German capital. Many recalled the west of the city as a 'sea of flames', with entire streets ceasing to exist. Barbara Wenzel described the damage in a letter to her brother:

> You cannot imagine the pile of rubble that is Berlin! Between the Zoo, Wittenbergplatz, Lützowufer, Einemstrasse there is hardly a habitable house still standing. The diplomatic quarter is all burnt out; Hansaviertel and Moabit are in ruins, and it's the same in Alexanderplatz, and from Oranienburger Tor via the Stettiner Bahnhof to Reinickendorf. All the big railway stations are badly hit: Leipzigerstrasse, Potsdamerstrasse; also the Arsenal and the Academy of Music. Kurfürstendamm and Charlottenburg are in flames . . . Last night Spandau was apparently hit very hard. Everywhere it is still burning, ruins are constantly collapsing.[41]

Goebbels, too, had the chance to witness the effects of 'total war' when he left his bunker beneath Wilhelmplatz on the evening of the 24th to drive to his country residence at Schwanenwerder to the west of the capital:

> What I saw was truly shattering. The whole Tiergarten quarter has been destroyed, so has the section round the Zoo. While the outer

façades of the great buildings are still standing, everything inside is
burned to the ground . . . you see nothing but remnants of walls and
debris . . . Groups of people scamper across the streets like veritable
ghosts. How beautiful Berlin was at one time and how run down and
woebegone it now looks![42]

In the aftermath, some sought to carry on as normal. Dieter
Borkowski attempted to get to school from his home in Kreuzberg
early on 22 November:

That morning, the tram only went as far as Hallesches Tor. I tried to
turn in to the Saarlandstrasse, [but] on both sides the house fronts were
in flames. Glowing sparks flew around the passers-by; like me many
people were running in the direction of the Anhalter Bahnhof, as one
could get down into the S-Bahn there, or via Potsdamer Platz into the
U-Bahn. Mountains of rubble, crying people in between, everywhere
clouds of smoke from still-burning houses.[43]

Missie Vassiltchikov had a similar experience trying to get to work
two days later. Having equipped herself with a pair of military goggles
and a headscarf, she gamely set off for her office in the nearby
Tiergarten. Her own street, Woyrschstrasse, was not too bad, but soon
the scale of the damage became apparent:

one block away, at the corner of Lützowstrasse, all the houses were
burnt out. As I continued down Lützowstrasse the devastation grew
worse; many buildings were still burning and I had to keep to the
middle of the street, which was difficult on account of the numerous
wrecked trams. There were many people in the streets, most of
them muffled in scarves and coughing, as they threaded their way
gingerly through the piles of fallen masonry. At the end of
Lützowstrasse, about four blocks away from the office, the houses
on both sides of the street had collapsed and I had to climb over
mounds of smoking rubble, leaking water pipes and other wreckage
to get to the other side.

When she turned the corner into Lützowplatz, where her office
was located, she saw that that building too was burning. Standing for

a few moments to take in the scene, she finally decided that there was nothing else to do but to retrace her steps and return home.[44]

Surveying the scene, Gestapo officer Otto Kramer made a list in his diary of the destruction wrought in the capital that week. It made for sobering reading:

> State Opera, German Theatre, National Gallery, Invalidenstrasse Museum, Hotel Bristol, Charité Hospital, City Hospital, French Embassy, Schulstrasse Maternity Hospital, Lichterfelde-East Rail Station, Swedish, Turkish, Iranian and Slovak Embassies . . . Jerusalem Strasse, Friedrichstrasse, Wilhelmstrasse, Unter den Linden, Alexanderplatz . . . Potsdam Station, East-West Axis . . .

He went on to note the suburbs worst affected: Pankow, Siemensstadt, Charlottenburg, Borsigwalde, Wittenau, Reinickendorf, Heiligensee, Neukölln . . . 'On the streets', he concluded, 'it looks like a battle-field.'[45]

The atmospheric effects of the raids were also substantial. Hans Liebig wrote to his wife on 29 November describing conditions in the capital: 'You can hardly breathe in the city for the smoke. When the sun came out on Wednesday, you just couldn't see it. We had to have a light on all day as the sky was a dirty yellow. You can't imagine it unless you have experienced it for yourself.'[46]

The bombing of that November week also hit Berlin Zoo. Located to the immediate south-west of the city centre and home to nearly four thousand animals, it found itself under attack on the night of 22 November 1943. Ursula Gebel, who lived nearby, recalled the tragedy:

> That afternoon . . . I had been at the elephant enclosure and had seen the six females and one juvenile doing tricks with their keeper. That same night, all seven were burnt alive. The entire zoo was destroyed by bombing. The hippopotamus bull survived in his basin [but] all the bears, polar bears, camels, ostriches, birds of prey and other birds were burnt. Every enclosure, except the animal hospital, was destroyed. The tanks in the aquarium all ran dry, the crocodiles escaped, but like the snakes they froze in the cold November air. All that survived in the Zoo was the bull elephant named Siam, the bull hippopotamus and a few apes.[47]

In the aftermath, grisly stories abounded about exotic animals from
the destroyed zoo finding their way into the city's parks and waterways, where they were often targeted by the hungry citizens of Berlin.
Hans-Georg von Studnitz noted in his diary the 'fantastic rumours'
that were circulating: 'Crocodiles and giant snakes are supposed to be
lurking in the hedgerows of the Landwehr canal. An escaped tiger
made its way into the ruins of the Café Josty, gobbled up a piece of
Bienenstich pastry it found there – and promptly died.'[48]

It is easy to dismiss such stories as so many urban myths, but the
account of one eyewitness suggests that there may have been a grain
of truth in them. Josepha von Koskull lived in nearby Charlottenburg
and on the morning after the raid was walking close to the burnt-out
Zoo when she saw a 'feral-looking Alsatian' coming towards her.
Taking pity on the creature, which she noticed seemed 'exhausted and
distraught', she was considering giving it her breakfast roll, when two
uniformed zookeepers appeared. The 'feral-looking Alsatian', it transpired, was an escaped wolf.[49]

After the ferocity of the attacks on the capital of that week in late
November 1943, the following month saw only a handful of major
raids. Of these, the worst was that of the night of 16 December, in
which a large RAF force bombed the same central and south-western
districts of the city – Charlottenburg, Wilmersdorf and Kreuzberg –
that had been hit three weeks earlier, at the cost of over six hundred
lives. Then, on the night of 29 December, the bombers hit the southern
and south-eastern suburbs, returning on two consecutive nights that
same week to bomb the same area, mainly Tempelhof and Neukölln.
As Ruth Andreas-Friedrich's laconic diary account of that week
suggests, the bombing had become strangely routine:

> The old year ended in horror; in horror the new year begins. Heavy
> night raid on December 29. Heavy night raid on January 1. The heav-
> iest night raid of the war on January 2.
>   We move rubble. We nail up corrugated board. Here we are without
> water, transportation, or current. The telephone is dead too, and we
> learn only by roundabout ways whether our friends . . . are alive.[50]

The last major raid of this period, that of the night of 15 February,
demonstrated not only the vastly enhanced offensive capacity of the

RAF, but also the effectiveness of Berlin's civilian defences. That night, 891 aircraft were dispatched to the German capital. Of these, some 800 planes – including more than 500 Lancasters – reached their target, and bombed districts across the city from Wedding and Pankow in the north, to Zehlendorf in the south. Yet, though tremendous material damage was caused, only 169 lives were lost on the ground. Astonishingly, the RAF lost more air crew over Berlin that night than the city 'lost' civilians.[51]

The 'Battle for Berlin' finally came to an end after a largely ineffective swansong on the night of 24 March 1944. Berliners had little reason to feel relief. Though the scale and destructive power of those raids seen during the winter of 1943–4 would scarcely be seen again over the German capital, the bombing would nonetheless continue – accelerate even – as the war proceeded inexorably towards its end. Indeed, in the last full year of the war, Berlin would be raided more than 150 times – every other day on average – with RAF Mosquitoes and daylight USAAF raids making the bombing a round-the-clock torment for those on the ground.

Bombing was an experience that was shared by all Berliners, regardless of their racial origins or their social standing; from foreign forced labourers to refugee Jews, from the well-heeled, petty aristocrats of Dahlem to the communist tenement-dwellers of Friedrichshain. As one observer noted: 'The bombs fell indiscriminately on Nazis and anti-Nazis, on women and children and works of art, on dogs and pet canaries.'[52] For many, bombing would become the overriding memory of the time, an ordeal that was almost emblematic of life in the Reich capital.

The universal nature of the experience meant that bombing could become a subject of almost obsessive interest. Many youths developed a talent for plane-spotting, despite the fact that they were all supposed to be underground by the time the raids hit. Benedikt Dietrich, for instance, was adept at swiftly identifying all kinds of enemy planes, helped by the fact that his father – the local air raid warden – had been issued with identification charts.[53] Others became experts in the technological aspects of the bombing; they would eagerly make enquiries at local bomb sites, and claimed to be able to identify the type of bomb dropped from the damage caused. Some became obsessed with collecting shrapnel, or even the strips of aluminium foil

used to jam German air raid defences. When Christabel Bielenberg
rushed into a shelter in the suburb of Dahlem in the autumn of 1944,
she noticed that the woman next to her was counting aloud:

> Suddenly, 'Eight', she said loudly and firmly, 'peace now until the next
> wave comes over.' Sure enough our refuge quietened itself and she
> removed her feet from the wall opposite. 'Eight? What's eight got to
> do with it?' I wondered if she had found some magic formula. 'Eight
> bombs in each bomb cradle,' she announced with professional exacti-
> tude, 'and we were obviously in direct line.'[54]

Impressed by the woman's knowledge of the intricacies of aerial
warfare, Bielenberg asked her how long she thought the raid would
last. '"Not long," she said, "an hour, perhaps two."' To Bielenberg's
astonishment, the lady – who was middle-aged and dressed in an 'odd
assortment of rather well-cut clothes' – went on to explain the bombing
tactics, the 'carpet raid':

> 'They send over high-flying pathfinder planes which drop lights, . . .
> Christmas trees we call them. They drop them at each corner of a large
> square – one, two, three, four' – she drew a square in the dust on the
> floor with the toe of her shabby button boot. 'Then, my dear, over come
> the heavy bombers and drop everything they have into the square. Friendly,
> isn't it?'[55]

But the subject that dominated conversation most overwhelmingly
was the destruction caused. As one diarist noted, there were few other
topics of conversation in Berlin:

> Alarm, alarm and still alarm. You hear nothing else, see nothing else,
> think nothing else. In the S-Bahn, on the street, in shops and buses, every-
> where the same scraps of conversation: 'completely bombed out' . . .
> 'roof taken off' . . . 'wall collapsed' . . . 'windows out' . . . 'doors out'
> . . . 'bomb-damage certificate' . . . 'lost everything'. It is as if there is no
> place anymore for the usual subjects.[56]

Most Berliners endured the Allied bombing campaign in the cellars
of their homes. There, following procedures and precautions laid down

earlier in the war, they hunkered down with their neighbours, friends and family and hoped for the best. Those who headed for the city's bunkers, meanwhile, lacked a little in camaraderie, but gained in the additional security that their purpose-built concrete refuge gave them. Yet, the bunkers were not generally popular. Many Berliners felt uneasy about leaving their homes, especially as an official instruction required them to leave their doors and windows open, so as to minimise the damage caused by the pressure wave of any nearby explosion. Quite rightly, they were concerned that such measures encouraged theft.

In addition, they hated the crush and panic they faced each time they wanted to enter the public bunkers, all of which operated on a first-come-first-served basis. As a result, many eyewitnesses recalled being faced with the inevitable knot of civilians all trying to enter at the same time, often driven to a frenzy by the wailing sirens. Ursula von Kardorff recalled trying to get into the zoo bunker in 1944: 'It was eerie', she wrote, 'a mass of people all running in the dark, with the flak already firing, all making for the entrances, which are much too narrow. Torches are lit and then the shout goes up of "Lights Out!" Then the people push and shove and squeeze themselves in, and one wonders how it all seems to sort itself out.'[57] French labourer Marcel Elola was more damning. Witnessing the crush to get into the bunker on Landsberger Platz in the spring of 1944, he recalled:

> When the sirens go off, a huge stream of people head in the direction of the entrance. It is terrible to watch, as the women and children are shoved and even trampled by men, who are just as afraid as they are. The air raid wardens are just not in a position to establish any authority: those in charge are either children or old men. There is not the slightest discipline.[58]

It could be more than just a nuisance. On New Year's Day 1944, twenty-one Berliners were trampled to death when the queue for a public shelter was panicked into a stampede by a nearby raid.[59] At Neu Kölln, in the summer of 1944, meanwhile, a large number of civilians were caught trying to enter a converted subway station. As the flak was already firing and the sirens wailing, there was considerable urgency, but for whatever reason those at the entrance to the shelter became stuck. It took soldiers ten minutes to clear the bottleneck, but by that time ten civilians had already been killed, asphyxiated in the crush or trampled underfoot.[60]

Inside the cellars and bunkers it was often little easier. The claustrophobic atmosphere was oppressive, the lack of privacy rankled, and there was the all-pervading stench of sweat, urine and halitosis – the inevitable consequence of cramming a large cross-section of humanity into a small space for any length of time. People tended to deal with the stress in their own way. Some babbled and talked incessantly, others prayed or fussed over their children. The majority were left alone with their thoughts. Ursula von Kardorff recorded the complexity of emotions that raced through her mind during a raid in the spring of 1944:

> Now and then the light goes out. I wonder if that's a bomb landing close by? Next to me there is a small child, quite calm. He has no idea. Will we suffocate here? Or be slowly roasted like in the bunkers in Hamburg? An unpleasant thought. I wonder if I have a guardian angel? . . . I wonder if my house is still standing. And, if it is, 'they' will certainly be back tomorrow anyway.[61]

For many Berliners fear was the defining emotion of the period. One did not simply 'get used to it'; rather, as many eyewitnesses suggest, it grew with each raid, layered with the gruesome experiences of loved ones or friends, the visions of destroyed buildings, and the memory of lines of corpses laid out for identification. Josepha von Koskull recalled the many horror stories that did the rounds, 'about being buried alive, about charred bodies that were shrunk to the size of small children, and that could be buried in a margarine tub. Often it was said that the impact of a heavy air mine . . . would burst one's lungs bringing death.'[62] Panic attacks were not uncommon. One diarist described a woman having a 'screaming fit' as she was being escorted up into one of the Berlin flak towers: 'She thought she would die there, "I have a husband and son at the front", she screeched. "I am not going up there". Finally, she was removed . . . I thought, if panic breaks out in here, God help us.'[63]

Even for those who managed to keep their fears in check, the experience was profoundly unpleasant. The same endless sitting in rather uncomfortable surroundings, with a small case at one's feet containing valuable documents and other necessities; the same staring at the bare walls, listening to the murmured prayers and sobs of those whom fate – and the RAF – had thrown together.

By far the worst part, however, was the sheer cacophony of a raid: the distant, menacing thud of falling bombs, growing louder and more threatening as the bombers approached. Though many reassured themselves with the mantra that 'if you can hear the bomb then it won't hit you', the noise was profoundly disconcerting:

> After the first impact, the light in the bunker went out. A burning candle was placed on the stairwell of each floor. Around us, whilst the bombs fell and death and destruction raged, there was breathless quiet. Somewhere a rumble started; a terrible rolling of thunder that comes nearer; the bunker rocks, but holds, and the rumble fades away. Then another one starts with terrible blasts, again it seems to roll towards us, comes close, and then crashes away into the distance. For a long time after the last explosion is heard, there is absolute silence in the bunker, amongst young and old. Then the realisation dawns, that it's over.[64]

For some, however, that terrifying crescendo of explosions did not dissipate, or rumble off into the distance. Near the end of a raid, Ruth Andreas-Friedrich and her partner were contemplating returning upstairs to their apartment, when a 'thundering hell' broke loose around them:

> we fall to our knees, slide along the floor like repentant sinners towards the pillar that is the single support of the house walls . . . Broken glass scatters around us. Masses of dark-gray dust whirl through the air. Smoke, flames, sulphur-coloured fog . . . We choke and cough. Fire to the right. Fire to the left. A deluge of flames from all sides. . . . Time stands still; eternity has begun . . . Stones topple; a storm thrusts a whirlpool of sparks through the shattered windows.[65]

Leopold Deutsch described another direct hit, on his home in Kreuzberg in the spring of 1944:

> With our backs to the wall, we heard the first detonations as they came closer and closer. The emergency light was switched on. Suddenly, there

was a particularly loud crash and the light went out, so the Hindenburg
lights were lit on the table. . . . Shortly afterwards, there was another
detonation. I watched as – almost in slow motion – the ceiling fell inwards
like a trapdoor close to the entrance. The Hindenburg lights went out,
and I could hear only the din of falling masonry and debris. The rubble
rose like the tide, until I passed out.[66]

Only a child at the time, Leopold was one of the few to be brought
alive out of the ruins of the shelter.

Renate Knispel recalled being rescued from what was left of her
cellar in January 1944. She and her family had only just reached the
shelter, when the building received a direct hit:

> One had the feeling that one's head would be ripped off. We were
> buried up to our waists. Beneath the rubble I squeezed my mother's
> hand. She squeezed back, so I knew she was alive. We waited to be
> rescued. Finally, there was a knocking on the wall from the people next
> door, and one of us knocked back. Then they knocked a hole in the
> wall and pulled us out one by one. We were taken through their cellar,
> in which we were astonished to see that the light still worked. When
> the neighbours saw us they started laughing. We did not understand
> until someone handed us a mirror. We were completely covered with
> a thick layer of grey dust.[67]

It is not surprising that the air raids provoked a fatalistic – even
apathetic – attitude among Berliners. Ursula von Kardorff reckoned
that such attitudes had become the norm: 'if it comes, it comes', one
acquaintance of hers averred, 'you cannot escape your fate'.[68] One girl
remembered her mother telling her in 1943 that the family would from
then on sleep together, with their heads all in the same direction. If
a bomb hit them, she reasoned, they would at least all die together.[69]

Those killed would be pulled from the ruins by their former neighbours, or by teams of soldiers or forced labourers thrown together
for the purpose. Marcel Elola recalled the grisly task of recovering the
bodies of a family from a collapsed house:

> With the others, we pulled out the three adults, or rather what remained
> of them. They were torn to pieces and their remains could be removed

in a washbowl. Then we pulled the little girl out of the rubble. Her body was in one piece, her eyes protruding. We laid her in the yard on a pile of stones. Her dress was hardly torn. She had often come to the factory and we had given her chocolate. Another image that I will not forget: this child, lying there on her back, arms crossed, as though she had just fallen asleep on the piles of rubble and ash; all that remained of her family.[70]

Initially, any unidentified corpses would be laid out in the street so that a name might be provided by neighbours and passers-by. After the larger raids, however, the potential shock caused by leaving large numbers of corpses on public display was such that the dead were laid out, incongruously, in school halls and gymnasiums. In many cases, the severity of the injuries meant that identification was almost impossible. When a girls' school on the Neuenburgerstrasse was hit early in 1945, the hundred or so corpses of the young victims were laid out in nearby buildings to be identified by their distraught parents, but their injuries were such that only a few of them could be named.[71] In due course, those few were handed over to their next of kin for burial. The remainder were interred in a dedicated section of a local cemetery.

For those fortunate enough to survive a raid, the first task was to check if their homes were still intact. Ursula von Kardorff was among those bombed out in the raid of 1 February 1944. While the attack was still raging, she had left the cellar and climbed the stairs, only to find her apartment burning fiercely and realise that there was little left to rescue. 'We dragged what we could find down the stairs', she wrote in her diary the next day, 'and simply threw beds, books, and cushions out of the window.' 'Somehow', she concluded, 'I always knew that it would come to this.'[72] Others were unable to salvage even the essentials. Erich Neumann could save only the family dog and a case of beer, when his mother's bar was bombed in 1944.[73]

In many cases, the bombed-out had nowhere to go. Official instructions held that they were to seek shelter initially with friends or family, but failing that they would be rehoused by the authorities. In the short term, the Nazi welfare organisation, the NSV, took care of refugees, setting up tents in the city's parks, while field kitchens – wheeled stoves with tall chimneys, known affectionately as *Gulasch-Kanonen* – dished up hot food and soup. Thus fortified, the bombed-out would begin an interminable round of office visits and form-filling, in search of new accommodation, replacement furniture and clothing, much of which came from 'evacuated' Jews.

Many, however, were reluctant to leave what remained of their former homes and preferred to camp out among their few rescued possessions. For some, it seems the act of repairing and making good represented a form of continuity, even of sanity. Ruth Andreas-Friedrich recognised this point. 'Why make repairs?' she questioned:

> Why do millions of people keep starting all over to build up what may be in fragments again within the next hour? . . .
>
> I think I know the answer. We make repairs because we have to, because we couldn't live another day if we weren't allowed to make repairs.
>
> If our living room goes, we move into the kitchen. If the kitchen is smashed, we transfer to the hall. If the hall is in ruins, we set up in the cellar. Anything so long as we can stay at home. The most dismal scrap of home is better than any palace somewhere else. That's why they all come back someday – the people whom the bombs have driven out of the city. They root among the stone fragments of their ruined houses; they go to work with shovel and broom, hammer, tongs and pickaxe, until one day a new home rises out of the charred foundation – a Robinson Crusoe stockade, perhaps, but a home nonetheless. You can't live if you don't belong anywhere.[74]

Thus many Berliners ended up living beneath canvas in a ruined shell of their home, without heating and lacking even the most basic creature comforts. As Ursula von Kardorff explained, that existence could be sorely trying:

> Our flat: without a door, windows, heating, light, water, telephone and gas, is worse than a wooden hut in the wilderness. A civilisation destroyed makes one feel completely helpless. Come the evening, when the dusk falls and the witching hour begins, it is dreadful: the banging of the window frames, the damp and the cold, and to cap it all, the melancholic darkness. I can't stand even an hour of it. It's just beyond my endurance.[75]

Another priority was to look for loved ones who were missing. That search could be made easier by the practice of pinning paper notes to the door frames or scrawling chalk inscriptions on the blackened walls of burnt-out buildings, detailing the fate and the whereabouts of those who had lived there: 'All safe and well from this cellar', they might read, or, 'Dear Gretchen. Where are you? Your Hans', or the more poignant 'We are alive. Luzie'. One eyewitness recalled arriving at his shattered home on Innsbrucker Platz to find a note in his mother's handwriting, stating that the family was alive and was living in Zehlendorf.[76] Missie Vassiltchikov also wrote a chalk message on the wall when she was bombed out, ostensibly for the 'various beaux' whom she hoped would still be calling for her: 'Missie and Loremarie are well, staying in Potsdam with B.'[77] In time, as people returned and read the messages, replies would be scribbled below.

Other inscriptions were soon to be seen among the ruins. The slogan *Unsere Mauern können brechen, unsere Herzen nicht* – 'Our walls might break, but not our hearts' – was commonly daubed on the capital's bomb sites, or printed on official posters or banners that were displayed in the rubble. Ursula von Kardorff was not impressed. 'Complete nonsense', she wrote in her diary, 'the sort of thing that only makes an impression on a blockhead.'[78] Others developed slogans of their own. One favourite quip of the later years of the war was to wryly repeat Hitler's election slogan from 1933: 'Give me four years, and you will not recognise Germany.'

Despite the large scale of death, destruction and suffering, civilian morale in the German capital did not collapse, as 'Bomber' Harris had anticipated. Berlin was subjected to one of the most concentrated bombing campaigns of the war, attracting the largest tonnage of Allied bombs – over 67,000 tonnes – of any German city.[79] Yet there was no civilian unrest and the Nazi regime did not crumble. There are a number of reasons for this. For one thing, Berlin simply did not 'burn' as readily as the RAF had hoped; its wide boulevards and stone-built avenues did not lend themselves to the ignition of the firestorms that had wrought such catastrophic damage to the old medieval cities of Hamburg and Cologne. For another, the death toll in the German capital was relatively low, amounting to around 50,000 casualties from air attack for the entire war.[80] In comparison, the wartime civilian death toll in London amounted to around 30,000, from the dropping of around 20,000 tonnes of bombs.[81]

One should not imagine, however, that the RAF's efforts had no effect on morale in the German capital. There was certainly an accelerating dilution of the faith that many Berliners – and indeed Germans as a whole – had in the Nazis. The regime had earned the loyalty of the German people primarily through their restoration both of the economy at home and of German 'honour' on the international stage and, to some degree, the outbreak of war in 1939 could be construed as an extension of these principles. But from 1943 – with the defeats at Stalingrad and Kursk, the collapse of Italy and the advent of large-scale aerial bombing – it would have been clear to many that the tide was turning.[82]

However, a number of factors effectively combined to prevent any open expression of dissent. Firstly, the Nazis were expert at manipulating public opinion through the use of propaganda, and this skill was honed still further in the latter stages of the war. Also, the vast majority of Berliners knew very well what fate awaited those who openly criticised the regime, or even began to conspire against it. There was a more 'positive' factor at play. The Nazi state delivered on its promises. Not only did it undertake a massive programme of bunker building for its civilian population – which far outstripped the paltry assistance on offer to Londoners during the Blitz – it also had extensive welfare networks and compensation schemes to help those who were bombed out. At a time when the civilian population was most reliant on the regime, the regime delivered.

Moreover, in place of that shrinking political loyalty, other loyalties emerged. The first of these was a default 'My country – right or wrong' form of patriotism that would celebrate German successes – even though it might be sceptical of the Nazi regime itself. This attitude was born not only of the common peril that Berliners faced, but also of the loyalty to the large numbers of young men from Berlin – sons, brothers and fathers – who were fighting in Germany's name at the time. As the British had discovered for themselves earlier in the war, when the Luftwaffe was pounding London and other cities, the most likely result of an air offensive is a strengthening, not a weakening, of domestic morale.[83]

Beyond that default patriotism, a network of self-help communities emerged based on the solidarity of an extended family, a particular street or even a single building. As one Berliner recalled of an air raid in 1943: 'We clung to each other. It did not matter whose hand we held or whom we embraced. In that moment the walls fell that divided Communist from Nazi, Mutti from fingernail-painted Frau Fuchs, the drunk from his sober neighbour and children from adults.'[84] In many cases, it would be these groups and these allegiances that would help to sustain Berliners through the brutal terminal phase of the Third Reich.

16

To Unreason and Beyond

The 18th of February 1943 was a beautiful early spring day. The clear blue sky over the capital would have lifted the public mood and encouraged Berliners to shed their hats, coats and scarves, constant accessories for the previous few months. Though spring itself was still a good few weeks off, the unusual warmth of the sun that day meant that Berliners could allow themselves to believe that another hard winter of war was behind them.

Joseph Goebbels was in a less optimistic mood, however. The German defeat at Stalingrad – announced barely two weeks earlier – still loomed large in the public consciousness. As the first serious defeat of German forces, and one in which the Nazis' time-honoured tactics of *Blitzkrieg* and encirclement had been successfully employed against them, Stalingrad gave the German people reason for profound reflection and concern. The most immediately affected were those who mourned the loss of their husbands, sons and brothers of the German 6th Army: men who had marched in resplendent triumph through Warsaw in the autumn of 1939, and who were now either dead or stumbling into an uncertain fate in Soviet captivity. Beyond that, many would have worried that such a catastrophic defeat would prove to be the high-water mark of the German advance – or, indeed, that Stalingrad would be the beginning of the end.

As Minister for Propaganda, Goebbels was duty bound to counter such negative opinions; to put an optimistic gloss on events, or at the very least steel the German people for a year of hardship. Yet, peculiarly, he felt himself hampered by the sudden outbreak of fine weather. 'Every ray of sunlight', he wrote in his diary, 'is an obstacle to the implementation of measures for total war. I would much prefer it if winter would prevail for a few more weeks, albeit in a milder form.

The worse the image of the war appears, the easier it is to draw the necessarily harsh consequences.'[1] The Propaganda Minister clearly did not see the world as other Berliners did that day.

That same evening, Goebbels was due to speak at a large public meeting in the prestigious Berlin Sportpalast: it would be one of the most important, and indeed infamous, speeches of his life. The venue was well chosen. The Sportpalast was a huge arena in the southern suburb of Schöneberg, which had made its name hosting cycling races, ice hockey and skating, but since 1933 had served exclusively as a venue for political rallies. For an event of this sort, it could accommodate up to 14,000 Nazi faithful, seated not only around the banked stands, but also massed in serried rows on the floor of the hall itself – little wonder, therefore, that Goebbels described the venue as 'our political grandstand'.[2]

In preparation for the speech, the Sportpalast had been carefully decorated. Garlands festooned the balcony, interspersed with swastika banners. At one end of the arena, a large stage had been constructed. A long, white platform spread across the hall, behind which senior Nazi dignitaries were seated. At its centre, a Nazi flag and a bank of microphones marked the position of the orator. To the rear, a stylised German eagle rose above the dais, leading the eye to two more galleries of seating, divided by a huge banner bearing the legend 'Total War – Shortest War' in a florid gothic script.

The crowd, too, had been meticulously prepared. Carefully selected for its political reliability, it was also intended to represent a cross section of the German people. Alongside ranks of wounded from the Eastern Front there were holders of the prestigious Knight's Cross, nurses, armaments workers, doctors, scientists, artists, engineers, architects and teachers. As Goebbels would later swoon before them: 'I see thousands of German women. The youth is here, as are the aged. No class, no occupation, no age remain uninvited.' 'At this moment', he would proclaim to his audience, 'you represent the whole nation.'[3] As he would also be heard by millions of Germans in their homes, their workplaces and in their barrack blocks, the 'whole nation' was indeed listening.

When he took to the stage that evening, Goebbels cut a rather peculiar figure. Elegantly attired in a double-breasted jacket, with the obligatory swastika band on his left arm, he seemed rather dwarfed by the lectern before him. He began his speech in a sombre tone,

recalling his previous appearance at the Sportpalast, three weeks
earlier, which, he revealed, had been listened to by the remnant of
German troops fighting within Stalingrad. 'It was a moving experience
for me, and probably also for all of you', he said, to think that those
'last heroic fighters . . . perhaps for the last time in their lives joined us
in raising their hands to sing the national anthem.' He then elaborated
on the meaning of the defeat at Stalingrad; that Bolshevism now im-
perilled not only Germany itself, but all of Western civilisation. Meeting
this threat, he said, was Nazi Germany's primary duty, for 'if we fail,
we will have failed in our historic mission. Everything we have built
and done in the past pales in the face of this gigantic task.'

Warming to his theme, and feeding off the growing and vociferous
enthusiasm of his crowd, Goebbels grew louder and more animated
in his delivery – gesticulating to all corners of the hall, posing with
his hands on his hips, or wagging his finger demonstratively. His
mouth, already cavernously wide, appeared to widen still further as
he spoke, until his whole head seemed almost to pivot around his jaw.
His voice, too, increased in intensity, occasionally dropping off to force
his audience to listen more carefully, and at other times rising to a
shriek. He stated that Stalingrad had opened the eyes of the German
people 'to the true nature of war'. With the future of all of Europe
hanging on the German success in the east, he argued 'total war is
the demand of the hour'.

> The question is not whether the methods are good or bad, but whether
> they are successful. The National Socialist government is ready to use
> every means. We do not care if anyone objects. We are not willing to
> weaken Germany's war potential by measures that maintain a high,
> almost peace-time standard of living for a certain class, thereby endan-
> gering our war effort. We are voluntarily giving up a significant part
> of our living standard to increase our war effort as quickly and
> completely as possible.[4]

Goebbels proclaimed that bars and nightclubs would be closed forth-
with; luxury stores, too, would be shut down, as they 'offended the
buying public'. 'What good are fashion salons today', he asked, 'what
good are beauty parlours?' Luxury restaurants, meanwhile, whose
demand for resources far outstripped what Goebbels considered

reasonable, would also be forced to close their doors. 'We can become gourmets once again', he mocked, 'when the war is over.' In the meantime, thrift and austerity was to be the order of the day. 'Life may not be as pleasant as it is during peace. But we are not at peace, we are at war . . . we must sacrifice our comforts to gain victory.'

With that grim forecast, which had been met by the crowd with rapturous cheers and shouts of approval, Goebbels reached the conclusion of his speech. Whipping his audience into a frenzy, he posed a number of questions in response to British allegations that the German people had no stomach for the war and had lost faith in victory.

'Do you believe in the final total victory of the German people?'

'Yes!' they bayed, with one voice.

'Do you want total war? If necessary, do you want a war more total and radical than anything that we can even imagine today?'

'Yes!' they replied, drowning out the speaker with an avalanche of applause.

'Are you determined to follow the Führer through thick and thin to victory and are you willing to accept the heaviest personal burdens?'

In response, the audience rose as one, shouting 'Führer command, we follow!'

'You have given me your answers', Goebbels concluded, 'you have told our enemies what they needed to hear.' Amid a cacophony of applause and cheering, he proclaimed the nation's new slogan in its struggle for final victory: *'Nun Volk steh auf, und Sturm bricht los!'* 'People, rise up and let the storm break loose!'[5]

Goebbels regarded his speech as a tremendous success. 'The atmosphere recalled a wild mood of mass hysteria', he wrote in his diary the following day:

> My speech made a profound impression. Even in the opening passages, it was interrupted by wild applause. The public's reaction was indescribable. The Sportpalast has never witnessed such scenes as there were at the end, when I posed my questions to the audience . . . I think that this speech will make an impression, not only on the Reich, but also on the neutral countries and even on our enemies . . . It could not have gone better.[6]

Albert Speer, who had been present at the Sportpalast, recalled that
he had never seen an audience 'so effectively roused to fanaticism' –
with the exception of Hitler's most successful public meetings.
Speaking with Goebbels later that evening, Speer had been regaled
with the Propaganda Minister's pseudo-psychological assessment of
the crowd's response: 'Did you notice?' Goebbels asked him, 'they
reacted to the smallest nuance and applauded at just the right moments.
It was the politically best-trained audience you can find in Germany.'[7]

For all the brilliance of his oratory, Goebbels allowed himself to
forget that the audience at the Sportpalast had been minutely stage-
managed. Not only had those attending the speech been hand-picked,
but the hall had also been rigged with a loudspeaker system, through
which gramophone recordings of ovations and cheers had been surreptitiously relayed, so as not only to enthuse the audience present, but
also to provide them with all the appropriate cues.[8] Such sleight of
hand, however, should not detract from the remarkable scenes
witnessed in the Sportpalast that evening. The audience had certainly
been manipulated and encouraged, but their fervour was no less
genuine for that. Ursula von Kardorff noted how grimly infectious
the fanaticism could be. 'One of our editors', she wrote,

> who was there as a reporter, told us how the masses had raved. He is
> a calm, thoughtful man and an anti-Nazi, yet he found himself jumping
> up with the others and came within a hair's breadth of shouting out
> along with the others, until he sat back down in shame. He said, if
> Goebbels had asked 'Do you all want to die?', they would have roared
> the same answer 'Yes!'[9]

The reaction among those Germans listening in their homes on
their radios is more difficult to fathom. Some would have been unimpressed by Goebbels' oratory and would have seen through the
propagandistic bombast. Foreign Ministry official Hans-Georg von
Studnitz, for instance, though largely loyal to the regime, questioned
the wisdom of raising the nation's morale by 'instilling people with
a terror of bolshevism'.[10] Ruth Andreas-Friedrich, meanwhile, was
more damning, describing the speech as a 'demonstration of fanatical
will'. 'Total, totaler, totalest', she mocked, 'I didn't know that even
ultimates could have superlatives. Probably people who are unsure of

themselves have to fall back on such things.'[11] Listening to the speech at home that night, Josepha von Koskull was outraged. 'What were they thinking?' she wondered of Goebbels' audience.[12]

There were many more, however, who had been deeply moved to hear their fellows so enthused, and shared the wave of hysteria. The weekly mood report compiled by the Nazi security service testified to the positive reception that the speech had enjoyed among the German people. 'Its effect', it reported, 'was unusually large, and on the whole very favourable. . . . In spite of its honest assessment of the seriousness of the situation, it has eased tensions and strengthened anew the people's optimism and their trust in the leadership.'[13]

It would be wrong to assume, therefore, that the German people had simply been manipulated by Goebbels. They knew very well that they had been seduced that night – but crucially, once their ardour had cooled, they realised that the essential thrust of the speech had been absolutely correct. If Germany *was* to win the war – and it was very clearly now an 'if', not a 'when' – a massive and fundamental mobilisation of the home front would be required, sacrifices would have to be made and privations endured. This was the 'total war' that they had agreed to.

This, too, is why there was a surge in public morale in the aftermath of what was otherwise an apparently grim message. Traditionally, the Nazis had been unwilling to present unglossed or 'unspun' truths to the German population: every setback was dismissed as temporary, every defeat couched as a 'tactical withdrawal'. Now, with Goebbels' unusual candour in the Sportpalast, the government had finally 'come clean' with the people; moreover, it had presented concrete measures by which the situation might be remedied. This new openness seems to have been widely welcomed.[14]

Yet, for all their new-found enthusiasm and determination, the German people realised full well that difficult times lay ahead. And the question remained to be answered how robust public morale would prove to be should German forces stumble to a string of further defeats. How would the German population react when they began to feel the force of 'total war' being visited upon *them*? It would not take long to find out.

Nineteen forty-three would prove to be a catastrophic year for Germany, with setbacks and defeats in every theatre of the war. The bad news began in the Atlantic, where German U-boats had been busily sinking Anglo-American supply convoys, in an attempt to disrupt the British war effort. The first half of the war had gone well for Admiral Dönitz's U-boat 'wolf packs', with the tonnage of Allied shipping lost far outstripping German losses, and the technological and tactical counter-measures of the Allies being slow to take effect. In the spring of 1943, however, a decisive shift occurred, most notably when long-range Allied aircraft closed the 'gap' in the mid-Atlantic, where convoys had previously not been covered by air patrols, and where the wolf packs had enjoyed their most fruitful hunting. Already by May, more U-boats were lost than Allied ships, losses that Dönitz conceded made the continuation of U-boat warfare 'impossible'.[15] Germany had lost the Battle of the Atlantic.

It is doubtful that the minutiae of the war in the Atlantic were fully appreciated by the Berlin public. But the tailing off of positive news reports from that theatre did not go unnoticed. The capital's rumour mill was alive with theories explaining the secret operations in which the U-boat fleet was now engaged. Some considered that the wolf packs were being massed for a decisive attack; others were more fanciful, believing that they were to be used to launch an invasion of Britain, or that they were ferrying much-needed rubber to Germany from Japan. Only the soberest and best-informed observers would have concluded that the U-boat war had actually been lost.[16]

For the majority, however, it was events in other theatres that dominated their thoughts that summer. In the war in the east, the Battle of Kursk that July was to prove a salient reverse for German forces. Intended as a return to the glory days of the *Blitzkrieg*, Kursk was envisaged by the Germans as an enormous pincer movement, to pinch off a bulge in the front line. Yet, German commanders soon discovered that the Soviet positions facing them were heavily reinforced, and the intended swift advance quickly became bogged down in a static tank battle of unimaginable and unprecedented ferocity. Though Kursk had been supposed to wrest the initiative from the Soviets, the sheer scale of heavy armour sacrificed there would spell the end of the Wehrmacht's offensive capacity. Thereafter, for the rest of the war, German armies would be engaged in a slow, torturous retreat towards their own capital.

To the south, meanwhile, the Allied invasion of Sicily that same month of July would also prove to be of profound significance. Not only did it help to make the central passage of the Mediterranean safe for Allied shipping, it also opened a long-awaited 'second front' in Nazi-occupied Europe. Nazi propaganda sought to downplay such developments, stressing the peripheral location of Sicily and boasting of the swift defeat that would be inflicted on the invaders. But few were fooled.

In time, the ramifications of the invasion of Sicily would prove even more critical. On 25 July, Mussolini was deposed. Two weeks after that Italy announced an armistice with the Allies, forcing the German High Command to commit large numbers of troops to the theatre in an effort to shore up its former ally. On the home front, meanwhile, the many thousands of Italian labourers working in German industry – and especially prevalent in a city such as Berlin – were no longer to be treated as friends and allies. Almost overnight, they became prisoners of war.

The true significance of the surrender of Nazi Germany's primary ally was kept from the German public. The event was treated by the German press as a minor development, with the *Deutsche Allgemeine Zeitung*, for instance, devoting only a single column to the story.[17] Hans-Georg von Studnitz noted the strange silence of the German media. 'Tomorrow is Mussolini's sixtieth birthday', he wrote on 28 July, 'but not a line about him will appear in the German papers. The man who has been presented to the German people as the greatest statesman in the world after Hitler disappears from the German scene unheralded and unsung.'[18]

While the news of Mussolini's fall and the defeat at Kursk was being digested by Berliners, another development – one whose implications affected the home front much more directly – filled them with foreboding. Though the RAF had been exercising its improved capacity for air warfare over Germany for much of the previous year, the fire-bombing of Hamburg in the final week of July 1943 brought home the stark realities of modern warfare to the German people.[19] In the aftermath of the attack, as Hamburg struggled to come to terms with the destruction, the rest of Germany was whipped into a frenzy by the horror stories emanating from the city, spread in many instances by shell-shocked refugees. Many would have wondered if this was what Goebbels meant when he spoke about 'total war'.

More seriously, the coincidence of these three developments caused a loss of public faith in the regime itself. Some still managed to fool

themselves into believing that Germany would be better off without
the Italians, or that the destruction of Hamburg would prove to be
exceptional. Others found solace in the supernatural. Ursula von Kardorff
recalled a horoscope reading that did the rounds of the capital that
summer, which predicted that the worst air raid on Berlin would come
on 27 August, followed by 'a sensational decision' in mid-September –
and, from May 1944, Germany would again have a king. 'Such is the
nonsense', Kardorff wrote in her diary, 'to which the people cling.'[20]

This almost mystical belief in salvation dovetailed neatly with the
growing popular desire for revenge. In the summer of 1943, rumours
began spreading about Germany's 'wonder weapons', which were popularly known in Berlin by the acronym 'Wu-Wa', after the German
'Wunderwaffen'. Though some dismissed such rumours out of hand, there
were many others who believed them, praying that the 'Wu-Wa' would
turn the tide of the war and wreak devastation among Hitler's enemies.
Hans-Georg von Studnitz recalled hearing the stories:

> For some time now rumours have been circulating about secret weapons
> which are about to be used and which will change the whole aspect of
> the war in our favour. Nearly everybody knows somebody who was
> present when these weapons were being tested. Some talk about a bomb
> which will be fired by rocket from an aircraft and contains an explosive
> force sufficient to wreck a whole city. Others declare that the new projec-
> tiles will be fired from specially constructed bases on the French coast.
> The people eagerly swallow these fairy-tales. Faith in the wonder-weapon
> is at present the one thing which stimulates their morale.[21]

For all Studnitz's scorn, the Berlin rumour mill was largely correct.
Early trials of the weapon that would become known as the V-1 'flying
bomb' had indeed involved launches from parent aircraft, while later
firings were planned from fixed sites on the French coast. Within
barely a month of his diary entry in August 1943, Studnitz would have
been surprised to hear Albert Speer publicly confirm that retribution
would be wrought against the western Allies using a 'secret weapon'.[22]
The first operational launches of the V-1 would follow in June 1944.

While some undoubtedly found solace in such rumours, others were
more realistic. Increasingly, opinions began to be aired which doubted
Germany's ability to fight on, much less to win. Doubts also began to

be expressed about the accuracy of German news reports.[23] Ruth Andreas-Friedrich spoke for many when she made the following acerbic comment in her diary about the 'tactical withdrawals' that were increasingly being reported from the Eastern Front: 'In the east they are resorting to more and more radical "shortening of lines". If you look in the atlas, these unadmitted retreats seem rather to lengthen the front. I expect we shall still be shortening our lines when they're ten kilometres from Berlin, successfully disengaging and victoriously resisting.'[24]

As 1943 drew on, therefore, morale in Berlin gradually deteriorated. The population, tired from its relentless exertions, shattered by the ongoing and intensifying air war, and crushed by the constant restrictions and shortages of rationing, sank increasingly into indifference. Hans-Georg von Studnitz recalled the mood in the prestigious Adlon Hotel in Berlin in the autumn of 1943, when one of Hitler's speeches was being broadcast:

> Public apathy was symbolised by the fact that the speech was not relayed to the dining room, as previously, and that in the small lounge where a loudspeaker was installed, not even a quarter of the hotel's guests bothered to listen. Most of the audience consisted of cooks, waiters and maids.[25]

Increasingly, Wehrmacht reports and the shrill pronouncements of the regime sounded hollow, and both were most frequently met with a derisory snort. As Lutz Ritter recalled, 'Nobody in my circle of friends took the "final victory" fantasies seriously any more.'[26] Public optimism about the war was becoming a rare commodity, supplanted by self-reliance and a grim determination to survive.

Whatever aspirations Berliners might once have harboured, after Stalingrad and the reverses of 1943 they were reduced to the simple desire somehow to escape the war with their lives. For some, such fundamental human instincts became paramount. As one diarist noted in the winter of 1943–4:

> Neither rubble shovelling nor pillow rescuing has anything to do with Nazi enthusiasm or resolution to endure. Nobody thinks of Hitler as he boards up the kitchen window. What everyone thinks of is that you can't live in the cold, that before evening falls and the sirens wail you must

have a corner where you can lay your head and stretch your legs – the way you choose to do it, and not the way someone else wants you to choose.[27]

As the public mood deteriorated through 1943, life in the German capital became exceedingly trying. The aspect that affected Berliners most immediately was the parlous state of public health. Already in 1941, the American Howard Smith had complained about the stench of halitosis – the result of a catastrophic decline in dental hygiene – which seemed to permeate the city, and noted the pale faces of Berliners 'unhealthily white as flour, except for red rings around their tired, life-less eyes'.[28] In the years that followed, public health deteriorated further, assailed by the stresses and strains of life in wartime, the sleepless nights and the enforced shortages of rationing. Influenza and the common cold quickly became endemic, while dysentery and scarlet fever were also on the increase.[29] Yet, as the example of Helga Schneider's family demonstrates, even those who did not suffer from any identifiable complaint were often in very poor health. 'We are all in a sorry state', she wrote:

> Opa has a painful swollen knee, but we have no painkillers, and Hilde has not been able to find any either . . . My stepmother is suffering from bilious colic and wraps her belly with woollen shawls, seeking comfort in massages she is given by Frau Köhler, the concierge of our building. I have scabs on my head, and Peter vomits yellow foam. Whenever I get up from a chair or out of bed, I immediately feel faint.[30]

By 1944, it seems, an extraordinarily bleak atmosphere had descended on the German capital. The Danish journalist Paul von Stemann recalled in his journal that it was a time of

> dullness, anticipation, fear and continuous bombing. It was a soul-less existence. The war seemed perpetual. The sameness of each successive day was blunting but the obliteration of all beauty was even more so . . . The flowers had gone, the books had been burnt, the pictures had been removed, the trees had been broken, there were no birds singing, no dogs barking, no children shrieking . . . there was no laughter and no giggling. No face ever lit up in a

warming smile, no friendly kiss or hug. There was still the sky above
... but then it was often effaced by the stinking and greasy carpets
of voluminous black smoke.[31]

Norwegian reporter Theo Findahl bemoaned the fact that the restrictions imposed by the regime now affected every aspect of life and that,
since Goebbels' new regulations had come into force, even the traditional refuge of the theatre or a cabaret show was now denied to the
capital's civilians. 'With a stroke of his pen', Findahl wrote, 'Goebbels
has abolished almost everything enjoyable in Berlin in the name of
"Total War". No theatres, no variety, no dance clubs, no wine bars.
Berlin has become the most boring capital city in the world.'[32]

It could also be one of the most surreal. Life in wartime could
produce some peculiar human responses, as people became inured to
the constant drama surrounding them and adopted their own idio-
syncratic survival strategies. Hans-Georg von Studnitz noted the rather
bizarre experience of his friend, Hans Flotow, who decided to walk
home through the centre of Berlin in the aftermath of an air raid:

> Firemen were still at work extinguishing the flames, intermingled with
> courting couples, an old gentleman with a little dog, girls in slacks wearing
> steel helmets, people with portable radios and men selling newspapers. A
> female voice was screaming for water. When Flotow turned round, a young
> girl asked him if he would like to take her home: she would show him a
> good time. When he reached home at last, he found that the neighbouring
> Magdeburgerstrasse was in flames. Hurrying across, he discovered Frau
> von Gersdorff in her burning kitchen, calmly making sandwiches for the
> firemen. In another room of the Gersdorff house lay the corpse of a man
> who had died several days before, covered with a tartan rug, a crucifix on
> the chest: the body could not be removed to the mortuary because of the
> incessant alarms. Hans went to bed at 7.00 a.m.[33]

The experience recorded by Ursula von Kardorff was perhaps less
searing, but no less peculiar. Over Easter 1944, she described in her diary
an excursion to the Spree bend in the heart of Berlin, in the area that
was supposed to form the centrepiece of Albert Speer's ambitious
remodelling of the capital. In the bright spring sunshine of that day,
however, the site made a bizarre impression:

There in the middle of this Hieronymus Bosch landscape, there is now
a lake, some metres deep, surrounded by the ruins of the former
General Staff building . . . and the wrecked ambassadorial villas.
Although it is forbidden, children play around the lake, building rafts
out of charred planks . . . All around the wild flowers bloom, yellow
and poisonous, but the air is clean and the weeds are green, and fish
have already made themselves at home. A macabre sort of idyll.[34]

The year 1944 brought a further deterioration of Germany's military
predicament. That spring, the US Air Force began their daylight raids
on the capital, spurred by their own growing capacity and by the
comparative weakness of Luftwaffe defences. Though Berliners had
become rather used to the night-time visits of the RAF, daylight raiding
was a new and disconcerting experience, not least because most people
were on the move or at work and thus some distance from their
usual shelters and their loved ones. As an SD mood report noted, the
American attacks brought about a marked change in civilian behaviour. Whereas the routine of night-time raiding had bred an attitude
of stoicism in the cellars, the daylight raids generated a 'pronounced
fear' and had led to instances of civilians literally 'running for their
lives' in search of shelter.[35] There were other novelties, as one diarist
explained:

> In contrast to the British night raids, which usually last for about forty-
> five minutes, the American daylight raids go on for two or three hours.
> Whereas the British prefer to attack on dark nights and in bad weather,
> the Americans like daylight and clear skies . . . The British drop their
> bombs quickly and at random – 'carpet-bombing' is their speciality –
> while the Americans prefer to take their time and make two or three
> trial runs over the target before releasing their bombs.[36]

The advent of daylight raiding afforded many Berliners the first
opportunity actually to see their attackers. It was a curious experience. Some eyewitnesses almost waxed lyrical about the 'silver birds'
of the USAAF, whose vapour trails scarred the blue skies above their
city. Yet, for all their brutal majesty, they were bringing death to the
capital and their straight and level bombing runs suggested a worrying
immunity to German air defences. Albert Speer was one of the many

who drew gloomy conclusions from the American attacks of that spring, believing that they sounded the death knell for German armaments production.[37]

In addition, rumours abounded in the first half of 1944 of the expected Allied invasion of occupied Europe. By that stage, not only were the Soviets beginning to threaten the borders of German-occupied Poland, but the long-awaited 'second front' in the west was also considered imminent. It was fast approaching the point where Reich territory itself would come under ground attack. After months of speculation and false alarms, when news of D-Day broke in Berlin on 6 June 1944 it was almost a relief. Certainly that was the tone adopted by the Nazi press. One journalist noted that the instruction from her editor was one of near-jubilation: 'Hurrah!', she wrote in her diary in imitation of the official tone, 'it has finally come, now we will show how we will chase [the Allies] away. Victory is finally approaching!'[38] Dieter Borkowski was one of those caught up in this perverse sense of optimism. Musing in his diary on his recent conscription to the flak service, he wondered if his call-up had actually come too late.[39]

Most Berliners were much more sceptical. One diarist noted the military situation 'visibly deteriorating', and remarked that 'one hardly dares to read the military's communiqués'.[40] The bad news came thick and fast that summer: the Allied invasion of Normandy in June was followed by the 20 July Plot and the attempt on Hitler's life. August then saw the liberation of Paris and the rising of the Polish Underground on the streets of Warsaw. It all amounted, as Hans-Georg von Studnitz recalled, to 'an avalanche of events, hurtling downwards with ever-increasing momentum'. The question of who was going to win the war, he believed, had now been answered: 'the collapse of Germany [is] regarded as inevitable'.[41]

In the circumstances, Berliners resorted to the sort of dark, wry humour for which they are famous. It was in evidence most often in the whispered jokes and quips that increasingly punctuated ordinary conversation in the city. It was not usually the cause of belly laughs – life was too grim for that – rather it would result perhaps in a half-smile, or a shake of the head. Many jokes centred on the leading figures of the Third Reich: Goebbels and Göring were the two most common targets for caricature. The voracious sexual appetite of the former was one popular subject, and it was quipped that the angel atop Berlin's

Victory Column was the only virgin left in the city, as she was the only woman beyond the diminutive Propaganda Minister's reach. Göring, meanwhile, earned himself ridicule for a number of reasons – not least his own 'larger-than-life' character and his legendary vanity – but most pertinently for his proclamation, early in the war, that he would change his name to Meyer if the enemy ever penetrated German air space. Accordingly, in the height of the air war, the capital's air raid sirens were popularly known as 'Meyer's Bugle'.[42]

The Nazi mania for abbreviations was also a natural target for humour. The 'German Girls' League', for instance, which was abbreviated as the BdM (for *Bund deutscher Mädel*) was often rendered as the *Bund deutscher Matratzen* (German Mattresses' League), or as *Bedarfsartikel deutscher Männer* (Commodities for German men). Painted on many walls in the German capital, the initials LSR indicated the location of the nearest air raid shelter, or *Luftschutzraum*. Towards the end of the war, however, LSR was popularly taken to mean *Lernt schnell russisch* – or 'Learn Russian quickly'.[43]

As this last example demonstrates, humour easily crossed over into subversion, especially as the fortunes of war turned against Germany. Towards the end of 1944 and early in 1945, dissent was increasingly expressed via graffiti, often scrawled on Nazi propaganda posters. One example involved the so-called *Schattenmann*, or 'shadow man', a life-size silhouette of a figure with a hat, which was officially painted on walls, often with the motto *Feind hört mit* – 'The enemy is listening' – to remind Germans to exercise caution and discretion in their conversations. In Berlin, however, as the war neared its end, the *Schattenmann* was often given the subversive title *Adolf türmt* – or 'Adolf scarpers' – thereby expressing the hope that the Führer himself would soon be on his way. And, as if the mysterious figure in a hat did not do enough to suggest a departure on a long journey, the *Schattenmann* was sometimes given a suitcase.[44]

By that late stage of the war, there were many in Berlin who would have welcomed the chance to 'scarper' themselves. Yet, the ties of family, community and work bound tightly for most, quite apart from the restrictions imposed by a regime keen to know precisely where its citizens were and what they were doing. Then, in October 1944, a new responsibility was foisted upon them.

All those males between the ages of sixteen and sixty, who were not already in military service, were to be conscripted into a newly formed 'National Militia' – the *Volkssturm*. The idea of the *Volkssturm* already had a long pedigree by the winter of 1944, having been inspired by the Prussian *levée en masse* of the end of the Napoleonic Wars and mooted in the last desperate months of the First World War. Now, with the Red Army encroaching on the eastern frontier of the Reich, and the western Allies poised at Aachen in the west, Hitler ordered the creation of this new force, whose determined defence of their own home towns, he expected, would turn the tide of the war.

For all the rhetoric, the *Volkssturm* was scarcely an impressive force. The Nazis had been so efficient in conscripting menfolk for military service that, with the exception of those of military age who were released from professions that were now deemed expendable, all that was left to recruiting officers were youths, old men and invalids. It was a fact not lost on ordinary civilians, who quipped, in a parody of the popular song, '*Die Wacht am Rhein*':

> *Lieb Vaterland, magst ruhig sein*
> *Der Führer zieht die Opas ein.*

> Dear Fatherland, set your mind at rest,
> The Führer has called the Grandpas up.

One potentially rich source of recruits was the legions of injured soldiers, recuperating in the hospitals of the Reich, and party agencies duly patrolled the wards, looking for anyone who was still fit enough to hold a gun and could be pressed back into service. Peter Siewert was one of the lucky ones. He had already been seriously wounded serving with the Wehrmacht in the Ukraine in the summer of 1943 and was recovering after a series of operations in a Berlin clinic. When his nurse suggested that he start picking at his injuries that winter, he immediately grasped the reason. By the time the *Volkssturm* recruiting sergeant arrived the following week, Peter's wounds were suppurating nicely, and, while much of his ward was marched off to fight again, he was deemed unfit for further service.[45]

Others employed rather less painful methods, feigning illness or procuring fraudulent doctor's notes. Ruth Andreas-Friedrich recalled her partner Leo Borchard visiting a doctor acquaintance in November 1944.

"'I think it's about time for you to be preparing for the Home Guard",
the doctor told him. "Better to have things ready in good time, and then
when the moment comes they won't look too new."' Borchard duly
picked up 'a predated weak heart and alarmingly high blood pressure',
which, in due course, would excuse him service in the *Volkssturm*.[46]

It was not necessarily cowardice that made people go to such lengths
to avoid service in the *Volkssturm*; neither should such behaviour be
glibly equated with opposition to the Nazi regime. Rather, there were
a number of quite understandable reasons why many Berliners sought
to avoid the call-up. For one thing, many were already buckling under
the strain of the war, and resented having to shoulder new responsibilities. For another, it was widely suspected at the time that the Soviets
would not treat *Volkssturm* men as legitimate combatants, and that
they risked being executed as spies or partisans, if captured.[47]

Nonetheless, many did as they were ordered and duly turned out
for the Berlin *Volkssturm*. After taking an oath and attending a rather
perfunctory four-day training period, they were provided with a simple
armband, reading *Deutscher Volkssturm*, and allocated to their local
battalion for further instruction. There were no formal uniforms, just
the order that bright-coloured clothing was inadvisable and that items
should be dyed *einsatzbraun*, or 'field-service brown'. Indeed, the
opening month of 1945 would see a nation-wide initiative to collect
clothing for the *Volkssturm*, donated by members of the public. The
result was that those men who turned out in uniform at all usually
wore a bizarre mixture of components, with Luftwaffe tunics being
paired with Hitler Youth caps or Wehrmacht overcoats.[48]

The training was also rather haphazard. If they were lucky, recruits
might undertake courses in map reading, tactics and fortification, but
many of them did nothing beyond the four-day induction. They might
also receive weapons. The standard-issue item for the *Volkssturm* was
the *Panzerfaust* single-shot, disposable bazooka, which was cheaply
produced and became the staple of the German defence against Soviet
tanks. Yet in practice, *Volkssturm* men were issued with whatever weapons
were available, including obsolete rifles and captured foreign weaponry.
The alternative was that they would receive nothing at all.

In November 1944 a mass oath-taking for new recruits was staged
in Berlin, timed to coincide with the commemoration of the Beer
Hall Putsch, a sacred date in the Nazi calendar. The main event was

held in the Wilhelmplatz, where many thousands of *Volkssturm* men gathered in the rain. Similar ceremonies were held at ten other locations across the city with the speeches relayed by loudspeaker. In all, over 100,000 Berliners took the *Volkssturm* oath that day:

> I swear before God this sacred oath,
> that I will be unconditionally loyal and obedient
> to the Führer of the Greater German Reich, Adolf Hitler.
> I swear that I will fight bravely for my homeland,
> and that I would rather die than surrender
> the freedom and the future of my people.[49]

Thereafter, Goebbels gave a short speech from the balcony of the Propaganda Ministry, in which he reminded the new recruits of their oath, spoke of their 'determination to fight' and their 'unshakeable will never to surrender to the enemies of the Reich'. Writing his diary that evening, he was predictably upbeat, noting that the new force 'made an excellent impression'. Clearly mindful of the criticisms that were already circulating, he concluded that it was wrong to view them as 'a levy of old men and children'.[50]

Few would have agreed with this assessment. The oath-taking in Berlin was certainly well attended, but it can have done little to improve the public mood. Though the creation of the *Volkssturm* was intended to demonstrate the determination of ordinary Germans to defend their home towns and cities against their enemies, in practice it smacked of desperation. The *Volkssturm* men, newly sworn in, marched in the drizzle along Unter den Linden and beneath the Brandenburg Gate, like the proud and victorious armies of the past. Yet with their greying hair, their assorted raincoats, flat caps and fedoras, and with a plethora of captured and obsolete weapons across their shoulders, they could scarcely have looked less like soldiers.

On the evening of 30 January 1945, a prestigious film premiere was held in the UFA cinema on Alexanderplatz. It was an auspicious day: the twelfth anniversary of Hitler's seizure of power had been chosen as the date for the presentation of Goebbels' newest propaganda spectacular – the film *Kolberg*.

Telling the story of the defence of a small German town during the Napoleonic Wars, *Kolberg* was a monumental undertaking. Produced in glorious Agfacolour, it was a feast for the eyes, with battle scenes of hitherto unrivalled grandeur and scale and the rather unusual feature of having its French characters speak French. Begun in 1943, it was the most expensive film of the Nazi era, costing an estimated 80.5 million Reichsmarks, about eight times that of most contemporary films. Six thousand horses were employed, as well as a hundred railway wagons full of salt, for use as snow in the winter scenes.[51] The film's director, Veit Harlan, claimed in his memoirs that 187,000 soldiers were drafted in to feature in the film's military scenes – more than had fought in the original battle. Though this claim must be treated with some scepticism, it is nonetheless clear that Harlan and Goebbels planned to 'create the biggest movie of all time'.[52]

The reason for this enormous outlay and expense – all during the most critical phase of the war and in a time of dire shortages on the home front – was obvious. Goebbels believed that *Kolberg*, with its messages about honourable sacrifice and the inspirational power of popular resistance against the invader, was of critical importance in galvanising Germany's civilians for the coming struggle against their enemies. He deemed it so important that he even wrote many of the set-piece speeches himself. The result, he immodestly confided in his dairy, was 'a true masterpiece . . . [which] is as important for the mood of the German people as a victorious battle'.[53]

Kolberg told the story of the Pomeranian town of the same name, which had been besieged by the French in 1807. Aside from the obligatory 'love interest', insisted on by Goebbels and played by Kristina Söderbaum, the main protagonists of the film were the town's mayor Joachim Nettelbeck, played by Heinrich George, and its military commandant, Colonel Lucadou, played by Paul Wegener. In the face of the French advance, the two characters disagree about how the town itself should defended. Lucadou is distrustful of the people and prefers that the fighting be left to the regular military, while Nettelbeck advocates the creation of a people's militia to fight the French. Their two positions are neatly summed up in the following exchange between Lucadou and Major von Schill, who is training the citizens of Kolberg into a viable fighting force:

LUCADOU. People, go home, leave this foolish playing at war – what will you gain by it? And as Officers do you support it? These good people perhaps meant well by this gesture but do you expect it to be of any military significance? On the contrary, as soon as things 'hot up' this civilian guard will only add to the confusion. Or do you disagree, Major?

SCHILL. If I may say so, yes I do. The people want what is right.

LUCADOU. But just look at them! What do they want?

SCHILL. That everybody should be capable of fighting. They want to become a people of soldiers; we can use that, Colonel. The salvation of the Fatherland lies with these people. It depends on their mood and attitude. If a fortification is besieged, then there can be no difference any more between civilians and soldiers.

LUCADOU. Ah, but waging war is a craft that has to be learnt.

SCHILL. Learnt, yes, but a *craft*, Colonel, it's not that. It's something that comes from the heart and the citizens of Kolberg have got that. They love their corner of the earth, and for this reason they'll be even better defenders than the soldiers . . .[54]

The scene, and the wider debate, was one that almost every Berliner would have recognised at once. But for the brief mention of Kolberg in the final paragraph, the entire exchange could easily be imagined in a Berlin street in the final months of the war. In another passage, particularly resonant with meaning for wartime Berliners, Nettelbeck discusses the defence of Kolberg with the Prussian general sent to marshal its forces:

> You weren't born in Kolberg. You were ordered to Kolberg, but we grew up here. We know every stone, every corner, every house. We're not letting it go even if we have to claw into the ground with our bare hands. In our town we don't give up. No, they'll have to cut off our hands to slay us one by one . . . we would rather be buried under the rubble than capitulate.[55]

The film then extols the virtues of selfless sacrifice in defence of the Fatherland. The lead female character, Maria, loses not only her father, her home and her two brothers, but also has to bid adieu to her beloved, Major von Schill. Yet, she is undaunted, believing passionately in the rightness of Kolberg's defence. 'You have sacrificed everything you had, Maria', she is told by Nettelbeck, 'but not in vain . . . You helped us win, you are great too.'[56]

The film's propaganda value was enormous. Finished reels were even parachuted into the French port of La Rochelle, where a German garrison was holding out behind Allied lines. The irony is that the impending crisis of the war meant that only a tiny minority of Germans had the time, the opportunity or the inclination to see the film. By now, legions of workers, young and old, were being conscripted into labour battalions to dig anti-tank defences; legions more were undergoing training for the *Volkssturm* and countless thousands were living as refugees in tent villages or in the remains of their damaged homes. Few had a mind for anything other than surviving the coming storm.

Even those who wanted to see the film would probably have been frustrated. Across the Reich, countless cinemas had already been destroyed by the air raids, and those that remained were usually closed that January, due to a lack of coal for heating. In Berlin, meanwhile, the flagship UFA cinema, Palast am Zoo, where most previous premieres had been held – had been destroyed. Of the city's four hundred other cinemas, all but around thirty had already been put out of action.[57] Even Goebbels, it seems, did not attend the premiere of his new 'masterpiece'. That evening, he too was distracted by the urgent necessities of war, discussing with subordinates a possible evacuation of the capital.[58]

Three days later, on 3 February, Berlin was subjected to a daylight raid of unprecedented ferocity. 'Today the heaviest raid that there has ever been on the city centre', noted Ursula von Kardorff gloomily. 'I had not thought that things could get any worse.'[59] That evening, she accompanied a colleague down to Alexanderplatz, where the scene of the *Kolberg* premiere was now a smouldering mass of ruins.

> We wandered amongst a tide of grey, bent figures, who carried their belongings with them. The bombed-out, heavily-laden creatures, who appear out of nowhere and disappear into nowhere. One hardly noticed when the sun went down, as it had been just as dark all day. . . . Why does no one stand on the street and shout 'enough! enough!'?, why is no one going crazy? Why is there no revolution?[60]

17

Ghost Town

At nine o'clock on the morning of his fifty-sixth birthday, 20 April 1945, Hitler was woken, not with congratulations, but with an urgent report from the front outside Berlin. Roused by his valet, Heinz Linge, he 'received' General Wilhelm Burgdorf through the closed door of his apartment in the Reich Chancellery bunker. He was informed that the Soviets had broken through German defences between Guben and Forst, to the south-east of Berlin, and that counterattacks had failed to halt their advance. Furthermore, he was told that the German commander on the spot had been shot for his failure to defend his section of the front. Hitler, it seems, was unmoved by this setback and addressed his reply to his valet rather than the waiting general: 'Linge', he said through the door, 'I have not slept yet. Wake me an hour later than usual at 1400 hours.'[1]

Later that day, after being woken as instructed, Hitler played for a while with his dogs, before lunching with his secretaries. 'The mood', Christa Schroeder recalled, 'was very gloomy as we ate.'[2] Then Hitler climbed up to the Reich Chancellery garden – now a mess of shell holes and the assorted detritus of war – where he received a group of Hitler Youth who had excelled in the bitter fighting against the Soviets. Looking hunched and jowly and wrapped up in a heavy field-grey overcoat, he moved along the line of boys, patting their cheeks, muttering platitudes and presenting them with Iron Crosses. After a short speech, he closed with an unusual '*Heil euch!*' – 'Hail to you'. There was no response from his wide-eyed child-soldiers.[3]

Hitler then disappeared back into the bowels of the Chancellery bunker to receive the birthday congratulations of his entourage. Admirals Raeder and Dönitz made an appearance, as did more regular visitors such as Himmler and Goebbels, and Hitler's doctors, Theodor

Morell and Ludwig Stumpfegger. A congratulatory telegram also arrived from Mussolini, now the much-diminished Duce of the so-called 'Italian Social Republic'. The mood was dark, however. 'The chorus of congratulations', Christa Schroeder noted, 'was much more restrained in comparison to earlier years.'[4] As Field Marshal Keitel recalled, most of those present merely stepped forward to shake Hitler's hand, making no specific mention of his birthday.[5] Others sought to persuade the Führer to leave the capital for the comparative safety of Bavaria. Only that evening was some semblance of a celebration held, when a few members of Hitler's inner circle – secretaries, cooks and adjutants – gathered in his small living room within the bunker for drinks. According to one of those present, Nicolaus von Below, 'the war was not mentioned'.[6]

It was all a far cry from Hitler's birthday of six years before. In 1939, Hitler had been at the very pinnacle of his prestige and power, and his capital had served as the pristine backdrop for military parades, festivities and grand ceremonial. Now, that capital was a mass of rubble, preparing itself for the final onslaught, and Hitler was 'tired, bent . . . and weak',[7] a man visibly diminished in the previous months, who now looked much older than his years. Rather than a birthday, there-fore, the events of that day must have seemed something like a wake. According to Hitler's pilot, Hans Baur, it was all very 'sad and gloomy'.[8] His private secretary Martin Bormann concurred, noting in his diary: 'Führer's Birthday: unfortunately not really a birthday atmosphere.'[9]

The mood beyond the bunker was similarly depressed. A few Berliners sought to commemorate that day, as they had always done. In the Olympic Stadium complex a parade was held with numerous groups of Hitler Youth and the girls of the Bund deutscher Mädel. 'Lift our Banners, in the fresh morning breeze',[10] they sang. There was little 'fresh morning breeze' to be had: the air outdoors was tainted with smoke and the event had to be held inside due to the threat of Soviet air raids. Elsewhere, slogans were daubed on the walls of ruined houses, proclaiming Berliners' loyalty: 'The Fighting City of Berlin Greets the Führer!' they read, or 'We Will Never Surrender!' Others were more ambiguous, reading 'For All This, We Thank The Führer!'[11]

A few in the city even seem to have used the occasion of Hitler's birthday for a bacchanal, probably sensing that the end was nigh. At a local Nazi Party office in Kreuzberg, for instance, the event appears to have got out of hand. 'Most Party comrades', said an eyewitness, 'were sitting or lying in the gutter; they were drunk . . . these "old fighters" of the Führer could hardly get up and some had vomit on their uniforms . . . If only [Hitler] could see them for himself.'[12] A similar scene was playing itself out in Wilhelmplatz, in the very heart of the city, where officials of the Propaganda Ministry were sitting drunk in a bunker in the converted crypt of a church. 'Its disgusting', Dieter Borkowski wrote in his diary, 'out there in the streets to the east and north of Berlin, the battle is already raging, but here in the remains of an old church . . . these drunken "Golden Pheasants"[13] sit and drink French red wine, which the Minister for Propaganda probably brought in to toast the "final victory".'[14]

This anger was no anomaly. According to the Danish correspondent Jacob Kronika, many Berliners were secretly hoping that this would be Hitler's last birthday:

Years ago they shouted 'Heil!' Now they hate the man who calls himself their Führer. They hate him, they fear him; because of him they are suffering hardship and death. But they have neither the strength nor the nerve to free themselves from his demonic power. They wait, in passive desperation, for the final act of the drama.[15]

Whether from disillusionment or from a sense of self-preservation, ordinary people were finally beginning to distance themselves from the regime. One young diarist summed up the attitude in the city. 'Back in the cellar. Today is the Führer's birthday. But no one has hung out a flag . . . Most people have already burnt their flags, also Party badges and similar have all been thrown away.'[16] A confrontation on a Berlin train that day demonstrated that the sense of resentment was becoming widespread. When a Party member clashed with an injured soldier over the former's high-handed attitude, he was told 'it's you and all the others that wear [the swastika] that we have to thank that we have wounded soldiers at all!'. The man was not alone in his protest; other passengers joined in, and when the argument was over one lady was seen surreptitiously removing her Party badge from her lapel.[17]

Although Berliners were certainly glad of the extra rations that were disbursed for the Führer's birthday, most had other things on their minds. The city was now gearing up for battle against the Soviets, whose armies were in the process of closing the ring around the German capital. Troops and materiel were being shunted around in a bustle of frenzied activity, while the city's last remaining policemen and firemen had been stood down and ordered to report to their nearest military unit. Ruth Andreas-Friedrich recorded conditions in what was now being referred to as 'Fortress Berlin':

> No express trains are moving in or out. All transportation is at a stand-still. Postal and telegraph services have ceased. We are cut off from the world, for better or for worse, at the mercy of the oncoming catastrophe . . . Beyond question Berlin is in danger. You can scent it in the air, read it in the distracted faces of men called up, the scurrying of steel-helmeted policemen and couriers.[18]

Helmut Vaupel, an officer-cadet undergoing training in Spandau, heard that day about the fate of the last batch of eight hundred recruits who had been sent out to the front: only eighty had survived. The carnage was such, he said, that even their otherwise hard-hearted sergeant major was reduced to tears.[19] Friederike Grensemann, mean-while, was sent home from work and arrived just in time to see her father leave to join the *Volkssturm*. As he departed, he gave her his pistol, adding, 'It's all over, my child. Promise me that when the Russians come you will shoot yourself.'[20] He then kissed her in silence and left. She would never see him again.

That evening, taking advantage of a break in the incessant firing and Soviet air raids, Ruth Andreas-Friedrich stole upstairs from her cellar to take a look at the city. The sky to the east, she noted, was now tinged with red, 'as if blood had been poured over it'. In the distance, she and her companion could make out the sounds of combat: 'From the east comes a grumbling like distant thunder. That's no bombing, that's . . . artillery. They're attacking the city.' The realisation was a sobering one, and they stood for a moment transfixed, lost in their thoughts. 'Before us lies the endless city', she wrote, 'black in the black of night, cowering as if to creep back into the earth. And we're afraid.'[21]

★   ★   ★

Surprisingly, given the urgency of the hour, German plans for the defence of Berlin were in a state of chaos. The capital had been declared a 'Fortress' in February, but little of any practical use had been done to prepare it for this role. A plan of sorts was then worked out in March, advocating the division of the city into eight defensive sectors, designated A to H. In addition, two concentric defence lines were to be constructed: one roughly following the boundary of the city and another along the line of the S-Bahn ring that circled the city centre. An inner defence line – codenamed 'Citadel' – was foreseen for the administrative district, centring on the island formed by the Spree River and the Landwehr canal, and encompassing both the former Reichstag building and the Reich Chancellery.

Within the city, German troops attempted to nullify the material superiority of the Soviets by targeting enemy armour with anti-aircraft guns and *Panzerfaust* bazookas. In engaging the infantry, meanwhile, they resorted extensively to ambushes. Red Army Marshal Vasily Chuikov would write of the Battle for Berlin:

> The Germans fought tenaciously . . . every dwelling, every block of houses had its machine-gun nest and its Panzerfaust grenadiers . . . They employed the following tactic: after the counterattack, they made a feint, as though it had failed, and pulled back. In the roomy villas, troops were concealed with machine pistols. Their job was to attack our assault formations on the flanks and from the rear, causing us heavy casualties with concentrated fire.[22]

There were a number of natural and man-made obstacles that could also be exploited. The city's river and canals provided a natural line of defence, and many of the bridges across them were mined in preparation. Moreover, the three formidable flak towers, located in an arc around the north of the city centre, made for obvious strongpoints in the defence network. Not only were they bristling with weaponry – much of which could be lowered to engage targets on the ground – their sheer size and strength made them ideal command posts.

Elsewhere in the city, improvisation was key. Barricades had been erected wherever possible, often consisting of disused trams or rail carriages filled with rubble. In some locations, iron girders were set into the ground to give strength to paving stones or railway sleepers that were stacked up to three metres high. Other positions were rather more formidable, featuring the working turret of a tank buried into the ground. Yet, for all the effort involved, such barricades were often afforded little respect by Berliners. As one of them quipped, the barricades would take only ten minutes for the Soviets to clear – 'nine minutes for the Ivans to control their laughter, and one minute for them to blast them into oblivion'.[23]

The number of troops available for the defence of Berlin totalled around 80,000, barely enough to man the outer defence line alone – and certainly insufficient to contend with the 1.5 million Soviet soldiers ranged against them.[24] What is more, that figure was made up of units of vastly differing quality and experience. Around half of them consisted of the cadres of the *Volkssturm*, many of whom lacked weapons and even basic training. The remainder, though regular troops, often comprised exhausted and makeshift formations, ranged alongside a core of battle-hardened veterans.

Morale among these myriad units was far from uniform. Many of those now fighting for their own capital – and in some instances their own streets and suburbs – were very determined. They were motivated not only by the Nazi habit of presenting a Soviet victory as a triumph for barbarism and the end of European civilisation, but also by the grim treatment they had been taught to expect from the Soviets. The atrocities at Nemmersdorf and Metgethen in East Prussia, in which dozens of German civilians had been raped and murdered by the Red Army, had been ruthlessly and systematically exploited by Goebbels. Many Berliners fully expected to witness similar scenes if their city were to fall.

There was also a distinct war-weariness in evidence, exacerbated no doubt by the bitter and protracted nature of the battle in the city, as well as the dawning realisation that the end was nigh. As one diarist from the makeshift Müncheberg Division recorded: 'Increasing signs of disintegration and despair . . . hardly any communications among the combat groups, inasmuch as none of the active battalions have radio communications any more . . . Physical conditions are indescribable. No relief or respite, no regular food and hardly any bread. Nervous breakdown from the continuous artillery fire.'[25]

Even within the SS there were rumblings of discontent, particularly among its foreign fighters. Berlin's defences had been bolstered by a motley collection of French, Dutch, Danes and others, the remnants of the multi-national Waffen-SS divisions *Nordland* and *Charlemagne*, raised to fight the Soviets. Many of them would fight courageously for their cause, with some being awarded the Knight's Cross during the Battle for Berlin. One of the latter was the twenty-five-year-old Frenchman Henri Fenet, who had the additional distinction of having been awarded the Croix de Guerre in 1940. He was presented with his Knight's Cross in a wrecked tram, by candlelight.[26]

Though Fenet was determined to fight to the bitter end, there were others who were actively seeking a way out of the impasse. Jacob Kronika recorded how a number of his fellow Danes, members of the SS *Wiking* Division,[27] pleaded for access to the Danish Embassy's bunker in the capital, so that they could sit out the remainer of the battle. As one of them explained: 'The Battle for Berlin will be over in a few hours. Like many others, I have allowed myself to be exploited by a regime, which is corrupt from top to bottom. I volunteered in good faith many years ago, but I do not wish to throw away my life for this.'[28] Such deserters were generally turned away by embassy staff.

The morale of the *Volkssturm* was even more fragile. Given that many of those called up were little more than children, it is sometimes hard to envisage the *Volkssturm* as a fighting force at all. Dorothea von Schwanenflügel was shocked to run into one such child-soldier, 'a sad-looking young boy', while she was collecting her rations:

> I went over to him and found a mere child in a uniform many sizes too large for him, with an anti-tank grenade lying beside him. Tears were running down his face, and he was obviously very frightened of everyone. I very softly asked him what he was doing there. He lost his distrust and told me that he had been ordered to lie in wait here, and when a Soviet tank approached he was to run under it and explode the grenade. I asked how that would work, but he didn't know. In fact this frail child didn't even look capable of carrying such a grenade.[29]

Among many *Volkssturm* units the overriding sentiment appears to have been a fervent desire to get home and avoid being killed. Erich Neumann found himself dragooned into a makeshift platoon, after he left his Charlottenburg home on his bicycle to find a doctor for his sick mother. Though only fourteen, he was given a 'used steel helmet',

had a K-98k rifle pushed into his hand – which was barely 10 centimetres shorter than he was – and was sent off to the western suburbs
of the capital. There he was fortunate to run into a family friend,
'Uncle Hermann', who would act as his protector:

> Uncle did not think much of heroism. The so-called battle consisted
> of a constant search for cover in stairwells and ruin. . . . Uncle Hermann
> thought only about survival, for us both. We left Spandau without a
> fight and marched west, as we thought the Russians were approaching
> from the east. Many others joined us and we quickly became a large
> group, albeit without a commanding officer.[30]

After deliberately avoiding any contact with the enemy, the group
finally ran into a Soviet patrol. 'Nobody', Neumann recalled, 'reached
for his gun.'[31]

They were fortunate not to have run into an SS patrol. Had they
done so, there is every chance that they would have been subjected to
a drumhead court martial and executed as deserters. Berlin saw
numerous such cases during those final days of the war, with most
victims being hanged from nearby trees or lampposts with a placard
placed around their necks detailing their offence: 'I am a traitor' or 'I
was too cowardly to defend my wife and children'.[32] Some of the offences
cited could be astonishingly petty. Two soldiers were hanged on
Friedrichstrasse for their failure to adequately maintain their weapons.[33]

In carrying out these tasks, the SS were no respecters of rank or
status. As one eyewitness noted, 'More and more people were hanged
everywhere, even men in uniform wearing the Iron Cross.'[34] Neither
did the military command allow wounded soldiers to be tended if
they suspected them of being traitors to the cause, or of having caused
their injuries themselves. 'In Prenzlauer Berg, a wounded soldier was
lying in the street', recalled Gisela Richter,

> who was crying out in pain, but was not allowed to be helped as he
> was a deserter. Other soldiers cast a wide cordon around him, which
> no one could cross, because [they said] 'the pig deserved nothing more'.
> He lay there crying on the pavement the whole day, and only that
> evening did an officer give him the coup de grâce.[35]

Dieter Borkowski was one of the lucky ones. He had left his position in an anti-tank unit in Friedrichshain in an attempt to check on his mother in nearby Kreuzberg, but had been picked up by an SS patrol, along with some foreign labourers, and had been taken to a command post in a nearby cellar. There he was abused by a young – and obviously drunk – SS officer who proceeded to read the order giving him the authority to execute 'traitors and deserters':

> The SS-Sturmführer pronounced the death sentence and poured a large glass of cognac down his throat. I almost passed out through sheer terror. The Frenchmen babbled in their language, no one understood them. We were to be taken up to street level – three SS soldiers were given the order – to be shot. Then I ran over to the drunken commander and burst out crying from fear; 'I am not a traitor, I don't want to desert!' I cried. The commandant waved to the SS men, who carried me away between them. I was taken up along with the French and Dutchmen.[36]

Though the foreign labourers were duly executed, Borkowski was fortunate. Just as his turn came, a report arrived informing the SS men that the Soviets had just crossed the Jannowitz Bridge and were now barely a kilometre away. Grabbed by the collar by the commander of the execution detail, Borkowski was roughly sent on his way. 'Get out of here', he was told, 'the next patrol will kill you anyway.' That night, the fear was still so fresh that he could barely write his diary: 'I would much prefer it', he wrote, 'if I could crawl into a cellar and sleep until the war is over.'[37]

The fate of the city's many remaining civilians, now huddled in their cellars, was hardly better. By the last weeks of the war, any semblance of 'normal' life in Berlin had become impossible. As Helga Schneider vividly described:

> We are vegetating in a ghost town, without electric light or gas, without water; we are forced to think of personal hygiene as a luxury and hot meals as abstract concepts. We are living like ghosts in a vast field of ruins . . . A city where nothing works apart from the telephones that sometimes ring, glumly and pointlessly, beneath piles of fallen masonry.[38]

As a result of such difficulties, most Berliners had by now taken up permanent residence either in their own cellars or in nearby bunkers and shelters. Given that many of them were already very well accustomed to spending time below ground during air raids, they were well prepared, with blankets and other necessities brought down from the houses above to provide a modicum of comfort. Else Tietmeyer spent the last week of the war in a cellar in Steglitz, which had 'children's beds, mattresses, a sofa and a comfy chair'. It was 'all very nice', she wrote to her children.[39]

But any extended stay in a cellar could be very trying, especially as the extreme emotions of the approaching conflict would be exacerbated by petty disagreements and rivalries, babies crying or squabbles over food. Hygiene, too, quickly became a major problem in these straitened circumstances. One Berliner found a novel use for her copy of Hitler's *Mein Kampf*, when her cellar ran out of toilet paper.[40] Helga Schneider, meanwhile, recalled that her cellar had only a single metal bucket to serve as a toilet. 'Located at the end of a long and gloomy corridor', she wrote, 'it gives off the most disgusting odour. There is an old man who would rather soil himself than go all the way to the bucket. As a result the stench we breathe is indescribable. Because we are permanently short of water, the wretched man can't even have good wash.'[41]

The public bunkers were no better. The flak towers, for instance, were quickly packed to bursting, with as many as 30,000 Berliners huddled together in their bare concrete halls and stairwells. Basic human hygiene was impossible, food was scarce and suicides were frequent. In one instance, two old ladies were found sitting bolt upright; both had taken poison and had been dead for days, but they had been propped in position by the crush of bodies around them.[42] Through it all, the flak guns on the roof continued to pound away at their targets, though they were most often lowered to aim at Soviet tanks on the ground. With every shot fired, the structure shook, the thunderous sound echoing through the building.

Those who ventured out of their refuges to search for food and water were often presented with a searing vision of destruction. Conditions outside the Zoo flak tower were particularly macabre. There, beneath its very walls, what remained of Berlin Zoo had become a Hades of broken and dying animals. Arno Pentzien was a soldier who witnessed a Soviet raid on the area:

Some of the bombs fall in a large basin in which there are pelicans and other seabirds, it is barely 20 metres away from us. We get a powerful splash from it, which was really not so unpleasant. However, at that moment, some of the large birds, which had been blown into the air, start falling dead around us. A large brown bear in a cage is bleeding heavily from a shoulder wound and roared and bellowed from the pain.[43]

Few of the animals would survive the onslaught.

By the final weeks of the war, the centre of Berlin had been reduced to a moonscape of bomb craters and ruined houses. The Swede Sven Frykman was leading a Red Cross humanitarian mission in the city in those final weeks and saw the conditions for himself during a night-time evacuation of former concentration camp prisoners:

Berlin . . . presented a dreadful scene. A full moon shone from a cloud-less sky so you could see the awful extent of the damage. A ghost town of cave-dwellers was all that was left of this world metropolis. We drove along the largest and most famous streets. The imperial palace, all the splendid castles, the prince's palace, the Royal Library, Tempelhof, the buildings along the Unter den Linden – hardly anything was left of any of these. Because of the moonlight which shone through all these empty windows and doorways, the city gave an even more grotesque impression than by daylight. Here and there a flame was still burning after the most recent bombing raids, and the fire brigades were at work. Burst pipes on some of the streets made you think of Venice and its canals.[44]

Moving about in the ruins could be perilous, but as one eyewitness recalled, Berliners had become 'fatalistic, scornful of danger . . . willing to risk their lives for a slice of bread or a spoonful of sugar'.[45] With the Luftwaffe now largely absent in the skies above the capital, the Soviet air force patrolled at will, routinely strafing vehicles or groups of civilians. Artillery was also a threat, and in one incident a bread queue on Steubenplatz in the western suburbs was shelled, with the loss of twenty-four lives.[46] In Adlershof, meanwhile, Eva Richter lost a leg when a Soviet grenade landed close to her while she was queuing for food. Already living as a refugee in the capital, having survived the flight from the eastern provinces now overrun by the Soviets, she was thrown into despair. As she gave her consent to an amputation the following day in hospital, she silently hoped that she would not come round from the operation.[47]

Despite the attendant perils, food *was* available in the capital, at least for those with patience, determination or ingenuity. On 22 April, an extra ration allocation had been ordered, by which jam, cereals, sugar, peas, coffee and meat were all made available, albeit after lengthy queuing and the presentation of the appropriate paperwork. In some instances, the authorities even seem to have taken a hand in ensuring that foodstuffs were distributed to the civilian population, even if it meant doing it themselves. As one diarist explained:

> Around midday a car arrived with policemen, stopped outside our house and asked after the [Schumann] grocery shop. I pointed it out to them, and they explained that they were to open the shop and sell its stock right away. Then they broke in, inspected what was there, took a few things for themselves; small boxes and larger bags (probably coffee beans and other choice things), handed over sale of the items to Frau L and some other people from the building, and then disappeared. In spite of the incessant firing, in a flash there was a huge crowd and a frightful crush.[48]

In the suburbs, especially, bakers and grocery stores could still be found operating near normally. In Buckow, for instance, the local baker was providing 1lb. loaves of bread to each of his customers right until the Soviets arrived and confiscated his supplies.[49] Quality could be highly questionable, however. Though wartime bread had already been adulterated with all sorts of dubious additions, standards often hit a new low at the very end of the war. One housewife was disappointed to find that the loaf she collected in late April was full of sand. She concluded, perhaps a touch generously, that 'mortar must have fallen into the mix'.[50]

Closer to the city centre, meanwhile, the situation was more difficult and the rumour mill was full of tips about where food stores might be found. Gerda Langosch recalled hearing that there were potatoes to be found packed into rail wagons at the Lehrter Station. When a member of her cellar was dispatched and discovered the rumour to be true, she found herself with enough potatoes to last for a few weeks. The following day, a local market hall was found with supplies of meat and butter, which was distributed among her fellows, with each of them receiving four pounds of butter and a sizeable portion of pork. 'The joy in the cellar', she wrote, 'was immeasurable.'[51]

Information was at a premium, as most Berliners had been effectively cut adrift from the momentous events that were taking place right outside their front doors. The newspapers had been replaced by Goebbels' *Panzerbär* news-sheet, which would peddle propaganda almost until the very end. Otherwise, the only sources of information were the military situation reports that would periodically be handed out or posted at local Nazi Party offices.[52]

Even radio, which had previously been such a staple source of information and entertainment, was going through a lingering demise. Most broadcasters had already ceased transmitting, particularly after the city's power had failed, and the majority of Berlin households had long since switched off, or run out of precious batteries. A service of sorts was, however, being maintained. Helmut Altner, a teenager serving with a ramshackle Wehrmacht unit in the area of Spandau, recalled the broadcast of a blood-curdling appeal by Goebbels himself, which was transmitted by Greater German Radio:

> Berlin will not be given up to the Bolsheviks . . . The Russian onslaught must be smashed in a sea of blood. Those traitors who hoist the white flag on their homes no longer have a right to the protection of the community. All the occupants of such buildings will be regarded as traitors . . . Berliners, the whole German nation is looking at you. Think about it! The hour before the dawn is the darkest, and our victory eagle will rise up into the sun of the new day radiant and magnificent![53]

Beyond such threats and desperate imprecations to hold out, there was precious little information of value to Berliners. The city was alive with rumours that spring, which reflected civilians' innermost hopes and fears. The most common of these was that Berlin would be relieved by the 'Armee Wenck', a semi-mythical force approximating to the remains of the German 12th Army, which was expected to lift the siege, but it was actually heading *away* from the capital.[54] It was also rumoured that the British and Americans had agreed terms with the Nazi leadership and were already racing to Berlin to assist in holding back the Soviet tide.[55] Others suggested that Hitler had already taken his own life or that the SS were planning to flood the city's underground tunnels. Most worrying for civilians were the stories of the mass rape of German women by the Red Army. Berliners did not know what to believe. As one diarist summarised: 'Rumours, rumours. We live on them, like rotting food, but we have nothing else.'[56]

This enforced ignorance also affected the city's defenders. Unable to accurately gauge the progress of the Soviet advance, even soldiers were often reduced to asking fleeing civilians whether the next street or the neighbouring suburb was still in German hands. One Wehrmacht staff officer in the *Führerbunker* even resorted to using BBC and Reuters reports in preparing his briefings: 'We found ourselves in a grotesque position', he recalled, 'whereby any situation report given to Hitler was based largely on information derived from listening to enemy radio.'[57]

In some instances, the telephone system could be used to good effect; armed with a Berlin phone book, one could track the progress of the Red Army by phoning various suburbs and seeing if a Soviet soldier picked up the receiver. It was a game the Soviets also played. Viktor Boev was a young Soviet interpreter, who was persuaded by his superior officers to pose as a German citizen and attempt to get through on the telephone to Goebbels himself. After a fifteen-minute wait and much questioning by the switchboard, Boev was finally put through to the Minister of Propaganda. After confessing to being a Soviet officer, he asked Goebbels some questions, such as how long he intended to hold Berlin, and in which direction he had planned his escape. He finished the conversation with a warning: 'Bear in mind, Mister Goebbels, that we will find you wherever you will be, and a gibbet has already been prepared for you.'[58]

By now, death was all around. While the Battle for Berlin produced large numbers of military casualties, among the civilian population suicides increased dramatically. There were numerous petty tragedies among them. When a young mother in a cellar discovered that her baby had stopped breathing, 'she sat in silence with the infant for a day and a night, before a break in the fighting allowed her to go out into the yard to bury him. When she did not return, however, the others in the cellar went to look for her. They found her, in her flat, hanging in the bathroom.[59]

Most suicides, were motivated not by grief but by fear of a future under Soviet rule.[60] So effectively had Nazi propaganda spread the image of the 'Bolshevik barbarian' that many Berliners preferred not to find out whether the stories were true. The urge to take one's own life appears to have been particularly keenly felt in the German capital, not least because Berlin was the primary target of the Nazis' looming nemesis, the Soviet army, and it was there that the Soviets were expected to take their revenge. In the capital, therefore, there were a number of very tangible encouragements to Berliners to take their own lives. Hitler famously gave cyanide capsules to his staff.[61] Elsewhere, the capital's health authority distributed cyanide on request, while the Hitler Youth handed poison capsules out at a concert of the Berlin Philharmonic.[62] According to the SS's own internal reports, suicide had become the single most discussed subject in the city:

> Many are getting used to the idea of making an end of it. The demand for poison, a pistol, or other means of ending a life is great everywhere. Suicide out of genuine desperation over the catastrophe that is undoubtedly to come is now on the agenda. Countless conversations with relatives, friends and acquaintances are dominated by such plans.[63]

There were many not shy of putting those plans into action. Some were high-ranking personnel who had good reason to fear capture and retribution. Hitler's SS doctor, Ernst-Robert Grawitz, had been one of the prime movers in the development of the Holocaust and in the medical experiments carried out on concentration camp inmates, and so was rightly fearful of falling into Soviet hands. On 24 April, he detonated two hand grenades beneath the table, as he sat down to dinner with his wife and two children in his villa in Babelsberg.

The vast majority of suicides were of ordinary Berliners, plagued by much more mundane concerns. Unable to face the coming battle, Erna Massow threw herself from the fourth floor of a staircase in the suburb of Smargendorf. Hanna von Beseler from Lichterfelde poisoned her eight-year old daughter and then overdosed on sleeping pills, as she feared that her husband, absent at the front, would not be able to protect her from the Russians.[64] In late April 1945, sixteen-year-old Lieselotte Grunauer noted in her diary that the district of Friedrichshagen had already seen around a hundred suicides:

> The pastor shot himself and his wife and daughter . . . Mrs H. shot her two sons and herself and slit her daughter's throat. . . . Our teacher, Miss K. hanged herself; she was a Nazi. The local party leader S. shot himself and Mrs N. took poison. It's a blessing that there is no gas at present, otherwise some more of us would have taken their own lives, perhaps we would also have been dead.[65]

In April 1945 alone, nearly four thousand suicides were reported in the capital.[66] Countless more went unregistered.

As the encirclement and siege of Berlin progressed, the official system of registering, collecting and burying dead bodies collapsed. As one journalist noted: 'Everywhere, one ran into handcarts or wheelbarrows with corpses in them wrapped in paper, and the carts were being pushed or pulled by the grieving families themselves.'[67] Corpses would be buried wherever space could be found; in cemeteries, certainly, but also in parkland and in open patches of ground. 'In the gardens and the parks', one Berliner wrote, 'everywhere, [there] are graves with crosses: "unknown *Volkssturm* man, fell on this and that date."'[68] In the absence of coffins, the dead would often be wrapped simply in newspapers or blankets, or even left to lie where they fell. 'The stench was so terrible', one memoir recorded, 'that people were fainting in the streets.'[69]

Burying the dead could be a difficult task, as one Berliner found when he resolved to bury his neighbours, who had committed suicide. 'They lay in the same room', he wrote, 'amongst bedclothes, laundry, scattered crockery and junk. All three had been shot in the head; terrible pool of blood. It was a dreadful job to get them out of there.'[70] There were further difficulties, not least because any prolonged activity outdoors ran the risk of attracting the attentions of the Red Army. In one instance, four civilians fell victim to a mortar attack, while attempting to bury a corpse from their cellar: 'Three men were apparently killed outright', a witness wrote, 'whilst a fourth, blown to the ground by the blast, pulled himself up into a sitting position, looked around in shock, and then fell over backwards. Dead.'[71]

The sight of a dead body quickly became commonplace. One young soldier was confronted with two corpses on a handcart after a fire had broken out in a nearby cellar. 'They were still burning', he recalled, 'their faces were already half charred and their clothes had been reduced to ash. I had never seen anything so gruesome.' Yet he surprised himself by his reaction: 'The image did not affect me much, everything was as though in a dream. One adapted oneself to the circumstances.'[72]

As the front line drew ever closer, Berliners also had to contend with the dreadful din of warfare. Since Hitler's birthday, the arrival of the Red Army had been heralded by a low rumble of distant artillery, and punctuated by aerial bombardments of growing intensity. However, as the front line neared, those sounds were transformed into a veritable cacophony of explosions, chattering machine guns and howling mortars. Klaus Sommer was recuperating in a field hospital in Tempelhof:

I was woken by the thunder of cannon fire, which had been audible in the distance for days but was now growing louder. It must have been about 5 in the morning. Everyone else in the room was awake . . . and it was clear to all of us that it was now deadly serious. We spoke only quietly and sparingly. Close to the ward a German flak gun must have been situated. It made an ear-splitting noise. Machine-gun and rifle fire were added to the mix . . . The windows rattled. There was no chance of getting back to sleep.[73]

One sound in particular struck terror into German hearts – that of the Soviet *Katyusha*. Mounted on the back of army trucks, it was a multiple rocket launcher, which was extremely effective at laying down a devastating amount of explosives in a short space of time. Its trademark howling wail, as its barrage was fired, caused it to be known to the Germans as the *Stalinorgel*, or 'Stalin's Organ'. For many Berliners, its fearsome howl alone was enough to convince them that the war was lost. Dorit Erkner recalled that when one heard its awful din, 'one thought only about survival'.[74] Describing a *Stalinorgel* attack, another reported: 'nobody dared leave the cellar. The house shook from the explosions, bricks and roof tiles fell, windowpanes flew out. It was as though the entire house was falling apart, piece by piece.'[75]

As the front approached, many civilians came into close contact with their own soldiers. Most instinctively gave help and shelter when it was needed, and – regardless of how much they wanted to keep the battle and all its participants at arm's length – provided whatever succour to the soldiers they could. Ruth Andreas-Friedrich was most accommodating when a young Wehrmacht soldier burst through her front door in the midst of battle, swiftly providing him with civilian clothes so that he could desert.[76] It was not always an easy decision, however. Gerda Langosch recalled the mixed emotions that resulted from the arrival of four young soldiers in her cellar: 'On the one hand, we felt sorry for the poor lads', she wrote, 'but on the other we couldn't be too friendly to them, or else they would not leave and would thereby put our own lives at risk. It was a terrible situation.'[77]

Soldiers of the SS could face a different reception. Identified as the most ideologically committed Nazis and closely allied to the regime, they struck fear into many and even provoked hostility. When Ruth Andreas-Friedrich was confronted by SS troops, she found it hard to hold her tongue:

'Open up!' comes a yell from outside. 'Open up!' . . .

The door flies open; I find myself staring into seven worn-out soldiers' faces.

'What is it?'

'Water!' says one of them hoarsely. 'Water!' They wear the SS emblems on their collars, the accursed runes of our mortal foes. They look as if they would collapse at any moment.

'We have no water,' I say. The men look at me like whipped dogs. 'Where's the front?'

They look at the ground. 'Along the canal. They've broken through. Over on the Priesterweg, too.'

'Well, then, be off with you.'

They make a hopeless gesture. 'Where to?' . . . We've lost our squad leader. They'll shoot us if we come without a leader.'

'My heart bleeds for you!'

The youngest of them tosses his head defiantly. 'Don't rejoice too soon. You people are the first that they will mash to a pulp.'

His neighbour nods . . . He gives me a hostile stare. 'Watch yourself, miss. Things haven't gone as far as you think.'

I slam the door. But I don't feel comfortable about it. Shouldn't I have given them a glass of water after all?[78]

But the battle could not be kept at arm's length for long: inevitably the front line had to pass through. Huddled in their cellars, Berliners often had no precise idea of the temporary hell that was erupting outside, but they could certainly feel and hear it. Dorothea von Schwanenflügel recalled her house being rocked so violently by a Soviet barrage that 'we feared that we would be buried alive like animals in their holes':

> Roof tiles were flung all over . . . windows were shattered and cracks appeared in the front brick wall. Shortly thereafter, we heard the chatter of heavy machine gun fire . . . As the noise got closer, we could hear explosions and rifle fire right in our immediate vicinity. We could even hear the horrible guttural screaming of the Soviet soldiers . . . Shots shattered our windows and shells exploded in our garden.[79]

Once the German soldiers had pulled out, the Soviets arrived. Most contemporaries recalled very clearly the moment they first saw a Red Army soldier. In some cases, it was only a glimpse, perhaps across the street or from a distance, but the olive green uniform was unmistakable. 'It was a terrifying sight', wrote one eye witness, 'as they sat high on their tanks with their rifles cocked, aiming at the houses as they passed. The screaming, gun-wielding women were the worst.'[80] Many also commented on their 'otherness'. 'Their faces make you scared', one Berliner wrote, 'they are Asians, with slitted eyes, protruding cheekbones, and greasy hair which sticks out beneath their forage caps.'[81]

Aside from the initial shock, for most the first encounter with Soviet soldiers usually passed off uneventfully. The first echelon were primarily interested in securing the area and ensuring that there were no enemy soldiers concealed there. Later arrivals, however, tended to be more demanding. 'Around 8 this morning the first Russians entered our house', wrote Ernst Schmidt.

> Questions at the point of a machine gun: 'Uhr?' [Watch], 'Parabell?' [Pistol], 'German soldier here?' After 10 minutes the next squad arrived. Again the same questions, especially the threatening demand for watches.
>
> As the morning progressed, it started in earnest. One squad dragged the wine racks out of the cellar and smashed them open in front of

the house . . . So it goes on. One squad after the other. Always the same
demands for schnapps and watches.[82]

The passion of Soviet soldiers for watches became legendary. Many
of them would have a number of examples – men's and women's – up
their arms, which they would compare and admire with tremendous
enthusiasm. Like many other Germans in Berlin at that time, Hitler's
pilot, Hans Baur, was also relieved of his watch. 'For the first time', he
recalled, 'I heard the later-familiar utterance "Uri-Uri" . . . My aviator's
watch, equipped with all the latest gadgetry, especially delighted [the
soldier]. It was decidedly superior to the other ten or twelve he had
already "found". At least, one assumed this from the satisfied look on
his face.'[83] Those who resisted could expect harsh treatment and physical assault; one woman in Friedenau was shot dead when she refused
to hand over her watch to a young Soviet soldier.[84]

The passion of Red Army soldiers for Berlin's women would also
become legendary. Estimates of the number of Berlin women who
were raped by Soviet soldiers in 1945 vary widely, but the capital's
hospitals put the total at between 95,000 and 130,000.[85] The true figure
is undoubtedly much greater. Few were overlooked: pre-pubescent
girls, nuns, grandmothers, pregnant women and nursing mothers were
subjected to the campaign of rapes. Even fugitive Jews and liberated
forced labourers received the same treatment. As one Soviet war
reporter recalled, the Red Army was 'an army of rapists'.[86]

The soldiers were generally straightforward in their methods. Though
a few employed a nominal 'courtship', crude flirting or the promise of
some sort of 'quid pro quo', in the vast majority of cases the soldiers
simply exercised their overwhelming power. The most perilous time for
Berlin women was after dark, by which time the soldiers were often
drunk and on the rampage. 'Throughout the night', one woman wrote,

we huddled together in mortal fear . . . a horde of Soviet soldiers
returned and stormed into our apartment house. Then we heard what
sounded like a terrible orgy with women screaming for help, many
shrieking at the same time. The racket gave me goosebumps. Some of
the Soviets tramped through our garden and banged their rifle butts
on our doors in an attempt to break in. Thank goodness our sturdy
doors withstood their efforts. Gripped in fear, we sat in stunned silence,

hoping to give the impression that this was a vacant house . . . Our nerves were in shreds.[87]

When they managed to gain entry to a building, the soldiers would select their victims. Younger women were favoured, especially those with blond hair. Plumper women, too, were often chosen, as they were seen as healthier than their slimmer counterparts. One eyewitness recalled the scene when a Soviet soldier sneaked into her cellar:

> Staggering from one support beam to the next he shines his torch on the faces, some forty people all together; pausing each time he comes to a woman, letting the pool of light flicker for several seconds on her face.
>
> The basement freezes. Everyone seems petrified. No one moves, no one says a word. You can hear the forced breathing. The spotlight stops on eighteen-year-old Stinchen resting in a reclining chair, her head in a dazzlingly white bandage. 'How many year?' Ivan asks, in German, his voice full of threat.
>
> No one answers. The girl lies there as if made of stone. The Russian repeats his question, now roaring with rage: 'How many year?'[88]

Such an interrogation would be followed by the words 'Frau, komm' – 'woman, come' – with which the grim selection was finally made. Occasionally, older women would step in to volunteer themselves, thereby protecting the younger victims. However, given the sheer numbers of Soviet soldiers roaming its streets, any reprieve thus gained tended to be temporary at best.

In many instances, the selection of the victims resembled a wild hunt for human prey. Often soldiers would return at night to search buildings where they had seen women during the day. Some young women would spend hours in hiding, while the building was ransacked by soldiers looking for them; one cough or creaky floorboard would have betrayed them.[89] Gerda Peters was hidden by her mother beneath a table in her apartment in Neukölln, while Soviet soldiers passed so close that she 'could have reached out and touched their boots'. Though Gerda remained undiscovered, her friend was not so fortunate and was dragged into the next room. Paralysed by fear, Gerda listened as the girl screamed out her name, over and over.[90]

Already injured by crossfire, Gisela Stange, a sixteen-year-old auxiliary nurse, found herself cornered by a Soviet soldier and thrown to the ground in an abandoned building. Guessing her attacker's intentions, she fought back, kicking the soldier in the groin with all her might:

> he screamed, and another soldier came to help him and pinned me down. I thought my last moments had come. I was kicked repeatedly in the face and noticed teeth falling from my mouth along with the blood. Luckily, an officer heard the tumult and brought it all to an end . . . Numerous teeth were missing, and some were broken, but I just thought: 'I have at least preserved my honour.'[91]

Those who fell into the soldiers' grasp were at risk not only of losing their 'honour'; those that dared to resist could be killed. In one instance a Berlin lawyer was shot for trying to protect his Jewish wife from Red Army soldiers. As he lay dying, he witnessed her being gang-raped.[92] Humiliation, abuse and physical violence were also commonplace. After one young girl had been raped by three Russian soldiers, they rummaged through the kitchen of her apartment, and when they found marmalade and coffee substitute, they smeared it into their victim's hair.[93]

Not all rapes were accompanied by violence and humiliation, however. As one eyewitness recalled, her assailants were sometimes far from the heartless monsters that one might have imagined. Some were young and shy, and liked to lie back afterwards and chat; others promised to return with food, or apologised in advance as it had been a long time since they had been with a woman.[94]

Occasionally, too, there was a crude *quid pro quo*. In one instance, Soviet soldiers selected young women from a queue outside a bakery, then disappeared with them inside the building. As an eyewitness recalled: 'After a while, the door would open again and the girl would come out carrying several loaves of free bread, and everyone knew why she had been so nicely rewarded.'[95] This was an aspect that was also identified by an Australian war correspondent, who arrived in the city later that summer. His interviews with Berliners revealed a curious world in which Soviet soldiers would arrive in the evening as rapists, but would often return the following morning to apologise, bring food and ask their victims not to report them. As one woman said of them, 'they were childish really'.[96]

Nonetheless, many Berliners devised methods to avoid unwanted attention. Some deduced that Soviet soldiers – whether out of fear of ambush or simple laziness – disliked climbing up to the higher floors of apartment blocks in their search for human booty.[97] Therefore, the rumour soon spread in the capital that the best place to avoid them was on the upper floors or attics. Those best equipped had a loft hiding place with a ladder that could be pulled up out of sight of marauding troops. Others went further: Rosa Hengst recalled clambering across the roofs in a bid to avoid Soviet patrols.[98]

Those in Dorothea von Schwanenflügel's cellar decided to decorate their refuge so as to make it resemble a Red Cross nursing station, 'complete with bandages, cotton wool in empty jam glasses, and face cream jars labelled as salves and ointments'. In addition, the women adopted the widespread practice of making themselves as unattractive as possible, 'smearing our faces with coal dust and covering our heads with old rags, our make-up for the Ivan'.[99] Some feigned illness – scarlet fever was a favourite – while younger girls cut their hair, wore trousers and pretended to be boys.[100] Nineteen-year-old Margot Hähnemann was even more cunning. After a couple of lucky escapes from Soviet soldiers, she was left as the only young woman in her cellar. 'In order to avoid further attacks', she wrote, 'I would occasionally pretend I was an idiot. I plaited my hair, rolled my eyes, pulled a face, dribbled and blathered to myself. It really scared the soldiers off.'[101]

The majority were not so fortunate or inventive, however, and for them the experience was both terrifying and humiliating. As one victim wrote in the aftermath of her ordeal: 'I feel so dirty, I don't want to touch anything, least of all my own skin. What I'd give for a bath or at least some decent soap and plenty of water . . . Where will this end? What will become of us?'[102] Another described how a twenty-five-year-old girl from her group who was raped 'became a stranger to herself and to us. In one afternoon she had turned into an old woman, with grey skin, drab hair and an absent mind.'[103]

It is thought that around 10 per cent of those raped committed suicide. Countless others would carry the consequences for the remainder of their lives: the shame, the failed marriages and the fear of intimacy. For some, the stigma would be even harder to shake off. It has been estimated that 5 per cent of children born in Berlin in 1946 were so-called *Russenkinder* – the products of rape between German civilians and Soviet soldiers.[104] Already damaged by their experience of the war and their complicity in the Nazi regime, many Berliners found these additional humiliations difficult to take. 'I must repress a lot', one of them recalled, 'in order, to some extent, to be able to live.'[105]

In the end, what many Berliners best recalled was the sudden irruption of silence. After months of often cacophonous noise – from the last Allied bombing raids to the arrival of the Soviets – the German capital was suddenly and strangely quiet. 'No shooting from the "Stalinorgans",' Gisela Stange recalled, 'no air raid sirens and bombs falling, no machine gun fire and a calm that I had longed for for years. It was so unusual that it was almost disturbing.'[106]

On the morning of 2 May 1945, this new-found silence was broken by an announcement from General Weidling, the commander of the Berlin garrison, who informed the city of the ceasefire:

> On 30 April 1945 the Führer committed suicide and in so doing deserted everybody who was loyal to him. You, German soldiers, were loyal to the Führer and were prepared to continue the battle for Berlin, although ammunition was in short supply and further resistance was pointless. I hereby declare an immediate cease-fire. Each hour you continue fighting prolongs the suffering of the people of Berlin and of our wounded. In agreement with the supreme command of the Soviet troops I order you to stop fighting immediately.[107]

The news spread slowly that morning. After the radio broadcasters had all left the airwaves, it had to be transmitted by word of mouth and by trucks mounted with loudspeakers. But gradually and cautiously, Berliners emerged out of their cellars, blinking into the light of a rain-sodden but peaceful day. Some were overcome with emotion. Ruth Andreas-Friedrich was simply delighted to have survived the war: 'Laughing and crying . . . for a long time we can't say anything at all, and when we finally do, it's just silly blubbering. They all appear, Frank, Dagmar, Joe, Heike and Fabian. They beam and act as if they are drunk. "Why, you did it! Why, you're alive!" Yes, we did it – life and liberty are ours.'[108]

Others were rather more circumspect, relieved that the war had ended, but still mindful that the perils that they faced were far from over. 'Things are quiet', one witness wrote that morning, 'we stand there in the pouring rain, speaking quietly and saying little . . . we wait.'[109] Berliners asked themselves what would become of the city's menfolk, now surrendering in their droves, as ordered? What, too, they wondered, would become of them, the city's ordinary civilians?

A few were not minded to wait to find out. On the very morning of the German ceasefire, Dieter Borkowski's group, which had previously occupied the flak tower at Friedrichshain, was ordered to attempt to break out towards the north. Emerging into the cool of a grey dawn, he paused a moment: 'I stood as though paralysed. "Is this the end?" . . . It was completely quiet. Is that a good sign or a bad sign? . . . It was a strange silence, hardly anyone dared to whisper. An eerie tension hung over our march into the unknown.'[110]

What Berliners were waking up to that morning was not peace; it was the absence of war. For all the relief that the fighting was finally over, they were also profoundly uncertain, with little idea of what to expect from their new overlords, and little concept of what new horrors might await them. 'Was it the end of one nightmare', one diarist asked, 'or just the beginning of another one?'[111]

Epilogue: Hope

With the signature of the unconditional surrender on 8 May 1945, peace finally returned to the German capital and, paradoxically, the precious silence of previous days was abruptly shattered by the sounds of Soviet soldiers celebrating. At the city's landmarks, such as the Brandenburg Gate or the Reichstag, crowds of Red Army men gathered to drink, carouse and fire their weapons into the air. For Berlin's hard-pressed civilians it could be disconcerting. One eyewitness recalled hearing the shooting and falling into a blind panic, thinking that the fighting had resumed, and packing a bag to escape the city.[1] Yet despite the hubbub, for most Berliners the uncertainty of the previous week eased and they began once again to move about the remains of their city, in the search for food or accommodation, with a little more confidence.

The scene that greeted them on those first excursions was one of unimaginable destruction. Few areas of the capital were untouched by the ravages of war. Entire districts had been rendered uninhabitable; buildings standing like so many broken teeth, with empty, gaping window frames opening into blackened voids where once had been apartments, homes and businesses. The streets in between were pitted with craters and covered by vast fields of rubble, through which makeshift footpaths snaked. Over it all, a pall of smoke and dust hung in the air, covering everything, choking the survivors and twisting and eddying in the cool spring breeze.

The detritus of war was everywhere. The city centre was the worst affected, being peppered with destroyed military hardware: tanks, anti-tank guns, trucks and vehicles of all types. The once-ornate gardens of the Königsplatz in front of the Reichstag building had been transformed into a battlefield, littered with artillery pieces, discarded weapons and the dead of both sides. Elsewhere, it was little rosier.

On Chausseestrasse, close to Friedrichstrasse in the very heart of the city, a half-track personnel carrier of the SS-*Nordland* Division stood abandoned in the middle of the road. On either side lay the bodies of its Swedish crew, gunned down presumably as they had emerged from the vehicle to engage the Soviet infantry. In the rear door was the crumpled body of the SS nurse who had been accompanying them.

Scenes such as these were replicated across the city. One eyewitness recalled an area in the west of the capital, which was a chaos of burnt-out vehicles and wrecked tanks. 'A dead-tank park', he wrote, 'crowded with buckled, broken, twisted wreckage and black and grey monsters of every kind, their caterpillar tracks sprawled out or looped up or broken into chunks.' It was, he said, like 'some ghastly workshop where Vulcan had indulged a whim to play with mechanical toys, until one day he became cross and in a fit of ungovernable rage smashed them all'.[2]

As if to exacerbate the chaos, Berlin had been thoroughly looted. From corner shops to department stores, few businesses had escaped the frenzy of 'liberation', with waves of looters passing through the city – Germans, foreign labourers and Soviets – like so many plagues of locusts. Ordinary homes and cellars, too, were ruthlessly targeted, with many German soldiers seeking civilian clothes so as to escape an uncertain fate in Soviet captivity. Soviet soldiers joined in the fun, showing themselves especially keen on women's underwear and kitchen taps. In the aftermath, the unwanted remains littered the streets, everything from broken items of furniture to smashed trinkets. For Margret Boveri, it was a thought-provoking sight: 'Only with all that which the Russians cart away, will we be able to judge how well-off we really were. For the moment, one cannot really imagine how it will all be tidied up, let alone how the houses will be rebuilt.'[3] To the inhabitants of Berlin, it must have seemed as though the city that they knew had ceased to exist. Little wonder that they would refer to 1945 as *Stunde Null* – 'zero hour'.

For their part, the Soviets had swiftly established an administration in the capital and had begun to restore order and distribute food. Margarethe Kopen was delighted to discover that rations were being distributed again in her district of Friedenau: 'For Germans', she wrote, 'there was a daily ration of 200 gr. of bread, 400 gr. of potatoes, 10 gr. of sugar, 3 gr. of salt, 2 gr. of coffee and 25 gr. of meat.' In addition, 'there is talk of a raised ration allocation and of an additional "gift" from Stalin, of coffee, tea and pulses.'[4] The Soviets also set up soup kitchens, distributing a steaming concoction to a wary but hungry populace: 'What could be better?' one diarist enthused. 'It is a wonder brew from the land of milk and honey. It tastes good and it fills your belly.'[5] Such enthusiasm was a rare commodity, however, as many Berliners – mindful of Nazi propaganda – still feared starvation under Soviet rule. For this reason, many still scoured the streets in that first week looking for any possible source of additional nourishment. As one diarist recalled:

> On the street-corner, I saw a woman with a large piece of meat and, on asking where it had come from was told that there was horsemeat nearby. I thought it was being handed out, so ran to find a still-warm horse on the pavement surrounded by men and women with knives and hatchets sawing off pieces of meat. So I pulled out my penknife, wrestled myself a space and joined in.[6]

For all the difficulty that Berliners faced, however, it was nonetheless a relief to many to note that Soviet rule proved more benign in that first week than had been feared. Seventeen-year-old Helmut Altner was surprised by his treatment when he was caught by a Soviet patrol trying to escape the capital with a group of refugees. Escorted back towards the city, he fell behind the column:

> We all have the same question inside us: 'What now? Will we be killed as we are told? Or do we have a short time before execution?' Suddenly one of the Russians stops and waits for me, as I am the last. 'This is the end!' I slowly go up to him. Then he takes my arm. I am afraid that he will take me aside somewhere where no one will see us, and put an end to me, but then I notice that he is supporting me, walking in step with me and guiding me. He gives me a cigarette and lights one for himself. 'War over! All go home!' he says to me. I am astonished. The immense tension of the last few days gives way inside me, and I am suddenly unable to hold back the tears, tears of relief that the enemy is human after all.[7]

The mood was still extremely tense, however. Women still had to fear for their honour and men of military age feared arrest or worse. Soviet soldiers meanwhile roamed the city with apparent impunity. Ruth Andreas-Friedrich described how Russian soldiers still turned up occasionally at her home: 'they go from room to room, look around, pocket what they like. They are not unfriendly, but not friendly either. They look through us, as though we are not there.'[8] Some were more confrontational. Jacob Kronika recalled a hostile stand-off between a Berlin family and a Soviet commissar: 'I am a Russian, a Communist and a Jew', the commissar began:

I have seen German crimes in my country with my own eyes. My father and mother were murdered by the SS because they were Jews. My wife and two children are missing. My home is in ruins. And what has happened to me has happened to millions in Russia. Germany has murdered, raped, plundered and destroyed . . . What do you think we want to do, now that we have defeated German armies?

He then stared at a young boy, the eldest son of the family:

'Stand up', he ordered. 'How old are you?'
    'Twelve' answered the boy quietly
    'About as old as my son would be today. The SS criminals took him from me.'
    His hand slipped beneath his uniform. He pulled out his revolver and pointed it at the boy . . .

With that, there was a commotion as the boy's parents tried to reach him, while others pleaded with the commissar that the boy was not responsible for the crimes of the SS.

The tension was unbearable.
    'No, no, no, ladies and gentlemen, I will not shoot', the commissar continued. 'But you must admit, I have enough reasons to do so. There is so much that screams for revenge.'
    He tucked the revolver back into his belt.[9]

Scenes such as these would be repeated across the city; and few of them would end as peacefully.

★   ★   ★

In time, the clean-up of the capital began. Most pressingly, the dead had to be recovered and laid to rest. The Soviet authorities, naturally, gave priority to their own dead, so only gradually was the wider task to be tackled. As a result, civilian and military casualties littered the pavements and lay in their thousands, unidentified and undiscovered, beneath the rubble, posing a serious health risk as the weather warmed. Theo Findahl recalled the body of a young man, which lay in a neighbouring garden; 'completely blue-black and threatening to disintegrate', he wrote.[10] There were countless others. The writer Fritz Raddatz noted that corpses were a common sight: 'in parkland, by the side of the road, often so plundered that one could not tell if it was a soldier or a civilian. Raped women with mouths wide open, their gold teeth broken out by looters. Some half-charred in the ruins of burnt-out houses.'[11] The stench could be difficult to stomach. One eyewitness described the city as 'a stinking jungle' consisting of 'dead horses with bloated bellies, splaying their legs in the air. Disembodied hands and arms, mutilated corpses and body parts blown against the house fronts by the explosions.'[12] As Raddatz wryly concluded, 'it was neither lilacs nor hyacinths that made the air smell so sweet that spring'.[13]

The famed *Trümmerfrauen*, or 'rubble women', also set to work, clearing the ruins, patiently passing buckets of debris down a line, stacking everything that could be reused and disposing of the remainder. For many of them, it was not a task that was entered into voluntarily. They were 'indignant at first', one eyewitness recalled, '[but] sensibly concluded that it would be wisest to work with a will and finish the task as soon as possible'.[14] For all their efforts, it was a process that would take many years to complete.

Amidst the chaos, one group of inhabitants was already seeking a swift exit: Berlin's legions of foreign labourers were mustering to make their weary way home. Those heading west and south – French, Belgians, Italians and Dutch – formed small groups with their few belongings piled onto prams, trolleys or handcarts. Some added a makeshift flag of their homeland to identify themselves to the Russians. Frenchman Marcel Elola left Berlin with nothing but the rags he wore, but he was able to get out of the city, negotiate the Soviet lines and cross the Elbe into the British-occupied sector of Germany. Within three weeks he would be home again.[15] Those labourers from the east,

EPILOGUE: HOPE

meanwhile, faced a more uncertain future. Though Poles and Czechs would generally be free to leave unhindered, those from the Soviet Union tended to be seen as traitors to Stalin's cause and would be treated as such, many spending years in the work camps of the gulag on their return.

For all the hard work and political uncertainty that the city faced, those first days of peace were also a time of reflection. On the evening of 9 May 1945, the Wehrmacht gave the last of its situation reports by radio. This time the broadcast was not sent from Berlin, but from Flensburg, near the Danish border, where the rump Nazi government had fled after Hitler's suicide in the capital at the end of April. 'Since midnight', it declared,

> the guns are silent on all fronts. On the order of Grand Admiral [Dönitz] the Wehrmacht has brought the now hopeless battle to a close. Thereby, the heroic, six year struggle is completed. It has brought us great victories, but also heavy defeats. The German Wehrmacht has finally honourably succumbed to superior force.[16]

Those proud words may have helped some Germans find succour or consolation. In the capital at least, however, no one was listening. Lacking electricity, most Berliners had already reverted to more direct and primitive sources of information – rumour and hearsay. Their concerns were also much more immediate: finding food, clean water and accommodation. Many thought about their loved ones away at the front, from whom nothing had been heard for many weeks. Others mourned those they had lost, or returned to the ruins of their former homes in the city and began the search for their friends and neighbours.

A few also reflected on the twelve years of Nazi rule, and on the fate that the nation and its once-proud capital had brought upon itself. The destruction of the city, Karl Deutmann wrote in his diary, had been 'pointless, criminal and unconscionable' while the Nazi regime itself had been one with 'worthless' followers and 'thieves and parasites in leading positions'. 'The world must not forget', he warned.[17]

Berlin and its inhabitants had endured much: not only the exuberant highs and horrific lows of Nazism, but also a ferocious air war and a ground offensive of unprecedented intensity. The city now lay in ruins, scarcely recognisable from the scene of such grandeur, such optimism – such hubris – that it had displayed on the occasion of the Führer's fiftieth birthday six years earlier. Those tanks that had once rattled down the East-West Axis were now blasted to smithereens across a thousand battlefields; those cheering Berliners, if they had survived at all, had been traumatised by the experiences of the intervening years. Of the stately backdrop the city had once presented, little remained. Only Speer's elegant lampposts still stood, lining the main boulevard just as they had done in 1939. Now pitted and scarred, even they had been pressed into service by the SS as makeshift gibbets for deserters.

Alongside the soul-searching and recriminations, there was also a renewed sense of hope. The change of the season did much to alter perceptions, ushering in a fresh optimism among the ruins. As one diarist noted. 'May has thrown a blossoming green girdle around the dead city . . . The breath of spring has chased away the stench of smoke, decay and corruption. It soothes the brows of the unburied dead, be they soldiers, men, women or children.'[18]

As the broken, splintered trees in the Tiergarten and on Unter den Linden struggled into leaf once again, Berliners were reminded of nature's resilience and of the cyclical quality of all life. The spring sunshine and the silence seemed to herald a change for the better. 'The sun shines again over the world', Helmut Altner wrote. 'No more shooting, no more dull thunder of a distant storm . . . no tacking of a machine gun, no chatter of an aircraft engine or roaring of a giant tank to remind one of war. The world lies at peace.'[19]

For the first time in many months, Berliners could look forward once again: 'The time of misery and death lies behind us like a bad dream', Altner wrote, 'and the future . . . has lost all its fears.'[20] The 'dead city' had endured much, but it would rise again.

Notes

Prologue: 'Führerweather'

• **1.** *Deutsche Allgemeine Zeitung*, 19 April 1939, p. 11. • **2.** Ibid., 18 April 1939, p. 2. • **3.** *Der Angriff*, 20/21 April 1939, p. 5. • **4.** Henrik Eberle and Matthias Uhl (eds), *The Hitler Book* (London, 2005), p. 43. • **5.** Ibid., p. 43. • **6.** Christa Schroeder, *He Was My Chief*, p. 70. • **7.** Ibid., p. 68. • **8.** Joseph Goebbels, *Die Zeit ohne Beispiel* (Munich, 1941), p. 102. • **9.** *Das Schwarze Korps*, 20 April 1939, p. 16. • **10.** *Deutsche Allgemeine Zeitung*, 20 April 1939, p. 12. • **11.** *Der Angriff*, 20/21 April 1939, p. 15. • **12.** *Daily Telegraph*, 20 April 1939, p. 13. • **13.** William Shirer, *This Is Berlin*, p. 39. • **14.** Alexander Stahlberg, *Bounden Duty* (London, 1990), pp. 98–9. • **15.** Shirer, op. cit., p. 39. • **16.** Ruth Andreas-Friedrich, *Der Schattenmann*, pp. 54–5. • **17.** Ruth Andreas-Friedrich, *Berlin Underground, 1938–1945*, p. 41. • **18.** Stahlberg, op. cit., p. 99. • **19.** Klaus U., correspondence with the author, October 2006. • **20.** Viktor Ulrich, *Geburtstagsparade: Berlin, 20. April 1939* (Kiel, 2004), p. 128. • **21.** Robert G. L. Waite, *The Psychopathic God: Adolf Hitler* (New York, 1977), p. 49. • **22.** Schroeder, op. cit., p. 70. • **23.** *Deutsche Allgemeine Zeitung*, 20 April 1939, p. 9. • **24.** J. Noakes and G. Pridham (eds), *Nazism 1919–1945*, vol. II (Exeter, 1984), p. 412. • **25.** Ralf Georg Reuth, *Goebbels* (New York, 1994), p. 247. • **26.** Adolf Hitler, *Mein Kampf* (London, 1939), p. 368. • **27.** Shirer, op. cit., p. 41. • **28.** Ibid., p. 40.

1 Faith in the Führer

• **1.** *Völkischer Beobachter*, 1 September 1939, p. 1. • **2.** *Der Angriff*, 1 September 1939, p. 1. • **3.** *Völkischer Beobachter*, 1 September 1939, p. 2. • **4.** *Deutsche Allgemeine Zeitung*, 1 September 1939, p. 6. • **5.** Wehrmacht proclamation of 1 September 1939, quoted in Max Domarus, *Hitler: Speeches and Proclamations 1932–1945*, vol. 3, p. 1745. • **6.** Günter Grossmann, *Die sieben mageren Jahren eines jungen Berliners*, p. 9. • **7.** Heinz Knobloch, *Eine Berliner Kindheit*, p. 93. • **8.** Ibid., p. 93. • **9.** Henrik

Eberle and Matthias Uhl (eds), *The Hitler Book* (London, 2005), p. 46. •**10.** Birger Dahlerus, *The Last Attempt* (London, 1948), p. 119. • **11.** Ibid., p. 117. • **12.** Albert Speer, *Inside the Third Reich*, p. 236. • **13.** See Thomas Wieke, *Vom Etablissement zur Oper: Die Geschichte der Kroll-Oper* (Berlin, 1993). • **14.** Giles MacDonogh, *Berlin*, p. 129. • **15.** Quoted in Domarus, op. cit., pp. 1752–4. • **16.** Quoted in ibid., passim. • **17.** Ibid., pp. 36–7. • **18.** Karl Wahl quoted in Wilhelm Deist et al., *Ursachen und Voraussetzungen des Zweiten Weltkrieges* (Frankfurt am Main, 1989), p. 25. • **19.** Author interview with Dietrich K., Berlin, October 2006. • **20.** William Shirer, *The Rise and Fall of the Third Reich* (London, 1964), p. 721. • **21.** Herbert Sonthoff, *Last Hours in Germany*, in *Atlantic Monthly*, November, 1939. • **22.** Author interview with Erich N., Berlin, October 2006. • **23.** Else Danielowski, *Kindheit und Jugend im nationalsozialistischen Deutschland*, CD produced by the Zeitzeugenbörse, Berlin, 2006. • **24.** Sonthoff, op. cit., p. 687. • **25.** Dorothea von Schwanenflügel-Lawson, *Laughter Wasn't Rationed*, p. 209. • **26.** Erich N., *Erlebtes*, unpublished manuscript, kindly donated to the author. • **27.** Recollections of Theodor G., Deutsches Tagebucharchiv (hereafter DTA), Emmendingen, ref: 540, 4, p. 5. • **28.** Knobloch, op. cit., p. 94. • **29.** William Shirer, *This Is Berlin*, p. 85. • **30.** Knobloch, op. cit., pp. 94–5. • **31.** *Neue Zürcher Zeitung*, 2 September 1939, p. 1. • **32.** Ruth Andreas-Friedrich, *Berlin Underground, 1938–1945*, p. 48. • **33.** *Der Angriff*, 3 September 1939, p. 11. • **34.** Andreas-Friedrich, op. cit., p. 49. • **35.** Margarete Behm, *So oder so ist das Leben*, p. 85. • **36.** The text of President Roosevelt's message is reproduced in Domarus, op. cit., vol. 3, p. 1762. • **37.** Michael Bloch, *Ribbentrop* (London, 1992), p. 259. • **38.** Winston Churchill, *The Second World War* (London, 1959), p. 161. • **39.** Shirer, *This Is Berlin*, p. 71. • **40.** Nevile Henderson, *Failure of a Mission, Berlin 1937–39* (London, 1940), p. 288. • **41.** Ibid., p. 288. • **42.** Ibid. • **43.** Schwanenflügel-Lawson, op. cit., p. 209. • **44.** Paul Schmidt, *Hitler's Interpreter* (London, 1951), p. 157. • **45.** Ibid., p. 158. • **46.** Domarus, op. cit., pp. 1782–3. • **47.** William Shirer, *Berlin Diary 1934–1941* (illustrated edition), p. 101. • **48.** *Deutsche Allgemeine Zeitung*, Extra, 3 September 1939, p. 1. • **49.** Henderson, op. cit., p. 289. • **50.** Helmuth James von Moltke, *Letters to Freya 1939–1945*, p. 35. • **51.** Shirer, *This Is Berlin*, p. 75. • **52.** Moltke, op. cit., p. 32. • **53.** Christabel Bielenberg, *The Past Is Myself*, pp. 13–15. • **54.** Domarus, op. cit., p. 1844. • **55.** Ibid., pp. 1847–8. • **56.** Bielenberg, op. cit., p. 67. • **57.** Moltke, op. cit., p. 39. • **58.** Shirer, *Berlin Diary*, p. 114. • **59.** Heinz Boberach (ed.), *Meldungen aus dem Reich 1938–1945*, vol. 2, p. 339. • **60.** Bielenberg, op. cit., p. 68. • **61.** Fred Taylor (trans. and ed.), *The Goebbels Diaries 1939–41*, p. 17. • **62.** Boberach, op. cit., p. 339. • **63.** William Russell, *Berlin Embassy*, p. 74. • **64.** Howard K. Smith, *Last Train from Berlin*, p. 67. • **65.** Russell, op. cit., p. 76. • **66.** Boberach, op. cit., p. 339. • **67.** Bielenberg, op. cit., p. 69. • **68.** Russell, op. cit., p. 77. • **69.** Moltke, op. cit., p. 39. • **70.** Andreas-Friedrich, *Berlin Underground, 1938–1945*, p. 51. • **71.** Taylor, op. cit., p. 20. • **72.** Ibid., pp. 20–21.

2 A Deadly Necessity

• 1. Blackout order of 23 May 1939 reproduced at http://
www.12move.de/home/bunker-bs/8dfgvo.htm • 2. Jörg Friedrich, *The Fire:
The Bombing of Germany 1940–1945* (New York, 2006), p. 363. • 3. Bundesarchiv-
Militärarchiv (hereafter BA-MA) RL41/1, 'Luftschutz-Berichte', 29 September
1939, p. 2. • 4. 'Berlin Orders Strictest Blackouts', in *New York Times*, 13
October 1939, p. 5. • 5. William Shirer, *This Is Berlin*, p. 69. • 6. *Deutsche
Allgemeine Zeitung*, 2 September 1939, evening edition, p. 6. • 7. 'Honk,
honk, honk', in *Time*, 16 October 1939. • 8. William Russell, *Berlin Embassy*,
p. 180. • 9. 'Honk, honk, honk', op. cit. • 10. Bundesarchiv, Berlin (hereafter BA-B), RL41/1. Luftschutz-Berichte, 17 January 1940, p. 2. • 11. 'Die
abgedunkelte Stadt' by Carl Haensel, in *Deutsche Allgemeine Zeitung*,
6 September 1939, p. 5. • 12. Ruth Andreas-Friedrich, *Berlin Underground, 1938–1945*, p. 48. • 13. Testimony of Josepha von Koskull, reproduced by the Deutsch Historisches Museum, Berlin, at
http://www.dhm.de/lemo/forum/kollektives_gedaechtnis/067/index.html
• 14. *Verdunkelung – Aber wie?* (Berlin, 1939), p. 4. • 15. Placard on display at
the 'Berliner Unterwelten Museum' at Gesundbrunnen Station, Berlin.
• 16. Quoted from an original 'Strafverfügung' of the Berlin Polizeipräsident,
in the possession of the author. • 17. Andreas-Friedrich, op. cit., p. 363.
• 18. Landesarchiv Berlin (hereafter LA-B), A.Pr.Br.Rep. 030-03 Tlt. 198B Nr.
1616, Tötungsdelikte, September 1939. • 19. LA-B, A.Pr.Br.Rep. 030-03 Tlt.
198B Nr. 1617, Tötungsdelikte, October 1939. • 20. LA-B, A.Pr.Br.Rep. 030-03
Tlt. 198B Nr. 1617, Tötungsdelikte, October and November 1939. • 21. LA-B,
A.Pr.Br.Rep. 030-03 Tlt. 198B Nr. 1620, Tötungsdelikte, January 1940. • 22. LA-
B, A.Pr.Br.Rep. 030-03 Tlt. 198B Nr. 1620, Tötungsdelikte, December 1940.
• 23. LA-B, A.Pr.Br.Rep. 030-03 Tlt. 198B Nr. 1617, Tötungsdelikte, October 1939.
• 24. See *Deutsche Allgemeine Zeitung*, 16 January, 1940, p. 7, 25 January 1940, p. 7,
and 27 January 1940, p. 7. • 25. Heinz Boberach (ed.), *Meldungen aus dem
Reich 1938–1945*, vol. 3, p. 696. • 26. 'Drei Todesurteile des Sondergerichts', in
Deutsche Allgemeine Zeitung, 23 December 1939. • 27. 'Blackout Robber Executed',
in *New York Times*, 26 January 1940, p. 2, and *Deutsche Allgemeine Zeitung*, 23 January
1940, p. 7. • 28. Quoted in Terry Charman, *The German Home Front 1939–1945* (London,
1989), p. 43. • 29. LA-B, A.Pr.Br.Rep. 030-03 Tlt. 198B Nr. 1617, Tötungsdelikte,
November 1940. • 30. 'Night Brings Home War to Berliners', in *New York Times*,
19 September 1939, p. 11. • 31. Anne O'Hare McCormick, 'Paris and Berlin: A
Revealing Contrast', in *New York Times Magazine*, 14 March 1940, p. 89.
• 32. Deutschland-Berichte der Sopade, quoted in Hans Dieter Schäfer (ed.),
Berlin im Zweiten Weltkrieg, p. 83. • 33. 'Night Brings Home War to Berliners',
op. cit., p. 11. • 34. All the following details of the Ogorzow murders are from

the Kriminalpolizei files held at the LA-B, A.Pr.Br.Rep. 030-03 Tlt. 198B
Nr. 1782–1789. The Ogorzow murders are covered in my article 'The Nazi
Serial Killer', in *BBC History Magazine*, May 2009. • **35.** See *Berliner Lokal-
Anzeiger*, 6 November 1940, p. 5. • **36.** LA-B, A.Pr.Br.Rep. 030-03 Tlt. 198B
Nr. 1620, Tötungsdelikte, December 1940. • **37.** Horst Bosetzky, *Wie ein
Tier* (Berlin, 1995), p. 176. • **38.** LA-B, A.Pr.Br.Rep. 030-03 Tlt. 198B Nr. 1784,
Abschrift, p. 6. • **39.** Kriminalrat Hans Lobbes quoted in *Der Spiegel*,
19 January 1950, p. 26. • **40.** *Völkischer Beobachter*, 30 December 1940, p. 5.
• **41.** LA-B, A.Pr.Br.Rep. 030-03 Tlt. 198B Nr. 1788, Kripo report, 23 December
1940. • **42.** Ibid., Kripo report, 23 December 1940 and 12 February 1941.
• **43.** Ibid., Kripo reports, 23 December 1940, 12 January, 1941 and 17 January
1941. • **44.** LA-B, A.Pr.Br.Rep. 030-03 Tlt. 198B Nr. 1789, Mordkommission
Koziol, 3 July 1941. • **45.** Ibid., 9 July 1941, p. 51. • **46.** See http://
de.wikipedia.org/wiki/Georg_Heuser • **47.** BA-B, R3001/123286, pp. 19–
24. Execution of Ogorzow. • **48.** Ibid., Kriminalpolizei Schlussbericht, 22
July 1941, pp. 159 and 189. • **49.** LA-B, A.Pr.Br.Rep. 030-03 Tlt. 198B Nr. 1620,
Tötungsdelikte, Statistical summaries for 1940. • **50.** Quoted in Norman
Longmate, *The Bombers: The RAF Offensive against Germany 1939–1945* (London,
1983), p. 200. • **51.** British Library, London, 'Blind Eye' (H₂S) Target Chart of
Berlin, ref. X. 5523. • **52.** For a discussion of the accuracy of H_2S, see Louis
Brown, *A Radar History of World War II* (Philadelphia, 1999), p. 324. • **53.** BA-B,
RL41/6, Pressematerial des RLB Präsidiums, 22 May 1944, p. 1. • **54.** Quoted
in Wolfram Wette, Ricarda Bremer and Detlef Vogel (eds), *Das letzte halbe
Jahr*, pp. 203–4.

3   A Guarded Optimism

• **1.** William Shirer, *This Is Berlin*, p. 108. • **2.** Ibid., p. 108. • **3.** Heinz Boberach
(ed.), *Meldungen aus dem Reich 1938–1945*, p. 442. • **4.** William Shirer, *Berlin
Diary 1934–41* (illustrated edition), p. 108. • **5.** *Deutsche Allgemeine Zeitung*,
21 December, 1939, p. 3. • **6.** Fred Taylor (ed. and trans.), *The Goebbels Diaries
1939–41*, p. 73. • **7.** *Deutsche Allgemeine Zeitung*, 10 December 1939, p. 1. • **8.**
Henrik Eberle and Matthias Uhl (eds), *The Hitler Book* (London, 2005), p. 53.
• **9.** Otto Tolischus, 'Inside Germany: The Mark of War', in *New York
Times*, 17 December 1939, p. 12. • **10.** E. Rinner (ed.), *Deutschland-Berichte
der Sozialdemokratische Partei Deutschlands*, vol. 7, p. 69. • **11.** Roger Boyes,
'Swastikas and twisted carols', *The Times*, 17 November 2009, p. 39. • **12.** Ruth
Andreas-Friedrich, *Berlin Underground, 1938–1945*, pp. 53–4. • **13.** Shirer, *Berlin
Diary*, p. 122. •**14.** Ibid., pp. 122–3. • **15.** William Russell, *Berlin Embassy*, p. 142.
• **16.** Otto-Herbert Leonhardt, *Spuren eines Lebens*, p. 89. • **17.** Shirer, *Berlin
Diary*, p. 124. • **18.** Christabel Bielenberg, *The Past Is Myself*, p. 70. • **19.** Howard

K. Smith, *Last Train from Berlin*, p. 38. • **20.** Boberach (ed.), op. cit., p. 1006. • **21.** Russell, op. cit., p. 235. • **22.** Smith, op. cit., p. 68. • **23.** Shirer, *This Is Berlin*, pp. 258–9. • **24.** Rinner (ed.), op. cit., p. 221. • **25.** Shirer, *This Is Berlin*, p. 269. • **26.** Boberach (ed.), op. cit., pp. 1127 and 1163. • **27.** Smith, op. cit., p. 68. • **28.** Heinz Knobloch, *Eine Berliner Kindheit*, p. 100. • **29.** *New York Times*, 15 June 1940, p. 2. • **30.** Ibid., 7 July 1940, p. 1. • **31.** Ibid. • **32.** Andreas-Friedrich, op. cit., pp. 56–7. • **33.** Ibid., p. 58. • **34.** Marie Vassiltchikov, *Berlin Diaries 1940–1945*, p. 18. • **35.** Shirer, *This Is Berlin*, p. 326. • **36.** See Götz Aly (ed.), *Volkes Stimme*, pp. 116–29. • **37.** Smith, op. cit., p. 66. • **38.** Roger Moorhouse, *Killing Hitler* (London, 2006), p. 80. • **39.** Reinhard Spitzy, *How We Squandered the Reich*, p. 308. • **40.** Smith, op. cit., p. 69. • **41.** *New York Times*, 19 July 1940, p. 7. • **42.** Shirer, *This Is Berlin*, p. 353. • **43.** Smith, op. cit., p. 69. • **44.** Boberach (ed.), op. cit., p. 1307. • **45.** *New York Times*, 4 August 1940, p. 56. • **46.** Hans Albrecht Schraepler, *At Rommel's Side* (London, 2009), p. 104. • **47.** See, for instance, Wolfgang Willrich, *Des Edlen ewiges Reich* (Berlin, 1939) or *Die Männer unserer Luftwaffe* (Berlin, 1940). With thanks to Gregers Forssling. • **48.** Tom Carver, *Where the Hell Have You Been?* (London, 2009), p. 25. • **49.** Author interview with Christa R., Berlin, October 2006. • **50.** On this subject see Fred Taylor (ed. and trans.), *The Goebbels Diaries 1939–1941*, pp. 390, 408 and passim. • **51.** 'Invasion of Russia is denied by Reich', *New York Times*, 20 June 1941, p. 4. • **52.** Boberach (ed.), op. cit., p. 2394. Report from 12 June 1941. • **53.** Max Domarus, *Hitler: Reden und Proklamationen 1932–1945*, vol. III (Wiesbaden, 1973), pp. 1731–2. • **54.** Ibid., p. 1732. • **55.** *Völkischer Beobachter*, 24 June 1941, p. 2. • **56.** Lutz R. correspondence with the author, December 2008. • **57.** Taylor (ed.), op. cit., p. 425. • **58.** Henry Flannery, *Assignment to Berlin*, p. 259. • **59.** Ibid. • **60.** See Hans-Rainer Sandvoss, *Die 'andere' Reichshauptstadt*, p. 462 passim. • **61.** Helmuth James von Moltke, *Letters to Freya 1939–1945*, p. 141. • **62.** Andreas-Friedrich, op. cit., p. 68. • **63.** *Die Weltwoche* (Zurich), 'Berliner Stimmungen', 5 September 1941, pp. 3 and 9.

4 Marching on their Stomachs

• **1.** Weather statistics from the Deutsche Wetterdienst at www.dwd.de/klima-daten with thanks to Walter Koelschtzky. • **2.** William Shirer, *This Is Berlin*, p. 195. • **3.** Ibid., p. 196. • **4.** Dorothea von Schwanenflügel-Lawson, *Laughter Wasn't Rationed*, p. 218. • **5.** *New York Times*, 16 February 1940, p. 6, and 19 February 1940, p. 6. • **6.** Ibid., 12 January 1940, p. 5. • **7.** William Russell, *Berlin Embassy*, p. 148. • **8.** Shirer, op. cit., p. 182. • **9.** Russell, op. cit., p. 153. • **10.** Heinz Boberach (ed.), *Meldungen aus dem Reich 1938–1945*, p. 721. • **11.** Ibid., p. 689. • **12.** *New York Times*, 17 January 1940, p. 10. • **13.** *The Times*,

22 February 1940, p. 7. • **14.** *New York Times*, 12 January 1940, p. 5. • **15.** *The Times*, 8 February 1940, p. 7. • **16.** Ibid., 16 February 1940, p. 7. • **17.** Boberach (ed.), op. cit., p. 720. • **18.** Russell, op. cit., p. 151. • **19.** Frederick Oechsner, *This Is the Enemy*, p. 126. • **20.** Shirer, op. cit., pp. 192–3. • **21.** Marie Vassiltchikov, *Berlin Diaries 1940–1945*, p. 4. • **22.** Russell, op. cit., p. 152. • **23.** Ibid. • **24.** LA-B, A.Pr.Br.Rep. 030-03 Tlt. 198B Nr. 1620 Tötungsdelikte, January 1940. • **25.** *Deutsche Allgemeine Zeitung*, 16 February 1940, p. 7. • **26.** See, for instance, *Deutsche Allgemeine Zeitung*, 15 February 1940, p. 7, and 16 February 1940, p. 7. • **27.** *Deutsche Allgemeine Zeitung*, 20 January 1940, p. 3. • **28.** Ibid., 29 January 1940, p. 4. • **29.** Boberach (ed.), op. cit., p. 705. • **30.** Ibid., p. 706. • **31.** Ibid., p. 685. • **32.** Ibid., p. 723. • **33.** Ibid., p. 662. • **34.** Ibid., p. 677. • **35.** Ibid., p. 687. • **36.** Ibid., p. 687. • **37.** *The Times*, 22 January 1940, p. 6, and Boberach (ed.), op. cit., p. 719. • **38.** *New York Times*, 14 January 1940, p. 34. • **39.** Boberach (ed.), op. cit., p. 649. • **40.** Howard K. Smith, *Last Train from Berlin*, p. 92. • **41.** *Deutsche Allgemeine Zeitung*, 20 January 1940, p. 3. • **42.** Ibid., 8 February 1940, p. 3. • **43.** Russell, op. cit., p. 151. • **44.** Otto Tolischus, op. cit., p. 13. • **45.** *New York Times*, 23 February 1940, p. 4. • **46.** Shirer, op. cit., p. 208. • **47.** See, for example, 'Genug für alle', in *Das Schwarze Korps*, 7 September 1939, p. 8. • **48.** *Der Angriff*, 2 September 1939, p. 14. • **49.** Quoted in Terry Charman, *The German Home Front 1939–1945* (London, 1989), p. 47. • **50.** Jeremy Noakes (ed.), *Nazism 1919–1945*, vol. 4, *The German Home Front in World War II* p. 512. • **51.** Rachel Becker, testimony, Yad Vashem Archive, ref: 03/1806. • **52.** Hans-Rainer Sandvoss, *Widerstand in Steglitz und Zehlendorf*, p. 191. • **53.** Noakes (ed.), op. cit., p. 525. • **54.** Richard Grunberger, *A Social History of the Third Reich*, p. 271. • **55.** See Norman Davies, *Europe at War* (London, 2006), pp. 356–7. • **56.** Noakes (ed.), op. cit., pp. 513–15. • **57.** Russell, op. cit., p. 157. • **58.** Smith, op. cit., p. 99. • **59.** Russell, op. cit., pp. 153–4. • **60.** Ibid., p. 154. • **61.** Ibid., p. 162. • **62.** Ibid., p. 142. • **63.** Smith, op. cit., p. 96. • **64.** Ibid., p. 95. • **65.** Ibid., p. 94. • **66.** Vassiltchikov, op. cit., p. 13. • **67.** 'Gestohlene Fleischmarken', in *Deutsche Allgemeine Zeitung*, 10 December 1939. • **68.** *Berliner Lokal-Anzeiger*, 19 April 1944. • **69.** Christabel Bielenberg, *The Past Is Myself*, p. 61. • **70.** Smith, op. cit., p. 92. • **71.** Vassiltchikov, op. cit., p. 34. • **72.** Author interviews with Renate K. and Renate B., Berlin, October 2006. • **73.** Smith, op. cit., p. 93. • **74.** Irene Guenther, *Nazi Chic? Fashioning Women in the Third Reich* (Oxford, 2004), p. 238. • **75.** Quoted in Richard Evans, *The Third Reich at War*, pp. 427–8. • **76.** Quoted in Russell, op. cit., pp. 206–7. • **77.** Smith, op. cit., p. 96. • **78.** Guenther, op. cit., p. 240. • **79.** Bielenberg, op. cit., p. 62. • **80.** Ruth Andreas-Friedrich, *Berlin Underground, 1938–1945*, p. 67. • **81.** Vassiltchikov, op. cit., p. 36. • **82.** Ibid., p. 34. • **83.** Reinhard Spitzy, *How We Squandered the Reich*, p. 312. • **84.** Quoted in Charman, op. cit., p. 137. • **85.** Smith, op. cit., pp. 109–10. • **86.** Boberach (ed.), op. cit., p. 4886. • **87.** Author interview with Benedikt D., Berlin, October 2006. • **88.** Bielenberg, op. cit., p. 70. • **89.** For more on this peculiar episode,

see http://wisconsinhistory.org/whi/feature/angora/ • **90.** Martin Kitchen, *Nazi Germany at War*, p. 82. • **91.** See Guenther, op. cit., p. 230. • **92.** Lutz Heck quoted in Hans Dieter Schäfer, *Berlin im zweiten Weltkrieg*, p. 164; English translation from Giles MacDonogh, *Berlin*, p. 142. • **93.** Grunberger, op. cit., p. 264. • **94.** Dieter Borkowski, *Wer weiss, ob wir uns wiedersehen*, p. 72. • **95.** Götz Aly, *Hitler's Beneficiaries*, p. 104. • **96.** Smith, op. cit., p. 85. • **97.** Göring quoted in Don and Petie Kladstrup, *Wine and War* (London, 2002), p. 65. • **98.** Aly, op. cit., p. 99. • **99.** Smith, op. cit., p. 86. • **100.** Boberach (ed.), op. cit., p. 5496. • **101.** Andreas-Friedrich, op. cit., p. 104. • **102.** See Malte Zierenberg, *Stadt der Schieber – Der Berliner Schwarzmarkt 1939–1950*. • **103.** Adam Tooze, *The Wages of Destruction*, p. 645. • **104.** Theo Findahl, *Letzter Akt Berlin: 1939–1945*, p. 21. • **105.** Grunberger, op. cit., p. 138. • **106.** Albert Speer, *Inside the Third Reich*, p. 357. • **107.** Lothar Gruchmann, 'Korruption im Dritten Reich – Zur "Lebensmittelversorgung" der NS-Führerschaft', in *Vierteljahrshefte für Zeitgeschichte*, no. 42 (Munich, 1994), pp. 571–93. • **108.** Ibid., p. 581. • **109.** Ibid., p. 590. • **110.** Wolfram Wette et al. (eds), *Das letzte halbe Jahr*, p. 376.

5 Brutality Made Stone

• **1.** 'Überflüssiger Pilz', *Berliner Morgenpost*, 14 January 2007. • **2.** Adolf Hitler, *Mein Kampf* (London, 1969 edition), p. 239 passim. • **3.** Quoted in Ronald Hayman, *Hitler & Geli* (London, 1997), p. 30. • **4.** For an overview of Nazi architectural planning, see Albert Speer (ed.), *Die neue deutsche Baukunst* (Berlin, 1943). • **5.** *Daily Telegraph*, 22 January 2006. • **6.** Albert Speer, *Inside the Third Reich*, p. 123. • **7.** Ibid, p. 119. • **8.** Quoted in Frederic Spotts, *Hitler and the Power of Aesthetics* (London, 2002), p. 348. • **9.** Speer, *Inside the Third Reich*, p. 122. • **10.** Norman H. Baynes (ed.), *The Speeches of Adolf Hitler* (Oxford, 1942), pp. 593–4. • **11.** Speer, *Inside the Third Reich*, pp. 97–8. • **12.** *Der Angriff*, 28 January 1938, p. 1. • **13.** *Völkischer Beobachter*, 28 January 1938, p. 1. • **14.** *New York Times*, 28 January 1938, p. 1. • **15.** *The Times*, 1 February 1938, p. 13. • **16.** Speer, *Inside the Third Reich*, p. 198. • **17.** Hans Reichhardt and Wolfgang Schäche, *Von Berlin nach Germania*, p. 142. • **18.** Speer, *Inside the Third Reich*, p. 199. • **19.** Reichhardt and Schäche, op. cit., p. 136. • **20.** Speer, *Inside the Third Reich*, pp. 197–8. • **21.** See illustrations of plans in Reichhardt and Schäche, op. cit., p. 128. • **22.** Speer, *Inside the Third Reich*, p. 195. • **23.** Speer (ed.), *Baukunst*, p. 11. • **24.** Lars Olof Larsson, 'Die Neugestaltung der Reichshauptstadt', in *Stockholm Studies in Art*, no. 29 (Stockholm, 1978), pp. 32–5. • **25.** *New York Times*, 28 January 1938, p. 11. • **26.** Reichhardt and Schäche, op. cit., pp. 142–52. • **27.** Larsson, op. cit., p. 78. • **28.** Hermann Mattern, *Eine Aufstellung von Sträuchern und Gehölzen für die Reichshauptstadt Berlin* (Berlin, 1938) • **29.** Speer, *Inside the Third Reich*, p. 127. • **30.** Ibid., p. 197. • **31.** Fred

Taylor (ed. and trans.), *The Goebbels Diaries 1939–1941*, p. 333. • **32.** Speer, *Inside the Third Reich*, p. 127. • **33.** Spotts, op. cit., p. 355. • **34.** Albert Speer, *Spandau: The Secret Diaries* (London, 1976), p. 145. • **35.** Quoted in Alexandra Richie, *Faust's Metropolis*, p. 473. • **36.** Johann Friedrich Geist and Klaus Kürvers, 'Tatort Berlin, Pariser Platz: Die Zerstörung und Entjudung Berlins', in *1945: Krieg – Zerstörung – Aufbau*, Schriftenreihe der Akademie der Künste (Berlin, 1995), p. 69. • **37.** LA-B, Pr.Br.Rep. 107, Nr. 140/3. • **38.** Reichhardt and Schäche, op. cit., p. 155. • **39.** Ibid., p. 47. • **40.** LA-B, Pr.Br.Rep, 107, Ac2133, Nr. 53a, p. 28. • **41.** Reichhardt and Schäche, op. cit., p. 173. • **42.** *Völkischer Beobachter*, 15 July 1938. • **43.** Paul B. Jaskot, *The Architecture of Oppression* (London, 2000), p. 99. • **44.** Ibid., p. 93. • **45.** Author interview with Marianne M., Berlin, July, 2007. • **46.** Geist and Kürvers, op. cit., p. 68. • **47.** Ibid., p. 75. • **48.** See Paul B. Jaskot, 'Anti-Semitic policy in Albert Speer's plans for the rebuilding of Berlin', in *The Art Bulletin*, December 1996. • **49.** Wolf Gruner, *Judenverfolgung in Berlin 1933–1945*, p. 75. • **50.** Inge Deutschkron, *Ich trug den Gelben Stern*, p. 100. • **51.** Correspondence of Anna Samuel quoted in Marion Kaplan, *Between Dignity and Despair – Jewish Life in Nazi Germany*, p. 171. • **52.** Susanne Willems, *Der entsiedelte Jude* (Berlin, 2000), p. 163. • **53.** Martin Gilbert, *The Holocaust: The Jewish Tragedy* (London, 1986), p. 213.

6 Unwelcome Strangers

• **1.** Albert Flammant, quoted in Claus-Dieter Sprink, 'Das System der Durchgangslager für ausländische Arbeitskräfte in Berliner Raum', in Helmut Bräutigam, Doris Fürstenberg and Bernt Roder (eds), *Zwangsarbeit in Berlin 1938–1945*, p. 79. • **2.** Statistics from Mark Spoerer, *Zwangsarbeit unter dem Hakenkreuz*, p. 9, and Ulrike Winkler (ed.), *NS-Zwangsarbeit* (Cologne, 2000), p. 17. • **3.** Leonore Scholze-Irrlitz, 'Das Durchgangslager für Zwangs- und Fremdarbeiter des Landesarbeitsbezirks Brandenburg in Berlin Wilhelmshagen. Realität und ihr Widerschein im kollektiven Gedächtnis der Betroffenen und Anwohner', in W. Meyer and K. Nietmann (eds), *Zwangsarbeit während der NS-Zeit in Berlin und Brandenburg*, p. 214. **4.** Kazimiera Czarnecka, quoted in Berliner Geschichtswerkstatt (ed.), *Zwangsarbeit in Berlin 1940–1945* (Berlin, 2000), p. 25. • **5.** Irena Pawlak, quoted in ibid., p. 50. • **6.** Aleksandra Reniszewska, quoted in ibid., p. 37. • **7.** Zdzisław Szubielski quoted in ibid., p. 67 and Jan Matusiak, in ibid., p. 74. • **8.** Quoted in Scholze-Irrlitz in Meyer and Nietmann (eds), op. cit., p. 217. • **9.** Vojtěch Fiala, quoted in Gisela Wenzel and Cord Pagenstecher (eds), *Totaleinsatz: Zwangsarbeit in Berlin 1943–45, Tschechische Zeitzeuginnen erinnern sich*, p. 54. • **10.** Official document quoted in Leonore Scholze-Irrlitz, 'Am Ende der Idylle', in Leonore Scholze-Irrlitz and Karoline Noack (eds), *Arbeit für den Feind* (Berlin, 1998),

p. 18. • **11.** Quoted in Scholze-Irrlitz in Meyer and Nietmann (eds), op. cit., p. 220. • **12.** Zdeněk Štych, quoted in Wenzel and Pagenstecher (eds), op. cit., p. 32. • **13.** Bräutigam, et al., op. cit., p. 32. • **14.** Cord Pagenstecher, *Lagerlisten und Erinnerungsberichte. Neue Quellen zur Topografie und ärztlichen Betreuung der Berliner Zwangsarbeiterlager*, p. 7, at http://www.cord-pagenstecher.de/pagenstecher-2004a-lagerlisten.pdf • **15.** Statistics from Bräutigam et al., op. cit., pp. 30–33. • **16.** Pagenstecher, op. cit., p. 6. • **17.** See François Cavanna, *Les Ruskoffs* (1979), quoted in Pagenstecher, op. cit., p. 6. • **18.** See Cord Pagenstecher, 'Erfassung, Propaganda und Erinnerung. Eine Typologie fotografischer Quellen zur Zwangsarbeit', in Wilfried Reininghaus (ed.), *Zwangsarbeit in Deutschland 1939 bis 1945* (Munster, 2001), p. 257. • **19.** Marcel Elola, *Ich war in Berlin*, p. 34. • **20.** See, among many others, Jan Fernhout et al. (eds), *Niederländer und Flamen in Berlin 1940–1945* (Berlin, 1996), pp. 155–6; also Václava Jobová, quoted in Wenzel and Pagenstecher, op. cit p. 47. • **21.** Zdeněk Štych, quoted in Wenzel and Pagenstecher, op. cit., p. 34. • **22.** Edward Homze, *Foreign Labor in Nazi Germany* (Princeton, 1967), p. 288. • **23.** Testimony of Vladimir P., quoted in Judith Hahn, 'Eisenbahnen, Flugzeuge und Zwangsarbeiter – Erinnerung an einen kaum bekannten Industriestandort im Berliner Wedding', in November 2007 newsletter of the Gedenkstätte Haus des Wannsee Konferenz. • **24.** Homze, op. cit., p. 280. • **25.** Spoerer, op. cit., pp. 124–5. • **26.** Zdeněk Štych, quoted in Wenzel and Pagenstecher, op. cit., p. 33. • **27.** Jekaterina Woronenko, quoted in Berliner Geschichtswerkstatt (ed.), op. cit., p. 102. • **28.** Bräutigam et al., op. cit., p. 27. • **29.** Daniela Kryjan, quoted in Berliner Geschichtswerkstatt (ed.), op. cit., p. 35. • **30.** Daniela Kryjan, Kazimiera Czarnecka and Jekaterina Woronenko, quoted in ibid., pp. 35, 28 and 102. • **31.** Pagenstecher, *Lagerlisten*, op. cit., p. 3. • **32.** Quoted in Spoerer, op. cit., p. 139. • **33.** Pagenstecher, *Lagerlisten*, op. cit., p. 5. • **34.** LA-B, A.Rep, 003-03, Nr. 113, Krankenblätter Ausländischer Zwangsarbeiter. • **35.** Pagenstecher, *Lagerlisten*, op. cit., p. 5. • **36.** Bräutigam et al., op. cit., p. 43. • **37.** Kazimiera Czarnecka in Berliner Geschichtswerkstatt (ed.), op. cit., p. 27. • **38.** Quoted in Spoerer, op. cit., p. 132. • **39.** Ladislav Derka, quoted in Wenzel and Pagenstecher, op. cit., p. 31. • **40.** Erich N., unpublished memoir, kindly donated to the author. • **41.** Elola, op. cit., pp. 36, 37. • **42.** Ibid., pp. 37, 38. • **43.** Bräutigam et al., op. cit., p. 48. • **44.** Ernst Kaltenbrunner, quoted in Martin Weinmann (ed.), *Das nationalsozialistische Lagersystem* (Frankfurt, 1990), p. xxxv. • **45.** Rimco Spanjer and Johan Meijer, 'Gefangene No. 652 in Wuhlheide: Gespräch mit W. P. de Wit', in *Zur Arbeit Gezwungen: Zwangsarbeit in Deutschland 1940–1945* (Bremen, 1999), p. 65. • **46.** See Werner Geltner, 'Als Häftling Nummer 46 im Arbeitserziehungslager Wuhlheide', in Christine Steer (ed.), *Versklavt und fast vergessen: Zwangsarbeit im Berliner Bezirk Lichtenberg 1939–1945* (Berlin, 2001), p. 60. • **47.** Quoted in Berliner Geschichtswerkstatt (ed.), op. cit., p. 105, and Fernhout et al., op. cit., p. 150. • **48.** Geltner in Steer (ed.), op. cit., p. 60. • **49.** See testimony of František Šlof, quoted in Wenzel and Pagenstecher, op. cit., p. 63. • **50.** Karin Brakebusch in Fernhout et al., op. cit., p. 181. • **51.** See Christine Steer, 'Das Arbeitserziehungslager Wuhlheide', in Steer (ed.), op. cit., p. 48. • **52.** Erna Krauss and G. F. Hartlaub (eds), *Felix Hartlaub in seinen Briefen* (Tübingen, 1958), p. 220. • **53.** Ursula von Kardorff, *Berliner Aufzeichnungen 1942–1945*, p. 208. • **54.** Quoted in Steffen Müller-Rockstroh, 'Wie es dort ablief, und was dort ablief, da drang nichts raus', in Scholze-Irrlitz and Noack (eds), op. cit., p. 118. • **55.** Quoted in ibid., p. 115. • **56.** See Ruth Zantow, '"... das sind doch Verbrecher ..."' Konzentrationslager Sachsenhausen – Aussenlager Lichtenrade', in Geschichtswerkstatt Berlin-Lichtenrade (ed.), *Direkt vor der Haustür. Berlin-Lichtenrade im Nationalsozialismus* (Berlin, 1990), pp. 301–37, quoted in Robert Gellately, *Backing Hitler*, p. 220. • **57.** Helmut Korthase, quoted in 'Eher unbeholfen als ignorant' in *Märkische Allgemeine Zeitung*, 2 March 2004. • **58.** 'Sondereinsatz Berlin' Reports, from 13 to 19 November 1944, quoted in Hans Dieter Schäfer, *Berlin im Zweiten Weltkrieg*, p. 239. • **59.** Wolfram Wette, Ricarda Bremer and Detlef Vogel (eds), *Das letzte halbe Jahr: Stimmungsberichte der Wehrmachtpropaganda 1944/45*, p. 128. • **60.** 'Sondereinsatz Berlin' Reports, from 18 January 1945, quoted in Schäfer, op. cit., p. 249. • **61.** 'Sondereinsatz Berlin' Report, from 29 November 1944, quoted in ibid., p. 247. • **62.** Quoted in Müller-Rockstroh in Scholze-Irrlitz and Noack (eds), op. cit., p. 117. • **63.** Brych Case, LA-B, A.Rep, 355, Nr. 949. • **64.** Case quoted in Victor von Gostomski and Walter Loch, *Der Tod von Plötzensee* (Frankfurt am Main, 1993), pp. 116–17. • **65.** See 'Tod in der S-Bahn', in Regina Stürickow, *Kriminalfälle im Dritten Reich Berlin* (Leipzig, 2005), pp. 151–66. • **66.** Rinus van Galen, 'Errinerungen an das AEL Grossbeeren', in Spanjer et al., op. cit., p. 70. • **67.** Quoted in Scholze-Irrlitz in Meyer and Nietmann (eds), op. cit., p. 217. • **68.** Hans-Rainer Sandvoss, *Widerstand in Pankow und Reinickendorf*, p. 211. • **69.** Quoted in Müller-Rockstroh in Scholze-Irrlitz and Noack (eds), op. cit., p. 116. • **70.** Larissa Safjanik, quoted in Lidia Chodirewa, 'Ukrainische Schicksale', in Steer (ed.), op. cit., p. 94. • **71.** Lidia Affanasjewna quoted in ibid., pp. 104–5. • **72.** Konrad Warner, *Schicksalswende Europas? Ich sprach mit dem deutschen Volk. Ein Tatsachenbericht* (Rheinfelden, 1944), p. 206. • **73.** Ursula von Kardorff, op. cit., p. 209. • **74.** 'Sondereinsatz Berlin' Report, from 3 January 1945, quoted in Schäfer, op. cit., p. 248. • **75.** René Schindler quoted in Schäfer, op. cit., p. 245. • **76.** Václava Jobová quoted in Wenzel and Pagenstecher, op. cit., p. 47.

7 A Taste of Things to Come

• **1.** *New York Times*, 26 August 1940, pp. 1 and 2. • **2.** Frederick Oechsner, *This Is the Enemy*, p. 172. • **3.** Martin Middlebrook and Chris Everitt, *The Bomber Command War Diaries* (London, 1985), p. 77. • **4.** Heinz Boberach (ed.), *Meldungen aus dem Reich 1938–1945*, pp. 1503–4. • **5.** Helmuth James von Moltke, *Letters to Freya 1939–1945*, p. 110. • **6.** Report of the *Dagens Nyheter* from 26 August 1940, quoted in *Dokumente Deutscher Kriegsschäden* (Bonn, 1962), Beiheft 2, p. 45. • **7.** William Shirer, *Berlin Diary 1934–41* (illustrated edition), pp. 209–10. • **8.** C. Brooks Peters, in *New York Times*, 26 August 1940, p. 1. • **9.** William Shirer, *This Is Berlin*, p. 112. • **10.** Boberach (ed.), op. cit., p. 1434. • **11.** Quoted in ibid., p. 1504. • **12.** Ibid., p. 1425. • **13.** Report in *The Times*, Friday 30 August 1940, p. 3, 'Bombed Target and Target Only'. • **14.** Ibid., p. 3, 'Jolt to Berlin Nerves'. • **15.** LA-B, A Rep. 001-02 700, 'Bericht über die Luftangriffe', 31 August 1940, p. 3. • **16.** Quoted in *Deutsche Allgemeine Zeitung*, 31 August 1940, p. 2, 'Wohnstrassen "militärische Ziele" Englands'. • **17.** Boberach (ed.), op. cit., p. 1514. • **18.** See reports from *Neue Zürcher Zeitung*, 29 August 1940, p. 5, and *New York Times*, 30 August 1940, p. 2. • **19.** Frederick Oechsner, *This Is the Enemy*, p. 172. • **20.** *New York Times*, 30 August 1940, pp. 1 and 2, 'Raids Anger Reich'. • **21.** *Deutsche Allgemeine Zeitung*, 28 August 1940, p. 1, 'Steigende deutsche Empörung'. • **22.** Nicolaus von Below, *At Hitler's Side* (London, 2004), p. 71. • **23.** Quoted in Max Domarus, *Hitler: Speeches and Proclamations 1932–1945*, vol. 3, p. 2086. • **24.** LA-B, A Rep. 001-02 700, 'Bericht über die Luftangriffe', 28 September 1940, p. 1. • **25.** Shirer, *Berlin Diary*, p. 212. • **26.** Boberach (ed.), op. cit., p. 1525. • **27.** Quoted in Werner Girbig, *Im Anflug an die Reichshauptstadt* (Stuttgart, 1970), p. 37. • **28.** Luftlage Reich report for 7/8 October 1940, quoted at http://chrito.users1.50megs.com/1940/okt/8okt40luft.htm • **29.** Fred Taylor (ed. and trans.), *The Goebbels Diaries 1939–41*, p. 154. • **30.** *New York Times*, 15 November 1940, p. 1. • **31.** Taylor (ed.), op. cit., p. 174. • **32.** Girbig, op. cit., pp. 42–3. • **33.** Jörg Friedrich, *The Fire* (New York, 2006), p. 55. • **34.** Girbig, op. cit., p. 34. • **35.** Luftlage Reich report, op. cit., for 23/24 September 1940. • **36.** Luftlage Reich report, op. cit., for 7/8 October 1940. • **37.** Shirer, *Berlin Diary*, p. 229. • **38.** Luftlage Reich report, op. cit., for 1/2 November 1940. • **39.** LA-B, A Rep. 005-07 500, DNS Bericht of 15 November 1940. • **40.** Oechsner, op. cit., p. 174. • **41.** Ibid., p. 174. • **42.** Henry Flannery, *Assignment to Berlin*, p. 53. • **43.** *New York Times*, 13 December 1940, p. 1. • **44.** Dieter Zimmer, *Zur Familiengeschichte* (unpublished manuscript). • **45.** H. Christa Billawala, *Enemy's Child* (unpublished manuscript), available online. • **46.** Testimony of Günther E., from DTA, Emmendingen, Sig. 51/1, 2, p. 34. • **47.** Testimony of Gisela

Richter, reproduced on the website of the collective memory project at the German Historical Museum – http://www.dhm.de/lemo/forum/kollektives_gedaechtnis/466/index.html • **48.** Zimmer, op. cit. • **49.** Author interview with Herbert S., Berlin, January 2007. • **50.** Otto-Herbert Leonhardt, *Spuren eines Lebens*, p. 104. • **51.** H. Christa Billawala, op. cit. • **52.** Leonhardt, op. cit., p. 103. • **53.** Shirer, *Berlin Diary*, pp. 223–4. • **54.** *New York Times*, 12 September 1940, p. 2. • **55.** Flannery, op. cit., p. 52. • **56.** Marie Vassiltchikov, *Berlin Dairies 1940–1945*, p. 28. • **57.** Report from *Dagens Nyheter*, 8 October 1940, quoted in *Dokumente Deutscher Kriegsschäden*, op. cit., p. 53. • **58.** Vassiltchikov, op. cit., p. 28. • **59.** Ibid., p. 32. • **60.** Elke Fröhlich (ed.), *Die Tagebücher von Joseph Goebbels*, vol. 8, p. 296. • **61.** Shirer, *Berlin Diary*, p. 209. • **62.** Girbig, op. cit., pp. 21–2. • **63.** Leonhardt, op. cit., p. 104. • **64.** Shirer, *Berlin Diary*, p. 209. • **65.** Percival Knauth in *New York Times*, 26 September 1940, p. 1. • **66.** Taylor (ed.), op. cit., p. 161. • **67.** Middlebrook and Everitt, op. cit., p. 104. • **68.** Taylor (ed.), op. cit., p. 176. • **69.** Shirer, *Berlin Diary*, p. 210. • **70.** LA-B, B Rep. 020-7794, 'Ereignismeldungen der Technischen Nothilfe, Berlin', Reports for night of 20/21 October 1940, and 14 November 1940. • **71.** Luftlage Reich report, for 7/8 October 1940, op. cit. • **72.** LA-B, B Rep. 020-7794, 'Ereignismeldungen der Technischen Nothilfe, Berlin', Report for night of 14/15 November 1940. • **73.** LA-B, B Rep. 020-7794, 'Ereignismeldungen der Technischen Nothilfe, Berlin', Report for night of 25 October 1940. • **74.** Author interview with Christa R., Berlin, January 2007. • **75.** Flannery, op. cit., p. 41. • **76.** Author interview with Kurt R., Berlin, January 2007. • **77.** Zimmer, op. cit. • **78.** Ruth Andreas-Friedrich, *Berlin Underground, 1938–1945*, p. 58. • **79.** *New York Times*, 12 September 1940, p. 2. • **80.** Taylor (ed.), op. cit., pp. 162–3. • **81.** Count Ciano diary entry for 27 September 1940 quoted in Irene and Alan Taylor (eds), *The Secret Annexe* (Edinburgh, 2004), p. 456. • **82.** Shirer, *Berlin Diary*, p. 223. • **83.** Andreas-Friedrich, op. cit., p. 58.

8 *Into Oblivion*

• **1.** *Jüdisches Nachrichtenblatt*, 12 September 1941, p. 1. • **2.** The American Consul General in Berlin, for example, noted that autumn that 'disapproval of the [*Judenstern*] measure' among Berliners was 'general'. Telegram from Leland Morris to Secretary of State, quoted in Saul Friedländer, *The Years of Extermination: Nazi Germany and the Jews 1939–1945*, p. 254. • **3.** Victor Klemperer, *The Language of the Third Reich* (London, 2000), p. 155. • **4.** Carolin Hilker-Siebenhaar (ed.), *Wegweiser durch das jüdische Berlin* (Berlin, 1987), p. 136. • **5.** Eyewitness account quoted in Rolf Bothe (ed.), *Synagogen in Berlin*, vol. II (Berlin, 1983), p. 101. • **6.** Sample document reproduced in Inge Deutschkron, *Ich trug den gelben Stern*, p. 222. • **7.** 'Merkblatt für die Teilnehmer an den

Abwanderungstransporten' reproduced in Annegret Ehmann et al., *Die Grunewald Rampe* (Berlin, 1993), pp. 84–5. • **8.** 'Die Aufforderung zur Deportation' reproduced in ibid., p. 83. • **9.** Documents reproduced in Götz Aly, *Im Tunnel*, pp. 82–3. • **10.** Deutschkron, op. cit., pp. 91–2. • **11.** Christian Dirks, '"Traurige Erlebnisse aus der Nazi-Hölle Deutschland". Zum Schicksal der Familie Scheurenberg', in Beate Meyer and Hermann Simon (eds), *Juden in Berlin 1938–1945*, pp. 205–13. • **12.** Deutschkron, op. cit., pp. 99–100. • **13.** Hildegard Henschel, 'Aus der Arbeit der jüdischen Gemeinde Berlins während der Jahre 1941–1943. Gemeindearbeit und Evakuierung von Berlin 16 Oktober 1941–16 Juni 1943', in *Zeitschrift der Geschichte der Juden*, no. 9 (1972), p. 35. • **14.** Letter of Hermann Samter, Berlin, 21 October 1941. Yad Vashem Archive, 0.2/30. • **15.** Henschel, op. cit., pp. 35–6. • **16.** Siegmund Weltlinger, *Hast Du schon vergessen?*, quoted in Hilker-Siebenhaar (ed.), op. cit., p. 134. • **17.** Henschel, op. cit., p. 37. • **18.** Ibid., p. 36. • **19.** Alfred Gottwaldt and Diana Schulle, *Die 'Judendeportationen' aus dem Deutschen Reich 1941–1945*, p. 134. • **20.** Heinz Bernhardt, quoted in Friedländer, op. cit., p. 310. • **21.** On Rumbula see Richard Rhodes, *Masters of Death* (Oxford, 2002), pp. 206–14. • **22.** Christopher Browning, *The Origins of the Final Solution*, p. 397. • **23.** Quoted in ibid., p. 396. • **24.** Henschel, op. cit., p. 40. • **25.** See the chronology of the deportations in Gottwaldt and Schulle, op. cit., pp. 443–67. • **26.** Quoted in 'Ich hätte ihn erschiessen können', in the *Frankfurter Allgemeine Zeitung*, 2 May 2008, p. 35. • **27.** Quoted in Ruth Andreas-Friedrich, *Berlin Underground, 1938–1945*, p. 74. • **28.** Quoted in Aly, *Im Tunnel*, p. 60. • **29.** Hermann Samter, quoted in Gerhard Schoenberner (ed.), *Wir haben es gesehen – Augenzeugenberichte über Terror und Judenverfolgung im Dritten Reich* (Hamburg, 1962), p. 297. • **30.** Ibid., p. 297. • **31.** Andreas-Friedrich, op. cit., p. 83. • **32.** See, for instance, Daniel Goldhagen, *Hitler's Willing Executioners* (London, 1996), p. 105. • **33.** Eric Johnson and Karl-Heinz Reuband, *What We Knew: Terror, Mass Murder and Everyday Life in Nazi Germany*, p. 369. • **34.** Ursula von Kardorff, *Berliner Aufzeichnungen 1942–1945*, p. 105. • **35.** Johnson and Reuband, op. cit., p. 74. • **36.** Primo Levi, *The Drowned and the Saved* (London, 1988), pp. 1–2. • **37.** E. Thomas Wood and Stanisław Jankowski, *Karski: How One Man Tried to Stop the Holocaust* (New York, 2004), p. 188. • **38.** Kardorff, op. cit., p. 326. • **39.** *Verfügung*, kindly supplied to the author by David Kolakowski. • **40.** Quoted in Johnson and Reuband, op. cit., p. 73. • **41.** On the raft of anti-Jewish measures, see Wolf Gruner, *Judenverfolgung in Berlin 1933–1945*, pp. 82–7. • **42.** See Karin Wieckhorst, 'Das Poesiealbum von Ruth Schwersenz', in Meyer and Simon (eds), op. cit., pp. 215–31. • **43.** Marion Kaplan, *Between Dignity and Despair – Jewish Life in Nazi Germany*, p. 188. • **44.** Quoted in Aly, *Im Tunnel*, p. 60. • **45.** Andreas-Friedrich, op. cit., p. 75. • **46.** Maria Sello, *Ein Familien- und Zeitdokument 1933–45*, unpublished manuscript, Wiener Library, London, ref. 20384, pp. 20–21. • **47.** Helmuth

James von Moltke, *Letters to Freya 1939–1945*, p. 183. • **48.** Kardorff, op. cit., p. 105. • **49.** Konrad Kwiet and Helmut Eschwege, *Selbstverwaltung und Widerstand Deutsche Juden im Kampf um Existenz und Menschenwürde 1939–1945* (Hamburg, 1984), p. 205. • **50.** Joel König, *Aufzeichnungen eines Überlebenden* (Frankfurt am Main, 1979), quoted in Ehmann et al., op. cit., p. 86. • **51.** See Barbara Lovenheim, *Survival in the Shadows*. • **52.** Kaplan, op. cit., p. 199. • **53.** Quoted in Johnson and Reuband, op. cit., p. 194. • **54.** Hilde Miekley in Gerhard Schoenberner (ed.), *Wir haben es gesehen* (Hamburg, 1962), p. 300; quoted in English translation in Goldhagen, op. cit., p. 105. • **55.** Quoted in Kaplan, op. cit., p. 198. • **56.** Götz Aly, *Hitler's Beneficiaries*, p. 331. • **57.** Dieter Borkowski, *Wer weiss, ob wir uns wiedersehen*, pp. 38–9. • **58.** Goebbels quoted in Aly, *Beneficiaries*, p. 118. • **59.** Howard K. Smith, *Last Train from Berlin*, p. 140. • **60.** Ibid., p. 140. • **61.** Wiener Library, file P IIIe, no. 1186, quoted in Richard Grunberger, *A Social History of the Third Reich*, p. 140. • **62.** Kardorff, op. cit., p. 22. • **63.** Kaplan, op. cit., p. 200. • **64.** *Gedenkbuch Berlins der jüdischen Opfer des Nationalsozialismus* (Berlin, 1995).

9 *An Evil Cradling*

• **1.** See Helmut Maier, *Berlin Anhalter Bahnhof* (Berlin, 1984). • **2.** http://www.monumente-online.de/07/03/streiflichter/ 06_Anhalter_Bahnhof.php • **3.** Original text quoted in Gerhard Dabel, *KLV, die erweiterte Kinder-Land-Verschickung. KLV-Lager 1940–1945* (Freiburg, 1981), p. 7. English translation taken from Jeremy Noakes (ed.), *Nazism 1919–1945*, vol. 4, p. 423. • **4.** Quoted in Guido Knopp, *Hitler's Children* (Stroud, 2002), p. 186. • **5.** Heinz Boberach (ed.), *Meldungen aus dem Reich 1938–1945*, vol. 5, p. 1622. • **6.** Fred Taylor (ed. and trans.), *The Goebbels Diaries 1939–1941*, p. 125. • **7.** Noakes (ed.), op. cit., p. 423. • **8.** Statistics quoted in Gerhard Kock, *'Der Führer sorgt für unsere Kinder . . .' Die Kinderlandverschickung im Zweiten Weltkrieg* (Paderborn, 1997), p. 136. • **9.** Ibid., p. 139. • **10.** See Claus Larass, *Der Zug der Kinder* (Munich, 1983). • **11.** Copy of an original 'Merkblatt für den Landaufenthalt der Berliner Jugend von 10–14 Jahren' (1940) kindly supplied by Mr Kurt Roth. •**12.** Heinz Knobloch, *Eine Berliner Kindheit*, p. 103. • **13.** Placard reproduced by the German Historical Museum, Berlin, at http://www.dhm.de • **14.** Jost Hermand, *A Hitler Youth in Poland* (Evanston, Illinois, 1997), pp. 6–7. • **15.** *Kinderlandverschickung 1940–1945 – 'Wen der Führer verschickt, den bringt er auch wieder gut zurück.'* Begleitbroschüre zur Ausstellung des Kunstamtes Steglitz, 1995 (Berlin, 1995), pp. 10–13. • **16.** Testimony of Gisela Richter, reproduced on the website of the collective memory project at the German Historical Museum –

http://www.dhm.de/lemo/forum/kollektives_gedaechtnis/466/index.html
• **17.** Martin L. Parsons, 'Kinderlandverschickung – An introduction to the expanded German Evacuation Scheme', in *Children in War*, November 2004, vol. 1, no. 3, p. 5. • **18.** Author interview with Dorit E., Berlin, September 2008. • **19.** Testimony of Gerhard R., from Deutsches Tagebucharchiv (hereafter DTA), Emmendingen, Sig. 240.2, p. 15. • **20.** Quoted in Noakes (ed.), op. cit., p. 427. • **21.** Testimony of Gerhard R., DTA, Emmendingen, p. 15. • **22.** Author interview with Dorit E., Berlin, September 2008. • **23.** See Erich Maylahn, *Auflistung der KLV-Lager* (Bochum, 2004). • **24.** Gisela Stange, *Der verdammte Krieg*, p. 28. • **25.** Ibid., p. 29. • **26.** Renate Bandur, *Meine KLV-Lagerzeit 1941* (Bochum, 1941), p. 15. • **27.** Author interview with Dorit E., Berlin, September 2008. • **28.** *Anweisungen für die Jungen- und Mädellager (KLV.-Lager)* (Berlin, 1943), pp. 29–34. • **29.** Timetables published in Dabel, op. cit., pp. 124–5. • **30.** Instructions quoted in *Kinderlandverschickung*, op. cit., p. 14. • **31.** Testimony of Gerhard R., DTA, Emmendingen, p. 12. • **32.** Martin Kitchen, *Nazi Germany at War*, p. 127. • **33.** Michael H. Kater, *Hitler Youth* (London, 2004), pp. 46–7. • **34.** Letter reproduced in *Kinderlandverschickung*, op. cit., p. 33. • **35.** Testimony of Gerhard R., DTA, Emmendingen, p. 3. • **36.** Erich N., *Erlebtes* (unpublished manuscript supplied to the author), p. 20. • **37.** Testimony of Gerhard R., DTA, Emmendingen, p. 3. • **38.** Hermand, op. cit., p. 6. • **39.** Erich N., op. cit., p. 20. • **40.** Testimony of Dietrich Sch., DTA, Emmendingen, Sig. 1069/I.1, p. 395. • **41.** Testimony of Dietrich Sch., DTA, Emmendingen, Sig. 1069/I.1, p. 393. • **42.** Kater, op. cit., p. 47. • **43.** Quoted in Noakes (ed.), op. cit., p. 422. • **44.** Quoted in Boberach (ed.), op. cit., entry for 30 September 1943, vol. 15, pp. 5828–9. • **45.** Letter reproduced in Bandur, op. cit., pp. 42–5. • **46.** Letter provided by Kurt R., Berlin, in correspondence with the author. • **47.** Ibid. • **48.** Hermand, op. cit., p. 12. • **49.** Ibid., p. 11. • **50.** Ibid. • **51.** Testimony of Gerhard R., DTA, Emmendingen, p. 18. • **52.** Hermand, op. cit., pp. 14–15. • **53.** Author interview with Werner L., Berlin, September 2008. • **54.** Testimony of Gerhard R., DTA, Emmendingen, p. 13. • **55.** Author interview with Werner L., Berlin, September 2008. • **56.** Quoted in Boberach (ed.), op. cit., entry for 30 September 1943, vol. 15, pp. 5828–30. • **57.** Reinhardt Crüger, quoted in http://www.zeitzeugengeschichte.de/audio.php?clipId=122&rel=MetaTopic&par=159&autostart=true • **58.** Christa Becker, *Enemy's Child*, unpublished manuscript, ch. 5, p. 1, available online. • **59.** Author interview with Dorit E., Berlin, September 2008. • **60.** Werner Girbig, *Im Anflug auf die Reichhauptstadt* (Stuttgart, 1971), p. 111. • **61.** Christabel Bielenberg, *The Past Is Myself* , p. 240.

10 *The People's Friend*

• **1** . Joseph Goebbels, 'Der Rundfunk als achte Grossmacht', in *Signale der neuen Zeit: 25 ausgewählte Reden von Dr Joseph Goebbels* (Munich, 1938), pp. 197–207. • **2.** Ernst Kris and Hans Speier, *German Radio Propaganda* (Oxford, 1944), p. 58. • **3.** Helmut Schanze, *Handbuch der Mediengeschichte* (Stuttgart, 2001), p. 468. • **4.** Wolfram Wette, Ricarda Bremer and Detlef Vogel (eds), *Das letzte halbe Jahr*, see, for instance, pp. 196 and 246. • **5.** Author interview with Ernst S., November 2008. • **6.** Richard Grunberger, *A Social History of the Third Reich*, p. 506. • **7.** Horst Bergmeier and Rainer Lotz, *Hitler's Airwaves* (London, 1997), p. 9. • **8.** *Die Wehrmachtberichte 1939–1945*, vol. 1 (Munich, 1985), p. 1. • **9.** Michael P. Hensle, *Rundfunkverbrechen* (Berlin, 2003), pp. 36–7. • **10.** Otto Herbert Leonhardt, *Spuren eines Lebens*, p. 113. • **11.** William Shirer, *Berlin Diary 1934–1941* (illustrated edition), p. 124. • **12.** Bernd Müller in Sven Felix Kellerhoff and Wieland Giebel (eds), *Als die Tage zu Nächten wurden*, p. 130. • **13.** BBC External Services, 'Hier ist England – Live aus London': *Das Deutsche Programm der British Broadcasting Corporation 1938–1988* (London, 1988), pp. 7 and 10, quoted in Eric Johnson, *The Nazi Terror* (London, 1999), p. 325. • **14.** Quoted in Robert Gellately, *Backing Hitler*, p. 186. • **15.** William Russell, *Berlin Embassy*, p. 87. • **16.** Ruth Andreas-Friedrich, *Berlin Underground, 1938–1945*, p. 48. • **17.** Ibid., p. 65. • **18.** Author interview with Lutz R., Berlin, September 2008. • **19.** Christabel Bielenberg, *The Past Is Myself*, p. 81. • **20.** Johnson, op. cit., p. 259. • **21.** Rochus Misch, *Der letzte Zeuge*, p. 196. • **22.** Heinz Boberach (ed.), *Meldungen aus dem Reich 1938–1945*, p. 366. • **23.** Quoted in Hans-Rainer Sandvoss, *Widerstand in Friedrichshain und Lichtenberg* (Berlin, 1997), p. 319. • **24.** Russell, op. cit., p. 134. • **25.** Marcel Elola, *Ich war in Berlin*, p. 62. • **26.** Fred Taylor (ed. and trans.), *The Goebbels Diaries 1939–1941*, p. 65. • **27.** Hensle, op. cit., pp. 134–6. • **28.** Ibid., p. 141. • **29.** Howard K. Smith, *Last Train from Berlin*, p. 80. • **30.** Author interview with Else B., Berlin, September 2008. • **31.** Boberach (ed.), op. cit., p. 3020. • **32.** Figures quoted in Hensle, op. cit., p. 135n. • **33.** Ibid., pp. 136–7. • **34.** Johnson, op. cit., p. 259. • **35.** Hans-Jörg Koch, *Das Wunschkonzert im NS-Rundfunk* (Cologne, 2003), p. 133. • **36.** See 'Hitler's "record collection" turns up in the attic of a dead Russian soldier', in *The Times*, 7 August 2007, p. 3. • **37.** Grunberger, op. cit., p. 515. • **38.** Ibid., p. 511. • **39.** See 'Badenweiler March', in *Time*, 5 June 1939. • **40.** Quoted in Koch, op. cit., p. 299. • **41.** Goebbels, Bundesarchiv, BA-B, R 58/1090, fol. 6, quoted in Koch, op. cit., p. 335. • **42.** Taylor (ed.), op. cit., p. 223. • **43.** Gisela Richter quoted at http://www.dhm.de/lemo/forum/kollektives_gedaechtnis/466/index.html • **44.** Author interview with Ernst S., November 2008. • **45.** Peter Jung in Kellerhoff and Giebel (eds), op. cit., pp. 81–2.

11 *The Watchers and the Watched*

• **1.** On 'Horst Wessel', see Nigel Jones, 'A Song for Hitler', in *History Today*, October 2007. • **2.** Bundesarchiv Berlin (hereafter BA-B), R58/3706/50-63, case file of Bruno W. • **3.** Ibid., p. 57. Report of 26 June 1942. • **4.** See chapter 5 of Michael Burleigh and Wolfgang Wippermann, *The Racial State: Germany 1933–1945*. • **5.** BA-B, Bruno W., case file, op. cit, pp. 57–9. • **6.** International Tracing Service, Bad Arolsen, Archive File 1516. • **7.** See statement by the Nazi jurist Hans Frank, quoted in Hans Buchheim, *Anatomy of the SS State* (London, 1968), p. 199. • **8.** From the *Deutschland-Berichte* of the SPD, no. 8. August 1938, quoted in Klaus-Michael Mallmann and Gerhard Paul, 'Omniscient, Omnipotent, Omnipresent? Gestapo, society and resistance', in David F. Crew (ed.), *Nazism and German Society 1933–1945*, p. 168. • **9.** Howard K. Smith, *Last Train from Berlin*, p. 199. • **10.** Friedrich Zipfel, 'Gestapo und SD in Berlin', in *Jahrbuch für die Geschichte Mittel- und Ostdeutschlands*, vol. IX/X, 1961, p. 277. • **11.** Ibid., p. 284. • **12.** Landesarchiv Berlin (hereafter LA-B), C Rep. 375-01-20 (Ministerium für Staatssicherheit der DDR, Abteilung IX/11, NS-Sondersammlung – Teil Berlin), Nr. 274. Though the headline figure for January 1945 was 1,067 individuals, 280 of these were listed as being seconded to various *Einsatzgruppen*, thereby leaving a figure of 787 for Berlin. • **13.** See Detlef Schmiechen-Ackermann: 'Der "Blockwart". Die unteren Parteifunktionäre im nationalsozialistischen Terror- und Überwachungsapparat', in *Vierteljahrshefte für Zeitgeschichte (VfZ)*, vol. XXXXVIII, 2000, pp. 575–602. • **14.** Interview with Benedikt D., Berlin, October 2006. • **15.** On the *V-Männer* in Nazi Germany, see Klaus-Michael Mallmann, 'Die V-Leute der Gestapo', in Gerhard Paul and Klaus-Michael Mallmann (eds), *Die Gestapo – Mythos und Realität* and Walter Weyrauch, *Gestapo V-Leute* (Frankfurt am Main, 1989). • **16.** Weyrauch, op. cit., p. 12. • **17.** Mallmann and Paul in Crew (ed.), op. cit., p. 181. • **18.** LA-B, Apr.Br.Rep. 03007 Nr. 1095. Jugendkriminalität, August 1940, case of Erich V. • **19.** From the *Kölnische Zeitung*, 24 July 1934, quoted in Alexandra Richie, *Faust's Metropolis*, p. 422. • **20.** Quoted in Eric Johnson and Karl-Heinz Reuband, *What We Knew: Terror, Mass Murder and Everyday Life in Nazi Germany*, p. 45. • **21.** Laurence Rees, *The Nazis: A Warning from History* (London, 1997), p. 65. • **22.** Quoted in Richard Grunberger, *A Social History of the Third Reich*, p. 146. • **23.** Smith, op. cit., pp. 119–20. • **24.** Ibid., p. 120. • **25.** On the case of Erich Ohser, see Topography of Terror Foundation (ed.), *The 'House Prison' at Gestapo Headquarters in Berlin. Terror and Resistance 1933–1945* (Berlin, 2005), pp. 128–35. • **26.** Interview with Margit S., Berlin, November 2007. • **27.** Grunberger, op. cit., p. 152. • **28.** Ursula von Kardorff, *Berliner Aufzeichnungen 1942–1945*, p. 107. • **29.** Smith, op. cit., p. 199. • **30.** See, for instance, *Time*,

406BERLIN AT WAR

11 April 1938. Also referred to in Wiener Library, London, eyewitness accounts by Holocaust survivors, File P II a/54. • **31.** Ted Harrison, '"Alter Kämpfer" im Widerstand: Graf Helldorf, die NS-Bewegung und die Opposition gegen Hitler', in *Vierteljahrshefte für Zeitgeschichte (VfZ)*, vol. XXXXV, 1997, p. 412. • **32.** Johnson and Reuband, op. cit., p. 355, Table 12.2. • **33.** Gernot Jochheim, *Der Berliner Alexanderplatz*, p. 99. • **34.** Zipfel, op. cit., p. 267. • **35.** Interview with Rosa R., Berlin, January 2007. • **36.** Ruth Andreas-Friedrich, *Berlin Underground, 1938–1945*, p. 154. • **37.** BA-B, R58/3193 & 3194, Reichssicherheitshauptamt Monatsstatistik. • **38.** Johnson and Reuband, op. cit., p. 349. • **39.** Harold Denny, 'Life in Berlin Gestapo Jail: A Study in Mental Torture', in *New York Times*, 6 June 1942, pp. 1 and 5. • **40.** Paul Gerhard Braune, quoted in Topography of Terror Foundation (ed.), op. cit., p. 47. • **41.** Günther Weisenborn, quoted in ibid., p. 48. • **42.** Denny, op. cit., p. 5. • **43.** Gerhard König and Inge König, *Das Polizeipräsidium Berlin-Alexanderplatz* (Berlin, 1997), p. 84. • **44.** Philipp Auerbach, 'Berlin-Alexanderplatz', in *Isar Post*, 24 June 1947. • **45.** Ibid. • **46.** Quoted in Gabriele Layer-Jung, 'Tatbestand Arbeitsvertragsbruch. Die polizeiliche Verfolgung von Zwangsarbeiterinnen in Berlin und Brandenburg während der NS-Zeit', in Berliner Geschichtswerkstatt (ed.), *Arbeitserziehungslager Fehrbellin* (Berlin, 2004), p. 67. • **47.** See the account of Richard Hottelet, 'Guest of the Gestapo', in *San Francisco Chronicle*, 3 August 1941. • **48.** Smith, op. cit., p. 166. • **49.** Christabel Bielenberg, *The Past Is Myself*, p. 230. • **50.** BA-B, R58/2284-54, 9 July 1937, Case of Prisoner Bartsch. • **51.** Testimony of M. Labussière at Nuremberg, quoted in Edward Crankshaw, *Gestapo: Instrument of Tyranny* (London, 2002), p. 128. • **52.** BA-B, R58/2284-53, 9 July 1937, Case of Prisoner Borbe, and R58/2284-225, 15 September 1936. • **53.** BA-B, R58/2284-226, 15 September 1936. • **54.** Fabian von Schlabrendorff, *The Secret War against Hitler* (Boulder, 1994), p. 312. • **55.** BA-B, R58/2284-229. • **56.** BA-B, R58/2284-227. • **57.** Albrecht Haushofer, *Moabiter Sonette* (Berlin, 1946), p. 48. English translation by the author. • **58.** Victor von Gostomski and Walter Loch, *Der Tod von Plötzensee* (Frankfurt am Main, 1993), p. 105. • **59.** Harald Poelchau, *Die Ordnung der Bedrängten* (Berlin, 1963), pp. 48–9. • **60.** Arnold Weiss-Rüthel, *Nacht und Nebel: Aufzeichnungen aus fünf Jahren Schutzhaft* (Munich, 1946), p. 39. • **61.** Harry Naujoks, *Mein Leben im KZ Sachsenhausen* (Köln, 1987), p. 30. • **62.** Weiss-Rüthel, op. cit., pp. 61–2. • **63.** Sepp Hahn, quoted at http://home.snafu.de/etz/sachsenhausen/klinker_2.htm • **64.** Richard Bachmann, *Betrogen und Vergessen*, Archiv der Zeitzeugen (Munster, 2006), p. 333. • **65.** Quoted in Anne Sudrow, 'Vom Leder zum Kunststoff. Werkstoff-Forschung auf der "Schuhprüfstrecke" im Konzentrationslager Sachsenhausen 1940 bis 1945', in Helmut Maier (ed.), *Rüstungsforschung im Nationalsozialismus* (Göttingen, 2002), p. 244. • **66.** Ibid., p. 241. • **67.** See Lawrence Malkin, *Krüger's Men: The Secret Nazi Counterfeit Plot and the Prisoners of Block 19* (London, 2006). • **68.** Interview with Adolf

Burger, London, February 2009 – text reproduced at http://historian-at-large.blogspot.com/2009/03/interview-with-adolf-burger-auschwitz.html • **69.** Günter Morsch and Susanne zur Nieden (eds), *Jüdische Häftlinge im Konzentrationslager Sachsenhausen 1936 bis 1945* (Berlin, 2004), pp. 206–7. • **70.** Adolf Burger, op. cit. • **71.** Weiss-Rüthel, op. cit., p. 142. • **72.** See Hendrik van Dam and Ralph Giordano, *KZ-Verbrechen vor deutschen Gerichten* (Frankfurt, 1962), p. 182.• **73.** Albert Christel, *Apokalypse unserer Tage: Erinnerungen an das KZ Sachsenhausen* (Frankfurt, 1987), p. 78. • **74.** Witness K. B., Sorge/Schubert Trial, 1958. Testimony cited in Gedenkstätte Sachsenhausen, Block 38. • **75.** See, for instance, Wolfgang Benz and Barbara Distel (eds), *Der Ort des Terrors. Sachsenhausen, Buchenwald* (Munich, 2006). • **76.** Manuela Hrdlicka, *Alltag im KZ* (Opladen, 1992), p. 73. • **77.** Archiv Sachsenhausen, D 1 A/1230, Bl. 017 and D 1 A/1232, Bl. 299Ra. • **78.** Archiv Sachsenhausen, D 10 A/01, Bl. 086.

12 *The Persistent Shadow*

• **1.** Karl Treuwerth, *Der Invalidenfriedhof in Berlin. Eine Stätte preussisch-deutschen Ruhms* (Berlin, 1925). • **2.** See Günter Hinze, *Der Invalidenfriedhof in Berlin* (Berlin, 1936), pp. 12–15. • **3.** See, for instance, Johnny von Herwarth, *Against Two Evils* (London, 1981), p. 171. • **4.** William Shirer, *Berlin Diary* (illustrated edition), p. 109fn. • **5.** *Völkischer Beobachter*, 27 September 1939, p. 2. • **6.** For details of Heydrich's funeral, see *Völkischer Beobachter*, 5 June 1942, pp. 1–2. • **7.** http://en.wikipedia.org/wiki/Ich_hatt%27_einen_Kameraden • **8.** Laurenz Demps, *Der Invalidenfriedhof* (Berlin, 1996), p. 81. • **9.** Ursula von Kardorff, *Berliner Aufzeichnungen 1942–1945*, p. 35. • **10.** See Rüdiger Overmans, *Deutsche militärische Verluste im Zweiten Weltkrieg* (Munich, 1999), Section 2.2 'Meldewesen im Zweiten Weltkrieg'. • **11.** Taken from chapter 7 of H. Christa Billawala's memoir 'Enemy's Child', published online at http://askpepper.com/enemysChild/index.html • **12.** Kardorff, op. cit., pp. 41–2. • **13.** See, for instance, http://www.relichunter.com/doclot.jpg • **14.** Author interview with Ursula S., Berlin, October 2006. • **15.** *Frankfurter Allgemeine Zeitung*, 2 May 2008, p. 33. • **16.** *Deutsche Allgemeine Zeitung*, 26 September 1939, p. 4. • **17.** *Das Schwarze Korps*, 15 October 1942, p. 7. • **18.** Death notice reproduced in Terry Charman, *The German Home Front 1939–1945* (London, 1989), p. 82. • **19.** *Deutsche Allgemeine Zeitung*, 21 January 1940, p. 5. • **20.** Oliver Schmitt and Sandra Westenberger, 'Der feine Unterschied im Heldentod', in Götz Aly (ed.), *Volkes Stimme*, p. 97. • **21.** Quoted in Heinz Boberach (ed.), *Meldungen aus dem Reich 1938–1945*, vol. 4, p. 1325. • **22.** Victor Klemperer, *The Language of the Third Reich* (London, 2006), p. 114. • **23.** Schmitt and Westenberger, op. cit., p. 101. • **24.** For information on German war graves, see http://www.volksbund.de/ • **25.** Text taken from a

Wehrmacht missing notice in the possession of the author. • **26.** Frank Biess, *Homecomings* (Princeton, 2006), p. 19. • **27.** Agnes Miegel 'From Mothers to Sons in the War', quoted in Jay W. Baird, *To Die for Germany* (Bloomington, 1990), p. 232. • **28.** See Karin Hausen, 'The "Day of National Mourning" in Germany', in Gerald Sider and Gavin Smith (eds), *Between History and Histories: The Making of Silences and Commemoration* (Toronto, 1997). • **29.** Quoted in J. P. Stern, *Hitler: The Führer and the People*, revised edition (London 1990), p. 19. • **30.** For the text, see, for instance, Craig Nickisch, '"Die Fahne hoch!" Das Horst Wessel Lied als Nationalhymne', in *Selecta*, vol. 20, 1999. • **31.** Baldur von Schirach quoted in Guido Knopp, *Hitler's Children* (Stroud, 2002), p. 49. • **32.** Sabine Behrenbeck, *Der Kult um die toten Helden* (Cologne, 1996), p. 501. • **33.** Goebbels quoted in Baird, op. cit., pp. 211–12. • **34.** Biess, op. cit., p. 24. • **35.** Karl Cerff, Propaganda Ministry, quoted in Behrenbeck, op. cit., p. 500. • **36.** Biess, op. cit., p. 22. • **37.** 'In Weissensee', in Kurt Tucholsky, *Gesammelte Werke*, vol. 4 (Hamburg, 1975), p. 123. English translation by the author. • **38.** Rachel Becker, testimony, Yad Vashem Archive, 03/1806. • **39.** Ibid. • **40.** Peter Melcher, *Weissensee* (Berlin, 1986), pp. 98–9. • **41.** Martin Riesenburger, *Das Licht verlöschte nicht* (Berlin, 1960), p. 19. • **42.** Ibid., p. 26. • **43.** Ibid., p. 40. • **44.** Becker, op. cit. • **45.** Liselotte Clemens, quoted in 'Rabbi tended Jewish flame through Holocaust', in *New Standard*, 20 April 1997. • **46.** Johanna von Koppenfels, *Jewish Cemeteries in Berlin* (Berlin, 2005), p. 45. • **47.** See the memorial at the site, Grosse Hamburger Strasse, Berlin. • **48.** Riesenburger, op. cit., p. 50. • **49.** Steve Lipman, 'The Last Rabbi of Berlin', in *The Jewish Week*, 20 April 2001. • **50.** Samuel Mitcham, *The Panzer Legions* (London, 2007), p. 134.

13 Enemies of the State

• **1.** Hans-Rainer Sandvoss, *Stätten des Widerstandes in Berlin 1933–1945* (Berlin, 1986), p. 35. • **2.** English text quoted in Hilmar Hoffmann, *The Triumph of Propaganda: Film and National Socialism 1933–1945* (Oxford, 1996), p. 171. • **3.** Jeremy Noakes (ed.), *Nazism 1919–1945*, vol. 4, p. 591. • **4.** Text reproduced in Wolfgang Benz and Walter Pehle (eds), *Encyclopedia of German Resistance to the Nazi Movement* (New York, 1997), p. 180. • **5.** It is widely suspected that there was an informer within the Baum Group named Joachim Franke. • **6.** Elke Fröhlich (ed.), *Die Tagebücher von Joseph Goebbels*, part 2, vol. 4 (Munich, 1995), p. 350. • **7.** Margot Pikarski, *Jugend im Berliner Widerstand* (East Berlin, 1978), p. 108. • **8.** See Herbert Lindenberger, 'Heroic or Foolish? The 1942 Bombing of a Nazi Anti-Soviet Exhibit', in *TELOS* 135, Summer 2006, p. 134. • **9.** Fröhlich (ed.), op. cit., p. 386. • **10.** Saul Friedländer, *The Years of Extermination: Nazi Germany and the Jews 1939–1945*, p. 349. • **11.** Lucien Steinberg, *Not as a*

Lamb: The Jews against Hitler (Farnborough, 1974), p. 35. • **12.** Avraham Atzili, 'Baum Gruppe: Jewish Women', in *Jewish Women: A Comprehensive Historical Encyclopedia*, at http://jwa.org/encyclopedia/article/baum-gruppe-jewish-women. Another account (Steinberg, op. cit.) states that she broke both her legs in the fall. • **13.** Lindenberger, op. cit., p. 129. • **14.** Hans-Rainer Sandvoss, *Die 'andere' Reichshauptstadt*, p. 22. • **15.** George Kennan, *Memoirs 1925–1950* (London, 1968), p. 108. • **16.** Total number cited in Hans-Joachim Fieber (ed.), *Widerstand in Berlin gegen das NS-Regime 1933–1945, Ein biographisches Lexikon*, 12 vols (Berlin 2002–2005). • **17.** Peter Hoffmann, *The History of the German Resistance 1933–1945* (London, 1970), p. 30. • **18.** Quoted in Luise Kraushaar, *Berliner Kommunisten im Kampf gegen den Faschismus 1936–1942* (East Berlin, 1981), p. 208. • **19.** Ibid., p. 324. • **20.** Quoted in Shareen Brysac, *Resisting Hitler: Mildred Fish-Harnack and the Red Orchestra* (Oxford, 2000), p. 379. • **21.** http://en.wikipedia.org/wiki/First_they_came . . . • **22.** Quoted in Martin Gilbert, *Second World War* (London, 1989), p. 228. • **23.** Hans-Rainer Sandvoss, *Widerstand in Mitte und Tiergarten* (Berlin, 1994), p. 272. • **24.** Benz and Pehle (eds), op. cit., pp. 239–41. • **25.** Helmuth James von Moltke, *Letters to Freya 1939–1945* (New York, 1995), p. 404. • **26.** Ruth Andreas-Friedrich, *Berlin Underground, 1938–1945*, p. 141. • **27.** Sandvoss, *Die 'andere' Reichshauptstadt*. • **28.** Kennan, op. cit., p. 108. • **29.** Reha Solokow and Al Solokow, *Ruth und Maria* (Berlin, 2006), p. 82. • **30.** The story of Otto and Elise Hampel was the inspiration behind Hans Fallada's novel *Alone in Berlin* (London, 2009) and the UK edition of the book contains an appendix which gives details of their protest. • **31.** Sandvoss, *Stätten*, p. 11. German text is 'Gross ist die Zeit, doch klein sind die Portionen, Was hilft es uns, wenn Hitlers Fahnen wehn! Wenn unter diesen Fahnen heute schon Millionen viel weniger Brot und kein Freiheit sehn!' • **32.** Heinz Boberach (ed.), *Meldungen aus dem Reich 1938–1945*, p. 400. • **33.** Ibid., p. 422. • **34.** Hans-Rainer Sandvoss, *Widerstand in Pankow und Reinickendorf* (Berlin, 1992), p. 124. • **35.** Josepha von Koskull, at http://www.dhm.de/lemo/forum/kollektives_gedaechtnis/078/index.html • **36.** Sandvoss, *Widerstand*, p. 159. • **37.** Dieter Borkowski, *Wer weiss, ob wir uns wiedersehen*, p. 120. • **38.** Ibid., p. 117. • **39.** Hoffmann, op. cit., p. 123. • **40.** Hans Bernd Gisevius, *To the Bitter End* (New York, 1998), p. 514. • **41.** Andreas-Friedrich, op. cit., p. 146. • **42.** Marie Vassiltchikov, *Berlin Diaries 1940–1945*, p. 85. • **43.** Hans-Georg von Studnitz, *While Berlin Burns, Diaries 1943–1945*, p. 189. • **44.** Ursula von Kardorff, *Berliner Aufzeichnungen 1942–1945*, p. 161. • **45.** Andreas-Friedrich, op. cit., p. 147. • **46.** Text of the speech is at http://www.answers.com/topic/radio-address-on-the-1944-bomb-plot • **47.** Theo Findahl, *Letzter Akt Berlin: 1939–1945*, p. 117. • **48.** Findahl, op. cit., pp. 120–21. •**49.** Kardorff, op. cit., p. 163. **50.** Andreas-Friedrich, op. cit., p. 149. • **51.** Kardorff, op. cit., p. 163. • **52.** Boberach, op. cit., p. 6684. • **53.** Studnitz, op. cit., pp. 189–90.

14 *Against All Odds*

• **1.** Nathan Stoltzfus, *Resistance of the Heart*, p. xviii. • **2.** Quoted in Gernot Jochheim, *Frauenprotest in der Rosenstrasse*, p. 122. • **3.** Quoted in Wolfgang Benz (ed.), *Die Juden in Deutschland 1933–1945*, p. 593. • **4.** Gad Beck, 'Da waren auf einmal Hunderte von Frauen auf der Strasse', in Nina Schröder (ed.), *Hitler's unbeugsame Gegnerinnen* (Munich, 1997), p. 138. • **5.** Hans Bloch, quoted in Wolf Gruner, *Widerstand in der Rosenstrasse*, p. 114. • **6.** Quoted in Benz (ed.), *Juden*, p. 593. • **7.** Quoted in ibid., p. 594. • **8.** Inge Unikower, quoted in Gruner, op. cit., p. 106. • **9.** Erika Lewine, quoted in Stoltzfus, op. cit., p. 220. • **10.** Ruth Bileski, quoted in Daniel Silver, *Refuge in Hell*, p. 129. • **11.** Quoted in Jochheim, op. cit., p. 122. • **12.** Charlotte F., quoted in Stolzfus, op. cit., p. xvii. • **13.** Ruth Gross, quoted in ibid., pp. 227–8. • **14.** Annie R., quoted in ibid., p. xx. • **15.** Ruth Andreas-Friedrich, *Berlin Underground, 1938–1945*, p. 92. • **16.** Gruner, op. cit., p. 115. • **17.** Ernst Bukofzer, quoted in Stoltzfus, op. cit., pp. 249–50. • **18.** Ruth Gross-Pisarek speech, at http://www.rosen-strasse-protest.de/interviews/index_interviews.html • **19.** The two schools are broadly represented by the historians Nathan Stoltzfus and Wolf Gruner. • **20.** See Gruner, op. cit., pp. 118–29. • **21.** See Document 34 'Fabrikaktion', dated 8 March 1943, in Wolfgang Scheffler (ed.), *Judenverfolgung im Dritten Reich* (Berlin, 1964), p. 95. • **22.** Rachel Becker, testimony, Yad Vashem Archive, ref: 03/1806. • **23.** Marion Kaplan, *Between Dignity and Despair – Jewish Life in Nazi Germany*, pp. 203 and 228. • **24.** Yitzhak Schwersenz, quoted in Wolfgang Benz (ed.), *Überleben im Dritten Reich* (Munich, 2003), p. 24. • **25.** Leonard Gross, *The Last Jews in Berlin*, p. 173. • **26.** Testimony of Kurt L., held at the Wiener Library Archive, London (henceforth 'WL'), ref: P IIId. no. 83. • **27.** Benz (ed.), *Juden*, p. 661. • **28.** Quoted in Kaplan, op. cit., p. 212. • **29.** Adam LeBor and Roger Boyes, *Surviving Hitler* (London, 2000), p. 76. • **30.** Ursula von Kardorff, *Berliner Aufzeichnungen 1942–1945*, p. 15. • **31.** Irma Simon, quoted in Kaplan, op. cit., p. 218. • **32.** Erich N., *Erlebtes*, unpublished manuscript kindly supplied to the author, pp. 30–31. • **33.** Ibid., p. 32. • **34.** Benz (ed.), *Überleben*, p. 25. • **35.** Case of Alfred B., WL, ref: P IIIg no. 1196. • **36.** Testimony of Rita M., Deutsches Tagebucharchiv (hereafter DTA), Emmendingen, ref: 542. • **37.** Testimony of Inge Deutschkron, WL, ref: P IIId. no. 192. • **38.** Benz (ed.), *Überleben*, p. 37. • **39.** Cioma Schönhaus, *The Forger* (London, 2008), pp. 92–5. • **40.** Benz (ed.), *Überleben*, p. 25. • **41.** Taped interview with Otto Jodmin (1985) available at the House of the Wannsee Conference Museum, Berlin. • **42.** See Reha Sokolow and Al Sokolow, *Ruth und Maria* (Berlin, 2006), pp. 83–9. • **43.** Case of Gerda W. WL, ref: P IIId. no. 411. • **44.** Quoted in Kate Connolly, 'I still feel her breath', in *Guardian*, 30 June 2001. • **45.** Kaplan, op.

cit., p. 208, quoting the work of Avraham Seligmann. • **46.** Franke case, Gestapo Schöneberg, quoted in Gruner, op. cit, p. 70. • **47.** Andreas-Friedrich, op. cit., p. 118. • **48.** Erich N., op. cit., pp. 33–5. • **49.** Wyden, op. cit., p. 132. • **50.** Author interview with Maria N., Berlin, September 2008. • **51.** Testimony of Charlotte J., WL, ref: P IIId. no. 26. • **52.** Hanna Sohst, quoted in Konrad Kwiet and Helmut Eschwege, *Selbstverwaltung und Widerstand – Deutsche Juden im Kampf um Existenz und Menschenwürde 1939–1945* (Hamburg, 1984), p. 156. • **53.** Case quoted in Kwiet and Eschwege, op. cit., pp. 156–7. • **54.** WL, ref: P IIId. no. 83. • **55.** See Christina Herkommer, 'Rettung in Bordell', in Benz (ed.), *Überleben*, pp. 143–52, and also Larry Orbach's memoir. • **56.** Barbara Lovenheim, *Survival in the Shadows*, pp. 83–9. • **57.** See Schönhaus, op. cit. • **58.** Quoted in Peter Wyden, *Stella* (New York, 1992), p. 160. • **59.** Larry Orbach, *Soaring Underground*, p. 1. • **60.** Testimony of Gerda W., WL. ref: P IIId, no. 411. • **61.** Quoted in Kaplan, op. cit., p. 210. • **62.** Quoted in ibid., p. 211. • **63.** Wyden, op. cit., p. 155. • **64.** Ibid., p. 156. • **65.** For information on the Berlin Jewish Hospital, see Silver, op. cit. • **66.** Testimony of Ursula F., WL, ref: P IIId., no. 458. • **67.** See Alfred Gottwaldt and Diana Schulle, *Die 'Judendeportationen' aus dem Deutschen Reich 1941–1945* (Wiesbaden, 2005), pp. 466–7. • **68.** Kwiet and Eschwege, op. cit., p. 150. • **69.** Silver, op. cit., p. 1.

15 *Reaping the Whirlwind*

• **1.** Dieter Borkowski, *Wer weiss, ob wir uns wiedersehen*, p. 24. • **2.** Helene Braun, 'Bis wir uns wiedersehen', in Sven Felix Kellerhoff and Wieland Giebel (eds), *Als die Tage zu Nächten wurden*, p. 49. • **3.** Report 'RAF left Berlin afire after three days', citing a Swedish eyewitness, in *New York Times*, 22 March 1943. • **4.** Statistics quoted in *Flight* magazine, 20 August 1942, p. 193. • **5.** Ulrich Walter in Kellerhoff and Giebel (eds), op. cit., p. 202. • **6.** Report 'Berlin Blow to Goering', in *New York Times*, 20 March 1943. • **7.** Ruth Andreas-Friedrich, *Berlin Underground, 1938–1945*, p. 91. • **8.** Ulrich Walter in Kellerhoff and Giebel (eds), op. cit., p. 203. • **9.** Report from 4 March 1943 in Heinz Boberach (ed.), *Meldungen aus dem Reich*, p. 4888. • **10.** Hans-Georg von Studnitz, *While Berlin Burns, Diaries 1945–1945*, p. 37. • **11.** Elke Fröhlich (ed.), *Die Tagebücher von Joseph Goebbels*, part 2, vol. 7, p. 460. • **12.** Fröhlich (ed.), op. cit., pp. 459–61. • **13.** Michael Foedrowitz, *The Flak Towers in Berlin, Hamburg and Vienna, 1940–1950*, p. 5. • **14.** Howard K. Smith, *Last Train from Berlin*, pp. 116–17. • **15.** Marie Vassiltchikov, *Berlin Diaries 1940–1945*, p. 48. • **16.** 'German Use of Smoke', in *Tactical and Technical Trends*, no. 6, 27 August 1942. • **17.** Werner Girbig, *Im Anflug auf die Reichshauptstadt* (Stuttgart, 1970), p. 153. • **18.** Statistics from John Norris, *88 mm FlaK 18/36/37/41 & PaK 43 1936-45* (Oxford, 2002), p. 28. • **19.** Hans-Detlef Heller, quoted in Rolf-Dieter Müller,

Der Bombenkrieg 1939–1945 (Berlin, 2004), p. 143. • **20.** Borkowski, op. cit., pp. 128 passim. • **21.** Michael Foedrowitz, *Bunkerwelten*, pp. 10–11. • **22.** Ibid., p. 19. • **23.** The Gesundbrunnen air raid shelter is administered as a museum by 'Berlin Underworld' at http://berliner-unterwelten.de • **24.** The figure of 430 completed air raid shelters in Berlin was quoted in correspondence with the expert on the subject, Michael Foedrowitz. • **25.** Rolf-Dieter Müller suggests 5 per cent, while Jörg Friedrich suggests only 2 per cent. • **26.** Foedrowitz, *Bunkerwelten*, pp. 118–19. • **27.** Marcel Elola, *Ich war in Berlin*, p. 78. • **28.** Testimony of Lore Kastler-Lindig at http://www.jfarchiv.de/archiv03/083yy57.htm • **29.** See Martin Middlebrook, *The Battle of Hamburg* (London, 1980), or Keith Lowe, *Inferno* (London, 2007). • **30.** Boberach (ed.), op. cit., p. 5542. • **31.** Studnitz, op. cit., p. 89. • **32.** Ursula von Kardorff, *Berliner Aufzeichnungen 1942–1945*, p. 58. • **33.** Ibid., p. 58. • **34.** Fröhlich (ed.), op. cit., vol. 9, p. 200. • **35.** Helmuth James von Moltke, *Letters to Freya 1939–1945*, p. 327. • **36.** Boberach (ed.), op. cit., p. 5582. • **37.** Andreas-Friedrich, op. cit., p. 100. • **38.** Borkowski, op. cit., p. 53. • **39.** Quoted in Martin Middlebrook, *The Berlin Raids* (London, 1988), p. 2. • **40.** Statistics quoted in Sven Felix Kellerhoff, 'Bomben auf Berlin', in Kellerhoff and Giebel (eds), op. cit., p. 21. • **41.** Testimony of Henning Wenzel, on the website of the collective memory project at the German Historical Museum http://www.dhm.de/lemo/forum/kollektives_gedaechtnis/053/index.html • **42.** Louis Lochner (ed.), *The Goebbels Diaries* (London, 1948), pp. 432–3. • **43.** Borkowski, op. cit., pp. 77–8. • **44.** Marie Vassiltchikov, *Berlin Diaries 1940–1945*, pp. 109–10. • **45.** Diary of Otto K., Deutsches Tagebucharchiv, Emmendingen, ref. 278. • **46.** Correspondence with the author. With thanks to Alexandra Freimuth and Michael Foedrowitz. • **47.** Ursula Gebel, 'November 1943 in Charlottenburg', in Kellerhoff and Giebel (eds), op. cit., p. 59. • **48.** Studnitz, op. cit., p. 140. • **49.** Testimony of Josepha von Koskull, on the website of the collective memory project at the German Historical Museum – http://www.dhm.de/lemo/forum/kollektives_gedaechtnis/077/index.html • **50.** Andreas-Friedrich, op. cit., p. 113. • **51.** German civilian losses are quoted in Kellerhoff and Giebel (eds), op. cit., p. 222. As for RAF losses – 43 aircraft were lost on the Berlin raid of 15/16 February, each of which had a crew of 7, thereby making a total of 301 aircrew lost – killed, captured or missing – for the mission. • **52.** Christabel Bielenberg, *The Past Is Myself*, p. 125. • **53.** Benedikt D. interview, Berlin, October 2007. • **54.** Bielenberg, op. cit., p. 167. • **55.** Ibid., p. 168. • **56.** Ruth Andreas-Friedrich, *Der Schattenmann*, p. 127. • **57.** Kardorff, op. cit., p. 108. • **58.** Elola, op. cit., p. 78. • **59.** The case is cited in Daniel Oakman, 'The Battle of Berlin', in *Wartime*, issue 25, 2004. • **60.** Jörg Friedrich, *The Fire: The Bombing of Germany 1940–1945* (New York, 2006), pp. 350–51. • **61.** Kardorff, op. cit., p. 120. • **62.** Testimony of Josepha von Koskull, op. cit. • **63.** Kardorff, op. cit., p. 108. • **64.** Testimony of Karl Deutman, on the website

of the collective memory project at the German Historical Museum –
http://www.dhm.de/lemo/forum/kollektives_gedaechtnis/008/index.html •
65. Ruth Andreas-Friedrich, *Berlin Underground, 1938–1945*, pp. 101–2. • **66.** Leopold
Deutsch, 'Verschüttet', in Kellerhoff and Giebel (eds), op. cit., p. 56. • **67.** Renate
Knispel, 'Warten auf Rettung', in ibid., p. 91. • **68.** Kardorff, op. cit., p. 76. • **69.**
Ursula Strumm's story, at News-press.com, posted 3 March 2009. • **70.** Elola,
op. cit., p. 80. • **71.** Testimony of Karl Deutman, on the website of the collective memory project at the German Historical Museum – http://www.dhm.de-
/lemo/forum/kollektives_gedaechtnis/008/index.html • **72.** Kardorff, op. cit.,
pp. 111–12. • **73.** Author interview with Erich N., Berlin, October 2006. • **74.**
Andreas-Friedrich, *Berlin*, op. cit., pp. 113–14. • **75.** Kardorff, op. cit., p. 90. • **76.**
Testimony of Martin Kühnau at http://www.jf-archiv.de/archiv03/083yy57.htm
• **77.** Vassiltchikov, op. cit., p. 119. • **78.** Kardorff, op. cit., p. 134. • **79.** See statistics presented in 'Historical Analysis of the 14/15 February Bombings of Dresden'
prepared by the US Air Force Historical Studies Office and available at
http://www.airforcehistory.hq.af.mil/PopTopics/dresden.htm • **80.** Statistics in
Uta Hohn, *Die Zerstörung deutscher Städte im Zweiten Weltkrieg* (Dortmund, 1991),
p. 135. • **81.** Statistics collated from Horst Boog, Gerhard Krebs and Detlef Vogel,
Germany and the Second World War (Oxford, 2003). • **82.** See Götz Aly (ed.),
Volkes Stimme. • **83.** Juliet Gardiner, *Wartime: Britain 1939–1945* (London, 2004), p.
408. • **84.** Taken from chapter 7 of H. Christa Billawala's memoir 'Enemy's
Child', published online at http://askpepper.com/enemysChild/index.html

16 To Unreason and Beyond

• **1.** Elke Fröhlich (ed.), *Die Tagebücher von Joseph Goebbels*, part 2, vol. 7, p. 369.
• **2.** See http://en.wikipedia.org/wiki/Berlin_Sportpalast • **3.** Original German
text of the speech is available in Joseph Goebbels, *Der steile Aufstieg* (Munich,
1944), pp. 167–204; English translation is at http://www.calvin.edu/acad-
emic/cas/gpa/goeb36.htm • **4.** Ibid., passim. • **5.** Ibid., passim. • **6.** Fröhlich
(ed.), op. cit., vol. 7, pp. 373, 375. • **7.** Albert Speer, *Inside the Third Reich*,
p. 354. • **8.** Willi A Boelcke (ed.), *The Secret Conferences of Dr Goebbels* (London,
1967), p. xx. • **9.** Ursula von Kardorff, *Berliner Aufzeichnungen 1942–1945*, pp.
33–4. • **10.** Hans-Georg von Studnitz, *While Berlin Burns, Diaries 1943–1945*,
p. 27. • **11.** Ruth Andreas-Friedrich, *Berlin Underground, 1938–1945*, p. 90.
• **12.** Josepha von Koskull, account 'Sportpalastrede' archived at
http://www.dhm.de/lemo/forum/kollektives_gedaechtnis/075/index.html •
13. Heinz Boberach (ed.), *Meldungen aus dem Reich 1938–1945*, p. 4831. • **14.** Ibid.
• **15.** Admiral Dönitz quoted in Peter Padfield, *Dönitz: The Last Führer*
(London, 1984), p. 295. • **16.** See Boberach (ed.), op. cit., pp. 5433–4. • **17.** Kardorff,
op. cit., p. 58. • **18.** Studnitz, op. cit., pp. 88–9. • **19.** See Keith Lowe, *Inferno:*

The Devastation of Hamburg (London, 2007). • **20.** Kardorff, op. cit., p. 61. • **21.** Studnitz, op. cit., p. 97. • **22.** Philip Henshall, *Hitler's Rocket Sites* (New York, 1985), p. 128. • **23.** Boberach (ed.), op. cit., pp. 5542–4. • **24.** Andreas-Friedrich, op. cit., p. 106. • **25.** Studnitz, op. cit., p. 113. • **26.** Lutz R., correspondence with the author, December 2008. • **27.** Andreas-Friedrich, op. cit., p. 115. • **28.** Howard Smith, *Last Train from Berlin*, p. 119. • **29.** Richard Grunberger, *A Social History of the Third Reich*, pp. 292–4. • **30.** Helga Schneider, *The Bonfire of Berlin*, p. 65. • **31.** Paul von Stemann, quoted in Terry Charman, *The German Home Front 1939–1945* (London, 1989), p. 176. • **32.** Theo Findahl, *Letzter Akt Berlin: 1939–1945*, p. 102. • **33.** Studnitz, op. cit., p. 158. • **34.** Kardorff, op. cit., pp. 129–30. • **35.** Boberach (ed.), op. cit., p. 6413. • **36.** Studnitz, op. cit., p. 172. • **37.** Speer, op. cit., p. 468. • **38.** Kardorff, op. cit., p. 150. • **39.** Dieter Borkowski, *Wer weiss, ob wir uns wiedersehen*, p. 110. • **40.** Studnitz, op. cit., p. 187. • **41.** Ibid., p. 190. • **42.** Grunberger, op. cit., p. 423. • **43.** Antony Beevor, *Berlin: The Downfall 1945*, p. 2. • **44.** Josepha von Koskull, at http://www.dhm.de/lemo/forum/kollektives_gedaechtnis/078/index.html • **45.** Author interview with Peter S., Berlin, September 2008. • **46.** Andreas-Friedrich, op. cit., p. 175. • **47.** Wolfram Wette, Ricarda Bremer and Detlef Vogel (eds), *Das letzte halbe Jahr*, pp. 131, 274 and 135. • **48.** See illustrations in Franz Siedler, *Deutscher Volkssturm* (Munich, 1989), pp. 128–9. • **49.** Original newsreel footage of the ceremony is at http://www.youtube.com/watch?v=ocOxi6ehkZ4 • **50.** Fröhlich (ed.), op. cit., part 2, vol. 14, pp. 208–9. • **51.** See Richard Taylor, *Film Propaganda: Soviet Russia and Nazi Germany* (London, 1979), pp. 216–17. • **52.** Veit Harlan, *Im Schatten meiner Filme* (Gütersloh, 1966), p. 182. • **53.** Fröhlich (ed.), op. cit., vol. 14, pp. 310–11. • **54.** English text quoted in David Welch, *Propaganda and the German Cinema 1933–1945*, pp. 227–8. • **55.** Quoted in ibid., pp. 231–2. • **56.** Ibid., p. 230. • **57.** Susan Tegel, *Nazis and the Cinema* (London, 2007), p. 187. • **58.** Fröhlich (ed.), op. cit., vol. 15, p. 284. • **59.** Kardorff, op. cit., p. 230. • **60.** Ibid., p. 231.

17 Ghost Town

• **1.** Heinz Linge, *With Hitler to the End*, p. 188. • **2.** Christa Schroeder, *He Was My Chief*, p. 176. • **3.** Artur Axmann, *Das kann doch nicht das Ende sein* (Koblenz, 1995), p. 418. • **4.** Schroeder, op. cit., p. 176. • **5.** Wilhelm Keitel, quoted in Walter Kempowski, *Das Echolot: Abgesang '45*, p. 44. • **6.** Nicolaus von Below, *At Hitler's Side* (London, 2004), p. 236. • **7.** Linge, op. cit., p. 189. • **8.** Hans Baur, *Hitler at My Side* (Houston, 1986), p. 183. • **9.** Bormann, quoted in Kempowski, op. cit., p. 9. • **10.** Elvira Stührmann-Boljahn, quoted in Kempowski, op. cit., p. 76. • **11.** Olaf Groehler, *1945: die Neue Reichskanzlei: Das Ende* (Berlin, 1995), p. 13. • **12.** Dieter Borkowski, *Wer weiss, ob wir uns wiedersehen?*, p. 194. • **13.** 'Golden Pheasants' was a phrase used to describe senior Nazi Party members, who were often seen dressed in an elaborate golden-brown uniform. • **14.** Borkowski, op. cit., p. 195. • **15.** Jacob Kronika, *Der Untergang Berlins*, p. 127. • **16.** Diary of Lieselotte G., quoted in Ingrid Hammer and Susanne zur Nieden (eds), *Sehr selten habe ich geweint* (Zurich, 1992), p. 310. • **17.** Quoted in Kronika, op. cit., pp. 129–30. • **18.** Ruth Andreas-Friedrich, *Berlin Underground, 1938–1945*, p. 271. • **19.** Helmut Vaupel, quoted in Kempowski, op. cit., p. 75. • **20.** Friederike Grensemann quoted in ibid., p. 81. • **21.** Andreas-Friedrich, op. cit., p. 273. • **22.** Vasily Chuikov quoted in Erich Kempka, *I Was Hitler's Chauffeur*, p. 128. • **23.** Peter S. author interview, Berlin, September 2008. • **24.** Antony Beevor, *Berlin: The Downfall 1945*, p. 287. • **25.** Diarist quoted in Tony Le Tissier, *Berlin: Then and Now*, p. 227. • **26.** Richard Landwehr, *Charlemagne's Legionnaires: French Volunteers of the SS, 1943–1945* (Silver Spring, MD, 1989), p. 140. • **27.** Though Kronika records the division as the *Wiking*, it is more likely that the men were from the SS *Nordland* Division, which was then fighting in Berlin. • **28.** Kronika, op. cit., pp. 169–70. • **29.** Dorothea von Schwanenflügel-Lawson, *Laughter Wasn't Rationed*, p. 342. • **30.** Erich N., *Erlebtes*, unpublished manuscript kindly supplied to the author, pp. 36–7. • **31.** Ibid., p. 37. • **32.** Cited in Kempowski, op. cit., p. 177. • **33.** Helmut Blümchen, at http://www.dhm.de/lemo/forum/kollektives_gedaechtnis/422/index.html • **34.** Schwanenflügel-Lawson, op. cit., p. 343. • **35.** Gisela Richter, quoted at http://www.dhm.de/lemo/forum/kollektives_gedaechtnis/467/index.html • **36.** Borkowski, op. cit., pp. 203–4. • **37.** Ibid., p. 205. • **38.** Helga Schneider, *The Bonfire of Berlin*, p. 55. • **39.** Else T., testimony at Deutsches Tagebucharchiv (hereafter DTA), Emmendingen, ref: 1303/IV, p. 7. • **40.** Elisabeth M., testimony at DTA, Emmendingen, ref: 256, p. 30. • **41.** Schneider, op. cit., pp. 64–5. • **42.** Anthony Reed and David Fisher, *The Fall of Berlin*, p. 425. • **43.** Cited in Kempowski, op. cit., p. 186. • **44.** Quoted in Sune Persson, *Escape from the Third Reich* (London, 2010), pp. 113–14. • **45.** Schneider, op. cit., p. 63. • **46.** Otto E., testimony at DTA, Emmendingen, ref: 224, entry for 26 April 1945. • **47.** Eva Richter-Fritzsche, in Kempowski, op. cit., pp. 81–2. • **48.** Testimony of Hugo B., in Hammer and zur Neiden (eds), op. cit., p. 362. • **49.** Christa H., testimony at DTA, Emmendingen, ref: 45, p. 5. • **50.** Margarethe Kopen at http://www.dhm.de/lemo/forum/kollektives_gedaechtnis/458/index.html • **51.** Gerda Langosch, at http://www.dhm.de/lemo/forum/kollektivesgedaechtnis/033/index.html • **52.** See, for instance, Margret Boveri, *Tage des Überlebens: Berlin 1945*, pp. 69–70. • **53.** Helmut Altner, *Berlin Dance of Death*, pp. 126–7. • **54.** See, for instance, Peter Gosztony (ed.), *Der Kampf um Berlin 1945 in Augenzeugenberichten*, p. 262. • **55.** See, for instance, testimony of Klaus Sommer at http://www.dhm.de/lemo/forum/kollektives_gedaechtnis/461/index.html • **56.** Hertha von Gebhardt, in Kempowski, op. cit., p. 180.

• **57.** Bernd Freytag von Loringhoven, *In the Bunker with Hitler* (London, 2006), p. 152. • **58.** 'Can I speak to Doctor Goebbels please?', in *Russia Today*, 15 May 2009. • **59.** Schneider, op. cit., pp. 115–16. • **60.** See Christian Goeschel, 'Suicide at the End of the Third Reich', in *Journal of Contemporary History*, vol. 41, no. 1, 2006. • **61.** See Schroeder, op. cit. • **62.** Gitta Sereny, *Albert Speer: His Battle with Truth* (London, 1995), p. 507. • **63.** Heinz Boberach (ed.), *Meldungen aus dem Reich 1938–1945*, p. 6737. • **64.** Goeschel, op. cit., pp. 162 and 164. • **65.** Lieselotte G., in Hammer and zur Neiden (eds.), op. cit., p. 312. • **66.** Goeschel, op. cit., p. 162. • **67.** Curt Riess, *Berlin Berlin: 1945– 1953* (Berlin, 2002), p. 23. • **68.** Hertha von Genhardt, quoted in Alon Confino, Paul Betts and Dirk Schumann (eds), *Between Mass Death and Individual Loss: The Place of the Dead in Twentieth Century Germany* (Oxford, 2008), p. 73. • **69.** Schneider, op. cit., p. 142. • **70.** Dr Schmidt, in Kempowski, op. cit., p. 296. • **71.** Hugo B., in Hammer and zur Neiden (eds), op. cit., pp. 361–2. • **72.** Testimony of Klaus Sommer, op. cit. • **73.** Ibid. • **74.** Author interview with Dorit E., Berlin, September 2008. • **75.** Testimony of Gerda Langosch, op. cit. • **76.** Andreas-Friedrich, op. cit., p. 290. • **77.** Testimony of Gerda Langosch, op. cit. • **78.** Andreas-Friedrich, op. cit., pp. 298–9. • **79.** Schwanenflügel-Lawson, op. cit., pp. 346–7. • **80.** Ibid., p. 347. • **81.** Marcel Elola, *Ich war in Berlin*, pp. 91–2. • **82.** Dr Schmidt, in Kempowski, op. cit., pp. 206–7. • **83.** Baur, op. cit., p. 199. • **84.** Testimony of Margarethe Kopen, op. cit. • **85.** Beevor, op. cit., p. 410. • **86.** Antony Beevor, 'They raped every German female from 8 to 80', in *Guardian*, 1 May 2002. • **87.** Schwanenflügel-Lawson, op. cit., p. 347. • **88.** Anonymous, *A Woman in Berlin*, p. 68. • **89.** Author interview with Ursula N., Berlin, October, 2006. • **90.** Author interview with Gerda P., Berlin, November, 2007. • **91.** Gisela Stange, *Der verdammte Krieg*, pp. 105–6. • **92.** Andrew Roberts, 'Stalin's army of rapists', in *Daily Mail*, 24 October 2008. • **93.** Anonymous, *A Woman in Berlin*, p. 263. • **94.** Ibid., passim. • **95.** Schwanenflügel-Lawson op. cit., p. 357. • **96.** Interview by Osmar White, at http://www.argo.net.au/andre/ osmarwhiteENFIN.htm • **97.** This opinion, expressed to me by numerous interviewees, is corroborated in *A Woman in Berlin*, p. 161. • **98.** Author interview with Rosa H., Berlin, October 2006. • **99.** Schwanenflügel-Lawson, op. cit., pp. 348 and 349. • **100.** Carl Diem, quoted in Kempowski, op. cit., p. 289. • **101.** Margot H., testimony at DTA, Emmendingen, ref: 264, p. 6. • **102.** Anonymous, *A Woman in Berlin*, p. 80. • **103.** Karin Finell, *Goodbye to the Mermaids: A Childhood lost in Hitler's Berlin* (Columbia, 2006), p. 178. • **104.** See Marlene Epp, 'The Memory of Violence: Soviet and East European Mennonite Refugees and Rape in the Second World War', in *Journal of Women's History*, vol. 9, 1997. • **105.** Quoted in Beevor, *Berlin*, p. 410. • **106.** Stange, op. cit., p. 110. • **107.** German text from Joachim Fest, 'Das Ende', in *Der Spiegel*, December 2002, p. 68. • **108.** Andreas-Friedrich, op. cit., pp. 311–12. • **109.** Anonymous, *A Woman* *in Berlin*, p. 131. • **110.** Borkowski, op. cit., pp. 212 and 213. • **111.** Schwanenflügel-Lawson, op. cit., p. 362.

Epilogue: Hope

• **1.** Anonymous diarist quoted in Antonia Meiners (ed.), *Berlin 1945* (Berlin, 2005), p. 70. • **2.** Richard Brett-Smith quoted in Tony Le Tissier, *Berlin: Then and Now*, p. 299. • **3.** Margret Boveri, *Tage des Überlebens: Berlin 1945*, p. 130. • **4.** Margarethe Kopen at http://www.dhm.de/lemo/forum/kollektives_gedaechtnis/458/index.html • **5.** John Stave quoted in Meiners (ed.), op. cit., p. 60. • **6.** Boveri, op. cit., p. 98. • **7.** Helmut Altner, *Berlin Dance of Death*, p. 229. • **8.** Ruth Andreas-Friedrich, *Der Schattenmann*, p. 309. • **9.** Jacob Kronika, *Der Untergang Berlins*, pp. 184–5. • **10.** Theo Findahl, *Letzter Akt Berlin: 1939–1945*, p. 184. • **11.** Fritz Raddatz in Walter Kempowski, *Das Echolot: 1945 Abgesang*, p. 429. • **12.** Findahl, op. cit., pp. 189–90. • **13.** Raddatz in Kempowski, op. cit., p. 429. • **14.** Brett-Smith quoted in Le Tissier, op. cit., p. 300. • **15.** Marcel Elola, *Ich war in Berlin*, p. 146. • **16.** Quoted in *Stern*, 'Der letzte Wehrmachtsbericht', 4 May 2005. • **17.** Karl Deutmann, at http://www.dhm.de/lemo/forum/kollektives_gedaechtnis/013/index.html • **18.** Ibid. • **19.** Altner, op. cit., p. 228. • **20.** Ibid., p. 230.

Select Bibliography

ARCHIVES

British Library Newspaper Archive, Colindale, London
Bundesarchiv, Berlin, Germany
Deutsches Tagebucharchiv, Emmendingen, Germany
Landesarchiv, Berlin, Germany
The National Archives, Kew, London
The Wiener Library and Archive, London

INTERVIEWS AND CORRESPONDENCE

Thessi Aselmeier, Renate Baudert, Eberhard Beigel, Horst Biesel, Rosemarie
Biesel, Frank Braun, Else Buchner, Benedikt Dardin, Leopold Deutsch, Dorit
Ebert, Dorit Furchheim, Marie-Louise Gericke, Rosa Heinrich, Irmgard
Hoferichter, Peter Jung, Luzie Kannewischer, Renate Knispel, Rita Krämer,
Dietrich Krüger, Edith Krüger, Ruth Lejeune-Jung, Gerda Lemke, Otto-Herbert
Leonhardt, Werner Lindner, Marianne Maasch, Erich Nieswandt, Jutta
Petenati, Wolfgang Pickert, Elisabeth Poschinger, Lutz Rackow, Eva Reichel,
Christa Ronke, Kurt Roth, Ernst Schill, Paul Schmidt, Peter Schmidt, Ursula
Schmidt, Kurt Schulz, Dietrich Schwanke, Margit Siebner, Hans Soost, Gisela
Stange, Gerda Steinke, Klaus-Jürgen Ulandowski, Ulrich Walter, Gisela Weber.

PUBLISHED MEMOIRS AND DIARIES

Altner, Helmut, *Berlin Dance of Death* (Staplehurst, 2002)
Andreas-Friedrich, Ruth, *Berlin Underground, 1938–1945* (New York, 1947)
— *Der Schattenmann* (Frankfurt am Main, 2000)
Anonymous, *A Woman in Berlin* (London, 2004)
Beck, Gad, *Underground Life: Memoirs of a Gay Jew in Nazi Berlin* (Wisconsin, 1999)
Behm, Margarete, *So oder so ist das Leben* (Berlin, 2002)

Bielenberg, Christabel, *The Past Is Myself* (London, 1970)

Borkowski, Dieter, *Wer weiss, ob wir uns wiedersehen* (Berlin, 1990)

Boveri, Margret, *Tage des Überlebens: Berlin 1945* (Munich, 1968)

Deutschkron, Inge, *Ich trug den Gelben Stern* (Cologne, 1978)

Elola, Marcel, *Ich war in Berlin* (Berlin, 2005)

Findahl, Theo, *Letzter Akt Berlin: 1939–1945* (Hamburg, 1946)

Flannery, Henry, *Assignment to Berlin* (London, 1942)

Fröhlich, Elke (ed.), *Die Tagebücher von Joseph Goebbels* (29 vols, Munich, 1993–2006)

Grossmann, Günter, *Die sieben mageren Jahren eines jungen Berliners* (Berlin, 2005)

Horstmann, Lali, *Nothing for Tears* (London, 1953)

von Kardorff, Ursula, *Berliner Aufzeichnungen 1942–1945* (Munich, 1976)

Kempka, Erich, *I Was Hitler's Chauffeur* (London, 2010)

Knobloch, Heinz, *Eine Berliner Kindheit* (Berlin, 1999)

Kronika, Jacob, *Der Untergang Berlins* (Hamburg, 1946)

Leonhardt, Otto-Herbert, *Spuren eines Lebens* (Mahlow, 2004)

Linge, Heinz, *With Hitler to the End* (London, 2009)

Misch, Rochus, *Der letzte Zeuge* (Munich, 2008)

von Moltke, Helmuth James, *Letters to Freya 1939–1945* (London, 1990)

Oechsner, Frederick, *This Is the Enemy* (London, 1943)

Orbach, Larry, *Soaring Underground* (London, 1996)

Reichel, Eva, *Eva im Glück* (Berlin, 2005)

Russell, William, *Berlin Embassy* (New York, 1941)

Schneider, Helga, *The Bonfire of Berlin* (London, 2005)

Schroeder, Christa, *He Was My Chief* (London, 2009)

von Schwanenflügel-Lawson, Dorothea, *Laughter Wasn't Rationed* (Alexandria, VA, 1999)

Shirer, William, *Berlin Diary 1934–1941* (London, 1997)

— *This Is Berlin* (London, 1999)

Smith, Howard K., *Last Train from Berlin* (London, 1942)

Speer, Albert, *Inside the Third Reich* (London, 1970)

Spitzy, Reinhard, *How We Squandered the Reich* (Wilby, Norfolk, 1997)

Stange, Gisela, *Der verdammte Krieg* (Berlin, 2003)

von Studnitz, Hans-Georg, *While Berlin Burns, Diaries 1943–1945* (London, 1964)

Süssmilch, Waltraud, *Keine Zeit für Puppen* (Frankfurt am Main, 2001)

Taylor, Fred (ed. and trans.), *The Goebbels Diaries 1939–41* (London, 1982)

Vassiltchikov, Marie, *Berlin Diaries 1940–1945* (London, 1985)

OTHER PUBLISHED PRIMARY SOURCES

Boberach, Heinz (ed.), *Meldungen aus dem Reich* (Herrsching, 1984)

Domarus, Max, *Hitler: Speeches and Proclamations* (London, 1997)

Gosztony, Peter (ed.), *Der Kampf um Berlin 1945 in Augenzeugenberichten* (Düsseldorf, 1970)

Kellerhoff, Sven Felix, and Giebel, Wieland (eds), *Als die Tage zu Nächten wurden* (Berlin, 2003)

Kempowski, Walter, *Das Echolot: Abgesang '45* (Munich, 2005)

Noakes, Jeremy (ed.), *Nazism 1919–1945*, vol. 4: *The German Home Front in World War II* (Exeter, 1998)

Rinner, E. (ed.), *Deutschland-Berichte der Sozialdemokratischen Partei Deutschlands (Sopade) 1934–1940* (Frankfurt am Main, 1980)

Schäfer, Hans Dieter (ed.), *Berlin im Zweiten Weltkrieg* (Munich, 1985)

Wette, Wolfram, Bremer, Ricarda, and Vogel, Detlef (eds), *Das letzte halbe Jahr* (Essen, 2001)

SECONDARY WORKS

Aly, Götz, *Hitler's Beneficiaries* (New York, 2007)

— *Im Tunnel* (Frankfurt am Main, 2004)

— (ed.), *Volkes Stimme* (Frankfurt am Main, 2006)

Aycoberry, Pierre, *The Social History of the Third Reich* (New York, 1999)

Beevor, Antony, *Berlin: The Downfall 1945* (London, 2002)

Benz, Wolfgang (ed.), *Die Juden in Deutschland 1933–1945* (Munich, 1988)

Bräutigam, Helmut, Fürstenberg, Doris, and Roder, Bernt (eds), *Zwangsarbeit in Berlin 1938–1945* (Berlin, 2003)

Browning, Christopher, *The Origins of the Final Solution* (London, 2004)

Burleigh, Michael, *The Third Reich: A New History* (London, 2000)

Burleigh, Michael, and Wippermann, Wolfgang, *The Racial State: Germany 1933–1945* (Oxford, 1991)

Crew, David (ed.), *Nazism and German Society 1933–1945* (London, 1994)

Evans, Richard, *The Third Reich at War* (London, 2008)

Foedrowitz, Michael, *Bunkerwelten* (Berlin, 1998)

— *The Flak Towers in Berlin, Hamburg and Vienna, 1940-1950* (Atglen, PA, 1998)

Friedländer, Saul, *The Years of Extermination* (London, 2007)

Gellately, Robert, *Backing Hitler* (Oxford, 2001)

Gottwaldt, Alfred, and Schulle, Diana, *Die 'Judendeportationen' aus dem Deutschen Reich 1941–1945* (Wiesbaden, 2005)

Gross, Leonard, *The Last Jews in Berlin* (New York, 1982)

Grunberger, Richard, *A Social History of the Third Reich* (London, 1971)

Gruner, Wolf, *Judenverfolgung in Berlin 1933–1945* (Berlin, 1996)

— *Widerstand in der Rosenstrasse* (Frankfurt, 2005)

Jochheim, Gernot, *Frauenprotest in der Rosenstrasse* (Berlin, 1993)

Johnson, Eric, and Reuband, Karl-Heinz, *What We Knew: Terror, Mass Murder and Everyday Life in Nazi Germany* (London, 2005)

Kaplan, Marion, *Between Dignity and Despair – Jewish Life in Nazi Germany* (Oxford, 1998)

Kitchen, Martin, *Nazi Germany at War* (London, 1995)

Kriesch, G. et al., *Berliner Alltag im Dritten Reich* (Düsseldorf, 1981)

Ladd, Brian, *The Ghosts of Berlin: Confronting German History in the Urban Landscape* (Chicago, 1998)

Le Tissier, Tony, *Berlin: Then and Now* (London, 1992)

Lovenheim, Barbara, *Survival in the Shadows* (London, 2002)

MacDonogh, Giles, *Berlin* (London, 1997)

Meyer, Beate, and Simon, Hermann (eds), *Juden in Berlin 1938–1945* (Berlin, 2000)

Meyer, W., and Nietmann, K. (eds), *Zwangsarbeit während der NS-Zeit in Berlin und Brandenburg* (Berlin, 2001)

Paul, Gerhard, and Mallmann, Klaus-Michael (eds), *Die Gestapo – Mythos und Realität* (Darmstadt, 1995)

Reed, Anthony, and Fisher, David, *The Fall of Berlin* (London, 1992)

Reichhardt, Hans, and Schäche, Wolfgang, *Von Berlin nach Germania* (Berlin, 1998)

Richie, Alexandra, *Faust's Metropolis* (London, 1998)

Sandvoss, Hans-Rainer, *Widerstand in Steglitz und Zehlendorf* (Berlin, 1986)

— *Die 'andere' Reichshauptstadt* (Berlin, 2007)

Silver, Daniel, *Refuge in Hell* (New York, 2003)

Spoerer, Mark, *Zwangsarbeit unter dem Hakenkreuz* (Munich, 2001)

Stargardt, Nick, *Witnesses of War: Children in the Third Reich* (London, 2005)

Stoltzfus, Nathan, *Resistance of the Heart* (New York, 1996)

Tooze, Adam, *The Wages of Destruction* (London, 2006)

Welch, David, *Propaganda and the German Cinema 1933–1945* (Oxford, 1983)

Wenzel, Gisela, and Pagenstecher, Cord (eds), *Totaleinsatz: Zwangsarbeit in Berlin 1943–45, Tschechische Zeitzeuginnen erinnern sich* (Berlin, 1998)

Zierenberg, Malte, *Stadt der Schieber – Der Berliner Schwarzmarkt 1939–1950* (Göttingen, 2008)

Index